Around
&Around
&Around

Roy Starkey

Published by Paragon Publishing, Rothersthorpe
First published 2015

ISBN 978-1-78222-388-7

Book design, layout and production management by Into Print
www.intoprint.net
+44 (0)1604 832149

Printed and bound in UK and USA by Lightning Source

For Steve

CONTENTS

INTRODUCTION

ROY STARKEY AND I went to school together on Merseyside in the 1960's. When Roy decided to build *Sea Loone* from scratch, he naturally turned to his friends for free labour and, in some cases, for advice and skills. My own contribution was minimal. I did some light work in the early stages of boat-building and gave him the run of my empty attic to cut some of his framing templates.

But that was not the end of my involvement. In 1978 I was there to welcome Roy and Jean when they sailed into George Town harbour in the Cayman Islands where I was then living. They had just completed their first transatlantic crossing.

Fast forward thirty years. Five years ago I began to receive parcels of Roy's hand-written manuscript from far away tropical islands. The first, I remember, was from Honiara in the Solomon Islands. My job was to transcribe Roy's scribbles into my computer and help him produce a readable story of his forty-year travels.

As the story unfolded on my screen, I became fascinated by each instalment. Finally, on hearing from Roy that *Sea Loone* had completed her third circumnavigation and was anchored in Grenada I flew down with Karen, my wife, to collect the final instalment. It was important, we felt, to spend a few days aboard *Sea Loone* in Hog Island to get some idea of Roy's life and the boat we had all helped to build forty years earlier.

Roy's lifetime at sea has been the fulfilment of a dream, a dream that many have but few actually follow. At first glance, Roy seems a rather remote and eccentric companion. But as you learn what drives him, you will find yourself in the company of someone who he solitary wisdom of the sea with a warm sense of humour.

His story takes place in many odd corners of the world so a good atlas is essential to follow the route. I know you will enjoy the trip

January 2015 Steven Williams

Book One

Period: 1970-1980

1

I WAS WALKING along the prom wall. It was a beautiful early summer day with the tide lapping on the concrete slope to my right and the sea stretching out to the northwest towards Ireland, an unusually calm sea. To my left was a narrow strip of sand dunes covered in marram grass in places and then a low bank with scraggly hedge and fence on top. Beyond that the market gardens started, small fields divided by privet hedges. Vegetables had been grown here since the early days, the dark ages maybe. There were dilapidated wooden sheds for packing and equipment in the odd overgrown corner. It all looked very rural and quiet on that sunny summer's day and may be, I thought, a possible place to start my project, my dream.

So I climbed over the bank and headed for a small plot where I'd seen some activity. The farmer I found fitted the scene, calloused and sun burnt. When I explained my need he replied with a Merseyside accent tinged with westcountry. I should go see Mr. Biddle down the lane. He had had a fellow with a boat in his packing shed. Great – a good omen maybe.

I found the packing shed and Mr. Biddle easily. All I needed, I explained, was a small plot of land on which to build a boat, a concrete boat. A water supply would be handy but not much else. So following him down the lane, past a small caravan and farm houses, he pointed out a small square of ground up against the seaward bank and fence line. There was a broken down shed and greenhouses with mainly broken panes of glass and he revealed under a clump of brambles, a water tap!

It was remote, quiet and idyllic, with the birds twittering and the insects humming. We quickly came to an agreement. I had my boat building site and was ten shillings a week poorer. I was away. After weeks of frustration I had a place to start. My mind buzzed with the thousands things I could do to get started.

Dr. Eddie White had been a lecturer in the Dept. of Zoology, Liverpool University and running graduate courses in fresh water biology. We had worked together for five years. He was now in New Zealand running a government department of ecology. He had invited me along as his assistant and already had some money allocated to a similar project we had been working on. Instead of Shap Fell in the English Lake District I would be on Lake Taupo in North Island. Instead of a free agent I would be a government scientist. I declined the offer.

I had a paper to finish off; an enormous amount of data to complete. My thesis sat in my little office. I had a big laboratory to close down and a little bit of money, now more or less at an end. The money paid my wages, small as they were. I had taken a holiday, staying with a friend on the Isle of Majorca in the Mediterranean, the first holiday in five years and I had come to a decision to walk away from it all and find another dream. To help me in that I had a University superannuation scheme which when cashed in was going to give me £700, a bloody fortune!

My wages had originally come from the Food and Agriculture Organization, the F.A.O. as part of a scheme studying bodies of freshwater in different parts of the world. Later they were provided by National Environmental Research Council of the British Government. The money had been reallocated to a Government Research Station as part of the Labour Government's policy of bleeding Universities. So Eddie had gone to New Zealand, and everybody else scattered to the wind. Me, I was going to build a bloody boat and leave Harold Wilson to get on with it. I would be in Tahiti or some other exotic tropical island and not give a toss.

So I was now paying rent on a flat in town and a piece of land some five miles away. I shared the flat in Wallasey facing Liverpool across the River Mersey, with Pamela, a vivacious blond bombshell. Her mother had been over the moon when I suggested Pamela come and share the flat. I was beginning to understand; Pamela was born to rule. I was ousted to the back bedroom and given the job of painting the bathroom. The boyfriend came to stay most weekends.

I had decided on the plans for the boat. It was to be more or less a Contest 33. I think it was Yachting World that waxed lyrical about this boat, made with fibreglass in Holland. They particularly pointed out a shallow beamy boat and then provided the drawings for the hull which was very helpful. Cutting up these little drawings and placing them on my microscope, I measured off all the intercepts with a vernier scale and soon had the off sets which I blew up, going from ten centimetres to one metre. I changed the propeller aperture to something simpler and altered the transom to make it vertical. I than played around with measuring the centre of lateral resistance, tipping moments, tons per inch immersion, and other things, all of which told me very little.

So I then magnified everything by ten again bringing the drawings to full size and the hull length ten metres. I drew out the frames on four sheets of hard board. This needed an area of about eleven square metres and by jamming the bed upright in one corner and the wardrobe in the other I could do the drawings in my bedroom.

A lot of nail holes appeared in the floor as I sprung the curvatures with a batten, no problem. But when I than transferred these shapes to planks I had acquired from dunnage in the docks the room became a bit of a mess. I cut the curves on a band saw in the University, but sanding them accurately was the last straw. The sawdust leaked into Pamela's room, into the dining room, everywhere. I suppose it was also a bit noisy. Fortunately cupid came to my rescue. The boyfriend wanted to move in and I had found a much more salubrious and cheaper place to live.

While building the frames I was preparing the building site. The first day I went out to Meols and the site did not start very well. It was a weekend and I had coopted some friends to help. The fifteen hundredweight Morris van I had brought back from Spain was happily booming down the Meols stretch when it lurched up in the air and then came crashing down on its front end. The inside front wheel had come off, we had driven up over it. The van came to a grinding halt. The wheel lay on the road behind us and next to it the hub cap with the five nuts sitting in it. We needed a trolley jack and quickly, the road tax sticker was a little out of date. We were very exposed. So some of us legged it off to the garage not too far down the road and pleaded for the jack. Back in a flash we had the wheel back on and everything was good.

There was always lots of timber around, old railway sleepers from the docks and roof trusses and beams from demolition sites. I soon had a huge building frame up, all seated on sleepers and ready for the boat frames to be hung. I often saw Mr. Biddle the farmer and the two farm labourers often came and had their lunch break with me. They were intrigued by the project.

Across the fields there was a construction site involved with a new sewer pipeline. The project was closing down and George, the farm labourer, pointed out that there was a caravan going begging if I wanted it. My new home! The caravan was going to cost five pounds. It came together with two gas bottles, a gas heater, lights and a cooker. It was a little rotten and the wheels didn't go round, but it only had four hundred yards to travel to arrive next to the boat frame. I cleared a way through the hedges and George dragged the caravan along with the farm tractor. I then set it up on bricks and moved in. I already had negotiated with Mr. Biddle and was paying another ten shillings a week. So it was now one pound a week all in, but there was no longer money coming in and the £700 had still a long way to go. The Contest 33 from its factory in Holland cost £8.056 completed. It was 1971.

I soon had the frames hanging up and standing back there was the boat in three dimensions. It looked enormous, I had some difficulties fairing up the shape, stringing battens around longitudinally. But a shipwright came to visit that had heard of our project and he showed me how to let the battens run naturally. His rule was that if it looked right it was right and so we nailed in the sheerline by eye standing on the shed roof to get it "right".

I bought the quarter inch reinforcing bars locally and more than a dozen rolls of half inch chicken mesh from a farming cooperative. The mesh was a serious expense. During the week I worked alone but often had visitors at the weekends. It was not easy to find your way down the lanes. Friends came to lend a hand, dreamers came to waste my time and occasionally really helpful people turned up.

The first was Dave, the policeman. I was just beginning placing the reinforcing bars and had a hacksaw to cut pieces to length. Dave arrived in his "Panda car". He immediately suggested that with that huge pile of reinforcing bars to cut up, I needed a pair of bolt cutters. I point out that they were outside my budget. He nodded, climbed back into his car and shot away. He reappeared four hours later with a pair of bolt cutters. They were large, heavy and had been obviously run over at some time but they worked perfectly. Dave explained that he had been into Birkenhead to one of the dodgy scrap dealers. He told them what he wanted and they happily came up with these bolt cutters for him to borrow sort of permanently. Through Dave I met Taffy who worked at night in a huge factory making spark plugs, but daytime making fibreglass boats in a warehouse down the docks.

The summer passed quickly. I had a lot of birds nesting in the hedges around me, a fox and a stoat had visited, the grass grew so fast I was losing things in it. The boat was taking shape and with each layer of reinforcing bars and chicken mesh becoming more substantial. But money was disappearing quickly so it seemed a good move to find some work for the winter and then take the following summer off to boat build.

In the bar of the Albion pub in Wallasey where I used to play darts, I knew a

Polish guy who was the general foreman on a huge tunneling project expanding the underground rail system under Liverpool. I made an appointment to see him and on the spot got the job as pit bottom man on their site down on the Pier Head. I was given a pair of wellies, a set of yellow waterproofs and a yellow hard hat and sent off on the bus to the Pier Head. The crane driver pointed at the changing shed and the primitive lift down the shaft. It was like descending into a bad dream. When I reached the bottom, a tunnel with a rail track sloped up hill. The roof dripped, the light bulbs flickered, a small stream flowed down into a pit at the bottom of the shaft. There was nobody there.

So I marched up the rail line to find a plastic sheet forming a tent some way up the tunnel and inside sat Roony's Loonies , seven miners mostly Irish, and the ganger, Roony.

I was invited to sit. It was tea break, but they were all looking at me somehow that made me nervous. I soon found why. There was a huge explosion and I fell off the plank. They roared laughing, the bastards. If they had to use explosives they did it then so the dust settled while they had tea. No matter things got better, but it was hellish hard work. I spent most of the twelve hours shift moving tons of mud and rock from rail trucks into a huge skip which was then hoisted up the shaft. I had a shovel in my hand most of the time but also had huge pumps to look after. They removed the water pouring down the tunnel walls.

The money I was paid was enormous but depended on how much rock was moved. I was a miner's labourer and earned more than a professor and by Christmas they made me a full miner, maybe a better qualification than any degree I had but it was hard. We worked a six day twelve hours shift and altered days to night each week. Sundays the job stopped for a day but I took on the job of watchman so in fact never had time off at all. Whether we finished at seven in the morning or seven at night we never saw the sun so it was easy to get confused as to whether we were working days or nights.

We had some early snow that winter. It was the last straw. Leaving work at seven I would take the train to Meols and then walk down the lanes to the boat site and my caravan. The problem was the shops were closed and I was doing night watchman down the tunnel on the Sunday. So I couldn't organize food. The night it snowed the roof vent blew off and I woke with a snowman alongside the bed and only minutes to pull on damp cloth and trudge down the lane to the train. At the pier head I'd changed into mud caked jeans, shirt and pullover, a pair of waders, the helmet and then down into the dripping tunnel. So I capitulated, phoned my mother and moved in with her for the rest of the winter.

We had so many accidents down the hole, all of which could have been really serious but Rooney's Loonies seemed to have charmed lives. We were given a lovely wooden shed which we pitched in the station we had dug out. It didn't last a week. We accidentally blew it up while starting an escalator shaft. Back in the plastic tent, that got destroyed together with the tea urn when a boggie with a full set of rail lines loaded on it got loose. Fortunately we all got time to climb the wall bars as it went under us. And then one daft Paddy used reverse to slow down the little electric train coming down the line. The fuses went and he was already going far too fast for him to screw the brake down. He shot past me as I hung from the roof. He was already off the rails and had ten tons of rocks behind him and heading for a solid rock wall. I found him quite unhurt surrounded by boulders, gibbering and needing a change of knickers.

They had dug a vertical shaft alongside the river at the pier head and we were digging the tunnel inland to meet another team digging down from Central Station joined with the old line this would then form a loop. We had a digging machine with a huge articulated boom to cut the sandstone. It had tracks and hydraulic legs to push it along. A skirt picked up the rock and deposited it in tipping wagons and we had two electric trains to move these wagons up and down the tunnel.

We had carved out a wider hole and a rough platform for the first station and Rooney had found two more workers in the pub who were to cut the lift and elevator shafts to the old station which was above and to the right of us. The first guy was an Australian who had worked the mines in Australia, his mate was a New Zealand Maori.... whose last job had been leading pony tracking expeditions in the Hindu Kush.

Using our power rock drills the newcomers drilled a pattern of holes in the side of the station, inserted the dynamite and tamped it all down. The idea is to set off a central charge milliseconds before the circle of outside charges goes off. This didn't happen so a large boulder took off and met our new tea shed after ricocheting across the tunnel. Hence the reason we were back in the plastic tent.

We weren't pleased; so a week or two later when our antipodeans had their accident we were more than amused. They had been cutting a steep sloped tunnel upwards for the escalator ... expecting to arrive somewhere in the old station, which didn't have any plans available. The last charge had exposed a brick wall which nobody knew about. They went to break it down with a jackhammer. It turned out to be an old drainage sump and was full of smelly sludge. It washed them down the slope and deposited them by the remains of the tea shed.

On a couple of occasions we stopped work for day-long arguments over the hardness of the rock. The hardness had an enormous effect on our ability to move forwards and with the bonus system the amount of money we earned. On a couple of occasions I took the opportunity to go up the hill and have coffee in the Zoology Dept of the University. The staff included three professors all earning less than me right then.

On another occasion, I took the train out to the boat site and was incredible lucky to arrive and find a electricity company wagon parked by the caravan. Two men were examining a wooden box which stood some twenty yards away in the next field. The box apparently belonged to the contractors that had been putting in the sewage pipeline. The electrical people were there to disconnect and remove the electrical supply in the box. Pointing to the skeleton of my boat I explained that electricity would be really handy in completing my project.

So I was given the name of someone to contact and they agreed, being good British workers, to do nothing. I found that I needed a letter to transfer the supply from the contractors which I soon had and then I had to put a basic circuit to my site and they would come back, examine my system, fix a meter and hook me up. I purloined a good length of armoured cable to run from the box to the old shed which I now had as a workshop. In the shed I put one light, one plug and a fuse box. No problem, a year later there were wires everywhere as you can imagine.

It was springtime and I wanted to get back to the boat. I had saved more than £1,000 which I had deposited in the bank. The government had taxed me more than 33% and even demanded I pay tax on the interest that money had already made in the bank. Bastards!

But now I was a lot more savvy. I got the company to dismiss me and went on the dole, the unemployment benefit. So I was back in the caravan with rent to pay at one pound a week and a van which needed tax, insurance and petrol, but the dole paid me six pounds a week so all my savings and even some dole money would go into the boat. When I was interviewed by the dole office they suggested I contacted Chester Zoo. I was not impressed and couldn't see any relationship between my work as a limnologist and feeding buns to elephants.

Work on the boat had got to a very boring stage. All the steel was in place and the eight layers of chicken mesh had to be tightly tied into the frame. This involved twisting off tie wires at more or less two-inch centres over the whole surface of the hull. The ties were pushed inboard and tied off inside. There were tens of thousands of them. It was lonely work and I lost myself timewise to the extent that one day I went to sign in on the dole queue and found I was a day out. Not easy to explain how you lost a day to a very aggressive civil servant.

The news of a boat being constructed down the lane in Meols spread around. I had a lot of visitors most of them asking very silly questions but amongst them arrived Tom and Jean. Tom I knew from bird watching on Hilbre Island not far away. They had been talking to Barry who was building another concrete boat in his garden not far away in Oxton and they were looking for a place to start themselves.

Mr. Biddle didn't mind another ten shillings a week so they began on plans they had bought to build a huge forty four foot boat. Within a few months another enthusiast appeared. He was from the south somewhere with a very pretty wife. With two huge building frames already a bit conspicuous I wasn't too keen on expanding but when Brian the newcomer mentioned he had a circular saw and a welding machine I was more than enthusiastic. Mr. Biddle got another ten shillings a week.

By midsummer the boat was ready for plastering. In concrete boat building this is an important day. All in all I had fifty odd people coming, friends from Wallasey from school days, from the rugby club, locals from the pub, other boat builders, a team of plasterers from Widnes and so on. I had two cement mixers hired, tarpaulins in case of rain, lots of buckets, food, a barrel of beer and a thousand other things.

The night before I nearly cut my thumb off making wedges I needed, using the circular saw. It got sewn up and bandaged but wasn't going to slow things down. The cement had to go on in one day. It had to be mixed exactly using sharp graded dried sand and precise quantities of water. I had Derek, a naval architect in charge of that department. Then there were poor buggers inside the boat who had to push the almost dry material through the mesh using the heel of their hands and working from the keel upwards. Each had a partner on the outside with a knitting needle to indicate where more was needed. As they moved away from the keel the work went faster. With the enormous extra weight on the structure its possible for part to sag disastrously, but it didn't happen.

By early afternoon the basics were done and my friend Sue and her gang were busy feeding people. The plasterers then took over, skimming the outside surface and the beer barrel was opened. One friend was a rep. for the brewery so we had all the gear in that department.

By teatime we had the whole thing covered in burlap sheets borrowed from the motorway construction and a sprinkler system to keep everything damp. It was going to be another month before that lot got removed so we could see the finished object. The day had been perfect.

Even wearing gloves a lot of people got cement burns, the smallest scratch turned black and hurt like hell. My bandaged hand for all my efforts suffered badly. The bandage was a solid black lump. A week later the cement mix got tested by the nurse's scissors as she went to cut the bandage off. The scissor failed and they even had difficulties with the circular saw they used for removing plaster casts. The thumb was a mess and is still a bit of a funny shape.

With the cement curing the next problem was the deck and the cabintop. I had already discarded a deck in cement with the reinforcement half completed. I decided it was going to be too heavy, so in a few minutes chopped weeks of work off and threw it aside. The next idea was wooden beams which I started laminating. I bought lengths of mahogany from another boat builder in Manchester who was getting offcuts from huge logs when they were milled. The problem was going to be attaching them as a beamshelf to the hull. The stainless steel bolts were horrendously expensive. The next idea was a flush deck using steel beams. These I acquired from a dilapidated Dutch barn a few mile away. There was an article in the local newspaper saying the police were investigating the strange disappearance of this barn and suspected a large group of "badies". In fact it was just one.

Finally I found a large quantity of foam sheets which I acquired for only a few pounds. Taffy, a friend of the local bobby, had a fibreglass business down at the docks and I had worked for him occasionally. He had a source of very cheap polyester resin from Manchester. It was reject stuff but worked perfectly well with lots of accelerator. It was only fifty pounds a drum. Fibreglass I could buy from Fibreglass Company also reject with little hard balls of fibres in it every so often. No problem I used two and a half drums of resin in the end but finished with a very strong well insulated foam sandwich deck and cabin top.

The gantry now had a roof and sides so it became a huge barn. That winter I had electric heaters under the roof so I could continue fibreglassing in the winter and I had to find another job to get more money coming in.

I took a job as a plumber's labourer at the shipyard in Birkenhead. Till this time my total work experience had been the University and the tunnel. Now I was in a completely different environment. It was us against the bosses and do as little as possible. I was bored to death but ship building and boat building do have a few things in common and if the men weren't that keen on working for the company they were more than keen on helping me out when I explained my project. Much the same attitude could be found in the pub or well basically anywhere. The idea of building a sailing boat and sailing off around the world was everybody's dream and if they couldn't realize it at least they could help my dream into reality. So during the next four years materials appeared out of the blue, timber, plywood, fastenings, paint etc. The stern tube got machined, the bollards got fabricated and so on.

A typical example would be the rudder. This was to be plate of quarter inch steel welded on a shaft with wooden cheeks and all shaped and covered in fibreglass. In the shipyard I could buy scrap steel from the company so on seeing a suitable piece in the skip I asked the foreman for a note to take to the office. When I explained what it was for he asked me if it was the right shape and if not why not tomorrow give him a piece of paper in the right shape.

So the next thing, there is my rudder with "scrap" written on it in the bin. So I find the man and asked for the note. He asks if I have a vehicle, so I say yes a large van in the car park. I give him a description and that night drove home with my rudder which had magically appeared in the back. We build a car ferry with very nice white paint and we built a destroyer with special underwater paint. A lorry arrived with all my plywood and later some beautiful hardwood.

A fishing boat broke its mooring in one of the big winter gales and drifted down the promenade wall. Right where the boat site is there is a kink in the wall, Dove Point. Here boats usually came to grief. The boat hit the wall a few times but continued down the coast half underwater. We followed it with the tractor and as the tide ebbed, the rise and fall can be thirty two feet on spring tides, we went out to retrieve the engine. It wasn't there. By this time I knew it was a two cylinder Lister diesel, just what I wanted for the boat. George, the tractor driver and my next door neighbour, walked with me back towards Dove Point and there was Tolley, another pirate from Hoylake, on the beach with another tractor. The engine had fallen out of the bottom of the boat right by our boat site. I had to borrow one hundred and fifty pounds and buy the engine from Tolley.

I bought a wooden mast in Norwich on the other side of the country. A friend and I brought it back on the roof of a Morris Traveller, it was forty feet long. and stuck out a long way fore and aft. My friend had to run forward to any halt sign to see if anything was coming and we had lots of flags at the back. It was hair raising and in the end the mast was obviously quite unsuitable. Eventually I brought a very cheap aluminium extrusion from another concrete boat builder in Bristol, who had the section extruded with his own die. I remember it was something like a minimum of a quarter of a mile before the aluminium company would do it!

By the final year at the boat site there were three large concrete yachts and George, the farm labourer, building a concrete fishing boat. Brian spent a lot of time there and his wife was finishing her PhD. She was offered a research post with a professor in California who had recently won the Nobel prize and she couldn't refuse. Tom and Jean were moving along painfully slowly. Jean who seemed a lot more dedicated was getting frustrated. She eventually packed her bags and went off to France picking grapes and later working in Paris.

By this time the boat looked close to completion. I got more and more visitors. I had a girlfriend who had done a lot of traveling including up to Base Camp Everest. Her name was Angie. She often stayed in the caravan and would sometimes go for early morning dips in the sea. One day she almost gave a poor old guy walking his dog a terminal heart attack. She had been wearing a diaphanous cheesecloth gown and after a dip in the sea, obviously nothing else. Not the sort of thing you expect to see flitting through the sand dunes at that time in the morning!

It is amazing the useful people you find in pubs and I was lucky to meet up with a guy in the transportation business one night and so mentioned the problem of me getting the boat to the docks to launch it. It finished off as a silly bet of one beer as to whether he could do the job. I couldn't get a crane down to the lane but had built a cradle under the boat which the lorry could drive under and we would than lower the boat using jacks.

And so the great day came and a huge lorry arrived with a very low flatbed trailer with lots of axles and wheels. There was one heart stopping moment when the cradle cracked but, with crude repairs, the trailer slid under the boat and we lowered it down, cutting off the ends of the beams once it was down. I had trimmed a lot of trees in the lane and had to push a few cables up in the air to pass under but the trailer caterpillared over the humps and bumps beautifully. The police met us on the main road and escorted the boat down into Birkenhead and down to the docks. At the docks I had a crane waiting and there was a big crowd of people, including all the people that had helped me over the years. It was now 1976. It had been five years of grafting and scrounging to get this far.

The champagne bottle broke nicely on the bow, the spare bottle got drunk and contrary to all skeptics, the boat floated. I named her *Sea Loone*, the "e" was added to avoid problems with registration as a British ship. A loon is a bird, normally in England they are called divers, they are very handsome streamlined birds but have a call resembling the howl of a lunatic or loony and me being Starkey or Starkers short for stark staring mad. The family once living on the river Lune above Kirby Lonsdale in Lancashire. Finally people often said you had to be mad wanting to go sailing out there in Liverpool Bay which is usually horrible rough, grey and cold.

I wasn't really worried that the boat might sink but in fact of the three concrete boats launched there around that time *Sea Loone* was the only one that decided to float.

Barry, who had built his boat in Oxton, had launched his boat some four months before. The reporters from the newspapers came but he also had the television cameras. Everything went really well, but not long after the cameras and the crane had gone they found water pouring in at a number of places. They recalled the crane and soon sorted the problem. The third boat which was launched after *Sea Loone* was a very sad story.

Eric, to become known as "Mad Eric", arrived at the boat site some years before. He was going to build concrete boats in his back garden. He had with him a model of the boat. It had more fins than one of those exotic goldfish with the googly eyes. I put him on to a couple of books on design that I had used and he scaled down a few of the fins.

Only a few month later he was down telling us he was about to cement his boat. So Tom and Jean, Brian and myself shot off down to see. Eric's house was a semidetached bungalow and he was using both his and his neighbours garden. There were two large fin keels and two small keels behind for the two rudders. There was quite a mixture of reinforcing bars and chicken mesh but it was good.

So a few weeks later we went to help the cementing day. Eric was a teacher and most of his helpers were teachers or teacher's wives or husbands. They didn't last the course. The four of us from the boat site were knackered by the end of the day and the hull wasn't really finished. We went back the next day to finish it off.

The boat was a little unusual. It had 30 odd windows from telephone kiosks, the engine had a radiator in the saloon, there were car parts for steering the two rudders. On another visit to the boat site he told us he had the mast up, well worth another visit. Sure enough there was a huge mast towering into the sky held up with huge cables and rigging screws from the same source as the telephone kiosks. The mast was a welded lattice of pipes and very easy to climb. By the time you had climbed up onto the boat and then up the mast you could see across the Wirral Peninsula to Liverpool and to the Welsh mountains. It was spectacular. I'm still not sure how he managed to put it up, but I know what happened when it came down, in fact I saw it. The mast had fallen into the garden and into another garden. It must have hit with such force that it had formed the contours of the ground and the hedge. Eric was not worried at all.

When it came to launching his boat, the original idea had been to take it through another neighbour's garden to the road, but unfortunately the new owner was not in agreement. Meanwhile the next door neighbour in the other half of the semidetached bungalow died and Eric had bought the property. So he bought an old digging machine and knocked this half of his property down, built a trailer and dragged the boat out onto the road.

Unfortunately I didn't know the exact day he was going to launch, until somebody came around and said I was urgently needed in the main basin of the dock. It was a disaster. The crane that Eric acquired had lifted the boat out too far from the wall. The crane had turned over with its boom narrowly missing Eric on the foredeck, before piercing the deck and then the hull and plunging it into sixty feet of water. Eric got caught up in the falls of wire, broke his hip and got dragged under. He was dead lucky to extricate himself and get to the surface where his cousin plunged in and kept him afloat. By the time I arrived Eric was in the hospital, the crane had one foot jammed on the wall, the rest in the water, the boat was not to be seen. The local crane company sent their largest crane to sort things out and some commercial divers arrived. The dock company was not happy, they had a large cargo vessel waiting in the river to come in and we were in the way.

The big crane tried to lift the smaller crane and couldn't do it so we had to wait for a huge one hundred ton crane to come from Manchester. The two cranes lifted the third like huge prehistoric monsters, but the boom on the crane kept on extending as the hydraulics were bust. They had to cut it off. The cost must have been enormous. With the crane out of the way the divers tried to put slings under the boat in the murk and mud at the bottom of the dock. I sat on the wall making drawings and suggestions. We pulled up a few bits but in the end only succeeded by putting a wire snotter, like a noose, around the transom, the back of the boat and lifting it up and out stern first, water poured out of the huge hole in the foredeck. The last blow was when they dropped the remains on a huge ships mooring bollard .

The following day I saw Eric in hospital. Propped up in his bed he said that he definitely felt the boat float for a few seconds before the crane speared it. He then showed me a drawing he was working on. It was the next boat.

The crane was doing a "foreigner" (a job on the side). It was working from some miles away on a refinery and not supposed to travel on roads and obviously not supposed to do private jobs on weekends. But as luck would have it, the crane driver was the union delegate in the refinery so he wasn't even sacked. The whole operation in the end must have cost a fortune. God knows who paid. That's Liverpool!

In the dock I tied next to an old dredger that was being cut up for scrap. They paid me to be the night watchman and with winter coming on I sometimes slept in their portacabin as it was much warmer than the boat. I still had the engine to hook up, finish the ballasting, finish the galley and put up the mast.

Jean who was now in Paris and working in a hotel was keen to join the crew when I left the next year and she was sending me money to make sure it happened. Angie was also keen to come but I hadn't quite got round to acquainting each with the other. And then there was Phil who had helped a lot in the building and Alan who had apparently some sailing experience. The two lads had sports cars which if sold would help to pay the trip. I was permanently broke. There was always something to gobble up whatever I had.

In the Spring Jean came back from France. It might have helped if I had some warning. Introducing Angie to Jean while one was lying naked in my bed didn't go down to well. I'd had exotic ideas that I could manage the two of them. After all Wharram with his catamarans down the road in Pembrokeshire had half a dozen girls as crew on his boat. No chance. Angie took off. Very sad!

We took the boat for a sail around the dock. The cotton genoa tore in half and then the rudder fell off. The shaft for the rudder was a heavy steel tube. Electrolysis had eaten into it like mice into cheese. The rudder stayed jammed in the lower pintle but separated from the shaft going up through the boat. It was lucky it did jam and not fall into the depths below.

Kenny my mate from Liverpool came to my rescue with his kid's snorkelling gear. It wasn't too deep so he attached a long tube to the snorkel and jumped in. He nearly collapsed his lungs apart from the hypothermia. Then a guy building a steel yacht over in Liverpool promised to come and give us a hand. He was a diver. The local scrap yard cut away the steel tube, the paper mill came up with a solid stainless steel shaft machined at the ends and a small coastal shipping company welded the shaft and plate back together and all this was done for free, fantastic.. A week later I had a much superior rudder back in place and I had hung some zinc anodes under the boat for the first time.

It was time for sea trials. So with the crew signed on for a day trip into the river we locked out of the docks, put the sails up and were swept down the river with the tide. It runs at up to nine knots in the Mersey so you go with it, quickly or slowly, but you go with it. Phil who is basically a very clean person was scrubbing the foredeck removing all the congealed dock grime when the Isle of Man ferry passed us. We nearly lost him. *Sea Loone* plowed into the tsunami left by the ferry and water a foot deep swept down the decks. There wasn't much wind and we couldn't go very far but we missed the tide to get back into the docks and only just managed to pick up a mooring down at the river mouth, New Brighton, before we got swept away to Ireland.

It was dark and low tide as we motored back up the river. We found some slimy steps next to the lock gates which lowered above us and tied up there until the tide rose high enough for the gates to open. Alan had planned to take his girlfriend out that night. When he didn't pick her up she panicked and the lifeboat was called out to look for us. We of course were invisible tied below the lock gates only a couple of feet of mast showed above the dock wall. Not a good start and the following week Phil and Alan found other more important things to do then go off sailing the Atlantic.

The boat was ready to go. The hull was a slightly expanded Contest 33 with an exaggerated shear line, a vertical transom and a six inch toe rail all the way around. The cabin top was supposed to resemble that of another yacht, an Erikson 35 but had not looked right until I lifted the backend four or five inches and eyed it from the roof of the wooden shed. The engine was the air cooled Lister diesel off the beach. The cooker was gas and out of the caravan. The two settees in the main cabin were pushed right up against the hull sides to give good floor space. One settee extended to make a double bed. Up forward was a work bench and narrow berth. The toilet had a louvre door as did the wardrobe opposite. Under the cockpit was a hell hole and a bunk for a contortionist, the chart table was like a school desk facing forwards with the top a single massive piece of teak donated by Martins Bank, St. Helens.

In the bilge there were two inflatable water tanks and the fuel tank from one of my Austin minis. There was a generator bolted to the Lister engine taken from the last of my Morris Minors. In the cockpit there was a beautiful S-shaped tiller laminated from dark red mahogany. Behind the tiller was a huge two speed winch donated by Rolls Royse and the navy. The mast was aluminium, its rigging, chainplates, the bow pulpit and stern rail all galvanized steel. The blocks were a mixture of sizes and shapes, the ropes from a company selling cheap rope ends. The main anchor was a new CQR, the second a large fisherman, a gift. The anchor chain was ex lifting chain welded together.

The sails were all second hand, the mainsail a bit small and the two jibs from a trimaran. The cotton genoa from a huge old racing yacht had disintegrated but I still have the big piston hanks from it today. We had navigation lights on the bow and stern and on top of the mast. We had a VHF radio, a depth sounder and a radio direction finder all made by Seafarer. We also had a large Phillips radio that could pick up short wave. The radios etc had all been very expensive and way too much to afford at this late stage in preparing to leave, that is until they fell off the back of a lorry.

Brian, building the largest of the concrete boats had been to sea before he worked for an oil company. He had a second mate ticket and the knowledge how to use a sextant. He generously sold me his old sextant, a beautiful bronze job made during the war. It was very accurate but difficult to read as it was vernier, rather than with a micrometer. The calculations were worse but Brian got some of it into my head. An old sea captain gave me his copy of Norries tables and some other navigation books, light lists and such like and I got some cancelled charts, most of them for the wrong places from a shipping line in Liverpool.

The summer passed. We were ready to go, the "we" being myself and Jean. We were penniless but some dubious source had landed us a complicated radio. It was of no use to us so we found someone happy to give us fifty pounds for it. That was enough, we were off. It was September 1977.

The leaving of Liverpool, a well known song so I wasn't going to be the first boat to leave. Liverpool sailing ships had been some of the best, the fastest and well known. The sea shanties invariably mention the port. When I was a small boy I remember seeing what must have been the last commercial sailing ship in the river, a three-masted brig carrying potatoes from Ireland. With the huge tides, thirty three feet on "springs", this was not a place for yachts such as mine. There were still a few small yachts on moorings in the river. I had been enthralled by slide shows in the yacht club on the old pier where some of the boats had cruised up to Scotland or over to Ireland in the 1960's. Fitting out the boat in Morpeth Dock there were just a few fishing boats, converted lifeboats and such like.

To see anything similar to *Sea Loone* I had to go each year to the London Boat Show. On one of those occasions I was amazed to find a real Contest 33 on display. What luck. I was invited around it by one of the salesman, who went on about the wonderful lines and beautiful underwater shape, the fin keels and balanced rudder. How many hours I had spent looking at exactly this while twisting a quarter of a million wire ties in the chicken mesh. Inside the boat the poor man lifted all the floorboards for me to peer in the bilges as I sneakily measure a few things. He must have felt sure of a sale. I was sorry for him and embarrassed when he couldn't get all the floors to sit back in place properly.

2

THE GREAT DAY broke clear with a fickle wind which at least wasn't going to be directly against us. I swung the engine over, flicked the decompression levers and the Lister started thumping away. We set off out of Morpeth Dock, the first and then second road bridges opened for us heading for the locks into the river.

Bob and his wife Andy were coming with us as far as Anglesey. They were from the "centre of the universe" which is apparently a suburb of Manchester. We also had two girls from the University. As the lock gates opened a slight swell rocked the boat. One poor girl shot below and spent the rest of the trip in the forward bunk filling plastic bags with sick.

We drifted up river for a while until the tide changed and then we were swept out into Liverpool Bay. As we passed New Brighton Bob and Andy disappeared below feeling ill and twenty miles out as we went over the bar the last temporary crew gave in. Jean and I were sailing the boat alone.

I had made a self steering gear operated by the winds. It seemed actually operated by the devil. Somehow we got to Anglesey the next day and as we entered the harbour all the crew miraculously recovered. The boatman at the yacht club offered us a mooring and ferried our crew ashore, Jean and I were left alone. The sailing season was ended so it was very quiet. We had a rubber dinghy given to us which we used going ashore. The technique was to pump it up and row like hell before it folded in half. Jean learned to row here by the sink or swim method. As she got blown out of the harbour she had to sort out her technique and get back before the dinghy deflated.

We dried *Sea Loone* against the harbour wall and cleaned off a thick crust of barnacles and sea squirts, all of which we had brought from the Mersey. The weather was terrible and day by day it got colder. We caught prawns in the rock pools and picked blackberries and mushrooms in the fields above us and the money slowly evaporated.

As time passed I realized that my greatest asset was Jean. She was no ordinary lady and had an unusual background. She was born and brought up in Yorkshire. Her mother, sometime after Jean was born became seriously ill with long periods of depression. Jean became the mother of the family which now included a younger brother. Running the household, cooking, cleaning, decorating, gardening and so on I don't think she had much time for being a child or even a teenager. She did manage to find time with her studies and was offered a place at Liverpool University to study medicine. I'm not sure how she met Tom, perhaps with his bird watching.

She was very committed to their plans to build a boat and sail north following Tillman's voyages around Greenland. She had given up on the medicine degree and was then working in a biscuit factory by day and twisting tie wires by night.

Having seen the huge amount of time and dedication she had put in, it was a real shame that they fought like cats and dogs. At the rate Tom was progressing even with Jeans efforts it was obvious the boat wasn't going to hit the water for many years. I think the night she came knocking on my caravan door in the pouring rain with broken glasses and crying her eyes out was the last straw for her and shortly after she left for France.

I had offered her the chance to come on Sea Loone if everything fell apart for her and if *Sea Loone* really did go sailing. I had said this without a great deal of thought but I realized when Jean started sending me bundles of French francs she was taking it very seriously. So when Phil and Alan changed their minds after the shakedown cruise and when the seasick crew left Holyhead, Anglesey, to return to Liverpool it was just the two of us.

It was more than five years since I had stood on the promenade wall and discovered the boat site. Each and every day apart from when I was digging the tunnel I had tried to do something, however small, towards building the boat. The total cost in materials, tools and rent had been two and a half thousand pounds. Had I included the real cost of some materials and labour and included my own labour especially all those hours tying bloody wires then it could probably have been cheaper to have bought that Contest 33 at the Boat Show.

As we watched the gales howling and the seas pound over the harbour wall, the money eeked away. On October 6th there was a break in the weather and we sailed out to sea heading south down the Irish Sea. We had waited three weeks for the weather to settle. The trip from Liverpool with six of us on board had passed without any problems. Now with only the two of us we were heading out into the Irish Sea. I seemed on a much bigger test. The daylight faded and we sailed vaguely south through the first night. Hanging onto the tiller looking into that blackness bouncing up and down on a really bumpy sea was not the dream. The nights were getting longer and it was a long time before there was a glimmer of dawn. The horizon cleared to show us no sign of land. We were truly at sea. A few gannets and kitiwakes flew past but other than that we saw nothing all day. It wasn't until late afternoon with us being pushed west that we saw what must be the coast of Ireland and as it got dark we picked up the loom of Tusker Rock Lighthouse. The following morning we passed the Smalls, an impressive lighthouse stuck on a very small rock. I had met a lighthouse keeper once on Bardsey Island when I was bird watching. He had worked on the Smalls and described how he walked around in circles all day.

We thought to spend the winter in Bristol and find some work to fill the empty piggy bank. On the third day we were off Milford Haven near the south west corner of Wales. We were cold, wet and salty. A small gale blew us into the Haven and when we arrived off the dock, the gates miraculously opened and a smiling dock keeper in a thick polo necked jumper waved us in. We didn't hesitate.

It was heaven, flat calm out of the wind. We tied up next to huge piles of lobster pots with the herring gulls hovered overhead screaming. I think they mistook us for a fishing boat. Across the way was the harbour office, Here we met Dundes Aires, the jolly man that had waved us in.

We filled in our first form, first of many to come. Name of boat, registration number, tonnage. I got as far as tonnage, Dundes stopped me. Nine tons he said was awfully heavy and the harbour was very expensive for heavy boats. So *Sea Loone* suddenly lost a lot of weight, in fact half its weight and we committed ourselves to pay ten shillings a week sometime soon.

We needed to make some money and quickly. Jean got a job serving in the local fish and chip shop. The shop had been recently taken over by a Chinese man. His children were going to the local school and had some English, the father not so good and the wife and her mother not at all. They had some relations in London. I thought they were pretty adventurous coming to live in the wilds of Wales. It was a bit of foreign land for me. I heard there was some work available unloading fishing boats on the docks. So I went and had a snoop around. It turned out that the Iceland cod trawlers from Hull which were now more or less redundant, were fishing for mackerel bringing them into Milford Haven to be sent off to Nigeria to feed the starving people there somewhere up country.

So early one morning I found myself amongst a crowd of locals in a small room with a raised podium one end. A large hairy old Welsh man was pointing down at different people and saying "I'll have you and you" but he didn't point at me. I called him Llewellyn, prince of Daveth and each day would find a good spot in front of him and stared. It took a while but he eventually pointed at me.

There was only work available when both a freezer ship and a trawler arrived. As they locked into the dock right next to my boat I was first to know and first waiting outside Llewellyn's office. The trawlers were huge carrying 500 to 1000 tons of boxed frozen fish. They were restricted to only catching twenty tons of fish per day. It took them twenty minutes once they isolated the shoal of fish. It took us maybe a day and a half to empty a trawler into the freezer ship alongside in a temperature of minus thirty two degrees centigrade. Throwing the boxes onto pallets was hard work but you never got warm and we all worried about frostbite in our toes.

I became a fixed member of the B-team with occasional invites into the A-team which was good going for an English outsider. There were quite a few injuries especially broken bones. I broke the end of my finger and for a few weeks had an easy job directing the crane driver standing on the relatively warm deck shouting insults to the crew below in the frost. When they realized the finger was fixed I soon got dragged down below again. The money we earned was phenomenal. One week when we had to work every day I came home with forty six five pound notes. I threw them down in the cabin and they fluttered around Jean's bemused head. This was ten times the money I had been earning in the shipyard.

If we were to get away we really needed this sort of money. We bought some sails from a local potato farmer. We bought an Aires wind wave steering gear which was like buying a third crew. We bought an inflatable dinghy to replace the deflatable. The list went on.

Tied alongside the dock near us was another concrete yacht, which had been launched not long before we arrived. The owner, Gordie, lived just up the hill and had built the boat here. He was a driller and travelled all over the world drilling holes in rocks usually for dams and bridges. We took his boat for a test sail, engineless, in the haven. The decks were flush and he had no rails so I fell over the side. Not serious except that at that time I couldn't really swim, so they had jibe around quickly before I disappeared under the waves.

To get back into the dock we had to take a run at it and get up enough momentum through the narrow locks. Healed well over I was a bit worried the mast might scrape along the wall and even maybe pick up Dundes, who was standing there also looking a little worried. Just as our bow nosed into the gates we lost the wind, shot upright with all the sails fluttering and flew through into the dock basin. Nobody could have realized that the three of us were absolute beginners.

Lobster fishing was a big thing along this rocky coastline but also some local divers had discovered crayfish. There were rock pinnacles just off the coast coming close to the surface from deep water. At certain times of the year these pinnacles had huge numbers of big crayfish sitting on them. The divers we met soon reduced the numbers. David, one of the divers said he would go down in those early days with a sack. The crayfish would be sitting on ledges, packed next to each other. He said it was like picking up five pound notes and stuffing them into the sack.

We went out with the divers a few times on an old fishing trawler. The technique was to find a pinnacle with the depth sounder, take a reading on the Decca, a not very accurate positioning device, chuck a diver over the side with a sack, a plastic bottle to fill with air to lift a full sack and a flag to wave when we returned and we could go off to find the next pinnacle for the next diver. One of the most successful divers was a professional violinist from Yorkshire, another had built a beautiful house on the cliff top with his profits. They were all a bit mad.

By the spring the trawlers had decimated the shoals of mackerel and what were left had disappeared along the coast as they always did. We spend a lot of money on the boat but still had more than £1000 to leave with. We were off to the Caribbean.

It wasn't actually until July that we finally headed out from Dale at the mouth of the Haven for Dunmore East at the entrance to the Waterford River in Ireland. The plan was to sail down to the south west tip of Ireland and then head south for Bayona on the north west coast of Spain. We wanted to be across the Bay of Biscay before any autumn gales. We would then sail out to Madeira and south again to the Canary Islands, which would be our starting off point to cross the Atlantic to the Caribbean.

Once I got the wind vane the right way around the Aires self steering worked perfectly. I could sit with Jean on the foredeck and look back at the boat ploughing through the water leaving a perfect straight wake, straighter I'm sure, than either Jean or I could have managed. The wind wouldn't allow us to sail directly for Dunmore initially but gradually came round so that by the following morning the course had curved around and the Aires sailed us into the river's mouth without us even touching the tiller, amazing!

On arrival, we made a big mistake. The harbour was full of yachts on a race from somewhere, but we had found a spot on the dock wall to tie up. Not long after we had a visit from the port Customs officer. Why weren't we flying a quarantine flag? We hadn't even thought about it. As punishment he was going to choose our boat as the boat to be searched for contraband. He started with a cup of coffee and we explained that we were not one of the racing yachts but in fact on our way to the Caribbean and which ever locker or cupboard he was going to look in was going to be full. He changed his mind, nice man.

Cross Haven is the yachting centre for Cork and the yacht club the oldest in the world established in 1720. We arrived for the beginning of Cork Week, not a good idea for us beginners. We managed to get a mooring rapped around our rudder right in front of the yacht club. The boatman helped us to untangle this. We didn't offer the boatman a tip as some other visitors had done. The boatman had pointed out that he was simply a member of the club doing the job by rotation. His signature was on the banknote proffered; he was the Governor of the Bank of Ireland.

Finally anchored properly we thought we'd have an evening beer in the yacht club. We were wearing jeans and pullovers, but the club was crowded with people in dinner suits and ladies in gowns. There was a huge dinningroom with linen table cloths and silverware. We went to sneak out when a familiar face asked us if we wanted a drink. It was a guy with a large motor cruiser we had met in Liverpool docks, he had been a national champion sailing dinghies. When we mentioned where we were off to, we became instant celebrities. For two days we were wined and dined even though we hadn't actually been anywhere. We felt like frauds but it was very enjoyable.

The Irish coast is really very beautiful when the weather cooperates. The people are warm and full of fun. The Irishmen I had worked with down in the tunnel in Liverpool had jokingly told me the story of a young Irishman who had got a job on a building site in Liverpool. He had to dig holes for fence posts. The ganger had got him started on the first hole and went off to supervise another part of the job. At the end of the day the lad was nowhere to be seen. He was more than six feet down heading for Australia. Nobody had told him to stop.

So when we sailed into Kinsale, I went to see another concrete boat I had been told about. It was being used as a tourist boat giving trips round the harbour. It had two telephone poles for masts but it was the hull that interested me. It seemed very Irish. The builders had dug a boat-shaped hole and then somehow cemented the sides of it. It not only floated but, seeing the people trooping on board for a harbour cruise, it was making money.

In Kinsale there was only a short piece of wall to tie up to, so up to ten boats rafted themselves up together. The inside boat scraped up and down the wall as the tide rose and fell. When I had tied into the flotilla I realized that the boat next to me looked familiar. It was flying the Dutch flag. Then it struck me; it was a *Contest 33,* the design I had borrowed from the magazine. This was a real one.

The owner looked almost annoyed when I pointed out to him that our two boats were roughly the same design. The decks were on the same level which surprised me. Ours was carrying so much more weight for the transatlantic cruise. The only real difference in the outside shape was that we were a tad longer.

Down below it was a different story. When I was invited onto the Dutch boat I noticed that the cabin felt much smaller. The lockers were placed on either side of the quarter berths and the folding table, which even when not open took up most of the floor space, was a permanent obstacle when you tried to edge your way forward. The Dutchman was sure I was mistaken when he came on board *Sea Loone* and easily walked upright around our spacious cabin.

We were still making lots of mistakes. We got very tangled up against the dock wall and when we tried to extricate ourselves, we managed to tangle our anchor with a French yacht and finished up abruptly alongside him. The French love dragging and bumping into each other. It's a kind of social outing for them so the captain was very friendly and helpful.

In Baltimore, a small gale blew up suddenly and I had to row out our fisherman anchor. While we were doing this they launched the lifeboat very close to us. They have a long steep ramp and the lifeboat half buries itself as it hits the water with a huge splash. It was very spectacular but no one seemed to have any idea where they were going.

We were leaving Baltimore to cross the Bay of Biscay for Cape Finisterre on the extreme the northeast corner of Spain; then down the coast a short distance to Bayonne. My bibles for building the boat had been Eric Hiscock's "Cruising Under Sail" and "Voyaging Under Sail." We were still using them for the trip. They instructed us to buy ten lemons presumably to prevent scurvy.

In Baltimore this was not straightforward. In the shop there was a box of lemons. But when Jean asked for ten the lady tut-tutted and started counting them. With her board Irish accent she said she had two for Mrs Flaherty, one for Mrs O'Leary and so on. It was a full box so she carried on like this for quite a while. Finally, she calculated that Jean could have four. Ah well, "aught's better than naught".

We motored out of the bay, set the sails and with the lightest of breezes, headed slowly south. Sherkin Island passed on the starboard side and out to the west was Clear Island and the Fastnet Rock. As we came out into the open sea we met the first real ocean swells we had encountered. They were like huge watery hills marching towards us in long dark ranks. In the valleys we completely lost the horizon. I conjured up images of these swells turning into huge breaking deluges in a gale. *Sea Loone* seemed to shrink under as if it were a mere flea on the huge rounded grey back of an elephant.

We threw the brass fish for the log in the water. The fish is about six inches long on a sixty foot line. It's attached to a Walker Patent Log bolted to the toe rail. As the fish spins, the log records the distance traveled through the water. There was also a little red dot on the flywheel which, if you timed so many revolutions, you could get an idea of the speed.

On the other side of the boat, we had the fishing line with a frayed rope lure on the end. It was not unusual for the lure and the log to get together and if we didn't see it quickly, it could be an interminable task trying to untangle the two.

Jean wrote down our departure time in the logbook noting that we had about five hundred miles of openocean to cover. The next landfall would be Cape Finisterre, the northernmost tip of Spain, with its large lighthouse perched on top. It took a few days to get used to the ups and downs in overcast conditions, with the wind not too strong. A pomerine skua came to visit which thrilled me. It is a bird.

It wasn't until the fourth day that things deteriorated. The wind started to pick up in the late afternoon and by dusk I had taken down our largest headsail and replaced it with the smallest. Then with a lot of difficulty and hanging on for dear life, I managed to reef the mainsail down to its minimum. By the time I had done this I was very wet, very cold and knackered. Jean pointed out that the barometer had plummeted, so from then on we watched it like a hawk.

The gale blew all night and the seas got bigger and bigger. Occasionally the boat seemed to freefall off a wave, heel over madly and crash into the next wave. We thought we had stowed everything away properly but now there was very little that wasn't on the move. Under the cockpit everything shot from one side of the boat to the other and back again. We were powerless to stop it. The noise was horrendous inside and out. I spent the night wedging things in place. Meanwhile Jean, seemingly unperturbed, made dinner.

Fortunately, it wasn't much of a gale but a good tester for us. A day later we were becalmed off Finisterre and that evening saw the loom of the light. We were slap bang in the middle of the main shipping route to northern Europe with ships passing us continuously. We sneaked in close to the land and the next day, dodging multitudes of fishing nets, we sailed into Bayonne a truly foreign port.

We spent nearly a month in Bayonne. Neither Jean nor I spoke any Spanish but we managed to communicate. Pepe's Bar in town was the center for the few yachts in the harbour. One pound bought us one hundred and forty pesatas which seemed to go quite far. But we still had to live carefully and frugally.

In the evenings, the local people fished off the wharf using long poles under the street lights. Jean discovered they were catching squid which was very edible and quite valuable. So, using her newly acquired smattering of Spanish, she went down to the local feritaria (hardware store) and bought herself a squid lure. The only lighting we had on *Sea Loone* was a Tilly lamp, (a pressurized paraffin lamp) hanging from the middle of the main cabin. It was easy to hang this over the side and attract lots of small fish. In turn, these attracted the squid.

Jean jigged the lure up and down in the bright halo of light beside the boat. As if by magic, from out of the darkness emerged the first squid. As it got near the light it shot forward to grab the lure in its tentacles. It wasn't a very big squid only about five ounces and it wasn't a happy squid being yanked up out of the sea onto the boat. It squirted black ink all over Jean and over the deck. The ink is indelible so Jean had black-spotted jeans and tee shirt and the deck had black splodges which weren't going away any time soon. But undaunted, she devised a new technique that involved getting the squid out of the sea and into a large bucket of water as quickly as possible. Needless to say you had to wear your oldest clothes and keep throwing regular buckets of water over the deck.

The idea caught on and soon there were fishing lights hanging off all the yachts in the harbour. We swapped a few squid for mackerel but it never developed into the big business we had hoped.

There were three other British yachts heading for the Caribbean and a German yacht that we were to meet again in Madeira. We drank a fair amount of beer and wine, enjoyed a fiesta in the village and did some more work on the boat. Jean was making two downwind spinnaker jibs from an ex-army parachute we had bought. I made spinnaker poles which were in effect, two lengths of timber with large piston hanks lashed to the ends. We had to drag the boat out against a wall to replace the transducer for the depth sounder and once that was done, we were set to leave to head out into the Atlantic bound for Madeira.

It took us eight days to get to Madeira and sighting land was really special. The morning was quite calm and misty. Although we couldn't see land, my sights with the sextant and the numerous lines I had drawn on the chart, said we were close. The radio beacon said the island was directly in front of us. It was then that Jean gave a sudden shout and pointed upwards. There were mountain tops towering above us several thousand feet; and yet we couldn't see land at all at sea level.

By midday the mist had burned off and we headed for a point around which we hoped to find some shelter and anchor. But just at that moment, the wind started to pick up. So, to save time we aimed for a point between the headland and a large rock. Once committed I started to get nervous in the rising breeze, but luckily we were quickly blown through the gap into calmer water.

As the sun set we anchored in deep calm water behind the steep peninsula. The wind picked up dramatically and in the pitch dark we dragged out to sea. The sea bottom dropped steeply and we finished with all our one hundred and fifty feet of chain hanging vertically. With no anchor winch we expended a lot of energy retrieving the chain plus the thirty five pound anchor, seriously huffing and puffing to get it all on deck.

I motored back up to the cliffs watching the depth-sounder. Eventually we seemed to get out of the wind under the cliff and with the water rapidly shallowing, we threw the anchor back in. The cliff seemed to hang right over us so I didn't get a lot of sleep.

The morning broke calm and clear. We could see the boulders and seaweed under the boat and sure enough we were far too close to the cliffs. The daylight showed us it had been a silly place to anchor. Fortunately, the anchor chain stayed clear of the rocks and we got off without a tangle, heading for Funchal the harbour.

Madeira being Portuguese, the paperwork on arrival was overwhelming. I received a booklet to be filled in page by page at the various offices where we were required to register .The town is perched on a mountainside and you could be sure that if Page 1 was from the office at the bottom of the hill, Page 2 would be at the top, and Page 3 at the bottom again. After being cooped up on the boat at least it was good exercise.

The harbor was small and crowded. We anchored with our stern tied to the harbor wall next to a group of other yachts. I used a fancy knot on the rope between the anchor chain and the boat but it came undone. Luckily we managed to retrieve the line by quick action with a grapnel. A few days later with another yacht coming alongside, I lost the anchor again. This time we had to get a diver to go down and find it; all very embarrassing. I think it's called learning by your mistakes. We were learning a lot.

The island is sub-tropical and very mountainous. All sorts of interesting things grow on its terraces and in the valley bottoms. There was no flat land left uncultivated. Jean brought home sweet potatoes, passion fruit, prickly pear, fresh figs and mangoes, none of which had we ever eaten before. We took a bus up into the mountains and walked for miles through orchards of apples, plums and walnuts. There were grapes, sweetcorn and huge bilberry bushes.

In the harbour we met a Liverpool couple who we had earlier met in Spain. Their boat, *Quark*, was registered in Southampton but the owner, Charlie, had been a fisherman in the Isle of Man. We were destined to meet again; in fact many times and as I write, over thirty years later, I saw them again only a few days ago.

We were invited to dinner on the German yacht – a large new steel yacht named *Kairos*. George and Helga Koch were old hands. They had sailed round the world years before in a small wooden boat. To us they appeared quite posh so Jean was gobsmacked to learn they had pinched all the oranges from the Royal Yacht Club in Bayonne. They had made marmalade with them. This had been exactly Jean's plan too, except that they had all suddenly disappeared before she had a chance to filtch them. Now she knew the answer to the mystery. The closest Jean got to the oranges was exchanging some soya flour for some of Helga's marmalade.

It was George who mentioned that the boat didn't have water tanks, only storage space for lots of little plastic containers. Knowing from experience how much water he would need for the long crossing of the Atlantic, the excess bottles were filled with red wine. I stored away that piece of information.

When we came down the hill after our bus trip, *Sea Loone* was not in the same place. Apparently an afternoon squall had caused a lot of boats to drag their anchors including even *Kairos*. One yacht had bumped into us and dragged us with her. By then we had seen the island and done the town. So the next day we did lots more paperwork for clearing out, then headed for the Canary Islands.

As we departed the island we saw something really stupid. The town had provide a large dustbin (trash can) for all the rubbish that the boats and ships brought ashore. The dustbin was emptied into a lorry.

On leaving we saw what happened next. There is a huge cliff just out of town dropping into the deep water ocean. The lorry backs up to the edge and tips the rubbish over. It would have been less trouble if the boats had just thrown their rubbish into the sea in the first place.

We were headed for Teneriffe in the Canary Islands. Teneriffe has a huge volcano which is visible for seventy miles on a good day. When we couldn't see it, we asked a passing tanker where we were and where it was. It's cheating in a way; but we heard another yacht. *Rapid Transit*, asking the same question so we didn't feel so bad.

The main harbour was no good for us so we moved up the coast to the fishing harbour, Darsena Pesquera. The engine wasn't behaving very well but we putt-putted the last bit through the harbour entrance. There was a fleet of Russia and Chinese tuna boats in port so we had to tie up alongside a pirate ship designed for robbing tourists. The yacht *Rapid Transit* arrived (the voice we had heard earlier on the radio) and tied up outside of us. It was a huge new aluminium racing yacht being delivered to America. So we felt like the meat in the sandwich.

Any yacht we were going to meet now would be crossing the Atlantic and there were at least eight. The harbour was wonderfully flat calm but very polluted. The whole place stank of fish, rotten fish. It was the beginning of October and we were stocking up the boat for the long ocean passage. A sack of potatoes, 450 pesatas and onions much the same. We had to take one of the gas bottles to be filled which we only managed with the help of the racing yacht.

Although busy, we managed to organize a barbecue on the dock wall. The fridge on *Rapid Transit* had broken down so their meat had to be eaten. The Russian trawlermen brought a huge barracuda and some black bread. There were a couple of guitars and a Danish sailor with a clarinet. A lot of dunnage wood got burned and the iron curtain got lifted. The Russians really enjoyed themselves and would have let their hair down if it wasn't for a guy standing in the shadows. He wasn't joining in, he apparently was the "party" man, watching.

The pirate boat had a few charters organized so we had to move. We finished off tied to a Taiwanese long-liner together with two other yachts. One was Black Squall. We had met the young English owner, Jerry earlier in Bayonne. The other yacht was a wooden boat flying the American flag. Her skipper or guardian, Johnny, was a Moroccan.

The Taiwanese were really happy to have us all alongside their boat. They were always offering us food and drink and didn't mind us clambering over their boat to get to the dock. In fact, they were tied to another long-liner so we had two boats to cross before we got to land. The inside boat was from North Korea. Talk about chalk and cheese. The Koreans were a very unsmiling lot

We had the boat stored up and we were going to sail down to Los Cristianos on the south coast but before we left, Johnny suggested we took the Taiwanese crew for a day out on his yacht. The idea was to sail north a short distance and anchor in the first bay where we could all go swimming. The Chinese were really keen so off we went; Jean and myself, Johnny and Jerry and lots of little Chinamen perched on the cabin top. This predates refugee boats but you can imagine what it was like.

It was only then, as we sailed into the bay that Johnny mentioned he doesn't have an anchor. There was a yacht already anchored, another American. No problem. Johnny motors over to ask if we can tie alongside for a short while. Now Johnny's English has the American twang but he hasn't the looks. The very presentable young lady who was reading under the awning looks down at us over her glasses. She notices we are a scruffy lot, full of yellow peril, a few other oddballs; plus an Arab pretending to be an American. Needless to say we were not invited alongside.

The only other possibility was a fishing boat. Here we were made welcome because the Chinese were carrying a number of bottles of whiskey, their favorite local tipple. It turned out that this was not an ordinary fishing boat. It was in fact the research vessel for the local Institute of Oceanography. When the chief scientist returned from his swim he found us well settled in. There was a little whiskey still left but we had drunk most of their red wine.

The scientist, Dr. Brown, was explaining that they were studying "the respiration of organisms in the third trophic layer." They had tanks full of sardines and once the sardines had used all the oxygen in the water, they floated to the surface. They were then transferred to the frying pan. Fast fried with fresh bread, they were delicious. When the last fish had succumbed, and the wine and the whiskey were finished and our crew had swum around the boat enough we headed off back to the fishing harbour. We finished the day as usual squatting on very low stools on the aft deck of the tuna boat with a huge bowl of rice and a huge bowl of "whatever". I say "whatever" meaning whatever floated in their tasty sauce, though most of it we found impossible to catch with chopsticks.

The Taiwanese were very friendly and seemed always very happy and smiling, but their life was really hard. The boats use Tenerife as a base and they fished the area between the Canaries and Africa. They used long lines which were miles long with thousands of hook baited with squid. They would be at sea continuously until they were full, usually six months. When they returned to Tenerife they would either fly home or stay for the next trip. They were terrible gamblers, so many lost all the money they earned.

Next we headed for Gomera, the southernmost island which was reported to have better water. We anchored inside the harbour and rowed ashore. Here we discovered an English couple living under a bush. They were going to spend the winter there but did say they were looking for somewhere more substantial. They came across to the harbor wall with us when we went to collect water. We had to pay fifty pesatas for the minimum amount which was a quarter ton. It came out of a fire hose which is a little difficult to control. But when we had filled everything we all had a huge shower. The bush dwellers loved it.

Gomera is supposed to be the most verdant island in the Canaries but was still looking like an ash pile to us. We did manage to buy some fresh vegetables and of course the ten lemons. Jean finally bought fifty eggs and we were ready for the off. So October 25th we sailed out of Gomera and headed west for Antigua over 2000 miles away.

There is a point southwest of the Canaries which is the place Eric Hiscock mentioned where one should be able to pick up the tradewinds and turn directly west for the West Indies. The old adage says that you head south until the butter melts, then turn right. Whatever we did we never really found the tradewinds.

It took us two days to drop Tenerife over the horizon behind us. Then in mid Atlantic we had westerly winds for a short while before a frustrating week of total calm. Finally we picked up a fair wind to blow us the last 400 miles.

The really great thing that happened was that, after a week or so of this, we became absolutely in tune with the boat. We unthinkingly reacted to each movement of the boat and tuned out all the normal noises from the rigging and the rudder. We found we instantly knew if there had been any changes in the wind, weather or equipment. Together we and *Sea Loone* became a single efficient machine sailing across the high seas.

Four days out I caught our first big fish, a dorado over three feet long. They are spectacular fish, gold with bright blue fins but it's sad to see the gold colour fade to silver as it dies. We ate it for dinner then tea and for breakfast. Jean preserved more with vinegar and onions. I couldn't face that last little bit. I was happy to eat eggs for a change.

We had a visit from some pilot whales. They are like large dolphins with blunt noses. A shearwater landed in the cockpit and stayed the night as did a swallow later on. A small barge passed us and said hello, a great motor sailing yacht passed and said nothing.

It was flat calm, we jumped over the side with a rope tied around us and swam. We noticed that the barnacles had arrived and were growing rapidly. These were goose barnacles with leathery stalks and a black and white body on the end. They grow up to three inches long which means they can seriously slow you down. By the time we arrived off Antigua they were mature.

The one problem we had which could have been serious was with the water. We had two inflatable water tanks in the bilge. As they emptied, they naturally creased but with the movement of the boat the creases worked back and forward until they split. We started to lose the water and we still had a long way to go. Fortunately we had four plastic Jerry cans which each held five gallons plus a couple of other containers. We were washing in saltwater and if it rained at all we tried to collect water off the mainsail. We did get one bucketful off the sail but it was pretty dirty and full of sand presumably blown from the Sahara.

When we eventually got closer to Antigua navigating with the sextant we also began picking up local radio including Radio Monseratt, good music and a navigational aid as well.

Finally, on the night of December 1st 1978 we picked up some lights and saw the island looming ahead of us. The coastal waters gave us an unpleasant bouncy last night at sea, so we were happy to see the dawn, get our exact position and head down the coast to English Harbour. Our first Atlantic crossing was behind us!

3

ENGLISH HARBOUR WAS one of the main bases for the British fleet in Nelson's time during the long war with France. Nelsons dockyard inside the harbour repaired and refurbished Britain's "ships of the line".

The only way we managed to spot the entrance was seeing the masts of some large yachts poking up above the overlapping headlands. Getting closer I realized that the headland we were heading for was fortified with crenellations like an old castle. I swung the old Lister over, dropped the decompressors and, with a sigh of relief, putt-putted our way through what we now saw was a very narrow channel between the headland to port and the jagged reef to starboard.

This was our first tropical island. We had crossed the Tropic of Cancer many miles back. I wanted to see the lush tropical jungle just as the boys had found in the book Coral Island and there in front of me was a long sandy beach with thick green vegetation immediately behind and covering the steep hillside above us. To our left was Nelson's historic dockyard with its half-timbered buildings and a lot of very large luxurious yachts. A few were anchored in the bay but most were tied with their sterns to the stone docks.

We dropped anchor in the outer bay, Freemans Bay, stowed the sails and sat back in the cockpit with a cup of coffee. It was 10 a.m. in the morning, the water brilliant turquoise and flat calm. There were white egrets stalking along the beach and a frigate bird cruising high above us. We had arrived, we had crossed the Atlantic Ocean but it had taken a long thirty five days.

I was champing at the bit to get closer to the tropical jungle. So, after a quick lunch, Jean and I pumped up the dinghy and rowed over to the beach, over the super clear blue blue water.

Close up, my "jungle" was not much more than a tangle of bushes and any idea of climbing the hillside was quashed. It was quite impossible to penetrate even a few yards and most every bush had serious thorns. Our temporary disappointment at the landscape was quickly redressed with a swim in the limpid water. Not long after this we both simply collapsed into a deep sleep, the first uninterrupted night since leaving Gomera over a month ago.

The charter season was apparently soon starting and scores of enormous yachts had begun to arrive, mainly from the Mediterranean, to meet their agents. The Nicholson family had run a charter business here for many years. There were varnished wooden schooners eighty to a hundred foot long, more modern sloops, and yachts with masts towering into the sky. All around we were dazzled by glistening brass work, and highly polished stainless steel. Very efficient crew were washing, scrubbing and varnishing. On one huge yacht, we were told, they didn't launder any linen; they simply bought it new for every charter. Another world!

That evening we went to celebrate Jean's birthday with a few beers. In the bar ashore we met Captain Bains from the BBC program "The Onedin Line". He had crossed the Atlantic with Giles Chichester on *Gypsy Moth V*. They had crossed the ocean in seventeen days which upset me. When I told Captain Bains that I recognized him, he was very condescending, this famous actor as seen on television. In fact I had seen him on the lock gates in Milford Haven and nearly knocked him in the water. He was in front of the BBC cameras and I was on my bike in a hurry to get back to offloading mackerel.

The next day, we walked over to Falmouth Harbour, passing a few very small wooden houses with lots of goats and chickens outside and small pikininis playing on the dry earth of the street. The water's edge was covered in mangrove bushes with a few local boats pulled up on the mud and a couple of sailing boats anchored off.

Jean had met some friends from Southampton who had been in English Harbour for a year and had found some work in the dockyard. They knew Alan Quigley, the Australian who had turned up in Liverpool before we left. He was due in the Caribbean after he had sorted out his problems when a Spanish ferry seriously squashed his boat in the Canaries. It was good to hear that work was available in the islands. Jean had just changed another sixty pounds and it didn't seem to go very far.

We had arranged to meet an old school friend of mine in the Cayman Islands where he was working for a bank. We had agreed to arrive for Christmas dinner. Steve and his wife had already been in Cayman for a few years but had seen the early stages of the boat building in Meols. It was already December so we had to keep moving to keep our date. Grand Cayman was in fact quite a long way away, 1000 miles downwind.

Jean had done some minor repairs on the mainsail and reattached some piston hanks on the small jib. I had scraped off some of the goose barnacles and collected a few jerry-cans of water. We swapped a few books and then cleared out. The clearance papers from English Harbour give the length of the boat and then the number of guns. Obviously things have not changed much from Nelson's day.

We planned to stop on Montserrat briefly, an island only thirty miles away before the long leg to Cayman. We were hoping to find a deserted anchorage as in our desert island dream and we wanted coconut trees which were missing in English Harbour.

We arrived in no time, current and wind behind us. Rounding a headland on the north of the island we found a sheltered bay with a valley rising up to some rocky volcanic hills. On the beach there were fifteen tall coconut trees. So we anchored, pumped up the rubber dinghy and rowed ashore.

On the beach there were a few open boats pulled up. A small stream meandered down the valley and we followed it. There were a few cattle which Jean was a little nervous of. They did look a bit wild. There were birds everywhere, a pair of hawks, egrets, grackles, terns, tropic birds with long tails, pelicans and iridescent hummingbirds. This was great.

There was no thick jungle as it was fairly dry but we found trees with odd fruits on them one of which we discovered was a gourd. There were pink and yellow butterflies, lots of red dragonflies and lizards; one green with a blue tail another looking like a miniature dragon doing vigorous push-ups every so often. In the stream bed was a turtle carapace some two feet across. We really should have collected it.

Heading back down to the beach we met the local landowner. He was travelling by donkey and swinging a wicked looking machete. They use these for all purposes cutting digging and anything else. He was very friendly explaining that he might visit England someday and would hope for the same treatment .One of his young relatives arrived and was sent shimmying up the nearest palm tree to throw down a coconut for us, a green one. The old man deftly lopped off the top and we drank the contents. The coconut water is cool and refreshing, the perfect drink for any castaway.. Having finished off the liquid the old man then fashioned a couple of spoons from the outside of the nut. These he used to scrape the jelly from the inner surface. It was delicious.

We spent the next day in the same place. We tried snorkeling in the shallow water but I needed to develop my swimming ability and Jean was having problems seeing very much without her glasses. In the end, we glued an old pair of Jean's glasses inside her mask so she could at last see the tiny brightly coloured fish and corals.

We were tempted to stay longer but it was already December 9th. Christmas was close but Cayman was still 1,000 miles away. So the next day we left. But before we did, Jean on her last amble ashore, found a crude piece of pottery on the ground. It was not complete but looked quite interesting. It turned out that it really was.

The following morning we set off downwind. We would be "latitude-sailing", more or less sailing along a line of latitude. A noon sight would tell us if we had wandered off the line of latitude and by measuring the height of the sun before and after noon could calculate our exact local time of noon which converted into longitude. Knowing the exact time was important for this and we had our quartz clocks bought from the Sunday Times before we left home. There were also some minor complications involving the equation of time but no matter.

We could estimate the distance run using the Walker log and trailing the spinner. But this didn't allow for the Gulf Stream current which was helping us along. The spinner was forever tangling up with the fishing line. In the end we decided to guess the distance and concentrate on the fishing. Not a bad idea but we still didn't hook a fish.

The trade winds were not blowing very strongly but we made steady progress with our cut-down parachute sails and primitive spinnaker poles. We had swallows visiting most nights. One would fly below and settle on the chart table for the night, a rather scruffy one we found dead in the morning which was sad.

We were to sail along the south coast of Jamaica but before that very inconvenient rocks called the Morant Cays were in the way. We had to make sure we passed during daylight hours. In fact we didn't see them till late in the afternoon. It was a great relief. We kept Jamaica to the north. We had been told stories of pirates and political unrest so when a strange boat came over the horizon we were on our guard. It was a long narrow canoe with a huge outboard on the back and two crew wearing very large Mexican style hats. They altered course and passed close by, waving and smiling. We were a bit abrupt so they wished us a good day and carried on towards the Jamaica Coast. They seemed such friendly people, when the next boat popped over the horizon we waved hello.

The next thing we know is, they are alongside, nearly taking off our spinnaker pole. They wanted some water, so Jean gave them water and each got a piece of cake she had just baked. They had been fishing on some reefs way to the south and had a couple of huge woven baskets in the boat. Opening one, they pulled out a huge crayfish and threw it in the cockpit. Now we were really happy. So much for the dangerous pirates.

The crayfish only just fitted in our largest pot and we had a long debate as to how long we should cook it. Whatever we did, it was delicious. We sat in the cockpit at sundown slowly drifting west in the lightest breeze pulling the poor crayfish into tiny pieces to discover that even the smallest piece of white meat was delicious. It was our first meal of crayfish and a memorable one.

The wind continued light and sometimes died altogether. Jean was imagining Christmas dinner of beans and corned beef somewhere off Kingston Harbour. Eventually on December 20th we only had 120 miles to go, so we should arrive the following day. Sure enough, on cue Grand Cayman appeared over the horizon. There's a huge feeling of satisfaction after making all these calculations and drawing all those lines to see your destination come into view.

I got a fright as we came close. I looked in the water and their below us were huge coral heads. I thought we were still in deep water and in fact we were. It was still really 100 feet deep but the water was so clear and those coral heads were so big that it looked like we were almost touching them. We sailed along the south coast and turned north up the west side of the island to arrive, later in the day, off the capital, George Town.

Steve came down to meet us. We threw the anchor in and finished up in a very nice restaurant eating steaks. What a treat!

In the morning we had to untangle our anchor chain from the coral reef where we dropped it. This was our introduction to Barry, one of the local diving instructors from Sunset House where we were to stay. Even with his help it took us a while to untangle the chain and retrieve the anchor.

Sunset House was a small dive lodge perched on the low coral ironshore cliff about a mile south of George Town. They kept a couple of dive boats, ex-landing craft, to take divers out. We anchored quite close to the hard black coral shoreline. On the other side of us, about one hundred yards out, was the drop-off. This is the edge of the reef shelf. It drops almost vertically into 600 feet of deep blue nothingness.

Steve and his wife Gill were great hosts. Adrian who owned Sunset House and his dive crew including Barry, couldn't have been more helpful but it became obvious we had problems! With the name British West Indies and the Cayman Islands flag proudly displaying the British Union Jack, we naturally assumed we would be welcomed to stay and find work. The reality was that after giving us a visa for one month, they then wanted us to leave. There was no way they were going to give us a work permit.

I tried to arrange some boat work in the scruffy marina in North Sound; and, at some stage, I was intending to teach navigation which I honestly didn't know enough about, I also tried to get a job at the local Mosquito Research Centre. Meanwhile, Jean tried for a nursing position in the hospital. We ran around desperately. There were lots of jobs but not without a work permit. Working without one was impossible as the island was so small.

In the meantime the engine was giving problems. The spline between the engine and gearbox wasn't meshing properly. It was the northwester the season when cold fronts sweep down through the Yucatán, the wind shifts to the northwest and huge seas make the anchorages on the west side of the island, where we were, impossible. When a northwester is forecast, the whole fleet of boats on the western coast moves around to South Sound and anchor behind the reef in very shallow water. The Sunset House dive boats were part of this flotilla so each time it moved Barry, a Scouser from Liverpool, would tow us there and back.

The £1,000 we had when we left England was rapidly disappearing particularly as Cayman was probably the most expensive island in the Caribbean with its offshore banking industry and fancy hotels on Seven Mile Beach. We had an invite to the New Year's party at the rugby club and Steve, Gill and Adrian invited us to a few barbecues with the divers. So between these and eggs or fishing over the side, we wouldn't starve. But some fish, like squirrel fish, were very boring and very bony.

The island magazine wrote an article about us and we were also invited to talk on the local radio, Radio Cayman. But by the end of January 1981, we were only given a one-month visitor extension. We heard that our friends Charlie and Jeanette on *Quark* had found work in the Virgin Islands. There were lots of charter boats there but it was going to be a hard sail with nearly 1,000 miles against the wind and current. *Sea Loone* was no racing boat. Into the wind we could only manage 60° which meant sailing two miles at an angle to make only one mile direct ahead. There was no question of using the engine. With only 12 hp when working properly, it wasn't a going to make much of a difference pushing nine tons of boat into steep breaking seas. In any event, its constant thumping noise and vibration would drive us mad.

Gill's girlfriend Pat, a dive instructor at Sunset House, was keen to come with us. She was an American with her diver certifications. We had acquired visas from the visiting American consul for Jamaica and, on the way to Puerto Rico, we could stop in Montego Bay on the north coast of Jamaica. This was not going to be a pleasant sail.

We departed George Town with a huge white ensign flying from the top of the mast. It had graced the clubhouse of the Cayman RFC (rugby club) for some time after they had stolen it from a visiting British destroyer. They presented it to us as part of our farewell.

We pitched and rolled for seven days on the way to Montego Bay. On the worst day we tore the backend off the small jib, we lost a forestay when one of the turnbuckle disintegrated, the fishing line somehow got caught in a sheet block and caused a hellish tangle and Jean got pelted by hail trying to have a shower in one passing squall. Oh and my watch stopped!

Jamaica in 1979 was experimenting with communism. The socialist government had invited the Cubans to help form farming cooperatives, a lot of property and businesses owners had fled the country, law and order was breaking down, and white people, "honkies", were being murdered in their beds. The Americans had managed to make the Jamaican dollar worthless so the supermarket shelves were empty. It was probably not the best time to visit the Island, but when we sailed into Montego Bay, we didn't know any of this!

We soon found out. The Montego Bay yacht club was deserted. There was only one yacht mast sticking out of the water in the middle of the bay, a huge luxury yacht once owned by Errol Flynn. The yacht club manager told us it was very dangerous to move around the town and the only place to leave our dinghy was at the yacht clubr which he would charge two dollars a day. Jean, in charge of our rapidly disappearing savings, was not happy.

Having cleared customs we had a few days to sort out and provision the boat. Luckily, fruit and vegetables in the market were good and cheap. We bought some akee a really strange fruit the nut of which is poisonous. But the attached fruit looks and tastes like scrambled egg when you fried it up in a little butter. Amazing.

Pat, who had survived the first leg well without being sick, managed to find us a spare turnbuckle. I had suggested she dive on the sunken wreck in the harbour but she wasn't keen; the water in the bay was filthy.

Before we left, the manager of the yacht club invited us to ride along with him on a visit to a farm inland where he was delivering some mail. Maybe he felt a bit guilty about charging us for the anchorage, but anyhow it was a nice gesture. We drove past scenes of real poverty and the locals when they saw us shouted "honky" in a not very friendly way. The place we were to visit was an old sugar plantation which was quite hilly and now all overgrown. The old plantation house was built from bricks and the other material brought out as ballast on the old sailing ships. It stood on the top of one of the small hills. The owner was very English and proper. He was living there with his elderly mother. The wife and children had been sent off to England. If he had also left the island, his property would have been seized. So they continued to live there hoping for better times.

We were invited for afternoon tea in the dining room. The dining table was mahogany with beautiful matching chairs which must have been Chippendale or something similar. The China tea set was again probably priceless. We were sitting in a museum. You can imagine how it must've been in the heyday of sugar and here the owner was now after generations of luxurious living isolated on his hilltop and farming a few dozen ducks. We left with some more akee, some paw-paw, bananas and a dozen duck eggs.

We had to make clearance just to sail along the north coast for the next stop, Port Antonio, at the east end of the island. As we left we were accosted by a police launch. We were already outside the shelter of the bay but they wanted to board the boat and search. The guy driving the boat didn't have a clue. He hit the back of our boat narrowly missing the self-steering gear and breaking off the log bracket. On his second attempt he hit us amidships and destroyed his own bow rail. He also nearly squashed the guy on his foredeck who was supposed to be coming on board. After some more shouting back-and-forth they gave up and went back to Montego Bay.

A few days later the Jamaica Navy came out to see us in a big, grey gunboat. If they rammed us we would really be in trouble. Fortunate they weren't cowboys. We gave them our route and expected arrival time in Port Antonio and they wished us well.

After Montego Bay, Port Antonio was a pleasant surprise. When I cleared in at the local police station I complained bitterly about the police launch. They were very apologetic and offered the use of their covered dinghy dock.

The people here seemed a lot morefriendly and were obviously very proud of their island. A small boy offered us a mango. Another said this was a very ordinary mango and offered to take us to a really good mango tree, a "numero onze" he said. Then he climbed into the tree and shook down some beautiful fruit.

By now we had quite a few boys around us and one of them offered to show us his ganja; that is, marijuana. We followed round the back of the town to his little garden. The plant was in a pot and about eighteen inches high. I recognized the distinctive leaves. Another child laughed derisively. "Come on man...look up there", he said pointing out a huge square of green on the hillside. These were the foothills to the Blue Mountains. That was his uncle's plantation and each plant, he assured us, was over six feet high. The coffee plantations had obviously moved over to a more lucrative crop.

A few years later when a new more conservative government came into power, the American government offered aid to rebuild the Jamaican economy that they had helped destroy. But the aid was conditional upon banning the growing of ganja too much was arriving in the USA. But the new Jamaica Government argued that the ganja crop constituted the major part of Jamaica's exports so they refused to do anything so silly.

Jamaica is famous for its waterfalls so we decided to visit one not too far away. This involves getting a local bus crammed solid with people sitting on wooden benches or hanging onto the outside. The roof was loaded with produce and animals.

We talked with a local carpenter on his way to work and when we got off the bus he got off as well. He said it was more important to him to show us Jamaica than go off to work. We were a bit sceptical but he really didn't want any payment. The waterfall was a disappointment so we were not tempted to climb up the valley into the jungle any farther

In the end, we walked downstream to arrive on a black volcanic sand beach. It was beautiful. We started walking back towards Port Antonio and passed a small village made entirely from bamboo. They were Rastafarians. Not knowing much about it, we left them to themselves and further on, arrived at the mouth of the Rio Grande. This was the same, quite large, river we had crossed on the bus much further inland.

There was a railway bridge nearby by which we decided to use to cross the river. We climbed the steep bank of the river and out onto the bridge. We were high above the river and the view was magnificent. Drifting down with the current were bamboo rafts. At the back was a guy with a large steering oar, in the centre a raised platform with a worn sofa on it. On this sat a couple of tourists surrounded by potted plants. The railway bridge was an old steel arched affair with a single track. We had to step from sleeper to sleeper.

Half way across there appeared from the other direction a four-wheel boggie. Two men pushed it along with wooden poles and in the middle sat a couple of ladies. They were carrying a load of groceries. By mistake I whipped out my camera to take a photo. Many Jamaicans, from following voodoo, consider photos take away part of their souls. So the friendly smiles quickly turned to rage. Hanging onto the girders at the side of the track and with the river running fast far below us, we felt a little vulnerable.. Thank God the boggie passed by without knocking us into the water and we were able to continue across to the other side before meeting any more angry locals or an express train.

We eventually got back to Port Antonio hitchhiking the last few miles. A small cruise ship had arrived in the harbour. This was obviously where the tourists had come from.

That evening across the bay, we came across the remains of what had obviously been one of the most prodigious sports fishing clubs. The guy running it, not that there was anything left to run, was a local Jamaican married to a Scottish lady. She had a pretty little daughter only four or five years of age, but there was obviously something wrong about this. The child was ebony black with little pigtails, really a very pretty little pikinini.

The mother laughed at my questioning expression and explained that she'd been in Jamaica for many years. One year she decided to take a trip home to Scotland to see the family. While away the husband "dallied". Nine months later there was a knock on the door and when she went to open it she was presented with the baby. She had been delighted! "No problem, mon!"

We did some more hill hiking but, after a while, Jean decided we should keep moving. She was tired of standing in long lines to buy groceries that were rationed at so much per person; even though, in the market, she could buy all sorts of fruits and veg. Before we left, she bought six oranges, ten grapefruits, thirty six limes and some cabbages all for about ten dollars. We weren't going to get scurvy.

We eventually left Port Antonio on March 10th without any problems. We put the boat hard on the wind again. We quickly left Jamaica far behind. We were heading across the southern edge of the Windward Passage ready to pick up the south coast of Haiti. Maybe we'd have an easier time of it keeping close to the Haitian shore. The winds dropped and our headway slowed.

The next day the hanks on the head sails were wearing away on the galvanized wire forestays so we had to replace some. The turnbuckles or rigging screws were also worrying me. We had broken one already and the others were suspect. There were ten of them altogether, two forestays, two back stays, two shrouds and four lower shrouds. They were made of galvanized steel and, despite my ministrations with boiled linseed oil mixed with varnish, they were rusty and kept jamming. We really needed modern yacht ones made in bronze or stainless steel, but they would cost a year's wages even supposing we had a job, quite out of reach for two people who didn't!

The Haitian coast when we found it seemed pretty deserted, no sign of life, and at night with no moon there was not a light to be seen. We had no alternative but to tack out to sea in the dark. Jacmel, the one port on that coast, had a reputation of being full of thieves and brigands, led by the Port Captain himself. So with enough problems already, we sailed on past.

The wind started to pick up as we approached Alto Vela, the island of the high winds, on the border between Haiti and the Dominican Republic. True to its name, high wind, the closer we got the more it blew. We had just repaired the head sail but now the main sail tore again. Then the luff rope got caught high up in the rigging so we couldn't get the sail down. In the end I had to shinny up the mast with the boat rolling like crazy, in order to cut the rope away with the bread knife.

The mainsail was badly torn so under the headsail alone we tacked south while Jean tried to make some repairs We had a good old Singer sewing machine which she used on the cabin floor feeding the sails through while turning the handle of the machine in what were now really big seas. This was very difficult.

Without the mainsail we were not going to make any headway against the wind. So we headed south and maybe a little west until we could put the sail back up. When we did get it back up it tore again within an hour. We continued south.

Two days after the first tear, we turned north again. When we saw land and got closer we saw it was Alto Vela, in exactly the same position we had last seen it four day before. Depressing! So we headed south again for a day and tacked once more. Sure enough there once again was Alto Vela but this time on our port side and ten miles downwind.

Eventually we managed to sneak past Cape Beata and at last started to make some real progress. But we felt bad about taking seven whole days of bashing into big seas, heeled over with seas washing over the decks, to make only a miserable ten miles. Sometimes I thought there must be nicer things to do.

Ten days later we were approaching Santo Domingo, the capital and main port of the Dominican Republic. We needed a break. A passing ship gave us some good directions as to how to navigate the entrance and tied up on the commercial dock. One hour and ten dollars later we got cleared in and with two armed guards looking after the boat we headed into town.

The market was fantastic, pottery, weaving, woodcarvings from Haiti, amber necklaces. With an amazing black market exchange rate for dollars Jean and I changed ten dollars and went on a spree. Pat went mad and changed $50 and then tried to buy the whole market.

The fire hose on the dock had good freshwater and a crowd of locals accumulated when the crew took advantage to have a shower in the morning.

I was sitting waiting in the Port Captain's office to do my clearance when a gun went off. Everybody shot to attention facing the window. They were raising the national flag in the square outside and giving me a serious fright.

We'd had our promised day off so now it was time to set out to sea again. It was really blowing by the time we reached Saone Island at the east end of Hispaniola. Heavy seas were already breaking and we had to cross the Mona Passage to Puerto Rico. Inevitably the mainsail tore again as did the small jib. The bow pounded into the seas, green water shot down the deck and often over the cabin top and the cockpit was always wet. On April 1st the tiller broke off. It was a beautiful laminated piece of mahogany. The spare was ugly and steel, but hopefully stronger. The next day a lower shroud gives way and I had to climb to the spreaders and replace the clevis pin.

We turned into Ponce on the south coast of Puerto Rico for another short break. I was knackered, Jean was exhausted, and Pat needed cigarettes. In the Mona Passage Pat had offered to make pancakes from a packet of mix she had in her luggage. They were inedible and she retired into her corner and hid in a cloud of cigarette smoke. In the meantime between repairing sails, Jean was rustling up pies, cakes and fresh bread in the cabin where, if something was not tied down, it was off and away.

We anchored off the Fishing Club in Ponce and had no problem clearing in with the American visas we had acquired from the American Consul for Jamaica. We had met him in Cayman. Jean's visa application had a picture of her standing on the deck in a very skimpy bikini. It was the only photo we had. The Consul liked it a lot!

With good cheap food available, we changed one of our last travellers cheques into $100 and spent most of it on canned food and such like. But we also splurged on buying a machete, a sort of large bush knife good for repelling boarders and keeping the crew in line. Jean also found a new shuttle for the sewing machine which she was really pleased with. Jean spent most of the time while sailing completely naked and wearing minimal bikinis in between. Pat was more conservative but in Ponce bought herself a bikini. Who knows what next?

There was another yacht in Ponce, a Swan racing yacht. The owner was in New York but the captain, a Belgian hairdresser, was a great guy. He got the job while on holiday in the Caribbean and since then had sailed the boat around to different ports as ordered by the owner. The owner always arrived with two pretty girls, models from his lingerie factory, one each. What a nice job.

The girls took advantage of his old skills and had their hair done. Then we all went over for a meal one evening. There was an ugly portable generator on the aft deck which really didn't look right but we soon discovered what it was for .Below deck there were purple drapes and lambskin carpets. The generator was for the vacuum cleaner, but also for use after dinner. It operated the blender for making fruit punches using the Bacardi rum from the distillery down the road. We got very drunk.

We left Ponce on April 9th. Jean wrote in her diary that we expected to be in St. Thomas, the Virgin Islands in two day's time; that is Wednesday, at the end of a very long hard sail.

At 6 pm on the Tuesday we were having dinner down below. The sun had set but there was still a little light. There was a good breeze and we were making good headway into the sea. Suddenly, there was rumble, a few bumps then absolute silence. The boat had stopped dead. I rushed out on deck. There was nothing there. No mast, no sails, no rigging. The boat was turning sideways to the swells and had started to roll dramatically.

The mast was in the water alongside us, held there by the rigging and a tangle of ropes. My first thought was that we had to get everything back. We had no money to replace anything. Maybe we could repair things. We would have to try!

It was really difficult with the rolling but we managed to tie the masthead to the bowrail. It tore away once as we rolled. The mast was full of water and very heavy. The second time I lashed it over and over and then moved to the other end.

The halyards were still on their cleats so we would winch it in. The mast had bent in the middle which helped. With both ends coming out of the water the mast became lighter as it drained and we could remove the boom. The mainsail was stuck where the mast had folded. I went along and bent all the stanchions. With this done, we could continue lifting the mast up over the side with the big winch on the aft deck.

It took us a while, all the time holding on grimly with the boat rolling madly. But at last we had everything on deck and tied down. By now it was well into the night but luckily there was a full moon. We were off the south coast of Viequez Island between Puerto Rico and the Virgin Islands. We could see the coast quite clearly so we took a break to decide what to do.

We had no detailed chart of the area but had been given a Caribbean Cruising Guide which mentions an American Naval Base in a place called Ensenada Honda. This seemed like a good place to head for to find help. The only problem was, when we looked on our chart, there were three places called Ensenada Hondas. This was because the words mean "deep bay".

After a bit of thought, we decided that the Naval Base was the Ensenada Honda downwind from us on the east coast of Puerto Rico. With any luck we could simply turn around and follow the coast. Hopefully we would be there next day even with our putt-putt engine.

While we were making our minds up what to do, a small coaster came past. We had no lights and the radio aerial had also gone for a swim. The girls persuaded me to try a flare. We had some old out-of-date flares and a smoke bomb from Liverpool. The flare nearly burned my hand off, the ship ignored it and I was quite relieved.

I went to start the engine. A couple of turns on the starting handle, drop the decompression levers and she started to fire. We turned to motor down wind; even at full revs we couldn't make progress into the wind. We headed west but, within minutes, the engine spluttered and died. With the rolling, the sludge at the bottom of the fuel tank had blocked the fuel line and filter. No problem; we had clean spare fuel in the metal jerry can. All we needed was the washing up liquid bottle for a funnel and we could feed the engine from the jerry can. We set off again.

Another small ship appeared. It was gray, looked very much like the US Navy, but again it ignored us and went past. The air-cooled engine was by now getting very hot. The hot exhaust was glowing in the cabin roasting us. But by 3 am we were already under the lee of Viequez Island and could see what we assumed were the lights of the naval base. The depth sounder was reading forty feet so we turned off the engine, threw in the anchor and took a break till dawn.

As the sun came up we started the engine again and headed towards the coast. A sports fishing boat came past and, seeing us obviously with problems, came over. He was very helpful, pointed out the navigation buoys and promised to radio the Navy for us.

For the next five hours we chugged along. Navy ships passed us, a landing craft motored by, and helicopters buzzed overhead but they all completely ignored us. We followed the buoyed channel past the main docks lined with big grey warships. Eventually, we dropped anchor in the back of the bay near to a marina. We had our flag on the bowsprit, another stuck amidships and our Puerto Rican courtesy flag on the stern. All shipshape, except for no mast and a tangled mess on the deck.

It was April 11th 1979. We had left Cayman on February 17th. So altogether it had taken us eight weeks to get this far with only a few breaks from bashing into the waves. The ship's log recorded 1,750 miles as we left Ponce and we had only fifty miles go to be in the Virgin Islands. But without a mast, it might as well been another thousand!.

Fortunately, we had stored up with food so we weren't starving but we only had two hundred dollars left in the world and I couldn't see that getting us out of our predicament. Pat was back on American soil and surrounded by a few thousand rampant sailors, she wasn't going to have any problems at all.

We rowed ashore to the marina where a Mr. Gore, the manager, promised to organize permission for us to stay awhile. Then we returned to the boat to sleep the night away.

Next morning dawned sunny and calm so we soon had the mast stripped and all the wires and ropes and sails sorted and stored away. We attached fenders to the mast and threw it back into the water. Then we towed it ashore and stored it behind the marina building.

One of the first people we met was a guy called Chauncey. He'd been in the Navy all his working life and was due to retire in a couple of years. He was a flyer, a member of a small group of guys who drank beer in the yacht club behind the marina and occasionally flew planes from the nearby airfield. They had a couple of F4 fighters and, more interesting to me, a P3 bomber.

So the first possible solution to my problem was to borrow money, buy a mast section in America and these guys would go and collect it for me. They explained they would have to cut a small hole in one of the aircraft's crossbeams to fit the mast, but assured me that wouldn't be a problem.

The whole project sounded pretty amazing to me but the plan was doomed to failure for another reason, money. After several frustrating attempts, I managed to contact my mother and explain that I desperately needed to borrow £1,000 to replace the mast, otherwise the boat was lost. I promised to return immediately to England and if I couldn't find a way to repay her, sell the boat.

I was sure the idea of selling the boat, finding a job and settling down would be music to a mother's ears. But apparently it wasn't. No money was forthcoming in fact she flat out refused and that was the end of it.

And so to Plan B which, it turned out, was lying right there behind the marina near my broken mast. Dennis, an ex-Navy guy had been out sailing at the same time as us when we lost the mast and had done the same thing however his mast had folded neatly in two whereas mine had folded and twisted at the same time. In other words his mast was repairable. The only two short straight parts remaining on mine were given away and used as struts on a Hobie Cat dinghy.

Dennis was about to buy a whole new mast. So we negotiated with him to buy the bare mast for the $100 we had left. Plus the girls offered to sand down the bottom of his boat and repaint it for him.

Many years later, I met Dennis again. When eventually his new mast arrived from California he sailed from Puerto Rico via the Bahamas, back to the USA. Pat went with him as crew. I'm not sure what he expected but as soon as they arrived at a small island in the Bahamas, Dennis sent Pat ashore to get some groceries. When she came back to the boat, she found only her suitcase on the dock. Dennis had sailed away, poor girl. Maybe he didn't like her pancakes either.

So now I had a mast to repair and there were lots of people around to help us but there were also things we were going to have to buy. We needed money for that and also to pay the small fee for being anchored off the marina. Membership of the yacht club had already cost us the price of one beer, thirty American cents, but it was a lifetime membership!

Jean solved the problem by taking a job varnishing a mast in the marina. Hanging on a Bosun's chair in her yellow bikini, she was good advertising for more jobs. All in all, we spent ten weeks at the naval base. Jean spent a lot of time painting and varnishing. At one time she was painting the navy golf club. She also did sewing repairs with our old machine and on one occasion the happy customer paid her double.

I got free membership of the Navy's Hobby Club which owned a huge shed full of woodworking equipment, some of which still worked. Here I carefully cut the folded section out of the mast and laminated a plug which I rammed into one end using a hydraulic jack. This I pinned and then rammed the other mast section onto the end of the plug until the two pieces came neatly together.

We counted ourselves lucky to have found Dennis's mast but even more lucky that, having cut the bad section out, the remaining pieces were exactly the right length! The half inch hole through the mast, half way up, to attach the fish plates for the lower spreaders was in exactly the right place; and the top section of the old mast, with the rollers for the halyards, slid neatly inside the new section in perfect alignment without me even bolting it.

After that my luck ran out. I waited around for a long time for a welding machine to weld the aluminium .The machine was due to be repaired any day but it never was. So I looked all over for suitable rivets. I never found these either. Finally I had two cheek plates rolled in the main machine shop and these I attached on the outside of the join by drilling and tapping the aluminium and using small machine screws. My last job was to paint the mast with some very exotic white paint normally reserved for rockets. Someone found some old rigging screws (mine had all got bent when the mast went over) and then we lashed out on a new forestay made of stainless steel which wouldn't wear away the piston hanks.

In the meantime life was not without its enjoyable interludes. We were asked to deliver a yacht from the marina to Culebra not far away. So we took a young guy with us who knew the reefs. It was an easy job. They sent a small plane to collect us and bring us back the next day. It was Jean's first time in an airplane which astounded the pilot.

We had caught a large tuna on the way over, so the three of us were crushed in the back of the small plane with the fish across our laps. Then, before we started, we heard the senior pilot giving instructions to his junior pilot about how to fly the plane. This made us all a little nervous, especially as we had been told that the short take-off strip had a reputation for the number of planes that had finished in the lagoon. We managed to get off the ground successfully and flew the short distance back to Roosevelt Roads and the huge airstrip there.

We glided down smoothly but hit the ground hard, bounced up in the air, down again, up again a number of times before finally the little wheels stuck to the tarmac. "Sorry about that", said our pilot sheepishly. He then explained that he usually flew 747s. "When you put them down on solid ground," he smiled, "they generally stay there!"

We sailed another yacht over to Vieques for a weekend with our friend Dalton aboard. He went to a lot of trouble showing us the correct way to duck dive and snorkel. By this time Jean had found a prescription mask and was rapidly turning into a mermaid. Even I was getting pretty good at it.

We usually snorkeled around the deserted bay naked but Dalton unfortunately had a problem. There were remora or sucker fish swimming around. Often they attach themselves to sharks to grab any food bits left over from the shark's dinner. They also nibble the parasites off the shark's body.

One remora decided that Dalton had a nasty parasite worm so proceeded to try to nibble it off. Fortunately the remora didn't succeed; but we got a good photo of the teeth marks on the "worm" where he tried. The photo went on the bulletin board at the yacht club and was a great hit!

The time had come for us to prepare to move on as soon as the mast could be re-stepped. We started to make plans. First, we set about acquiring the supplies we would need, from the shops in San Juan, but we had a problem. Having come into the naval base from the sea we had no official passes or paperwork. How were we to get back into the Main Gate with no papers? The problem was solved by John our pilot to Culebra. He had two ways to help us, a father who was the skipper of a nuclear submarine and an old VW car.

Pasted onto the windscreen of the VW was the official Admiral's sticker. When we approached the gate, the guards fell over themselves to pile out of the little gatehouse and stand to attention as we passed through. We didn't even have to stop and the same thing happened on the way back into the base.

We had some stuff to sell to make us some more money. Jean had acquired some scuba diving equipment that could be sold and I decided to sell the old bubble sextant, a wartime relic I had from Liverpool.

Another money-maker occurred to us. We had seen land crabs for sale in the market, alive and tied up for a price of eighteen dollars for twelve. We had also seen thousands of these huge blue crabs strolling through the undisturbed mangroves inside the naval base. So one night, armed with sticks and buckets and two Tilly lamps, we set out into the swamp. Fortunately we didn't get lost but the mosquitoes and no-no's had a ball when they saw us. No-no's or no see'ums are minute sand flies with a viscious bite. Where we weren't covered in bites we were covered in mud. We saw only two crabs and they shot down their holes as soon as we approached.

Another sign for us to leave was the heat. Summer with the hurricane season approaching sees a huge build-up of heat and humidity. In the marina, the mosquitoes and the no-no's were getting so bad that we had to put up screens to stop them getting in the boat. With our pressure paraffin light and the cooker going, it was unbearable down below. Not only was it stifling but the no-no's were small enough to get through our netting. They began to arrive anytime, day or night especially after rain. Life aboard was becoming unpleasant.

At last, on June 11th 1979, some naval engineers came down to the boat with a lovely big crane and lifted my rebuilt mast into place. As soon as it was fixed, we flew our monster White Ensign donated by the Cayman Rugby Club from the top of it and got ready to leave.

On our last day, people came from all over to bring us goodies for the trip. A yacht that had just arrived donated all their unused cans of food from their Atlantic crossing and our good friend, Tina, gave us the 1979 nautical almanac. We got bottles of gin and rum. Then more rum and wine, even a bottle of champagne. Someone gave us fishing gear and whatever we still needed, we could buy cheaply at the Navy PX (grocery store).

The boat takes shape ...

Loading onto the trailer

Raising the mast

Ready to splash!

Stern trawlers in Milford Dock

Anchored off Montserrat

Jean and our first dorada

Jean

Crossing the Rio Negro, Jamaica

Dismasted

Leaving Horta, Azores, for Milford

Returning to Liverpool, broke

4

ON JUNE 21, 1979 we said our final goodbyes and sailed out of the Naval Base. We had a new mast, another mainsail we had butchered from something much bigger, a new forestay and a mishmash of rigging screws holding the mast up. We had one hundred and sixty three dollars still in the piggy bank most of which had been earned by Jean painting and varnishing.

There's an old Hurricane adage "June – too soon". But the season had officially started three weeks ago, on June 1st. We could have carried on to the Virgin Islands but the charter season was finished so there would be little work in the boat yards and marinas. More to the point, the boat would be vulnerable.

So after a long discussion, we decided to put our tails between our legs and sail home. Looking back, it was probably a bad decision but whatever.

We left Bahia Honda and anchored that night on a sandy reef just to the north. The water was clear so we scraped off weed and shellfish under the boat. The following day we upped anchor and set sail due north. The weatherman in Roosevelt Roads had given us a clear forecast but here they were reporting a tropical depression 375 miles east of Martinique and coming our way. It was about to be upgraded to a tropical storm. The next upgrade would be Hurricane!

We panicked and shot off West along the north coast of Puerto Rico to find shelter in San Juan harbour, the main port. We arrived in the night but the miserable little channel buoys were difficult to pick up especially silhouetted against the lights of the big city behind. No sooner had we followed a line of buoys into the back of the harbour than we went aground on a mud bank. However it didn't seem such a bad place to be landlocked and on the mud so instead of worrying, we went to bed.

In the morning, a customs launch came past and were good enough to stop and pull us off the mud. We found a better place to park ourselves and stayed another night. By this time tropical storm Anna had blown itself out but, just in case, Jean took the opportunity to go through our sails again to make sure every seam and fastening was secure, before heading back out to sea.

In any event our bananas and pineapples were already ripening so there was no hanging around. The next day we were off, heading north to avoid the doldrums. You have to sail a fair way north leaving Bermuda to port and then turning east for the Azores.

On the 27th, five days from Midsummer's Day, we were by my reckoning 23° 30 minutes north. I took out the sextant to do a new sight but realized that the sun was directly above my head at this time of year. So no possibility of closing the horizon. A few days later I again took out the sextant but now I knew the sun was to the south of me. Unfortunately the chronometer had decided to stop working. But we were a long way from land so there's no panic about shallow water or getting blown onto a lee shore. The next day, with the chronometer ticking again and having picked up the time signal on the radio, we get a fix. Ten days later, we turned for the Azores, 800 miles to the east.

I was just thinking how easy it had been so far – too easy – when the two forestays come tumbling down. Luckily the head sail kept the mast upright but it was bending backward crazily. A bronze clevis pin holding the fishplate for the two wires at the masthead has sawn itself in half. We ran around like scalded cats and eventually pull up the new stainless steel forestay on the spare halyard; but it was still a bit slack with the rope halyard.

The next day the sea had calmed off a bit and with the mainsail pulled in to reduce the roll, I climbed to the top of the mast with a pelican hook on the end of the forestay. The idea was to quickly hook this into the topmost fitting. I had to jam my fingers between the mainsail and the mast as I climbed. The higher I got, the more the mast wanted to throw me off. I couldn't wrap my legs around it so I had to rely only on my hands. When I got to the top I tried to jam the hook into the hole. But it wouldn't go. Swearing and with my arms about to give up, I managed to squirm back down onto the deck, my fingers completely frozen up. We were no further ahead.

That night the wind picked up and the following day we had a full gale, huge seas and pouring rain. We idled along with the main sail reefed. This was the new mainsail which we had cut to shape on a tennis court in the naval base. A sailmaker would be horrified the way we went about it. It had torn a few times but was so much better than the old one which had been completely rotten when we discarded it, more patches than original canvas.

Luckily the mast stayed upright and when the sea had calmed down, I attempted to climb up it again. This time still with the main up but also pumping oil out of the toilet to flatten the seas, I made it up and down successfully and attached the forestay with a shackle. When Jean tightened up the rigging screw on the bow, we no longer had to worry about the mast, but my fingers had frozen up and it took a few days before I could even hold a cup of coffee comfortably.

By now we were in the shipping lanes. Every day we had ships passing in the night and there were always lights somewhere on the horizon. Some ships came really close. We had to make sure they saw us. Listing on the radio, the BBC shortwave service had reported that two tankers had collided off Tobago with forty men missing. It made us very nervous.

Our navigation lights were useless. They had already corroded and the battery never had enough charge to last more than an hour or so. We kept a Tilly lamp, pressurized paraffin, on the cabin top giving a really strong white light all around. The single white light may have puzzled a few people but at least they knew we were there.

We hoped to speed up now that the rigging was secure, but the wind stayed light and often disappeared. We amused ourselves catching a huge Portuguese man-of-war jellyfish. They have a nasty sting but are a gorgeous pink purple and mauve. We got a few nice pictures as it floated around Jean's mixing bowl. All sorts of plankton and weed also floated past and one day a huge octopus drifted past only a few yards away. It gave me a few bad dreams imagining an arm reaching up in the cockpit and pulling one of us down into the depths. It certainly looked big enough to try.

The light winds and calm seas continued until we thought we'd be out there for ever. But eventually, on July 24th 1979, we sighted the Azores, the island of Faial. With land in sight we motored all day and came into the main harbour of Horta. We tied alongside the stone wall after a hairy few minutes of teamwork, me shouting down instructions to Jean under the cockpit, who was changing gear with a Stiltson wrench on the old gearbox.

During the night the wind picked up and was soon howling. Maybe I was only really half asleep because I heard the stern mooring line break with a sort of cracking noise. I was on deck in seconds calling for Jean as I jumped ashore with another line. I tried to hold the boat but the wharf was slippery with straw and muck from a boat loading cattle the day before.

Jean jumped ashore from the bow and took the line behind me trying to pull the boat back in. It was only with the help of two locals that we eventually succeeded. The locals were really embarrassed. Jean had found a T-shirt and her glasses before joining me, but no knickers. The Azores is Catholic and very conservative. As they pulled they had had Jean's bare bum in their faces!

Horta Harbour is famous for its long seawall plastered with the names of whaling ships and now yachts. There were two sailing ships in port. Both were Baltic traders, one original and one converted into a brigantine with yards and square sails. The first had come up from South Africa, the other from Puerto Rico the same as us. They had, however, cut the corner, got stuck in the doldrums and ran out of fuel. We had taken thirty five days but they took even longer.

There were two other yachts both coming from Ireland. One was from Cork, a teacher Tony with two lads as crew and on a summer cruise to Gibraltar and back to Cork. The other boat was returning to Belfast from the Caribbean. The boat was a Belfast Lough One Design, a wooden racing yacht but not happy after a few years in the tropics and patched all over with fibreglass.

Once ashore, we decided to change twenty dollars from the kitty. It made almost 1,000 escudos. A meal at the local Graciosa restaurant was only fifty escudos including five courses and a shelf on the wall for you to store your unfinished bottle of wine for the next visit. Things were not expensive and on top of that people were incredibly generous, often refusing payment.

Tony had a huge sack of potatoes delivered to his boat as a gift and one day in the restaurant, a local shopkeeper joined us to share his wine. He suggested we all visited his shop and choose something to take home to our families again for free.

I visited Orton, a local who had acquired an enviable reputation for doing scrimshaw on whales' teeth. It is an old seaman's art where you scratch a picture or design on the polished tooth and run ink into the scratches. Polished up a second time you have an ink drawing or engraving.

In his cellar, Orton had a workshop for sanding and polishing the teeth and then engraving them. There were sacks of teeth which he said he used to be able to buy for eighty pounds a hundredweight but were now one thousand five hundred for the same amount.

As whaling was now banned, the teeth were becoming much more valuable. But in the Azores whales were still hunted. In fact a whale was caught from Pico, the next island and one was sighted from Horta. We were invited to join the chase boats when they left the harbor. They were small motorboats which brought the whale back in. The whaleboat which caught the whale was an open boat with I think eight rowing, one steering and the main man in the bow with the harpoon. The only help they get from the other boats were extra coils of rope if the whale sounded very deep.

Each island had its own whaleboat and a spotter high up on the island who set off a cannon when he saw anything. I don't think they caught many whales each year but they do lose one man each year on average.

I really wanted a whale's tooth. Orton had promised to draw a picture of *Sea Loone* on one if I provided a photo. When we returned to his cellar a few days later he had ready two small identical teeth each with *Sea Loone* scrimshawed on it. He also showed me a huge tooth he had finished with a scene of whale-hunting. It showed a square-rigged ship, whalers and the whale. A rich American visitor was going to give him a fortune for this, he said. So we were absolutely obliged to have ours for free.

Jean had met a local who had recently bought a small lorry. Previously he had had a donkey train. The discussion in French, which Jean decided he might understand better than English, finished with him agreeing to take her on a tour of the island. Maybe he didn't realize that he was taking a boatload of us, but anyway it turned out to be a great day.

There were fifteen of us from the sailing boats in the back of the lorry. He first took us up to the tip of the volcano. We scrambled down into the caldera. Down was easy but climbing back up the 1500 feet to the top again showed how unfit we were after weeks on the boat.

We traveled across the island to the site of the volcanic eruptions of the 1950s, passing fields edged with blue hydrangeas, orange patches of montbretia and pink roses. Further on we saw burnt out cottages and layers of ash and then the top of the old lighthouse sticking up out of the new hills of pumice.

We had to stop occasionally while our driver pointed out his cargo, listing all our different nationalities. The last stop was for dinner at American Mary's where the hamburgers were okay but the fried limpets and small crabs, pretty awful. Mary was branching out from the restaurant trade into bed and breakfast. The beds were in the caves in the cliff behind the restaurant. As we descended into Horta in the evening the view across to Pico was breath-taking; a huge perfect cone rising straight out of the sea thousands of feet into the sky.

Time was passing we really wanted to get across the Bay of Biscay before the equinoxial gales. The locals were keen for us to stay for special celebrations of transformation from whaling to yachting. But we were adamant.

Peter and Jerry, the lads on *Bali Hai* with Tony, went to paint a green shamrock on the seawall with the name of the boat. They did a nice job but there was nearly a murder when Sam came along, dipped his hand in a pot of red paint and covered the shamrock with the red hand of Ulster!

In preparation for our departure, we stored up vegetables and then decided to invest what little money we had left in a few pounds of good rolling tobacco for 330 escudos and five bottles of Brandy for 500 escudos as long as we provided the bottles.

Tony left first and a few days later Sam with Eric his crew and then us. The Baltic trader *Frie* stayed on, as did most of the others. So it was that on August 3rd 1979, with a fair light breeze, we set out for Cape Clear an island off the southwestern tip of Ireland where we were hoping to meet friends from Liverpool.

There were no trade winds this far north; we could expect mainly westerly winds, but very variable. And that is how it was for the first week or so. We tore the mainsail again and Jean again repaired it. There were lots of ships so we had to keep watch at night. The barometer slowly climbed until it reached 1038 mbar and we were becalmed. We amused ourselves catching plankton.

By now we could pick up the BBC home service and listen to the shipping forecast. They mentioned a depression arriving and early Monday morning, the 13th, the barometer started to drop. By midday we had all the sails down and the wind was howling. The shipping forecast for Fastnet mentioned the possibility of Force 8 gale-force winds and the seas were starting to build up dramatically.

We were running downwind but as some of the largest seas pass us the self steering gear wasn't managing too well. The stern was getting thrown sideways. So I put out a very long hawser and attached my heavy tyre fenders to the end, trailing them behind us. This seemed to help keep us in a straight line. Later that evening there was a break in the BBC radio program to advise Imminent Force 9 to 10 gale in the sea area Fasnet". I think they were a wee bit late!

By morning the seas were majestic huge breaking lines of water marching towards us with scudding spume on the surface between. As each sea passed, our stern picked up and the boat shot forward. Occasionally the tyres at the end of the hawser would surface and surf after us. The Aires wind vane heaved and pulled back and forwards to keep the boat straight. It was doing an amazing job but occasionally even with the tiller full over, we would broach and be sideways on, vulnerable to the next big sea.

When this happened, Jean pulled the sliding hatch back and I'd dive up over the drop boards into the cockpit to heave on the tiller until the boat came straight. As soon as it was straight again, I dived back below and Jean would slam the hatch closed.

I got caught out on a few occasions doing this. One time, which I will never forget, I looked up to see a huge breaking wave standing vertically above me, towering well over the height of the mast. I ducked into the bottom of the cockpit and hung on for dear life and held my breath. The boat was submerged. When we eventually surfaced the cockpit was completely full. I sat praying that the drains would empty before the next sea arrived. I banged on the hatch and when Jean pulled it open I dived below like a rabbit with a ferret on his tail.

Still listening to the radio we began to realize this was not your normal average gale. There was a huge fleet of ocean racing yachts taking part in the Fasnet Race and we were among them. Yachts were being badly mauled, rolled over and dismasted. Rudders were being torn off, keels coming loose. People were being swept overboard. People were abandoning yachts. People started to die.

Sea Loone was heavy and slow and so seemed to stay fairly straight when we surfed down the huge seas. We were managing. The next day, August 14th, 1979 the sky cleared momentarily and we looked out on a seascape that was spectacular. Lines of breaking seas were marching towards us with the smaller waves, their tops blown off, turning to spume that covered the whole surface of the sea like a fast-moving fog. It was all brilliant white. As each sea passed, the stern lifted up and we surfed. Then as it passed as a rainbow formed above and along its breaking edge.

There was no let-up in the wind but as time passed we got more used to it. Jean actually made bread. It was her way of keeping her mind away from thinking about what was happening around us.

Tuesday, Wednesday and into Thursday it still blew. Each time I woke from a short sleep I heard the depressing high pitched singing of the wind in the rigging Maybe it went from really awful to just awful. We could do nothing about it. We drew a circle on the chart assuming a daily drift of seventy miles. We had no idea how much longer it would be before we hit land. We were getting blown rapidly to the west, so the Scilly Islands, off the southwest corner of England, were going to be our nemesis if it kept going much longer.

Friday dawned grey but with much less wind. In the morning a container ship passed really close. It was the *American Legacy*. We called them on the VHF radio and they went out on the bridge to see where we were. They couldn't see us. Eventually by giving them compass directions they were able to see us but I'm sure we were only visible momentarily as we crested a wave-top.

Like us, they were corkscrewing horribly and I felt quite sorry for them. But using their new satellite navigator they were able to give us our position. We were fifty miles or so from the Scillies. That meant that, from the time we'd been under bare poles and dragging our tyres, we had been doing three knots, quite fast for us.

By Saturday, the storm had abated enough for us to put up our sails, pull in the tyres and head for Milford Haven. We got a sextant sight but then the clouds closed and again the forecast turned nasty. We had no charts so made a map up using an old AA (Automobile Association) manual. It was actually quite good.

By the time we sighted Lundy Island it had started to rain and to blow again. Eventually the Milford Haven Conservancy that monitors tanker traffic in and out of the Haven talked us in on the VHF using their radar. When we saw St. Agnes Head at the entrance we were looking up at the huge cliffs. The visibility was awful and we were very close. It was already 6 p.m. so we turned into Dale just inside the Haven and threw out the anchor. It was Monday August 20th. We were finally home! We slept like logs.

It's not normally easy to get a good night's sleep that first night. Without the movement of the boat the sounds of sails and rigging, you keep on waking up. But that night we both slept until the sun woke us shining through the cabin windows.

High tide was not until afternoon so we motored up to Milford docks and picked up a mooring buoy to wait for the gates to open. No sooner had we turned off the engine than a dinghy rode out to us. It was Brian, the third member of Biddle's boat bunglers from our original building site where *Sea Loone* had been born. He had heard us on the VHF the previous day while he was working offloading a tanker in the Haven. A long way from the River Mersey where he normally worked. We piled into the dinghy and rowed ashore to the pub fifty yards away.

By the time the pub closed after lunch there were quite a few of us in the bar. By now the harbour gates were open so we motored in and tied up. We invited everybody on board and, in the meantime, put up flags, including the big naval white ensign and the yellow quarantine flag.

One of the pub regulars went off to inform customs of our arrival. Out came all the booze from the Naval Base, rum, gin, wine and even the champagne! We were starting to have fun until we heard the clump of Size-13 boots on the deck. A large red faced gent in a blue uniform was poking his head through the hatch He had lots of stripes and scrambled egg on his cap. He looked extremely serious. It was the Chief of Customs.

He told us that whoever had gone to see them had been arrested for drunkenness and pointing at the huge bottle of rum in the boat, asked what it was. When I told him it was rum, he ordered a large one for himself and a smaller one for the apprentice behind him. He threw his hat into the corner and the bureaucracy was over with.

We spent the next couple of week sorting ourselves out. The mackerel boats were gone and there wasn't much work around. I got a job for only one night guarding a barge full of explosives moored out in the Haven. It was money for old rope. I was amused in the morning when the labour arrived to offload the explosives onto a freighter also arriving. They were the old guys I had worked with on the mackerel boats two years earlier, before we set out for our trip to the Caribbean. They were wondering not only how I had got on since I left; but now how I had got such a cushy job having only been back a day.

We were going to have to carry on back to Liverpool to find more work. So Brian's girlfriend came along as crew and we set off up the Irish Sea to Holyhead, picked up Brian there and continued on to the Mersey. In Holyhead we had a huge dinner of roast belly pork with lots of crackling. Unfortunately it didn't go down too well, or stay down too long, with Brian. He fed the fishes all the way across to Liverpool!

There was lots of wind and we arrived off the bar at dawn. The main sail tore and Jean repaired it for the last time as we sailed up the Mersey on the flood tide. We picked up a mooring off New Brighton to wait for the lock gates to open; then with all flags flying, motored into Birkenhead docks and round to Morpeth dock. This was where we started from. We had come full circle.

We had quite a reception. The lock keeper had wanted us to wait for a freighter to enter first but Kenny Hall, who had been an enormous help in the building of *Sea Loone*, intimidated him. Kenny is rather large and noisy. We shot through the lock pirouetted for the crowd and then tied up. Two years had passed, it felt like a lifetime.

We were back in Morpeth Dock two years on from leaving. It felt as if we had just stepped out of a time machine which had projected us back two years. Nothing seemed to have changed. However, our perception of it had changed dramatically. I suppose you could say we were a lot more worldly.

The newspaper in Milford Haven and then in Liverpool wrote some articles and we had our pictures even on the front pages. Then the BBC came to interview us and we had a half hour to waffle on the local station, Radio Merseyside. So we were in the limelight for a short while, famous for the day. On one occasion we were invited to Glasson Dock near Lancaster where a fleet of concrete yachts had been launched. They were all large boats and a long way from finished. In the evening we were plied with beer and asked loads of questions. Within the hour, the conversation turned to radar and which was the best system to buy. It seemed to me a good idea to buy a few masts and sails first. Our fame hadn't even lasted the evening.

By late 1979, Jean and I didn't have to discuss our next plans. It was obvious we were going to go again. At that time, the country was depressed. Unemployment was at a record 10%, winter was arriving, and the pallid faces of the people, to us, made them look anemic and ill. We had to find some work, make lots of money, save it all up and sail away in the spring.

Looking back at the last trip, the boat had held out well apart from the mast, the rigging and the bloody mainsail. The obdurate attitude of the Cayman Islands government not allowing us to work was what really ruined our plans, but by then we were so far downwind there weren't any easy alternatives. However we knew there was work available. Jean's friends in Antigua were doing well and *Quark* had found work in the Virgin Islands. Plus we had our own experience of good work at the Naval Base in Puerto Rico. So there was no shortage of possibilities.

The new mast had worked well but we had to replace the rigging and rigging screws .They were still all galvanized and not a huge expense. A friendly potato farmer in Pembrokeshire had sold us some more of his sails, beautifully made by Ratsey and Lapthorn and still in good condition even though made in 1963 but we desperately needed a strong, new mainsail and it was going to be expensive.

The engine was working well although the spline in the gearbox was still a bit iffy. On the whole the trip from Britain across the Atlantic and back we'd only used ten gallons of diesel so we hadn't asked much of it. We had thrown away the flexible water tanks. The company refused to compensate us with money but gave us new improved tanks. We sold them on. We now used ten litre plastic bottles which stowed nicely under the floors and could be filled with other liquids such as wine and rum on the occasion.

So there wasn't a lot of work to do on the boat, the main thing was to fill the piggy bank as full as possible, as quickly as possible.

Through Kenny Hall who had greeted our homecoming so enthusiastically, Jean found a job machine-watching. Kenny's mate owned a small factory making tiny bolts and screws. The machines spat them out at a rate of knots and made lots of money. Jean's job was to look after them and keep them fed with wire. I signed on the dole and then worked with Taffy in the warehouse next to the boat. We were making fiberglass boats ranging from canoes to fifty foot trawlers. I got paid no money but came to an agreement that after so long, I could borrow a mould for a small fibreglass fishing boat and pop out a hull with Taffy paying for the materials.

A week later, two large steel pilot launches came into the dock and moored next to me. They were built just up the river and were destined to go to Guyana. They still had finishing off work to be done here in the dock and I was offered the job as watchman. The hourly pay was not good but the hours were twenty four seven so in the end the weekly wage was not bad.

I got *Sea Loone* craned out of the water next to the pilot boats and we moved on board one of them. We ran the generator for heat and light.

By Christmas 1979, I had a fishing boat out of the mould. I parked it next to *Sea Loone* and ran a power cable from the pilot boat to *Sea Loone* and the fishing boat. By this time it seemed a good idea to give up the dole. I was so busy I really didn't have enough time to go and sign on.

Time passed rapidly. 1980 had arrived and it wasn't much fun camping on the pilot boat through winter and as watchmen I couldn't go anywhere not even to the pub. I laid out sheets of fiberglass and made a cabin and wheelhouse on the fishing boat and found some heavy mahogany beams from a demolished railway loading platform to make the heavy rail and rubbing strake.

The pilot boats were finally finished and we took them out on the River Mersey for trials. The day we chose there was a very high tide. We had to run the measured mile to see what their maximum speed was. The sea was already lapping up to the road on the nearby promenade. As we charged along we were leaving a huge wake. One old man walking his dog had to run for his life as the wave chased them along the sidewalk ...

With the pilot boats gone, we put *Sea Loone* back in the water and moved back on board. I couldn't afford to put an engine in the fishing boat but got lucky one day when Kenny called to say that there was an auction of boat parts in Liverpool. A company that had been making very expensive luxury cabin cruisers had gone bust and was selling all the stock.

When we arrived the only people there seemed to be the pirates from Morpeth Dock and Coburg Dock on the Liverpool side of the river. Nobody knew anything of the value of the stuff and they were accepting ridiculous offers. I saw one guy offered a few pounds for two plastic bucket toilets except that the second one was a state-of-the-art bronze job worth a fortune! I bought a lot of cleats and stainless fastenings and a fancy steering ram and cables for the fishing boat; plus a few windows for it. So apart from no engine the fishing boat was looking pretty good.

Spring 1980 had sprung and now it was summer. *Sea Loone* was ready to go with a new mainsail, rigging and a new paint job. Her topsides now sported a gleaming white coat of paint replacing the red which had faded badly in the tropical sun. We had spent all the money we had earned especially on the new mainsail but we had a fishing boat to sell. It seems nobody had any money and although we reckoned the boat without the engine was with maybe £5,000 pounds, when we were offered only £2,000 we snatched it.

On July 30th 1980, at 3 o'clock in the afternoon we motored out of the dock into the river and sailed away!

We had £2,000 pounds in travellers' checks and £96 in cash. Last time when we left Liverpool we had fifty pounds, most of which we spent on beer waiting for the gales to finish in Holyhead, Anglesey. Even after working so hard in Milford Haven we had left with only £1,000. So this time we had twice as much as last time – enough we hoped that, with care, would last us three years. Of course, we expected to find ways to make more. We were confident that we could find work on the other side of the Atlantic but more important, we were really confident in our own ability to handle whatever the ocean threw at us.

The now infamous Fasnet gale had been really unpleasant but when expensive racing boats had broken up, *Sea Loone* had suffered no damage at all. And when experienced yachtsman had panicked, and some died, Jean had been making bread!

Book Two

Period: 1980-1989

1

HAVING EXPERIENCED the storm the previous August, we were not going to hang around before leaving. We plan to leave as soon as possible; to sail down the Irish Sea, down the south coast of Ireland and then head on south to Spain.

Of course man proposes, God disposes. So we were becalmed only twenty miles out of Liverpool on the bar and then got caught in fog off Anglesey. Fog was a new experience for us at sea. When the fog cleared we were quite lost and there was a gale forecast. We eventually found a protected bay with a number of moored fishing boats. We had huge problems anchoring in the rising wind but eventually grabbed a mooring. The bottom was covered in long strands of slippery Kelp. So much for the experienced world sailors. We had to ask where we were when we went ashore. It was Nefyn on the Lleyn peninsula.

We had wanted to call into Milford Haven but passed it by in a hurry to get south. Gordie, our friend from there with another concrete boat had just returned from a job in the mountains of Peru. We had been invited out to Peru for his wedding but were sent no plane tickets. Now he was back in Milford with his new wife. Never mind.

When the gale gave up we headed across to Ireland and sailed once more into Dunmore East on the Waterford River. The following day another gale blew from the southwest and with hardly a break blew for the next ten days. There were other yachts there also waiting for a chance to sail on down the coast but it was quite impossible. Eventually when a break came, we all left. We no longer felt we had time to cruise the coast so we headed south for Finisterre and Bayona as quickly as we could.

It was a full moon on August 26th 1980 and in the morning we dropped anchor in Bayona eight days out from Ireland, eight days and a few gales, but no dramas.

It was warm and sunny and for the moment, calm. With Biscay behind us we could relax a bit. Jean found a ten pound note in one of my pockets so she bought a chicken in the market and having eaten that, we had a few beers ashore. The head, feet and other bits I put in a net and made a crude trap from a bread tray. When I pulled it up there was a three pound octopus in it. A very lively octopus.

What do you do? The octopus knew. It quickly slithered out of the trap onto the deck and was on its way over the side. Jean tried to grab it and it wrapped its tentacles around her arm. I had a knife but didn't want to stab Jean's arms so we just danced around.

With all this going on, a French guy on a boat nearby saw what was happening and shot over. Sticking his fingers into the octopus mantle he tore him off Jeans arm and then deftly turn the animal inside out. This didn't exactly kill it but it certainly slowed it down. We then bashed it and stabbed it until it was dead at the same time covering the deck with black ink. . Jean had red marks all over her arm from the suckers and it seemed to have bitten her as well.

We then cooked it and tried to eat it but we found that octopus meat was as tough as boots. We obviously hadn't got cooking techniques sorted; but we did find the beak in the center of the tentacles that it given Jean the nip.

There were a number of yachts around us all, like us, heading south for the Canary Islands and then across the Atlantic. A few days after we arrived another yacht sailed in. As it got closer I began to think that the blue hull looked familiar. Then I saw a strange flag at the port spreader. The flag was from Peru. It was Gordie and his new wife, Miriam!

They had spent a month or two in Milford Haven but Miriam had been unhappy that no one spoke Spanish, not even Gordon and of course she didn't speak English or Welsh for that matter. You'd have thought that it would make for a very quiet relationship, but not so.

Miriam, unlike Gordie, was the life and soul of the party, any party. She vividly described the great trip across Biscay by comparing the size of the "ollas", waves in Spanish, with those in the film she had just seen, the Poseidon Adventure.

Gordie still had a lot of work to do on the boat. He had no engine, no bow rail, no stanchions, no selfsteering gear etc. so they were returning to Milford Haven in a few weeks. As it was, Miriam was not happy with the local people she met. They didn't speak "proper" Spanish. She didn't understand them well and more important they didn't understand her which really upset her.

A week later, we pulled up anchor to leave, motored out into a flat calm and waited for some wind. The horizon turned grey, then black and purple black so we turned back and re-anchored. That night it blew like hell and boats started to drag. A huge French concrete boat dragged into another large yacht in front of us and they both started dragging down on me. I kept on letting out more chain and then rope to keep away from both the boats. In the end both yachts moved away leaving their anchoring gear behind. One had to be towed as his engine wasn't working.

By morning the wind had fallen away to nothing and way up in front of me was a fishing boat pulling up his fishing net that he had set the previous day to catch prawns. Alongside the fishing boat were dinghies from the two French yachts. There was a lot of activity so I rowed over to see what was going on.

The fishing boat had a huge tangle of net alongside mixed with a lot of chains and a few anchors. They unshackled the two anchors, returned them to the Frenchman, and then unraveled all the chain. As they pulled up some more net another anchor appeared and they went to unshackle that. Yes, I can count to three, it was my anchor with my boat still hanging on it. I persuaded them to stop. The chain wasn't really tangled too much and we threw my anchor back in. The fisherman found the whole thing very amusing which was good, seeing as we left them with horribly tangled net and no sign of any prawns.

There were a couple of boats I gave some basic lessons to in using a sextant. Everybody now had cheap quartz clocks which were amazingly accurate. So it only took a few minutes to show them how to first do a noon site for latitude and then a series of sights across noon, graph the results, apply the equation of time and find longitude by time.

One of my pupils was a Swedish guy also on his second trip to the Caribbean. He explained that the first time he simply used dead reckoning, that is pointed the boat in the right direction and then made estimates of his speed. The further he traveled, the more Spanish stations he could pick up on his radio so he assumed he was too far south. He altered course and started picking up Caribbean music. No problem, mon! Of course even this technique was fairly sophisticated because you needed a transistor radio. The simplest way was still to head south until the butter melted and then turn right!

On *Sea Loone* I had a really nice sextant sold to me very cheaply by my friend Brian on Biddle's boat site. I had been made in 1941 by the Hezzanith Instrument Company of London. The mirrors were still good but the vernier was not easy to read quickly. I had Nories Tables but now I carried Air Navigation Sight Reduction Tables which made things so much simpler. Before the first trip I had bought a quartz clock offered by the Sunday Times for only £10. I now had two of them. If the clocks didn't agree I had one large portable radio with lots of shortwave bands to pick up time signals from the BBC or America.

Time was passing so in mid-September 1980 we set off again together with Gordie and Miriam. Once out on the open sea Gordie turned south to follow the coast to Lisbon and we set off southwest for Madeira.

Seven days later as the sun rose we came into Funchal. We anchored off the harbour and again spent time up in the mountains catching a bus early in the morning and spending the day walking. On one occasion we found a huge walnut tree shedding its nuts on the ground for us

A small motorized barge was anchored behind us. It had ICI written on its little funnel. It seemed to me that he may have come from the River Mersey, so I paddled over to see. Sure enough, the barge came from Runcorn. It had been sold to an American and was on its way to Florida. There were three Americans on board and one young lad from Warrington.

This wqs my first meeting with Jerry Jamieson. He was delivering the boat to Fort Lauderdale and then returning to Stuart, Florida, just north of there. He had a construction company building docks and marinas. The lad from Warrington had been told the streets were paved with gold. When we had dinner with him that night, Jean and I were told much the same Jerry left us with instructions how to find them and the promise of a huge long dock where we could come and tie up while we made our fortunes.

Thoughts of making our fortunes were soon out of mind however because the weather deteriorated rapidly. The wind began to blow on shore and the seas picked up dramatically. With all our chain out, the seawall was not far behind us. The bow started dipping into the waves and I was getting seriously worried. I was not sure our little Lister engine would make headway against the wind and waves and there wasn't enough room to try and sail out. I got the engine turning over anyway and only minutes later, the bow rose up on one big wave, the anchor chain came tight and then broke close to the bow.

Before the bow could fall off, I put the engine in gear and prayed that we would move forward I held my breath and watched my markers on shore. Ever so slowly we were moving forwards. We crabbed out to sea and then angled ever so slightly to starboard and crabbed our way behind the seawall out of the breaking seas and into the harbour.

Inside was crowded with ships, barges, yachts, tugboats and nowhere obvious for us to tie up. There was still a huge surge inside the harbour which could easily damage us. Further in we passed a large Dutch steel yacht who kindly offered to have us alongside. We managed a hair-raising U-turn and eased alongside. Luckily there were a few tyres floating around in the harbour which I snagged and used as extra fenders.

It blew all night and even with two layers of fenders between us and *Windensee*, the Dutch yacht, their wooden rail had some damage. Fortunately they were not too worried and in the morning we found a barge even further into the harbour that we could tie up.

When the sea calmed down we found an enthusiastic French diver on a yacht. Without my chain and anchor we were stuck with only an old fisherman anchor on a short length of chain. Maybe we were lucky but I knew exactly where the boat had been, having lined up things on shore to see if I was dragging. The diver went down from where I positioned the dingy and found my lost chain immediately.

With the anchor back on board it was time to go. The previous time we had been in Madeira everyone had had problems and now again. A beautiful island but a horrible anchorage and harbour.

I went into town for a few odd things and to make the paperwork to leave. When I came back, *Sea Loone* seemed to have disappeared and so had the barge we had been tied to. I finally found them still attached together at the other side of the harbour. The tugboat driver hadn't had a problem with us attached to his barge so suggested to Jean that she might enjoy a little trip around the harbour.

We left the next day and had a pleasant uneventful four days sailing down to the Canaries. We were soon tied up in Darsena Pesquera the fishing harbor in Tennerife, together with a variety of tuna boats and a number of yachts. Many of us had already met in Bayona or Madeira and some we were to meet again years later. We wanted to leave to cross the Atlantic at the beginning of November 1980 so we had to start organizing stores and water.

From the fishing harbour it was not a long walk to San Andres, a small village, with an imported white sand beach. We became very friendly with a small bar where we'd have a drink and maybe some tapas which the owners were keen to try on us. Mussels, small pieces of octopus, different fish etc. – he always had something tasty and interesting.

One day he invited us to come to a dance he was having. The bar was only a couple of square meters, but in fact behind it there was a large enclosed courtyard with a latticework of vines above. I don't know that the owner realized how many of us would arrive but it was a wonderful evening with a local band. Unfortunately, an elderly gentleman collapsed on the dance floor but one of our sailor group, a Belgian, was a doctor. He helped the old man before an ambulance could arrive and we were all made very welcome as his medical assistants. After that it became difficult for any of us to pay for our drinks.

Jean and I went into town to revisit Dr. Brown at the Institute of Oceanography. We got a tremendous reception and work stopped for the day. It was two years since we had boarded his research vessel with our crazy European friends and our crew of Taiwanese tuna fisherman. The refrigerator in Pepe's office was still full of cold beer and we spent the day reminiscing.

A few days later we had an invite from the Institute to a special celebration for one of Pepe's students who had received a special accolade. We were going to a special restaurant for lunch on the other side of the island.

Pepe picked us up in his car and we eventually drove down a very bumpy track into a farmyard. This apparently was the restaurant famous for its servings of pork. Our Spanish was minimal and Pepe was just about the only person we could communicate with. There were maybe a dozen noisy students .We all started into the bottles of red wine laid out on the long table.

The meal started with crackling, small pieces of crispy fried skin. They were delicious and next came some ribs. This Jean and I thought was the second and main course and chomped down. The final seventh course was a huge roast with rice and vegetables. By this time we couldn't eat another thing. Each course we'd thought was the last.

November was approaching. We set off down the coast to Los Christianos from where we were going to leave for the Caribbean. When we arrived we were forced into anchoring in shallow water close to the beach to avoid the ferryboat which came in and out. There was a swell running which became larger and larger. The waves were breaking behind us and running right over the beach and onto the road.

The small Norwegian yacht anchored close in had a few waves break right over it before another yacht managed to get a line on her and tow her out. The yacht next to me was showing its propeller as it went over the swells. Time to get out, I thought! Apparently all the bays had similar problems and the brand new marina in Grand Canary was being destroyed.

There was a small half built enclosed boat harbour in the southern corner of Los Christianos protected by a seawall. It had no bollards to tie to and no jetties; simply a few mooring buoys. By the time we arrived, a dozen yachts had jammed themselves in and had created a spider's web of lines. We joined the web. At least we were out of the swells. The seas were spectacular! I would have hated to be in the hurricane winds that had produced such seas.

On November 9th 1980 we set out again across the Atlantic. We had five dozen eggs, thirty five lemons, a load of spuds, and a locker full of tins, Also 68 gallons of water were in two gallon plastic containers under the floor. No more flexible tanks this time!

It had taken us thirty five days the last time and similarly from Puerto Rico back to the Azores. That's really slow. So this time we were expecting to do much better. Two days out with hardly any wind we had only done 70 miles. We could still see the top of the volcano on Tenerife!

We sailed on. We had a northerly swell which made us roll horribly when we had the wind behind us but for days on end the winds were against us; and in between, flat calm. During the crossing, we saw two ships, four yachts, three whales and we caught a huge dorado which Jean preserved in bottles using the pressure cooker.

2

LATE ON SATURDAY, 13 December 1980 we came in sight of Barbados. We were being boarded by swarms of big flying fish whose soft white flesh is delicious. We arrived late in the evening and hove-to off the island to enter the harbour in the morning. The crossing had taken yet another frustrating thirty five days!

As we came, in the local radio was playing Beatles music continuously. It would've been nice had it been just for us but in fact John Lennon had just been murdered in New York, not good at all.

The two lighthouses on the south side of the island didn't appear to be working so we waited till dawn to sail into Carlisle Bay. There we found a whole fleet of yachts about a dozen of whom we already knew. To clear-in we were forced to motor up a narrow creek into the center of Bridgetown where customs had a small wharf. We had managed to lose reverse gear so stopping alongside was going to be interesting. Fortunately there were quite a few yacht people on the wharf to grab hold and slow us down .We nearly dragged a few into the water before we stopped.

One person commented on how wonderful our little old engine sounded "just like an old fishing boat". He had to shout of course, but at least he didn't have to experience (as we did) the thumping vibrations on board that went with the sound.

On the way into the creek we had seen a small black steel yacht we knew from two years ago when tied alongside the Taiwanese fishing boat. Jerry was a young English guy and had been here for all that time because he had been so broke he couldn't afford to pay the light dues you had to pay to leave. So he stayed. He had been offered a job skippering a small freighter which operated out of Barbados and we were invited to dinner on the ship.

That evening we found the freighter tied up in the Creek together with a load more disreputable looking vessels. Jerry's ship, the *Michelle C*, was in fact in good condition, an old Dutch coaster with some very nice accommodation aft, two large holds and a crane forward.

When he first took the job, aged only twenty, he was flown to Venezuela with an engineer and a cook deckhand. He had to bring the ship back to

Barbados, It had been in dry dock. The mate was ill and so not available so it was a case of push this lever and see what happens turn that wheel and pray. I had been nervous coming up the creek with *Sea Loone*. I couldn't imagine how he felt bringing the *Michelle C* up the creek the first time. But now he was experienced master and had been up and down the islands many times.

While in Liverpool we had acquired stacks and stacks of charts all out of date rejects from a large shipping company. It was not easy for my friend to find the relevant charts but eventually we did very well and we had a lot of duplicates. With all the boats around us we sold off our spares and made a little money but soon we were going to have to seriously start looking for work. By the time we left the Canary Islands we had already spent £225 of our £2,000. We had had no serious expenses except to weld our anchor chain again. We'd also bought a new nylon anchor warp.

The rest have been spent on fuel and gas, food and the main expense, beer. Here in the Islands, beer was expensive. We had no refrigeration so drinking in bars became a luxury. It was more common to invite people, or be invited on board for rum punches usually made with a fake orange powder which, even with the rum, was horrible.

Windensee, the yacht we had tied to in Madeira had a great party on the boat for 1980-81 New Year. *Passing Through*, another Dutch boat had another huge party during which a new baby crawled to the side and fell overboard. I was, by chance, the only one to see this happen so was able to scoop him out before any real damage was done. I returned the baby to its mother who, I'm sure, was going to keep a closer eye from there on. We were to meet again in Florida.

The crew of the Australian boat, *Polar Bear* was trying to drink the island dry. They were in fact all Finnish so might succeed. We were to meet again in Cairns many years later. *Equinox* we would visit in New Zealand and *Prologue* in Sydney. A small English catamaran was anchored close by on his way to Vancouver Canada. We were to meet again many years later in New Zealand by which time he had circumnavigated and got into the Guinness book of Records. He was the smallest catamaran to do it and probably also the slowest!

Onshore in the local beach bar we met Rodney Fox. I'm not sure what he was doing on the island but this was the man that almost got bitten in half in Australia by a great white shark. One evening he showed a film of these huge white sharks but the most impressive thing was to see the teeth marks front and back around his body.

Jean described Bridgetown as a dump and it was. The fruit and vegetables were all imported. In fact, *Windensee*, the Dutch yacht sailed off to Dominica to bring back oranges to make some money. The Bajans grew no vegetables or fruit and they brought in cheap labour from the other Islands to cut cane.

To add insult to injury, when we left they wanted 45 Bajan dollars for "light dues" but the lighthouses didn't work! We left.

We sailed overnight with our two spinnaker poles out and in the morning there was the mountainous island of St. Vincent. To the left was a smaller mountainous island, Bequia, where we were heading. These islands, unlike Barbados, use the East Caribbean dollar as their currency The French islands use francs. The Virgin Islands in the north use American dollars. So it was important to know how they all related to each other and for us, to our British pounds.

In 1981, the pound was quite strong so for one pounds we could get 4.5 Barbados dollars, EC$ 6.7 (East Caribbean dollars), 10.9 French francs and US$2.15.

We anchored close to the beach in Admiralty Bay and paid our 47.50 EC dollars to clear- in. It was a lovely bay. To the left there was an old slipway, then a wharf with trading schooners tied up, a line of shops, a few cottages and then bush. To the far right, and separated by a rocky headline was a long sandy beach backed by palm trees; the stuff of dreams, my dreams anyway!

Anchored close in front of us was a small, what looked like, local boat with a gaff rig, a long boom and bowsprit and a flush deck. The owner turned out to be a charming German who had the boat built there on the beach. We were invited on board. The boat was only twenty six feet long and below there was only headroom for sitting. Under the floor was a huge anchor for use in hurricane and otherwise as ballast. The boat was really strongly made, the frames cut from hardwood trees growing on the hillside behind the beach. The bollards and samson post were some sort of ironwood or lignum vitae, the planking was mahogany sailed up from Venezuela. On the beach one of the Bequia two-bows was being built. This boat, *Plumbelly* was a little longer and a little fatter. Of course there was no engine.

Klaus, the owner, came for dinner and astonished us by explaining that he had only just returned here from a trip around the world. He had passed through the Panama Canal and between Galapagos and the Marquesas Islands had an amazing fast passage. This was the one leg on a cruise around the world which worried me. Having been so slow in our crossings of the Atlantic, I wondered how long that passage, half as long again, would take us. But he was a much smaller boat and had done it in only twenty three days.

Maybe we could do the same if and when we got that far. He did say that the winds were unusually strong and that running down the steep seas, the bowsprit spent so much time in the water that there were goose barnacles growing on its end!

We hiked all over the island, found a beautiful deserted beach on the windward side and found huge mango trees dropping the fruit on the ground plus a gourd tree one of which we picked and brought back to the boat.

Bequia people are great sailors and there were a number of small ships and trading schooners owned and operated from Admiralty Bay, trading up and down the Caribbean. One large schooner, the *Friendship Rose* provided a ferry service back and forwards to St. Vincent. Kingstown had a big market and a botanical gardens we want to see. So for five dollars we took off very early in the morning.

Hoisting the mainsail was a sight to see. Two groups of huge musclemen, stripped to the waist, heaved on the gaff, one lot pulling up the throat and the others following with the peak. The main boom stuck out over the stern to a distance far longer than the total length of *Sea Loone*.

The seas roar between the islands when the tradewind pumps. As soon as we left the harbour and the channel we heeled over and flew along. I was standing near the stern where a great argument started up between the skipper and the mate over how the mainsail was set. Eventually they agreed to let the boom out a little more. The loosed about two feet of rope on the mainsheet but with the numerous blocks it went through, I doubt the boom moved more than three inches. The odd wave would come over the side so it was a good idea to duck now and again. The flock of sheep penned up in the bow were going to arrive very wet.

We had until mid-afternoon to shop in the market but first we took a taxi up to the Botanical Gardens. Here we found a ten -year-old guy who showed us all the wonders of his tropical garden complete with local names and Latin names. Here was Capt. Bligh's first breadfruit tree brought from the Pacific. We were given lemongrass to make tea and saw our first nutmegs. We loaded up with fresh vegetables and fruits in the market. Then, carrying our precious load of fruit back down to the dock, we found ourselves a sheltered spot among the deck cargo of the *Friendship Rose* and made the return trip. We were pleased with ourselves.

If anything, the return trip was rougher or maybe some of the passengers had spent too much time in the rum shop in Georgetown. There was soon a line of passengers hanging over the lee side and one large lady making her offering on the windward side which cleared the deck behind. We were happily sitting on sacks of flour with our groceries until we realized that an army of weevils was abandoning the flour and invading our stuff. After hanging our bags in the rigging, we shook the wretched weevils out of our clothes.

We were pretty sure we would find some work in the Virgin Islands where *Quark* had already been now for more than a year; so we decided to jump from island to island up the chain of islands to Antigua and then go downwind a little to the BVI, the British Virgin Islands.

The first jump was from the Bequia round the back of St. Vincent to St. Lucia. We set off late one afternoon, flew across the channel and were behind St Vincent as the sun dropped. In the shadow of the huge mountainous island, the wind dropped so we sat there bobbing up and down most of that night.

By dawn we edged out from behind the North Cape. Gusts of wind heeled us over dramatically and rough seas built up. A hasty reef in the main and we flew across to St. Lucia hard on the wind with water flying everywhere and a few other things flying around down below. This seemed to be typical Caribbean sailing, either no wind or too much wind, with the sheets pulled in and the boat heeling over madly. We raced behind the Pittons on the south coast of St. Lucia. With the wind momentarily freeing off we zoomed along farther behind the island, the wind then dying into fits and spurts.

Late in the afternoon we found our way into Marigot Harbour. I say "found our way" because the narrow entrance is not at all obvious. The place was almost deserted; just a small hotel on the left and some houses up on the hill to the right. The body of water inside was surrounded by mangroves which made a really safe anchorage in any weather. We shared the anchorage with a couple of the other boats and also shared the mosquitoes that came out at dusk. The next day we set off for the next hop, Martinique and its main town, Fort de France.

The wind had eased a little or maybe turned slightly more south which was in our favour. The trip across was almost pleasant and for once we didn't arrive salt-encrusted. We even caught a small tuna. We tied up the dinghy on a scruffy wharf behind the city bus station. It wasn't pleasant. It seemed to be also the public urinal. The city was big and busy so we stayed only long enough to buy baguettes and a pineapple. Then we were off on the next hop to Dominica.

We knew already that Dominica was maybe the least developed and poorest of the Windward Islands. There certainly didn't seem to be any breaks in the solid forest covering the mountains. Portsmouth, in a large bay at the north end of the island had a good anchorage and was apparently was a good spot to buy fruit. Behind the islands we had to occasionally run the engine if we found ourselves sitting in the same spot for an hour or so. However, when I turned the engine over to motor into the bay, I found we had used up all our diesel.

We were still a fair way out so pulled in the sheets and started beating into the bay. At the same time two rowing boats appeared heading rapidly towards us. Each had two rowers and were fast moving. Pulling alongside they tied themselves off and began to barter for selling us fruit. With two large wooden rowing boats dragging behind us we were seriously slowed. So the first negotiation was that they'd only get business if they let go and allowed us to sail to our anchorage.

It took two tacks to get up near the beach and chuck in the anchor. By then, we had four rowing boats and a raft alongside. I asked who had the cheapest grapefruits just to get things going. The cheapest guy was then accused by the others of stealing his grapefruits. He still got my business but I divided the rest of our business with the other boats. Grapefruits were three for only one EC dollar.

The raft which was called *Kontiki* was owned and built by two little kids less than ten years old. They got my order for limes and I bet they were stolen also. But anyway when they returned, I asked them if they would prefer a good football which I had found, to actual money. They were quite indignant. They were businessmen. They didn't have time for football. "Give us the money!" they demanded.

The north side of the bay finished in a hilly peninsula on which there was a fort, Fort Shirley. It was built by the British to protect the bay and throw a few cannonballs north in the direction of Guadeloupe, the French island. We tramped up a rutted path in the jungle and came to some very dilapidated ruins. The fort had been finally overrun by the French and the guns tipped over the steep hillside into the water way below. Having poked around the ruins a bit we found the guns in the shallow water, huge cast-iron things with a crown stamped on the barrel. They must have been murder to move around. It was no wonder they still sat where they landed years ago.

Before we left we took a couple of jerry cans with us to find the Long House south of town where Geeste Bananas had a wharf and packing plant. We hoped for some diesel. Sure enough, we found we could fill our jerry cans and at the same time look around.

The banana boat arrived from Britain every couple of weeks. The bananas arrived the same day from all the small farms in cars and, and probably by bus and donkey also. The hands of bananas were separated, washed, boxed and loaded on the ship before it moved on to the next island. They had been picked green so would ripen the day they arrived in England.

Back in the port of Liverpool, the bananas would ripen while the ship sat anchored offshore waiting for trade disputes between owners and unions to be settled. At that time, that could take weeks. In consequence, Geeste's had moved to Swansea where the bananas we saw were heading.

Next stop, Guadalupe, another French island. We found a little cove, Anse de la Barque to anchor for the night where a small crayfish climbed in my fish trap, very nice. There were fish traps with their floats everywhere. It was difficult not to get tangled up when sailing at night. We had left early in the morning in the dark to do the final leg north to Antigua and English Harbour where we had made our first landfall two years before. This time, we avoided getting caught out by the nightfall, thrashing across the channel over night to arrive off English Harbour in the early morning.

In the two years we had been away, it was obvious that English Harbour had become a lot busier. In the middle of the harbor was a yellow buoy with instructions on it for us to tie up and wait for the authorities to clear us. When customs and immigration arrived, they explained that there was a daily fee, not much but I could see this was the thin end of the wedge.

We moved well inside the harbor and anchored off the Governor General's garden. This was a good move as there was a wild orange tree in the middle of the lawn. It was covered in oranges. Jean had met the Germans again in Fort de France and was still upset that they had beaten her to the orange tree in Bayona. So miraculously, that night a sack of oranges appeared on *Sea Loone* and the next day our marmalade factory got going. These wild oranges are impossibly bitter with hundreds of pips but they are perfect for marmalade.

The pips boiled in a net with the rest of the mixture, helps the marmalade set.

The stone head that Jean had found in Montserrat on the last trip had gone back to England with us. There we had sent it to the Liverpool Museum, who then sent it on to London. When it was returned we were informed it was an Arawak head made by the people who lived in these islands before the Caribs arrived about a thousand years ago. The head was part of a piece of their pottery. We were sent pictures of similar pieces in the museum but our piece was certainly more interesting than most.

Desmond Nicholson, one of the sons of the wellknown local family, was a keen archaeologist. He was in fact a bit unworldly and they called him Dizzy Desmond. When we showed him our head he was very enthusiastic and borrowed it to photograph and measure. Later, he took us to see what he had discovered in and around English Harbour but it was all made from red clay and quite different.

Some months later we were contacted by the Montserrat Museum who had heard from Desmond. They wanted us to donate our piece in exchange for a lifetime of free entrance to the museum. How generous. It's still on the boat which is probably just as well; if it was now on Montserrat it would be in under a mountain of ash.

One afternoon sitting in the shade and on a veranda overlooking *Sea Loone*, Jean's friends showed us their feeding bottles with red tips hung under the eaves to attract hummingbirds. The hummingbirds would come and hover right in front of my face, little iridescent beauties not much bigger than bumblebees. On the wooden uprights of the veranda there were little dragons maybe three inches long. They would occasionally stop and do press ups maybe just to keep fit.

After a few beers at the yacht club in Falmouth and a climb up to Shirley Heights to take in the fine view of the harbour and the surrounding island, we left. We were off to the Virgin Islands and where hopefully we would find gainful employment.

We passed Montserrat, Nevis and St. Kitts and Saba, a steep volcanic cone on which people manage to live. The following day we passed between Ginger Island and Virgin Gorda into Drakes passage. We beat up into St. Thomas Bay off the marina in Virgin Gorda and threw in the anchor on a sandy spot between the coral heads. Clearing in was easy enough, although the official was not very friendly. We were getting used to the surliness. It wasn't particularly reserved for the ex-colonial masters and was best ignored.

We met Charlie and Janet on their yacht, *Quark*, in the marina. Charlie was now the engineering manager for North South Yacht Charters which operated out of the marina. Charlie was a brilliant mechanic on diesel engines, outboard engines and anything else that could go wrong on a yacht. With a lot of very well used yachts for charter, Charlie was kept very busy but for us, Jean and I, there didn't seem much going on.

The yachts were normally rented out bare boat, that is, without a crew, but if the people didn't have enough experience or confidence they took a skipper. This was hopefully a job I could be doing. On larger boats there were cooks, stewardesses and jobs which Jean could do plus the odd bit of boat cleaning.

We sat around for a while but business didn't seem to be exactly booming then, suddenly, a week later, we both found ourselves with work. I was to take a Canadian family out for two weeks on a Morgan Out Island 41, a forty one foot ketch which sailed like a dog. Meanwhile Jean was to go out on the company's brand-new huge forty eight foot yacht just delivered from Canada. She was the cook and there was also a captain. The charterer was a very rich American lady with her teenage son who wanted to go windsurfing.

I had never sailed around these islands having only just arrived so had no knowledge of the anchorages, the restaurants, the landings, shops or watering places .The booklet the Charter company provided described me as a great skipper and know all, even a fine cook!

As soon as we got started I had to explain the new rules. I did not cook. Then I explained that each day was going to be an adventure for all of us. They were nice people, the two young kids under control and the wife was prepared to cook. For the first couple of days things were fine. Then the water ran out and they need to do laundry so I had to find a marina. No problem, but water and laundry every three days was going to take a bite out of the holiday. So I suggested they severely restrict their water use and didn't change's clothes so often. I suppose I could have suggested wearing less. That was how Jean solved any laundry problems but probably not a good idea for a family.

With clean clothes and our tanks filled with water, we set off again. But that evening disaster struck. The cooker used alcohol in a pressure tank under the sofa. This had to be regularly pumped up which was very inconvenient. Also, the burners had to be preheated before turning them on. We were all a bit nervous of this. That evening, the wife went to start the oven and a huge sheet of flames licked over the deckhead and out the open hatch. The husband went to throw water at it, which might have been more of a disaster, but just at that moment the wife screamed and fell back onto the sofa. The husband went quickly to attend to his wife while I turned everything off and the flames subsided. Disaster was narrowly averted! There a little soot around but fortunately no real damage. No one was injured.

It was decided that there would be no more cooking. No problem, every bay has its own restaurant or even a choice. My contract stated that if they ate out they had to also feed me which was fine by me. So we sailed from island to island and bay to bay and then they wanted to go to Anegada. This island was on an exposed reef to the north and east. The approach was through very shallow water.

The boat wasn't very keen on sailing to windward or tacking about. It was better to start the engine. So we motor sailed to windward arrived, ate lobsters and then sailed back down wind into quieter waters. Unfortunately they wanted to do it again.

This time, we set off to windward again and not far from Virgin Gorda disaster struck again. The shackle holding the roller furling gear and the huge head sail, broke. The large steel drum at the lower end flew up in the air together with the sail, then came down very close to us in the cockpit. I shooed the kids and the wife below while the sail took off into the air again and fluttered down on the mizzen mast

I turned the boat downwind and eventually the sail picked up and flew off forward again. Then I gradually brought the boat around and the drum and sail swung back in towards the port side. I got the husband to grab the roller and lash it any which way to the main shroud. The two of us then bundled up the sail and we set course back to the marina in Virgin Gorda.

When we arrived at the marina, I was surprised to find the new prize of the fleet was also back together with Jean. Their story was really good. They had sailed up into Gorda Sound only a few miles away. There the son wanted to go windsurfing every day and then wanted hamburgers on shore every evening, so Jean had not been exactly busy. However, when they decided to move to another part of the Sound, the boat started to fill with water. The water rapidly came over the floorboards, the engine and the batteries before skipper found the problem. Fortunately for everyone, he knew the type of boat and had heard of the same problem happening before. They had lost the propeller shaft, and that leaves a big hole!

After stuffing a rag in the hole they had had to be towed back home. The water had got into the engine and the electrics. The charterer was not happy. Neither was the company who no longer had a fancy new boat to charter.

Meanwhile, I had got the tangled mess on my boat sorted. The sail had a tear in it from the mizzen so was going to have to be repaired. The manager promised some sort of a sail for us in the morning so that we could continue.

That evening I was planning to go with my lot to the Marina restaurant when Jean arrived to say I was invited out with her lady charterer for a meal. The manager had foolishly offered to cover the cost of the evening out for her and her guests prior to their leaving. Jean's lady was going to take full advantage. We got cleaned up and then took a taxi to the Rockerfeller restaurant up the coast a mile or so. We started with escargot in the shell and went through the menu. The wine waiter offered us the wine list and the lady ordered the best. After a few glasses of wine I kept the company entertained with tales of the high seas. We never saw the bill but it must have been huge.

The following morning with the small jib borrowed from the manager's boat, I went out and finish the charter with the Canadian family. There were no more hiccups. Jean had a few more days stewardessing but it was becoming a little quiet, so we decided to move over to Tortola and see what was happening there.

Maya Cove, a few miles east of Road Town, the main town and seat of the central government, was home to another charter company, West Indies Charters. It was also a favorite anchorage for people like ourselves. There were five or six yachts there and everyone seemed to have a job, some full-time, with different charter companies. The anchorage inside the barrier reef was shallow and perfectly sheltered, the people helpful and friendly.

When I was eleven years old I had joined the Liverpool Botanical Society together with my sister. On many occasions I was the sole youngster with a group of elderly ladies hiking through the sand dunes on the Lancashire coast or in the hills of Wales. At school I formed the Wirral Ponding Society and dragged school friends from pond to pond dredging up water beetles, water scorpions and other nasties. In the garden at home, I had frogs and newts and some rare toads.

Later I fell in with birdwatchers, a large group of whom spent a lot of time on Hilbre Island in the River Dee estuary. It was only a ten mile bike ride from home but the island was only accessible at low tide across a few miles of muddy sand. The only full-time resident on the island was a warden employed by the local authority and living in an old brick house. In my later days at school through the time until I started building the boat the warden was Peter Bailey with his wife Barbara.

They had visited the boat occasionally when I was building it, often bringing me fresh goose eggs. Now they were here in the Virgin Islands. We found them not far along the road from Maya in East End. Peter was involved in a marina building project and Barbara was doing a little teaching. She also worked at the hospital.

We reminisced about the time on Hilbre and the characters in the birdwatching group and then Peter explained the situation in the Virgin Islands.

At that time, the Virgins- at least the British Virgin Islands – were pretty undeveloped and laid-back. Nobody locked the doors, nobody had heard of drugs. There were no problems. The Government however were not going to allow anyone to share this paradise. To extend your visitor's visa involved an unpleasant interview with the immigration department each month. A work permit was almost impossible unless sponsored by a large company and one could never become a permanent resident. The closest thing to permanent was to become a "belonger" but that gave no guarantees if you upset the wrong person.

It was March. I got a job with West Indies Charter but only for two days. I had to sail with the charterers for the two days to make sure they were competent to finish the charter on their own. In fact, my job was to teach them enough in two days that they weren't going to wreck the boat in the time remaining. We sailed downwind to West End stopping one night in Norman Island. In West End I jumped off and got the bus home. The charterers were stuck with beating back to windward.

After Easter, the charter season was finished more or less until the next season which started in December. They haven't been much happening anyway and now with the hurricane season looming, things were not looking good. A few of the charter companies didn't look too healthy and the others weren't going to be taking on any permanent staff.

Our financial situation was looking pretty good. Out of the original £2,000 in traveler's cheques we had spent nearly £300 pounds to get as far as Barbados and altogether £570 pounds until now, March, in the Virgin Islands. With our charter work between us Jean and I had earned US$1,185 which more or less replaced what we had spent.

The work we had done was illegal. We were paid basically fifty dollars a day all found. The government of course knew what was happening and preferred to keep the situation that way rather than allow any permanency. Sailing around the islands was pleasant and not exactly hard work. The charterers were normally okay apart from the continuous string of questions. I was in fact a glorified tour guide.

We decided to move on and head for Florida where Jerry Jamieson on the barge in Madeira promised us the streets were paved with gold. Before we left Road Town we invested in some booze. At that time, a bottle of rum, vodka or gin cost less than a dollar if you bought by the case. So we bought three cases. We seemed to spend as much on alcohol as we did on food so this seemed a good long-term investment.

From the Virgin Islands we sailed to Culebra which we knew from delivering the yacht from the Naval Base two years before. Once there, we planned to call into the Naval Base again just to say hello and maybe pick up some cheap tinned food from their PX or commissary.

Between Culebra and Roosevelt Road Naval base we knew there was the Seven Mile Reef. We headed to pass by its southern end. With a good breeze behind us and our two downwind parachute sails out on poles we were sailing fast. We were towing two fishing lines behind us.

We saw the marker on the reef and steered to leave it to starboard. Then there was a sudden grinding noise beneath our keel and, looking over the side, we found ourselves flying over masses of huge coral heads. I let the sheets go on the two headsails but the poles slammed into the forestays and broke. At least we had started to slow down though we were still grinding over thousands of heads of staghorn coral.

Looking forward, I spotted a clear area with a sand bottom. We veered towards it and, without hitting anything solid, arrived in a sandy pool only eight feet deep. Jean got the engine going and we motored around in circles while we cleared away the mess of sails and broken poles on the foredeck. We also pulled in the fishing line to find that, on one, there was a very battered looking three-foot barracuda that we had dragged through the coral.

We were close to the marker by now and when I climbed up the mast to the spreaders, I could see the reef ended not too far away if we continued west. The marker maybe indicated the middle of the reef which seemed a bit silly. There was no way to retrace where we had come so we took a deep breath continued across the reef. We smash through some more coral, avoiding the solid stuff, and popped out the other side of the reef into clear water. The "Sea Loone Channel" across Seven Mile Reef saves a few miles but I don't recommend it.

We sailed past all the warships coming into Rossy Roads and anchored off the marina without a problem. We were welcomed by our friends but things had changed! The oil crisis had severely affected the Navy. No more air-conditioned luxury, no cheap PX and, to cap it all, some US fighter planes had been blown up in San Juan, so security was tightened.

We stayed a few days then retraced our steps along the south coast of Puerto Rico stopping in Ponce. We then crossed the channel to Santo Domingo to see the market again. There we bought some amber jewelry, a turtle shell and some pottery.

Jamaica was still having problems so we sailed on to Cayman. There we discovered we might have problems arriving in the USA with our cases of liquor. They apparently don't allow yachts to bond on board so we were persuaded to sell our stock. We made a good profit so it wasn't hard and were careful to keep a small stock of liquor for socializing in port over the next few months. In this part of the world, the hurricane season starts officially in June but it was rare for anything to appear before late-July. Still, we were cautious and, as it was now May, we didn't want to be caught in the Gulf of Mexico.

Leaving Cayman, we headed for the Yucatán Channel. All the water in the Caribbean is forced into this channel between Mexico and Cuba. This then forms the Gulf Stream which sweeps past the southern tip of Florida, turns north and flows out into the Atlantic. We had little wind and have no idea what the current was doing with us. Fortunately, as we approached the western tip of Cuba, a ship came over the horizon and over the VHF radio a clipped British accent gave us our position. We actually had called the ship and asked for them to "confirm our position". But they didn't ask what we thought, which was just as well as we might have been embarrassed by our own guesswork. With whatever wind we had, we sailed a few miles. But basically we just got swept along. I got a few sights with the sextant and we played with our radio direction finder which confused us more than helped.

3

WE NEVER SAW land until, having rounded Key West, we saw a bank of brown fog on the horizon one morning. We picked up some red and white striped chimneys and realized that the fog was in fact, rush-hour in Miami! I thought of all those years in Liverpool under a similar haze without it being as starkly obvious as this.

Leaving Miami behind we passed Fort Lauderdale, with more striped chimneys, then followed the buoyed channel into West Palm Beach. We had a book and charts for the Intracoastal Waterway into which we now found ourselves sailing.

We found the customs wharf. The paperwork was straightforward in contrast to the rigmarole we had gone through in England to obtain an indefinite American Visa. We were given a stay of six months and as long as we surrendered the ship's papers to the customs, *Sea Loone* could stay indefinitely. As the customs guy put the papers in a drawer, I saw another British ship's registration, the blue book. They were for *Passing Through*, the crazy Dutchman's yacht we had last seen in Barbados.

Having finished with the officials, we set off along the waterway intending to find a place to stop, go ashore, drink a cold beer and buy some fresh food. Our first lesson was to keep well inside the channel buoys. We had done only one hundred yards before we found ourselves aground.

After kedging off, we set off again and turned into Little Lake Worth. Here we anchored in the middle, pumped up the inflatable, and rowed to the shore which was fringed by very fancy homes with little docks at the bottom of the garden usually with a large sports fishing boat tied up. However we headed for a small marina in front of a large building with Lake Worth Yacht Club written on it.

We rowed up to an empty wharf and tied up. As we did this, a uniformed character arrived on a moped. He had a fancy hat, a badge and a bloody great gun on his hip. Without preamble, he told us that he was from the Sheriff's Department and that if we stepped ashore we would be shot. Not much of a welcome to America! We paddled back to the boat.

An hour later another yacht passed us and anchored further up the lake.

We rowed over to ask where we could go ashore. The answer was basically, you can't. It was all private property with gunslingers hiding in the bushes. However, all was not lost if we rowed to the top of the lake where there was a road bridge across the creek. Here if you were athletic you could climb onto the bridge, tie off the dinghy and there was a convenience store down the road. Marvelous!

We had been at sea for nearly two weeks so having done the shopping trip we returned to the boat and slept. With the difficulties in navigation, the amount of traffic, and the lack of good winds we'd had had little sleep on the trip from Cayman. So here on the lake, *Sea Loone* was absolutely still. With no wind even the rigging was silent. We slept.

With no reason to hang around the next morning we set off north. The breeze picked up so we set the sails motoring at the same time. Maybe sailing on the Intercostal Waterway is not allowed. We got some funny looks from passing stinkpots, motorboats. We had to steer which was very boring. With the sails pulling we were not doing badly and bridges opened up conveniently as we approached.

It was going swimmingly until we arrived at Jupiter Inlet. Here we had to do a sharp right and left passing under a large bridge carrying a main road north. We swung around the first turn nicely and the bridge went to open for us. Then we caught the incoming tide from the inlet and slowed to a crawl. The sails were pulling, the Lister thumping, but we only crept up to the bridge. The bridge man was frantically waving for us to move faster as the road traffic was building up. But by the time we were through the bridge the main highway was blocked for miles!

We made a tight left hand turn and then, with the tide behind us, we saw the next road bridge. As we got closer nothing happened so we tooted our horn, still nothing! We did a sharp jibe around and dropped the sails. This guy must have heard from the other bridge! In the end, he made us wait twenty minutes before he opened the bridge.

By tea time we were looking for somewhere to anchor for the night. There's nowhere. Eventually, we simply drifted into the side and throw in the anchor. Opposite was a huge mansion with a lawn the size of a cricket pitch. There were full size black and white plywood cows on the lawn, say no more.

By noon the next day we have arrived at the St. Lucie Inlet and turn left to follow the St. Lucie River to Stuart. We have directions how to find Jerry's dock but no idea what it's going to look like. We only know there is a large schooner tied to the dock on which he lives.

We are careful to stay inside the channel markers and eventually make out what can only be the dock. It was a bit disappointing and as soon as we edge towards it, we hit shallow water. We anchor at the edge of the channel but we are a long way out.

When someone tells you in Madeira that he owns a dock hundreds of feet long, and you are from England, you envision substantial stone and concrete docks. Having seen docks in the Caribbean, then maybe you modify your ideas. But the dock we saw was no more than a wooden pier sticking out two hundred feet into the River with less than two feet of water under it and maybe four feet at the very end. *Sea Loone* draws six feet. The schooner we saw had to be aground or in a mud hole. At the end of the dock there is a barge with a crane and a couple of small boats tied alongside.

We rowed over checking the depth with our oars. It was shallow. Jerry was on the dock with his wife, Lucy. The schooner *Warlock* was a copy of the Chesapeake oyster dredger which Jerry had built in concrete. Jerry had seen us approaching. They were pleased to see us and we were soon sitting in the cockpit of the schooner *Warlock* sipping drinks.

When I pointed out that we needed more than six feet of water to come alongside his dock, Jerry assured us there would be no problem and he'd sort it out the following day. When I pointed out we were going to need to find work and make some money, he said we'd sort that out too on the following day. So we drank more rum and, feeling more optimistic, returned to *Sea Loone* and slept again like logs.

The following day with an ugly steel tugboat blowing out a channel with its propeller and then pulling us towards the dock, we eventually found ourselves alongside in a pool of water into which we just fitted. We weren't exactly afloat and bumped the bottom occasionally when the wake of a passing boat arrived. With a long gangplank we could jump onto the dock with *Warlock* opposite us.

It was really hot and humid. The mosquitoes in the evening were in their millions so we had to have screens on all the hatches as soon as the sun began to set.

I explained my plans to Jerry. We need enough money to carry on through into the Pacific by the Panama Canal and we also needed a more powerful engine to get through the canal. Jerry had two barges working, both driving pilings. Each barge had two men working them. Then he had another one or two doing odd jobs and working in a timber yard where they sold wood pilings and treated lumber. There was also a carpentry crew that built the docks. He subcontracted this crew as a unit.

All the workers were in fact subcontractors. At that time he didn't need any more workers but this would soon change, he said. The four guys working the barge were paid only by the footage of pilings placed. The rate was simply a dollar a foot and the story was that they could make as much as $1000 a week. For me this was the stuff of dreams. The shipyard in Liverpool where I worked had been paying me the equivalent of fifty dollars a week so a twenty times increase was crazy. I was determined to take over one of these jobs by fair means or foul.

Meanwhile Jerry had come up with another proposition. The *Warlock* was made in concrete and had a few problems. If I was to effect some repairs and offer Jerry my Lister engine he would come up with some basic wages and a Volvo marine diesel which they had acquired.

The engine was from a wrecked boat they had salvaged. It was almost new and producing thirty five horse power. It was more than twice as powerful as the Lister and was water cooled so probably less noisy. The only problem with the engine was it had a sail drive rather than the standard gearbox but I felt this could be easily altered.

The weather continued to be oppressively hot and humid so before we got down to work, Jean and I decided to take the opportunity to go and see Jean's aunt. It was now early June so we had until August before the hurricane season was upon us when we would need to stay close to the boat.

Jean's aunt lived in Vancouver, British Columbia. Our idea was to do a car delivery there and then back. Under the heading of travel opportunities, the Miami Herald advertised people needing cars delivered all over the country. The deliverer pays for the petrol and that was it. Very simple. So the next day I bought the paper and there was a car needing to be delivered to Spokane in Oregon just across the border from Vancouver.

I telephoned the number and spoke to the company organizing the delivery. The car had to go immediately and could I pick it up the next day, Friday. Hell, we hardly had *Sea Loone* tied up securely but this was a chance not to be missed.

I jumped on the Greyhound bus down to Miami the next morning. Knowing I was going to have to drive back, I tried to make head or tail of the spaghetti junction as we motored into Miami. After only a few minutes in the office in which my British driver's license was admired because it didn't run out till 2015, I deposited fifty dollars and was presented with a brand-new little Mazda car.

From Miami back to Stuart was a nightmare. At one stage I turned right on a dual carriageway to find myself on the wrong side of the road and with traffic heading straight for me. Fortunately the grass verge in the middle wasn't too much for the Mazda.

The next day we were packed and were off. Jean is a non-driver so I had a long trip ahead. In fact we did it in less than a week stopping in motels at night. We had hoped to find a quiet spot to park the car each evening to camp. In fact we only found a suitable spot once in the whole trip. Land was fenced and private and there were no little lanes and roads off the highway without a gate.

In Georgia, we stopped for petrol but couldn't understand a word the guy was saying, nor he us. After Georgia, maybe Louisiana, we drove through a historic site that had a manicured parkland and a large museum. We stopped and joined a party being lectured to about a famous battle which it taken place here. We got some funny looks when I asked if it was a battle among "yourselves" or against us. I didn't expect them to know anything about Agincourt or Waterloo for God's sake.

In Mississippi, we stopped for coffee and the blonde, blue-eyed waitress was amazed that we came from England. "Just like the people the other week" she said. "They came from the Philippines"! She then introduced us to the other waitress who, she said "came from the boondocks". In other words, she was even less worldly than she herself.

In a hotel in the Rocky Mountains, which had apparently once been a whore house, the owner was surprised that we knew nothing of the imminent Royal wedding in London. He had his plane ticket booked and was going to see Prince Charles married to what's-her-name.

We delivered the car to the owner, recouped our fifty dollars, hitchhiked down the road, stopped to collect some dust from Mount Saint Helens (that eruption must have been spectacular) and finally caught a bus across the border to Canada. There we were met by Jean's aunt and her family.

In one week we had gone from hot and humid Florida with malls, fast food, flashing signs etc. to rather cool English Properties, a suburb of Vancouver and all very proper.

Jean's cousin, a dentist, invite us to take a flight with him in his aeroplane. We drove to the private airfield and were shown the machine parked in its garage. It was small with a glass bubble on top and took two people, one sitting behind the other. We pushed it out into the open. This was Jean's second flight after our delivery job in the Caribbean and this was a plane even smaller than the first.

While they flew off I talked to the guys working on a plane in the next garage. It was a seaplane and it had a propeller facing the wrong way. The three guys that owned it were plumbers. They were repainting it for the next fishing season.

Apparently they flew north, found a remote lake, landed and fish for trout and salmon. Again, I thought back to the ship yard in Liverpool where a plumber would live in a terraced house, spend the weekend in the pub at the end of the road, put a few bob on the horses and maybe have ten days in a holiday camp in the summer.

I had my turn in the aeroplane. Unfortunately close to the city we were not allowed to do any aerobatics but the view of the city below, and then the mountains and coastline, was fantastic.

We determined to go out to one of the islands to meet Jean's family's friends who had taken early retirement there. They had built and operated a little restaurant on Galeano Island off Vancouver Island. They opened only one night a week with a fixed menu. They were fully booked all summer and closed for six months in the winter when they bought a round the world ticket and went traveling. It didn't seem like too much work but in fact us they grew all their own vegetables, smoked bacon and ham, baked all sorts of things and picked and preserved whatever fruits were in season.

Sylvia and Ken met us off the ferry from Vancouver and we drove up the island to where they lived. The restaurant was on the road which ran the length of the island but their home was along a footpath through forest. It was an amazing A-frame construction perched on the cliff edge facing the mountains of Vancouver Island to the west.

The main room had a potbellied stove in the center with the flu going up through the roof. The sleeping accommodation was on a platform jutting out into the room and accessible only by a ladder. The huge glass window looked out onto the sea partly obscured by the strange peeling trunk of an arbutus tree growing on the cliff edge. They had built it all themselves even to splitting the cedar shakes for the roof. Here as on the mainland, huge logs have washed ashore all along the coast so there was no shortage of building materials.

In their winter travels, Ken and Sylvia had been to many of the places we hope to visit so we had lots of stories from them. Here on Galeano Island where they had already been for some years, they had started living in glorious isolation but now, more and more people were arriving and houses were being built all around. So they were already looking to move on, maybe somewhere more remote to the north.

That first morning when I awoke, I looked out and staring back at me through the window, sitting on a branch of the arbutus tree, was a bald eagle. What a start to our stay. Galiano Island was one of two strings of Islands close to Vancouver Island. Many were uninhabited, rocky and forested. The channels in between, or so we were told, were full of salmon. So we decided to spend a bit of time fishing.

Ken found us a Canadian canoe with upturned ends and two paddles. First we went with hook and line and finding bait was easy. At low tide the rocks were covered in oysters and mussels. Much better were the gooey ducks. These were huge clams maybe four or five inches across living buried in the sand. Conveniently they squirted a jet of water when you passed to show us exactly where to start digging.

We tied the canoe to some kelp fronds. These seem to have flotation buoys on the end and we dangled our hooks in the water. The Eagles soared back and forwards across the cliff edge. We noticed little furry animals playing in the seaweed close to the shore. They were mink. Soon we were pulling in coddling which looked very edible.

After a few days of hook and lining we decided on something a bit more adventurous. We were getting reasonably good paddling the canoe in a straight line so with a borrowed tent we loaded up to go across the channel to the next string of islands and spend a few days on which ever one we fancied. It was all reliving the English children's novel, "Swallows and Amazons" by Arthur Ransome.

We had seen killer whales from the ferry. They came every season to feed on the salmon. As we crossed the channel a pod consisting of maybe a dozen passed close by us. The male dorsal fins stuck maybe six feet out of the water. Fortunately they ignored us and to be truthful we weren't really worried.

We found a perfect campsite in a narrow channel between two small islands. At low tide channels little more than one hundred feet wide and maybe four or five feet deep. It seemed the perfect place for our attempt at salmon fishing so we pitched the tent. At dusk we strung our gill net which I had brought all the way from Florida, across the channel. The tide was rising

Late at night and in the pitch dark I was woken by the sound of an engine. A boat of some sort was coming into the channel. It was crazy. The channel was too narrow and the water too shallow for whatever was coming through. Then the engine suddenly stopped and I could imagine our net wrapped tightly around the propeller; then us being questioned about a fishing license and then prison!

Minutes went by and then the engine started again and the boat was moving away. I couldn't sleep so at the crack of dawn I crept out and down to the water's edge. It was low tide but not like the previous low tide. The channel was completely dry and our net was lying there with three large fish flapping around for all to see. I dashed down, bundled up the net, fish and all, and dragged it into the forest.

It was a disaster! The net was a tangled mess, full of vicious little crabs and three inedible dogfish. We buried the net – end of salmon fishing!

Ken and Sylvia wanted to visit their son who was running a campsite up in the Cascade Mountains on the mainland. They suggested we all went, camped on the way .Coming back they would drop us off in the Okanagan Valley east of Vancouver where we could try and find some fruit picking which might be a little less nerve-racking than salmon poaching.

The campsites were in fact concrete squares for parking camper vans. We had a serious argument one night having pitched our two little pup tents in the weeds alongside the concrete square where we had parked Ken's little French car. For two little tents, the Canadian Mounty look-alike wanted to charge us twice as much as a huge motor home opposite us which sprouted TV antenna, and air-conditioner and with the family car bigger than ours, hooked on the back!

No matter, the mountains were impressive. One night we camped on the shore of Englishman's Lake which was really special. As we ate supper and watched the sun drop over the hills, the loons flew in to roost, or maybe nest, in the reeds on the lake. We heard their strange mad call for the first time.

Loons or divers as they are called in Britain, are seen off the coast where *Sea Loone* was built, but only in the wintertime, and you never hear them calling. I was enchanted by the sound and then to top it off, as the light faded, a beaver paddled past us, only feet away.

Ken and Sylvia dropped us off in the Okanagan Valley and we hitchhiked up to Eastern Kalowna where there was an employment office for casual fruit pickers. We had arrived before the apple season started but the cherries were ripe and cherry picking was our forte. We found the office, organized by the government to find workers for the fruit growers, but then we hit a brick wall. We were told that, as foreigners, we would have to apply months ahead and would only be employed if local people were not available. The employer would have to advertise, so on and so on.

As we were being told all this by one guy, another behind him was shaking his head and indicating we should ignore the speaker and leave. So we left and, as we walked outside, a pickup truck pulled up. The driver asked us if we were looking for work so we explained the problem. He said he would pick us up around the corner in five minutes. So an hour later we were camped under one cherry tree and surrounded by one hundred more all dripping with cherries. We each had a bucket and a ladder. The deal was a dollar twenty five per bucket each of which would hold ten pounds of cherries.

In the afternoon we managed to pick a total of twenty four buckets. At that rate, we were not going to make a fortune. Still with the cherrywood campfire in the evening, it was a pleasant place to stop for a while.

In the mountains we had been on the lookout for bears and Jean had listen to the stories of bears coming into your tent at night looking for food. Of course she also knew all about Pooh Bear and his liking for jars of honey or maybe jam. So before she went to bed she hid our jar of jam in the cleft of a convenient cherry tree. In the morning it was gone. So when the farmer arrived Jean asked if there was a bear problem. He looked at her very strangely and assured her there were no bears in the valley. The jam jar of course was in the tree next along.

The next day we managed twenty buckets each but spent eight dollars on beer and another thirty four dollars on groceries. We kept at it, got better at it, but it was hard work up and down the ladders all day. We moved from dessert cherries to pie cherries which meant instead of making sure you also took the stalks, you now wanted no stalks. Should have been easier and quicker but it wasn't much and then without stalks a lot more cherries fitted in the bucket. We finally packed it in having made the huge figure of $252.50. We had been the farmer's hardest workers and he was sad to lose us. He gave us a couple of broken buckets and allowed us to take as many cherries as we wanted.

It was four hundred miles back to Vancouver, far further than we thought. We handed our cherries to whoever gave us lifts and eventually made it back to English Properties. When we arrived we discovered that a bear wandered through the house next-door while we were away in the mountains. We had seen neither hide nor hair. .

We took our remaining bucket of cherries back to Ken and Sylvia and also boxes of strawberries we had picked from a pick your own farm near the ferry terminal. Leaving the strawberry field, I was bloated. If Jean hadn't dragged me away maybe I would have exploded.

August was rapidly approaching. It was time to start thinking of the boat and hurricanes. We want to deliver a car down the West Coast and then maybe across to New Orleans en route to Florida. But there was nothing available so in the end we agreed to deliver an Oldsmobile Cutlas to Baltimore. We could travel across Canada and then crossing to the US at Niagara Falls. The car was huge compared with the Mazda so that we could camp in it and save hotel room costs.

On July 28th we left Vancouver. The weather was miserable. It rained and rained and the road through the mountains was a mess. We had hoped to see at least one glacier but they were all in the clouds and the bears were obviously sheltering somewhere to. It rained across Alberta, Saskatchewan and across Manitoba.

On the shores of Lake Superior we stopped at Max's Café for a coffee and the owner solved the problem of finding a bear. We slept in the car on the water's edge and early in the morning followed the sign off the main highway saying Dump. So, there was a large hole all filled with rubbish and two bears sorting through it. I jumped out of the car with the camera and went to take a picture. The nearest bear turned towards me and raised itself up on its back legs. It suddenly looked huge and menacing so I clicked the shutter and ran. When I jump back in the car and slammed the door, Jean pointed out that as I ran one way the bear ran the other way into the forest. But I had my picture.

After the Trans-Canada Highway we followed the North Lakes Expressway or some such name. Apart from in Alberta, the roads didn't do justice to their fancy names. After viewing Niagara Falls, we paid forty five cents to cross the bridge and found ourselves back in the USA.

We drove through New York State stopping unsuccessfully to look for wild turkeys. Then we drove on into Pennsylvania and Annapolis where we hope to find John, the Admiral's son from Roosevelt Roads Naval base.

We inquired at the forces recruitment office and John arrived and steered us to his house. It was a complete mess with hardly any furniture and John's half completed concrete yacht hull was lying upside down in a jungle of weeds in the back garden. There was a bed for us to sleeping in.

The following day we delivered the car to Baltimore. Without any travel opportunities available to Florida we decided to catch the Greyhound bus which was going to cost us $230 for the two of us. So we returned to John's house in Annapolis for the night and it turned out a very strange and horrible night.

John had invited two friends for the evening. They turned out to be gays, queer as a nine bob note. We were drinking and they were smoking pot. Whatever it was I had drunk or smoked I suddenly felt very peculiar and helpless. I retired to our room with Jean and had a very uncomfortable nervous night. In the morning we couldn't leave quick enough.

The bus trip took twenty four hours. We had a glimpse of the capital buildings in Washington, flew through Virginia and the Carolinas, back into Georgia and then Jacksonville, Florida where we picked up the slow bus to Stuart.

We arrived back in Stuart, Florida on August 5th at 3 pm. Jean had eight dollars left in her purse. We had spent £550 pounds plus $50 deposit plus $200 in cherries money. So all in all, about £670 pounds for 8,000 miles.

As soon as we had got settled in back on the boat, Jean and I started work on Jerry's schooner. In the end we replaced all the bulwarks, tore out and rebuilt the whole transom and replaced the woodwork. In return we got paid one hundred or so dollars a week and acquired a new engine. In September, Jean found a job across the road working in the kitchen of the Something Fishy restaurant and continued working there for almost a year. The pay was minimal, around three dollars fifty per hour, but considering what happened with me it was great having the regular money coming in.

In October, I got a job on the barge that I had been wanting but didn't last much more than a week. We were setting a line of pilings in Port Salerno down river from Stuart. The technique was to jet a hole in the sea bottom with high pressure water and then slide in the wood piling. With no rocks or reef in the way it was a fairly rapid operation but the pilings had to be vertical and nicely in line with each other. On this job, we were using a hammer consisting of a large steel tube with a half ton weight welded on the top of it to tap the piling the last foot or so. Then lifting the hammer I was waggling the piling to line it up nicely with the others.

It was while I was doing this with one of the pilings that the hammer let go and came down on my left hand which was resting on top of the piling. Bob, my partner on the barge, jerked the hammer back up but three of my fingers were dangling loose held only it seemed by the skin.

That was the end of any dock building for me for a while. In fact when we eventually were allowed into the local hospital once Jerry had signed his life away for me, the first doctor reckoned it was the end of my three fingers. A lengthy stay in hospital loomed with a huge bill of more than $1,000 per day.

Fortunately they had to bring in a private orthopedic surgeon. He was horrified that they hadn't even bothered giving me painkillers. By then, my hand was very painful and had ballooned out. In the end he sent me home with a load of pills and an appointment for the next week when maybe the swelling would have died down and with the assurance that I'd still keep the fingers.

It wasn't until mid-November that the surgeon could operate on my hand. It was a day surgery and a cost of thousand dollars which Jerry was going to pay. I was contracting to Jerry although illegally, Jerry was still supposed to be insured which of course he wasn't. The surgeon put a pin in the little finger but left the others to sort themselves out .The middle finger in fact had a tendon stuck in the broken joint which could have been sorted out, the other finger was a mess.

By this time the barge was working on a big project to build a marina for a development called "Sand Pebble" on the Intercostal Waterway. The pilings were square concrete and they were having problems so I got the foreman's job. It was not well paid but when you are left-handed and your left hand is smashed, there's not much you can do.

I had a theodolite and a measuring tape to make sure everything was in the right place and in line. There were two long docks going out from the shore through the mangroves with a T-piece at the end of each and lots of finger piers for the fancy boats the new condominium-buyers were expected to have.

In the New Year my hand was much better. The three fingers no longer hurt but didn't do very much. But anyway I took over the barge again and worked through till April to finish the job. It wasn't easy to get the square pilings well in line. Overnight, they often settled down a few inches or leaned over. The pilings were also really heavy and getting them loaded onto the barge from the shore was a painful operation

We would drag them out through the water and then lift and lower them carefully onto the deck. If one happened to drop even a little bit the shock could start a leak in the rusty old hull .We would have to shoot inside the barge to make sure we hadn't sprung another leak. Between resetting, piling, re-floating the barge, maintaining the old P and H Crane, the push boat and the big six inch petrol driven water pump, there wasn't much time left for making money driving pilings.

The crane was a typical example of Doss Marine's construction equipment. To lift the heavy weight there was a bowl of sand. When the brake band slipped you threw in a handful of sand.

However if the lift continued when you didn't want it to, you used a can of WD-40. You quickly sprayed WD40 into the machinery and it slacked off.

The most nerve-racking operation was lowering the boom which would always try to go into freefall. A long length of reinforcing bar moved around in the right way operated a dog which jammed in the gears and stopped this happening. But suddenly stopping the boom shook the whole barge so again you had to dive below into the barge and look for leaks. If a leak started you used a rag with a screwdriver jammed in it and a bucket of hydraulic cement. A dollop of cement had to go on the outside so a mask and snorkel were always handy.

When the Sand Pebble contract was finished in April 1982, we had no work other than a bit of dredging with a drag line. Throwing out the bucket on a rocking barge was as difficult as fly fishing.

During this operation I managed another emergency visit to the hospital. A fire ant managed to bite me. Fortunately, it was only one bite but the effect was dramatic. I turned bright pink all over, went blind and my pulse went off the charts. At one stage I actually felt myself drifting away. The hospital could do nothing and eventually after four or five hours I came right.

In the next few months it happened twice more, the second time almost the same as the previous time. But the last time when a dozen ants climbed up my leg and bit me in unison, the effect was minimal. I had developed an immunity. Thank the Gods it was only one ant the first time.

There was one week in which there was no work at all and our barge lay idle at the end of the dock. However, Doss Marine did have another job going building a seawall and it was not going well so Bob and I and the two guys from the other barge went to see what was happening.

There were three people on the job using a backhoe and one of our big pumps. The wall was heavy aluminum sheeting, each piece slotting into the next with a capping piece and a small sheet behind as a tieback every four yards. They had dug the initial trenches and then with two jets of high pressure water were forcing the sheets down into the ground. The problem was them jamming up. They had only managed five sheets in a week, a total of twelve yards and there was half a mile to go.

The four of us took over, re-digging the trench and then jetting and shaking the sheets, while at the same time, belting them with sledgehammers. The next sheet slid in easily and then the next. But if you stopped shaking and banging even for a second, the whole thing froze up.

So we went back to the office. The two guys from the other barge didn't want the job. It didn't pay well and didn't really go with their image and the fancy cars they drove. Bob, my partner had serious debts to pay, college debts and payments on his truck so we agreed to have a go with one of the other workers. We were to be paid eight dollars an hour.

There had been no problem with the American immigration department over extending our stay and having deposited the ship's papers with customs boat could stay forever. Still, we planned to leave at the end of our second hurricane season, say November, so saving up was important.

Work on the great seawall dragged on into September. There were problems over the permits which stopped the job now and again and the backhoe was continuously giving trouble. We'd twice nearly lost it in the mangroves and had had to borrow a huge front-end loader to pull it out.

Bob and I needed two more workers. One was forced on us, the bank manager's son, a favour for the banks' loan to the company, I assumed. He was totally useless and I gave him the boot.

Jean finally finished at the restaurant which went broke. Both the cook and the restaurant owed her money. The owners were two brothers and one had run off with all the money. So after a succession of guys on our job, Jean came to work for us digging in the tieback plates as we moved along.

In October we finally backfilled the seawall and landscaped it a bit. On the last day the back wheels fell off the backhoe. We had had enough, we walked away. There were problems with the company getting paid and we were owed a fair bit of money. But while we waited to get paid we took *Sea Loone* to the Marina.

There we hauled her out and scrubbed her off. There were wheelbarrows full of growth. We had motored up to the Marina with the new engine but with so many barnacles and sponges and sea squirts on the bottom we hardly moved.

In November we put the boat back in the water, stocked up with food and were set to go. Dave, the young lad from Manchester had a girlfriend who worked in the company's bank and had promised to tip us off when Doss Marine actually had any money in the bank. Probably after me booting out the son, the bank were offering no credit.

So when we got the word, I asked for a meeting with Jerry and Jack and demanded the final $2,000. I said we were set to leave and if I had to leave without getting paid then I would leave behind two sunk barges, easily done with a few taps from a sledge hammer. I had lost my English reticence and they believed me. Next day we got paid, so everything was fine.

We set off down the river back along the waterway to West Palm where we cleared out for the Virgin Islands. We left Florida on November 27th, 18 months after we first arrived. We had saved $9,500 and we had a new engine, the 35 hp Volvo Marine engine with electric start, alternator and a gearbox. The latter gave us forward and reverse but rarely neutral. Still it was exotic after the Lister.

We also had a new dinghy, a little Avon inflatable, a new large stainless steel cooker, new sails for downwind and spinnaker poles to go with them. We also had a new Nikon underwater camera and Bob persuaded me to buy a stainless steel shotgun on offer in Woolworth's.

So we'd spent a lot of money improving the boat but we had also lost a lot of money on foolish things like a Camper Van which never worked properly and squandering money on trips to Disneyland and taking my mother deep-sea fishing when she and her boyfriend came to visit. But after all that we had, in fact, done quite well. Squashing my hand had seriously slowed us down in our moneymaking but we had an education which served us well later. We also had some stories to tell.

Firstly the education bit. When I was told I could earn $1,000 a week working on a Doss Marine barge, I believed it. In fact I was surprised there wasn't a crowd of people clamoring for the job. I then discovered that the Americans are just as lazy as the English when it comes to the workers. Employers on the other hand, promise the earth and rarely deliver. The big lesson for me is that it's not a good idea to keep accepting excuses when you're owed wages.

On the barge it took fifteen minutes to pick up a piling and jet it into the ground which gave me twenty dollars. At that rate, I could easily make $80 an hour or $1,000 a week. But when the barge is so rusty it will sink if you shout at it, when the crane is fifty years old and dangerous, when the tug boat is called Drut, (normally spelt the other way round) and when you have to push the barge for miles to pick up the piling and then miles in another direction to the job, then of course everything takes a little longer. On top of that, we had to spend days repairing motors, plugging holes and so on, without one foot of piling being driven.

So I put all this down as useful things to look out for but the big big thing was to throw away my English reticence. I used to say "Well, yes I think I could do that". But no more! Now it was, "Of course I could do that, done it all my life... do it with my eyes closed!".

Bob, my partner on the barge, had a degree at the local university in marine construction. He could do anything. Well so could I. I climbed up in the crane, pulled levers, trod on pedals and quickly found out what they did. I could push our huge barge into marinas full of expensive boats and drive the backhoe through the mangrove swamps. No problem!

One evening sitting on Jerry's schooner drinking rum, he told us how he had designed and built the launch platform for the moon rockets in Cape Canaveral. On another occasion we employed a welder to do some work in the timber yard. The following day he came to me to ask how you weld. I'm sure there are more brain surgeons in Florida than there are mosquitoes. So thirty years on I'm a plumber, miner, boilermaker, paper maker, famous artist and anything else you want me to be, no problem. Oh and I forgot... a writer!

There were also some good Florida stories. The best is my brush with the underworld, the Mafia. It started the day I met Jerry in Madeira. The barge had been bought by a Mafia boss in Chicago and Jerry's partner in the marine construction company Capt. Jack Doss, was apparently a retired Mafia man from Chicago. Why they gave the Jack the title of "Captain" I don't know and I thought you only retired from the Mafia with concrete boots.

Anyway between launching moon rockets, Jerry was also a ship's captain and when I first met him in Madeira, was delivering the barge to Florida. When we arrived in Florida they had already arrived in Fort Lauderdale with the barge. They had had to stop a ship in mid Atlantic to scrounge some oil. Then they had stopped in San Juan, Puerto Rico and then blithely motored on to Fort Lauderdale and up a creek to the yard they had organized. But without clearing in again with customs.

Dave the young lad from Manchester was still on the boat in Fort Lauderdale helping with the major refit including a new engine. Not associated with the barge, Dave had met someone in a bar in Fort Lauderdale, had been flown to the Bahamas and then had crewed a high-speed cigarette boat back to Florida – a drug run. Another boat was used as a sort of decoy. It was stopped and the crew put in jail. Dave had been lucky. He was on the boat with the goodies which wasn't stopped. So now Dave had a $5,000 dollars in the bank, a very lucky man.

Months later the barge was to be taken around to the West Coast of Florida to be hauled out. As they motored out into the Gulf Stream they were stopped by the customs and Coast Guard. Jerry, coming from San Juan had assumed he didn't need to clear into mainland USA so just motored in. The highly vigilant drug-watch boats, planes and radar had missed a one hundred foot barge and the owners had done nothing about import licenses, seaworthiness certificates or anything else.

In fact the Mafia boss apparently ran a very lucrative business stealing expensive cars in Chicago and selling them statewide. He had decided to go into the import business. The barge was refitted to sail to Jamaica pick up the cargo of conch for making conch chowder. The fact that they had no refrigeration made that a little difficult so Jamaican Blue Mountain marijuana or grass would make a good alternative. Obviously, the man knew little about seas and ships.

I was amazed that people in this business could be so naïve but the next chapter in the story was straight out of a comic book.

Close to Christmas Jerry came back to the dock with a TV in his arms. He had bought it very cheaply as a present for his father. At the same time

Crazy Eddie, a good friend of ours with a big welding shop, had bought a small runabout boat on a trainer and some carpets from the same guy. Over the next few days this guy sold a load of other things. He was a member of the Mafia gang from Chicago and was staying in the Mafia bosses holiday home on the beach. He was wanted for questioning in Chicago and so was having a little holiday to let the heat cool. All good stuff, straight out of Mickey Spillane.

The problem was the stupid bugger was selling the contents of the boss's house. When the boss found out obviously he was a little upset.

One morning Bob and I took the truck down to the timber yard where Capt. Jack has his office and, I kid you not, there was a black Cadillac parked outside and two guys in dark suits and sunglasses marching into the office. These were the enforcers putting out the word that if everything isn't returned immediately everyone will get fitted with concrete shoes. Gosh!

Jerry didn't hesitate and went off to his dad's place to ask for the Christmas present back. However Crazy Eddie was another story; he came from Georgia and had a load of rifles in the pickup truck and always a little chrome .22 pistol in his pocket. He's only little but he once cut his chin in half with a chain saw, so he wasn't pretty. He was a serious rebel redneck and they chew up and spit out Yanks especially those from as far north as Chicago.

For two days there was an impasse. Crazy Eddie was giving nothing back and he had his mates posted on the roof of his house with some serious weapons. I was waiting for the hit team to come with Tommy guns from Chicago it was like a real live gangster film until Eddie chickens out and returns the stuff. The thief was never seen again so at least I assume he got his concrete boots.

I have never really got the hang of American politics especially with the idea of democracy, equality, fraternities and all that. It's the lobbying maybe which seems a little like bribery but I had a wonderful chance of seeing the system in action. While we were there in Stuart the local County was having elections, Jerry had been invited to, I think it was called, hustings – a meeting of the party faithful. Jean and I went along.

The meeting was held on the ranch of a famous film star. I'm not sure who he was but they had a rodeo circuit with stands, horses, horsey people, a country band, and pom-pom girls dancing in miniskirts. Then, right in the middle of it all, a sky diving team landed. Being a political rally, I would have expected to hear speeches and someone explaining their plans and policies for the next year. But there was nothing like that ,just a huge barbecue with whole animals being roasted on spits and, more my speed, free cold beer being given away from the back of a huge refrigerated truck.

I found myself at the back of a long line of would-be beer drinkers. I was getting hot and sweaty and not in the best of moods. From the conversation around me, I suddenly realized what the gathering was all about. It was a get-together of all the people who wanted favours from those who might soon be elected as their political representatives. That's why Jerry was there. He needed his dredging permits and was there to support the guy who had promised to push through the dock building and land development plans. Everyone else had a similar agenda.

So I was not surprised when a pretty girl came up to me holding a very large hat. It was full of large bills, lots of money. I asked what the money was for and she told me it was to support "our" candidate. I explained to her that she would do better if she got me a free beer as quickly as possible. Then I would be more likely to vote for the candidate she was supporting.

She didn't understand and continued to poke the hat at me for a few more minutes. At last she left me alone. Presumably she decided I was mad. Eventually I got my beer but it wasn't very cold and tasted horrible. Later we found that "our man" got elected and months later our seawall got its retrospective permit. Democracy at work.

Of course there were lots of other interesting parts of the American way which amazed, shocked or confused us .There were certainly opportunities to do well but in the background always less fortunate people living in what for us was unbelievable squalor and poverty. It was unfortunate that at the very end of our stay the most harrowing incident occurred.

We had an elderly man who occasionally worked with the carpentry crew building the decks on to our pilings. He was an artist, a good sculptor and often had to be persuaded not to start sculpting the tops of the pilings. He was over 70 years of age, well-dressed and a real ladies man. He lived in a caravan. He arrived at our boat one morning and asked me if I would buy his electric tools, drills, saws, planers and such. I assumed I was the last resort. I had to explain that 110-volt tools were no use to me. He was desperate for some for some money and explained the problem.

Not feeling well, he had gone to the hospital in Stuart the same one I had had a frosty reception from with my hand. They had diagnosed that he had serious cancer, that he had no insurance so they could do nothing.

They sent him up the road to the next hospital in Fort Pierce. Of course, Fort Pierce sent him back to Stuart because that was where he lived. I'm not sure how much help the small amount of money from his tools was going to bring. A week later we saw him and he said nothing had happened. There been no rallying around of friends and no government agency offering to help. I could imagine him going back to his caravan awaiting a painful slow death.

4

As the Florida coastline sank over the horizon we had no regrets about leaving. The last-minute struggle to be paid for the sea wall job and then the incident with the old man had left a bad taste in our mouths. Though we now had an engine which could push us through the Panama Canal and enough money to last us a few years sailing across the Pacific to Australia. So with a sense of excitement we looked ahead to the next landfall.

We had cleared for the Virgin Islands but in honesty hadn't really expected to get there. Let's face it, the last time we had cleared the Cayman Islands and headed east to the Virgin Islands was a disaster. This time, with charts for the Bahamas only one hundred miles across the Gulf Stream, we were going to hop from island to island in a generally easterly direction. Then, if we were having problems going further east, along the North coast of Hispaniola and Puerto Rico, we could turn south through the Windward or the Mona Passage and head directly for Panama.

As it was the Gods smiled on us. Firstly a southerly wind pushed us north of all the Bahamas and then a northerly change sent scudding east. Eventually the strong cold northerly winds lasting ten, days left us becalmed just north of San Juan, Puerto Rico. We were within spitting distance of the Virgin Islands.

Then light winds plus the new engine motoring for a few hours, brought us into Culebra, just east of Puerto Rico. We stopped and rested for a few days, eating snapper we caught under the boat. We couldn't believe how easy it had been, two weeks of relatively easy sailing compared with, last time, more than a month beating our brains out. Now we were sitting within a few miles of where, last time, the mast jumped overboard.

It was another fifty miles to Road Town in the British Virgin Islands. There was little wind and we motored most of the way clearing in on December 13th in plenty of time for Christmas.

We sailed around to Maya Cove, met all our friends and got the news of the previous year or more we had been away. There had been a suspicious death, a sailor was thought to have drowned his wife, the usual charter boat disasters and the story of a famous yachtsman who had only just left the cove. The story about Hal the famous sailor was amusing.

Having written lots of books, including his experiences of over 50,000 miles of sailing, he was above talking to the rest of the boats. But when one guy early morning and in a great rush to start a charter job, dropped his anchor, moved to a mooring and then shot off to work, the famous man snagged his anchor, claimed salvage and proceeded to use it to anchor his own boat.

The boats in the cove were flabbergasted. The water is only ten feet deep and clear. The anchor was not lost. A meeting was held, a bottle of rum or two consumed and a plan made. The next time the famous yachtsmen went off to town two people dived in and retrieved the anchor and returned it to the owner. A few days later when a norther came through and the wind picked up, the famous yachtsman's boat began to drag. The rest of the sailing community watched as he pulled up his chain. Replacing his anchor was a toilet bowl!

We had Christmas dinner with the Bailey's from Liverpool. They were now "belongers" and well-established here. Unfortunately their other guest was an ex-commodore of the Royal Air Force yacht club. He flew a blue ensign instead of the common red ensign of most British ships.

He was very upset about the white ensign at the top of our mast. It had been stolen by the Cayman Islands Rugby Club from HMS Scylla and given to us for Christmas in 1978. The silly man had rowed over and asked to see my "warrant". When I explained it was a Christmas decoration and an act of piracy, he threatened to have me arrested. Oops!

New Year's Eve, with the ex commodore off charter skippering, we had dinner with his wife. She got so drunk she nearly fell over the side. I rather liked her.

With the arrival of 1983 we thought we needed to get moving again. Having cleared out, we sailed together with the Baileys across to Virgin Gorda. Here we had dinner together in Gorda Sound and then in the morning we planned to leave and head towards Guadaloupe..

So much for Plan A. All night Jean had terrible stomach pains. We sailed back to Road Town and by lunchtime a police car was touring the island looking for the local anesthetist. By tea time Jean no longer had an appendix!

The same day, two large gray warships anchored off Road Town. While Jean lay in bed recovering in the hospital, I spent time in the pub with the naval officers from the ships. They told me they had just come up from the Falklands Island full of naval commandos. .Jack, as the crew are called, was ashore for the first time after their little war. Road Town has a rum distillery so I could see that the combination was going to be a disaster!

There were skinny, white, spotty Glaswegians swimming naked among the posh yachts in the Marina all swigging bottles of rum. The bars were bursting but there was no trouble. On the Saturday night the Marine band came ashore. They gave a fantastic concert in the town Square. After that they were all the salt of the earth and the toast of the town.

Poor Jean had a rumbling stomach for a while but eventually we set off and beat out southeastwards to Guadalupe. From there we hopped down the islands, Dominica, Martinique, St. Lucia, St. Vincent and back to Bequia. Here we met "Plum Belly" again. In the 18 months since we had last seen him, he had sailed his boat across the Atlantic to Brazil and back to Bequia.

Grenada had had a revolution, a communist takeover. We could stay only in St. Georges. The south coast was out of bounds. There were stories of secret submarine bases and a huge airfield was being built. In town, there was now a vegetable cooperative with prices regulated. Also, clearing-in seemed a bit more organized. Otherwise nothing much seemed to have changed.

There was supposed to be large numbers of Cubans on the island but we never saw them. On the Sunday on the main cricket pitch behind the harbour there was a military parade. In front there were fifty or so islanders with smart uniforms and weapons marching in time then behind them twice as many with bits of uniform and old wartime rifles, behind them again were a lot more with no uniform no sense of timing and pretend wooden guns. There was a good band, lots of flags and everyone's having a good time. Two weeks later we left and they got invaded.

In Grenada we foolishly decided to charter *Sea Loone* to a young Swiss couple. They were looking for a lift to Columbia where they were going to spend some time. They had a backpackers book "South America on a Dollar a Day".

It sounded a bit optimistic to me especially as, at that time, Colombia had a bad reputation for drugs and crime. It had even put me off ever going. Anyway, we agreed to sail to the ABC Islands with them, Aruba, Bonaire and Curaçao, Dutch islands. From there they could easily get to Columbia just to the south.

They agreed to pay twenty dollars a day including food and drink. We set sail along the coast of Venezuela where they could see some of the offshore islands which were impossible to visit without a boat.

The charter didn't start well. I did the paperwork to clear out and we would be sailing overnight to the first of the offshore islands in Venezuela. Just before we left the Swiss guy climbed a tamarind tree at the yacht club and fell on his head. He was unconscious. We called an ambulance. As we wheeled him into the emergency room we were stepping on a trail of blood from another customer.

Luckily, the hospital could find no serious injuries so our guest was returned to us and we left. The only problem was he had lost his memory. He was sleeping in my bunk when we left. Imagine waking up in the middle of the ocean on a strange boat with strange people!

The day we arrived in Margarita Island the Venezuelan government had devalued their money. After doing lots of paperwork with the officials, we went to the bank where there was a huge crowd of people. That first day they would only change American dollars not travelers cheques or other currencies. Fortunately we had US dollars.

We found the prices were as yet unchanged in the shops so we went on a spending spree Later, on the mainland, I gave a truck driver in the village a one hundred dollar bill to fill our two jerry cans with diesel. We expected some change but couldn't believe it when he gave us back ninety eight dollars. For twenty gallons it was two dollars. Polar beer was ten cents a can. Venezuela was "barato", cheap! By this time the guy had regained his memory and we had pulled a huge splinter of wood out of his leg which the hospital had missed.

I was snorkeling around one day not far from the boat when I saw what I first thought was the antenna of a huge lobster sticking out from under a rock. But it wasn't. Not sure what to do, I called the Swiss girl over in the rubber dinghy. She hovered above me and I dived down under the rock.

She was more than a little surprised when I came up and flopped in the dinghy with a five foot long green iguana. What he was doing ten feet down under a rock I don't know. We called him Cousteau and he lived on the boat for a while. He ate only oranges, wasn't very active and we finally put him ashore. He immediately ran for the water and swam away. So there are marine iguanas in Venezuela and they are much more colorful than the ugly gray ones on the Galapagos Islands.

We only saw a couple of other boats the whole time in Venezuela. The offshore islands were amazing, the sea life amazing. There were huge sponges full of lobsters. There were big pink conch shells everywhere. I saw a dozen huge ones crawling along the bottom just from standing on the deck.

Arriving in Bonaire, the Swiss couple left the boat. They had rarely left the boat to see the land, rarely gone swimming. A picture I took sums it up with Jean sitting naked on the beach sorting shells she picked up and the Swiss couple fully clothed sitting in the shade a few feet away. I wondered if they would survive in Columbia especially on a dollar a day.

Spanish Waters in Curaçao is a fantastic natural harbour and we spent some time there before heading on along the coast of Columbia to the San Blas islands in Panama. With a gill net under the boat we were catching lobsters overnight.

There were lots of stories floating around about piracy off the Columbia coast all associated with drug trafficking. We were advised to stay well off the coast and not stop in Cartagena. I think it wasn't quite so serious and we later met a guy on a boat smaller than ours who had a story to tell.

He was sailing alone early one morning almost becalmed when he was approached by a large Columbia fishing boat. He was naturally a little nervous. The fishing boat came alongside and asked the name of his boat. When he told them they asked if he was sure it wasn't another name. No it wasn't. The fishing boat departed.

In the afternoon it came back and they suggested that even though he wasn't the boat they were looking for, could he take their cargo and sail north with it. He explained he was heading for the Panama Canal so they motored off together with their bags of white powder.

Between Curaçao and Panama is around 600 miles. It can be windy with a rough sea. We were still, in 1983, using my old vernier sextant but many yachts now had satellite navigators. I had seen one a few years ago on a Danish coaster. The workings took up a box the size of the wardrobe but now they were only half a shoebox and priced a little less than $1,000.

As we approached the Panama coast clouds came over and finally we had to stop and wait for some clear skies to find out where we were. Dead downwind, the San Blas islands sheltered behind a line of reefs. There was nothing other than coconut palms more than a few feet out of the water so we dared not get too close until we fixed our position. The mountains of Darian on the mainland are almost permanently covered in cloud. We waited two days, hove to in big breaking seas, before I was able to plot a position and head into the reefs.

As we picked up Hollandaise Island, we hooked a huge sailfish, over nine feet long. Too big to get on the deck, we tied it to the rail with its tail still dragging in the water astern. Navigating around the islands, avoiding the reefs and battling with a large fish kept us busy. A large bull shark joined in the fun and went to bite a piece out of the tail of the sailfish. He missed and bit a piece out of the paddle of the selfsteering gear instead. We eventually arrived in calm water behind the island and anchored off a coconut fringed white sand beach straight out of paradise.

The people of the San Blas islands are Kuna Indians. Small, fierce, people, they were never conquered by the Spanish and are still self-governing within Panama. We had only been anchored an hour or two when we were visited by the local resident in his dugout canoe. His name was Jamie.

He spoke Spanish and a little English besides his own Kuna language. He was living on the island with his wife and baby, tending the family coconut plantation. He was very happy to receive the major portion of our huge sailfish and returned in the evening for a glass of whiskey. He told us he had cut the fish into strips and was smoking it using coconut husks. He returned some of it to us a few days later when it was cured.

The Kuna people had problems with visiting yachtsman and in their villages customs had to be followed. The visitors, they grumbled, picked up coconuts on the beach not realizing that they were all owned by someone. They were sure that their problems with albino children were caused by sneaky sailors coming ashore at night.

However Jamie and ourselves, we had no problems. Jamie regularly visited us on the boat to acquire more English and sup a glass of whiskey. We even had dinner, sopa kuna, one night in his home, a round straw construction with a fire burning in the middle.

Jamie's dugout canoe was rotten. I tried plugging some of the holes in the bottom but not very successfully so when Jamie wanted to return with his family to his village we agreed to transport him. The village, Nargana, was quite a long way away, on an island close to the mainland.

When we arrived, Jamie went to talk to the two chiefs for permission for us to come ashore. We paid our respects and could then do as we pleased. Some of the houses had iron roofs but most were still rounded thatch construction. They had access to electricity and I even saw Christmas decorations with lights.

The huge Catholic Church dominated the village which took up the whole small island. It was the first time we had been amongst truly native people and the Kunas had preserved most of their language and culture. They was serious Catholics but behind this were still all the old customs and then there were new ones one of which really amused me. There was a hotel in the village and a menu posted on the wall. There were three courses one of which was Kellogg's cornflakes!

Quite a few yachts were arriving all heading eventually for the canal. Approaching San Blas using his new satellite navigator, one of the yachts had been called up by a passing ship. They had given the ship its position and advised that a serious change of course was necessary to arrive in the canal. The era of asking ships to confirm your position was ending. In fact, in this case it had been reversed.

Porto Bello, only a day's run from the canal, is famous for once being the port from where the Spanish shipped all the golden treasures they had acquired from the Incas and others. It's also famous for being one of the rainiest places in the world which it demonstrated the day we arrived by completely filling the rubber dinghy twice.

The town was a ruin. There were old fort ramparts, a huge church in ruins, ditches overflowing with rubbish, ugly black vultures scrounging around, and the people all seeming to be very poor. We sat in a scruffy bar on the waterfront together with an all-black guy who told us the story of Captain Morgan the pirate.

It was a perfect setting and he told a good story. As you sail into the deep narrow bay there are forts set up high on either side of the steep hills. In front is a long castellated wall armed with huge cannons. So an enemy coming into the bay would be fired on from three sides and quickly sunk.

Morgan knew this but there was a mountain of treasure in the town and he had a plan. He had co-opted all the pirate ships in the Caribbean to help him and they landed a few miles up the coast, traveled through the forest and came to Portobello from behind. Not one cannon faced them and the town was pillaged. Morgan still wasn't satisfied. Next he marched his men across the isthmus where the canal now is and arrived in Panama City which they also sacked and pillaged. When they sailed away they had enormous mountain of treasure which they divided between them.

It had been an act of piracy so Morgan was not a respectable person however rich he was. However being the cunning Welshman that he was, he sailed back to England and gave his treasure to Queen Elizabeth. She being a good politician made him the first governor of Jamaica so he had gained his respectability and she had got rid of a nest of thieves and pirates in Jamaica as they also became respectable under Morgan and the Spanish in Hispaniola were faced with a nasty neighbour.

We passed between the two long breakwaters at the entrance to the Panama Canal and anchored amongst a small fleet of yachts on the flats. It was already May. April and May are the months to cross the Pacific to the Marquesas. Then one has until November to sail through the Pacific islands before the cyclone season starts.

The yachts that had already left were reported to be having enormous difficulties. The Humboldt Current had almost stopped and the trade winds had just about disappeared. There were all sorts of strange phenomena and they started calling it the year of the El Nino. It apparently happened every fifty years or so. It did not seem a good time for us to set off so we changed our plans and headed up the west coast to Costa Rica and wait there for things to get back to normal.

With the water temperature rising when the cold Humboldt Current stopped, many creatures were dying in the Galapagos Islands, including the marine iguanas. In the Marquesas they had a cyclone, the first for a long time though not a very strong one. Even the weather in Australia was affected.

Colon at the beginning of the Canal was not a place to hang around. It was dirty, ugly and full of thieves. So we pushed ahead to get our transit organized. The canal was still owned and run by the Americans in 1983, so one day we were ushered into this huge office with an imposing desk and the headman sitting glaring at us.

He knew we were a British ship and demanded if we know a woman called Margaret, also English. I immediately realized who he was talking about. We had met Margaret Hicks in Bequia. She was a retired teacher sailing a small 21-foot yacht around the world. She had already taken part in a transatlantic race with the boat and had developed a great technique if she had any problems. In Bequia, she had four or five dinghies tied alongside. They were helpers to whom she served drinks while still in their dinghies. They fixed the engine, the sails and the rigging while she simpered.

The large American behind the desk had been given the same treatment.

Every day she arrived and poured out her problems to him. Too small and slow to go through the canal alone, the yacht was going to have to be towed. Finally, he told us with the big grin how he had sorted the problem. One day, a German arrived in his office. He had a large yacht with a large powerful German engine. He was told that it wasn't large enough or powerful enough to transit unless of course he towed Margaret out of his life.

Sea Loone had to be measured in order to arrive at its "Panama Tonnage". Then a certificate was issued and the date could be fixed for the transit. Our Panama tonnage was thirteen tons. That meant there was a fifty dollar fee for measuring and another fifty dollars to be deposited to pay for the passage. The exact figure would be calculated later and any excess money returned to us. I gave him my mother's address and in fact most of that fifty dollars was returned a few months later.

While all this was going on, Jean was helping other boats to go through as a line handler. You needed four line handlers on each yacht. She would jump on the train at the other end and then come back. So when our day came we had three friends whom Jean had already helped, plus the pilot provided by the Canal Company.

Arriving in the first lock, the pilot told me to stop in the middle. Arriving in the middle I stopped, which meant turning off the engine as we had no neutral. The pilot was not happy but there was no alternative. We took up the lines of from either side with a huge ship in front of us as the water roared in. The water swirled all around us in a nerve racking rush especially when you knew of all the disasters that had happened. Anyway, we got up the three locks without incident and sailed through the Banana Channel which was used by small boats. Half way we stopped for a swim in the fresh water of the lake and Jean did the laundry. We motored the fifty odd miles across the lake, passing drowned forests and entered the cut dug through the mountains close to the first of the down locks.

At that moment the engine lost its oil, spraying it everywhere half-way up the bilge. I dived into the mess to see what had happened. Fortunately it was simply the pipe to the oil pressure gauge that had broken. So I yanked the whole thing out and blocked the hole. I told the pilot we would be away again in a few minutes. He looked skeptical and then started shouting and waving his arms. The crew, being keen French sailors, had all the sails up and we were sailing into the lock. It would've been really interesting but I had the engine going again and we did the whole thing conventionally.

The last lock down was a nightmare with a ship coming in behind me before I got tied up. But we survived and when the gate opened we shot out into the Pacific Ocean. It was actually low tide with mud banks either side of us and rusty piers and pilings. We anchored off the yacht club but they were so unfriendly we didn't stay. Instead, we sailed out to a little island some ten miles away where we anchored. There we could still get a ferry back into town. Toboga Island as it was called, grew the best pineapples I have ever tasted.

We had kept in touch with "Mad Brian", the third of my Biddle's Boat Bunglers in Liverpool. He had agreed to find us a satellite navigator in England and fly out with it to Panama. After all those frustrating days off San Blas, and with the price of a Sat Nav now only half of what it was, we had decided to invest. The thought of pressing a button and getting a position after years of sextant sights, almanacs, and tables was just too tempting.

Brian was to fly into Panama City and sail with us up the coast to Costa Rica. For him it was a test sail to see if he would enjoy it and if not then give up his half completed boat and move on to something else. He had already spent eight years on the project.

The very first night anchored off Taboga Island a nasty squall came through and *Sea Loone* occasionally buried its bow in the short seas it produced. By morning, it had already passed but it had been a sleepless night and Brian was a little nervous. We sailed out to the Perlas Islands. Brian was already talking about leaving.

Heading north around Punta Mala, very well named, the sky turned purple black. In front of us a tornado developed. We heard a roaring noise as it sucked up a solid six foot column of water thousands of feet into the sky, up into a black cloud. It wasn't just Brian who was nervous! Behind us was a squall line with solid sheets of rain. We turned and ran for that like an ostrich putting its head in the sand. At one stage the column of water broke and receded for a moment back up into the clouds. But before we could breathe a sigh of relief, it re-formed, curling and twisting even more fiercely. We finally motored into the curtain of rain and saw the funnel cloud no more. God knows how close we came to the tornado and certain disaster!

Brian by now was on deck with binoculars looking for a road or a village where we could drop him off. But the coasts was all cliffs and impenetrable rain forest. The next night we had two anchors out in a bay on a small offshore island when another squall hit us. Lightning, wind and rain lashed us and we dragged onto the reef. We needed a third anchor.

Unfortunately to get the third anchor out of the bilge, the large fisherman anchor, we had to move Brian. He had taken so many sleeping pills to try and get some rest that we couldn't move him We had to drag him out of the way, get the anchor on deck and then into the dinghy. We then rowed the anchor out and kedged ourselves off in the pitch dark. Brian remained oblivious.

The next day we looked on the chart and saw what looked like a perfectly sheltered bay called Bahia Honda. It looked like a good place for a little break. I think it was an old volcanic crater and had a small island in the middle. The island had a village on it and Jean and I went ashore to look around.

The people were similar to the Kuna people of San Blas but not very friendly. Everywhere over the island were huge holes about six feet across and often quite deep. The only explanation we got was that they were planting trees but that was obviously not true. The children offered us broken pieces of pottery, supposedly pre-Columbian.

We thought nothing more about it. A few days later we sailed into Golfito just across the border in Costa Rica. Golfito is a banana town, hot humid and surrounded by lovely jungle. We anchored off a large dilapidated looking hotel. We were going to be here a while until the conditions in the Pacific improved. Brian saw the road, found a bus and was gone.

The hotel was run by Whitey and Barbara, Americans from the south, Okies I think as opposed to Arkies. Good people! There were three other yachts anchored with us, two French and one American. The French guys were waiting like us to get to French Polynesia.

I was in my element. The hills behind us were covered in forest full of creepy crawlies, butterflies, birds of all kinds and so on. Opposite us there was an island covered in forest. On the island an American was living commuting back and forth in a big dugout canoe or ponga. We spent some time with him and he explained the large holes dug around the island in Bahia Honda. The people had been digging up old burial sites looking for pottery, stone sculptures and gold ornaments. The gold ornaments were called waki-waki's or some such name. They could be very small and delicate but sometimes quite large. They were obviously very valuable.

Ron, the American, lived in a small wooden house with a veranda. Here he had two small toucans in a cage and three or four parrots all flying free, including two huge red blue and gold macaws. You had to take care eating a meal on the veranda or a macaw might come flying in to land on your head or the table and your food would be blown to hell and gone.

I decided to find some waki wakis. The technique used is to tramp through the forest prodding the ground with a steel rod. If you hit a stone then you dig it up. If this stone is round and smooth, a river stone, then you continue to prod and hopefully find a whole circle of rounded stones. So here lies the treasure. You start digging with lots of roots and stones in the way and you may have to go down more than fifteen feet. Even then, if the former occupant of the plot was poor, you may only find some pottery.

Ron had already found a circle so I started digging. As I dug Ron's green parrot found me, sat on a branch and started to talking to me. It was very hot and tedious work and after days and days, with the parrot I gave it up. My next project was to capture butterflies the huge blue morpho butterflies in particular. I tramped everywhere with my butterfly net and kill jar getting some very funny looks from the locals. But it was good advertising and with Whiteys help they all knew I was interested in creepy crawlies. Boxes started arriving at the bar with huge stick insects and praying mantis and a really huge rhinoceros beetle which I still have.

One day, leaning on the bar, Whitey was talking with two locals. In between them they had a large parcel wrapped in sacking. It was moving. The bar faced a large open area with an ornamental pool in the middle. The hotel rooms opened into this area.

When they undid the parcel a large very live crocodile was revealed.. Whitey immediately decided he would be a good tourist attraction even though there were no tourists there. But anyway, with lots of help, the sacking was carefully cut away and the crocodile was thrown into the ornamental pool.

That night the crocodile crawled out and visited one of the rooms which caused a bit of a stir. The following day I was at the bar having a beer with a retired American originally from Mississippi, when behind us we heard a wet slapping noise. Looking round, there was the crocodile all six or seven feet of it, coming to join us.

From his days in Mississippi, the American said he knew just what to do. He told me to go for the tail and he would grab the head. There was no time for discussion. He dived on the creatures head so I grabbed the base of the tail I was getting thrown everywhere but at least the American had the crocodile's mouth closed. We eventually got it back in the pool with a little help. Faulty Towers had nothing on this place!

There were a number of interesting people passing through and drinking at Whitey's bar. A few miles north, gold had been discovered and there was a mini gold rush going on. Rich fortune hunters arrived followed by a group of little Chinamen. Vanilla plantations were another prospective fortune being discussed.

I met a German guy one day, Winfried Zigan. He was living down the coast and was a keen surfer. He had settled in Costa Rica with a wife and little baby. The land he had bought sounded really interesting. We agreed that next time he came to town I would return with him to see where he lived.

So one day we set off on the first leg of the journey. We were squashed in with a number of other people in a four-wheel drive vehicle heading for Pavones. We passed through a huge banana plantation, crossed a few rivers and arrived on the beach at Pevones, a place famous as one of the best left or right-hand surfing breaks in the world. That night we stayed in a small farmhouse or finca together with a couple of visiting surfers. In the morning Winfried collected his horse and another for me. We had a day's ride ahead and I had never been on a horse in my life!

Fortunately the horse wasn't very big, was fairly docile and the saddle had a large lump in front which I could grab hold of when things got rough. We followed the beach and the cliffs rose higher and higher on our left as we proceeded. At one point we had to wade into the sea to pass a rock promontory and Winfried had organized to be at this point exactly at low tide. A few miles later a large river broke through a cleft in the cliffs and the horses had to take to the water again. As my horse jumped down the bank I nearly went over the front and was only saved by the lump on the saddle which tried to castrate me.

We rode along arriving in the late afternoon at quite a large house he had built from timbers cut and sawn up on the site. Above us the forested cliffs towered over us and a small stream dropped in a series of waterfalls .It was diverted finally into an old fiberglass boat next to the house and used as a bath. There were two narrow plateaus, ancient beaches, as you climbed the cliff and here Winfrey and his wife grew vegetables, fruit trees and coffee bushes. In places there were crude ladders to help with the climb.

The ridge at the top of the cliffs covered in massive, uncut, jungle formed the border between Panama and Costa Rica. It was quite pristine. There were tapirs, tigers and other rare animals around. As I leaned back to stare upwards there were bearded vultures with huge wingspan's circling and the sounds of hundreds of other birds filled my ears.

That evening we sat down on the veranda looking out to sea with massive surf breaking on the shore and as the sun set the howler monkeys started making their indescribable racket. We ate and then saddle sore and tired. I slid under mosquito net and slept like a log even though the nightlife pulsed around me. In the morning, Winfried admitted that the mosquito nets were not for the mosquitoes. They were for the vampire bats!

The following morning we were going hunting. The family often ate monkeys and toucans which didn't go down well with me although I still have a monkey skull and toucan beak on the boat. There were other things to hunt, rodents which resembled deer and pecaries which resembled small pig.

Pecaries had a fierce reputation. They roam the forest in family groups of sometimes over one hundred and if provoked will attack. They have been known to kill people, even bringing down horses and riders.

It was still dark as we set off scrambling up a stream bed into the steep forest. Winfred was decked out in camouflage shirt and pants and carried a .22 rifle with telescopic sight. With his army boots and floppy hat he definitely looked the part as the great White Hunter. I followed along in faded old shorts, a T-shirt and flip-flops with my binoculars round my neck.

The going got more and more difficult and we eventually had to leave the streambed and scrambled up the steep eroding bank. Using some tree roots I arrived some fifty feet above the stream ahead of Winfred and peered over the lip. I glimpsed a line of animals threading its way through the trees and heading our way. Ducking down, I signaled to Winfried and he cautiously slid his gun up and sighted on whatever I had seen.

Looking again myself I realized I was looking at a line of pecaries getting very close. Meanwhile Winfried had fogged up his telescopic sight. Eventually, he took aim and fired. The lead pig charged straight for us and sailed over our heads. It landed with a great crash in the stream below. Winfried followed it down and, after a quick look back at the rest of the pig family coming my way, I followed him. I wasn't staying to explain why we killed grandfather. The peccary had a bullet in its shoulder but the fall had broken its neck and it was quite dead.

Having concentrated on squinting through his telescopic sights, Winfried had never seen the rest of the animals so hadn't been worried as I had been. We tied the peccary onto a long pole and headed home with the animal strung between us. In fact, we were back before noon and spent the afternoon removing the long bristles which covered the body then we skinned and butchered it. We ate well that night and for the next couple of days that I stayed.

Water supply was not a problem and Winfrey was building a second hydroelectric system powered by the stream adjacent to the house. Having damned the stream high up he had a pipeline down to a high speed waterwheel and a generator. A small unit already supplied a limited amount of electricity for lights, refrigeration and for a drying chamber for bananas.

Access to town was the only problem. The surf made landing on the beach almost impossible, the broken whaler and a catamaran proved this. They had not lasted long. The horse ride was long and difficult and I was not looking forward to having to return alone. All this time Jean was alone on the boat in Golfito, so I couldn't stay longer.

Early the next morning we went to collect the horse Winfried had borrowed for me. The poor thing had blood all over its flanks from where the vampire bats had been having a feed. We washed the horse off in the surf and then loaded it up with bags of fruit and even a small tree I had to deliver to Whitey. I climbed on board and set off along the shore.

The horse was pretty lethargic and I had to beat him with a stick now and again to keep him moving. At one of the small river crossing, I jumped off to have a leak and a drink. It took me a while to find a bolder I could climb onto to remount. We were a bit late for the tide passing round the point but managed without getting sucked out by the backwash from the huge waves.

From there the path left the shore and we were in woodland. The sun was dipping towards the horizon and I was urging the horse along when suddenly he stopped dead and reared up. Standing on the path in front of us was a giant anteater. Standing upright, his long snout in the air, he was waving his huge front claws at the horse. He didn't stay more than a minute but I was enthralled. Only a few minutes later a troop of squirrel monkeys chased us, shaking the tree branches above our heads.

With the last of the light, we arrived at the finca in Pavones where I would stay the night. The innkeeper farmer helped me off the horse unloaded the sacks and the tree and led the poor animal away to do whatever you do with them after being abused all day.

In the morning I got a lift on a large canoe with an outboard engine. After following the coast for a while we headed up into a wide river mouth and then turned off through some mangrove swamps and came out in the harbour close to the hotel.

The previous evening while Jean was ashore, thieves had broken into the boat and made a terrible mess. They had stolen our portable radio, our camera, fifteen cartons of cigarettes which I had just bought for our Pacific crossing and some small change which had been lying on the table. Poor Jean was really upset and Whitey had his rifle out taking potshots at any canoes coming near the boats.

We put out a message on the village grapevine that there was a reward of twenty dollars for the return of the stolen goods and we informed the local police. A few days later two detectives arrived in plain clothes and straw hats. They had discovered where the stolen goods were, somewhere up a local river. They had a motorized canoe available but needed money for petrol. Surprise surprise they needed twenty dollars.

We invested the twenty dollars and within an hour we were given the receipt from the petrol station. The detectives took off to recover the stolen goods. The next day they arrived at the hotel happy and smiling with the goods. They had failed to find the camera but they had our radio, a little battered but still working and they had ten cartons of the cigarettes. The only problem with the cigarettes was they were a different sort, very strange but I'm not that fussy what I smoke.

The two French yachts had left for Cocos Island and we were set to follow them. The whole time in Golfito I had been looking for a parrot and at the last moment Whitey found us a beautiful Mealy Amazon. We called him Plod and organized a perch for him over the chart table where he soon settled into life on the ocean waves.

Before we left, Jean scoured the market for fruit and vegetables and found a chicken farm for some fresh eggs. Whitey and Barbara gave us a great sendoff and we headed out of Golfo Dulce into the vastness of the Pacific Ocean.

5

COCOS ISLAND IS some 500 miles out into the Pacific Ocean and in October and November there is not much wind. What wind there is, is mainly from the south and interspersed with thunderstorms and heavy rain but it felt good to be back out on the water again. Plod the parrot was happy on his perch above the chart table and kept us amused with his antics.

The new satellite navigator showed its worth as we got close to the island which is only five miles by three miles. It appeared out of the clouds and rain looking quite forbidding. The steep cliffs rose into forested mountains and in a few places waterfalls cascaded directly into the sea. Stephan and Guy with the two French yachts were already anchored in Chatham Bay so we joined them. The bottom was a steep, sandy, slope outside the reefs, so not easy to set the anchor in. We rolled dramatically.

The Costa Rican government had two conscript soldiers stationed in the next bay. They had hiked over the hills and were firing their guns to attract our attention so I went and picked them up. They were farmers from central Costa Rica and so not happy doing the "Robinson Crusoe" thing for their country; especially as their supply ship was more than three months late and their radio and refrigerator had both broken.

They guzzled down Jean's cake, drank some coffee and smoked my cigarettes until one of them turned green and ran to the side to throw up. I ferried them both back to the beach and made an agreement that I could shoot two pigs while on the island. We had dinner with the French guys. They had shot a number of wild pigs but with the recent rain the pigs seem to have disappeared.

Still, the next day I dug out my gun, keen to do the great white hunter bit. Since buying it in Woolworths in Florida, I hadn't actually fired it, nor, for that matter, any other gun. So I was a little nervous. It was a Winchester pump-action, 12-bore shotgun made of stainless steel with a very short barrel. They called it a riot gun. With a pocket full of buckshot cartridges and a large knife, Jean ferried me ashore and I set off up the steep path into the forest. The other guys were surveying the beach area with a metal detector.

After a hard climb I came out onto a plateau with quite a large area devoid of trees, presumably caused by a fire. The grass was high but in the middle in a small clearing stood a deer. My heart started hammering, I switched off the safety catch and aimed the gun. I tried closing my right eye but couldn't do it. Then tried the other shoulder. No good. In the meantime, the deer ignored me. I sidled closer until I was within 100 feet then aimed and fired. The deer ran away. After all that, I had missed!

The next few hours I trekked through the forest but saw no more deer and no pigs, although I could see the ground had been torn up everywhere by pigs. I retraced my steps and came back to the grassy clearing and there was another deer.

This time I took my time and got within fifty feet, fired the gun and the deer fell down dead. I was elated but with a tinge of guilt for murdering such a lovely creature. But the Great White Hunter prevailed.

The deer was small no bigger than a large dog so I tied its feet together and slung it on my back for the steep climb down to the beach. Jean was impressed and that evening, six of us ate on Stefan's boat with his crew doing the cooking.

At Whitey's place in Golfito we'd heard about the "Cocos Treasure". In the harbour, we knew that an American was fitting out an old minesweeper with a helicopter platform. He was said to have bought or found a Chinese treasure map and was organizing a huge treasure hunt. We had already heard plenty of tales of the English pirate treasure, the Spanish conquistador treasure and so on but I don't think anything had ever been found.

Anyway the treasure dream was keeping Stefan, Guy and their crew well occupied. The following day I saw them digging a serious hole near the beach as I passed by on my next hunting trip.

Jean had made me an ammunition belt with a scabbard for a knife so I was really looking the part. I climbed again up to the grassy plateau and sure enough there was another deer. This time I got down and crawled closer but was stopped by a deep ravine between me and the animal. Still, I was really close so I slowly stood up with the gun at the ready.

At the same time the deer sat down so that I could see just his ears. Patience is a virtue. I waited and eventually the deer stood up again and looked across at me. I pulled the trigger, bang, and the deer continue to look at me. I suddenly realized what I had to do. I pulled back the slides and then fired again. The deer fell down.

A long detour around the ravine found me beside the deer in about ten minutes. It was huge. I managed only with difficulty to drag it under the shade of the trees but then what was I to do with it. Finally I got to work with a knife separating the two back legs without disturbing the guts. I should really have cut out the back fillet. But with two hind legs over my shoulder and I was already seriously weighed down.

By noon I was back on the beach where the "French hole" had grown huge. Their metal detector was going wild. By tea time Jean already had a lot of the venison bottled, the pressure cooking hissing merrily. The French treasure turned out to be only an old steel ax head, a great disappointment after all the excavation work. But some days later. Guy found a really unusual small shell while diving. It was a murex, maybe a new species, which could be very valuable to a collector.

Sea Loone continued to roll annoyingly at her anchorage and we thought about leaving. The arrival of a fleet of shark fisherman made the decision easier. They were catching large sharks, mainly hammerheads, cutting off their fins and throwing the rest back in the water. With shark bodies drifting round the bay, we left.

Galapagos is due south and against the wind and current. We had to cross the equator and pay our dues with Neptune. In fact having crossed with due ceremony we tacked about as the wind was heading us and late in the day, crossed the equator again. Eventually, having crossed again, we arrived in Academy Bay on the island of Christobal.

To visit these islands you needed a permit from the Ecuador government but this was almost impossible to get. The yachts which pass through depend largely on the goodwill of the Port Captain to be allowed to stop and see the amazing wildlife. For me, as a zoologist of course, this was something I had really looked forward to for a long time. I had been told that the authorities had really relaxed the rules so I was hoping we would be able to stay a week or two.

We approached the Bay in the early morning. There was thick fog and it was quite chilly. The water was cold. An hour before, we had nearly run over an albatross sitting on the water like a large goose and oblivious to our approach. The island was dry and rocky, the hills covered in cloud. As we rowed up the creek to the landing jetty having anchored out, we were excited to see what we could find.

The first thing we saw as we stepped ashore was a marine iguana, an ugly gray with a ragged crest along its back like some ancient dinosaur. It was right there on the jetty. I was sure it had been placed there for the visitors but of course that wasn't true. They were everywhere and, like the albatross, showed no fear of us.

The second sighting was a little bird. We had sat down in the shade in the first café and were drinking a cold beer. The little brown bird landed on my glass and cheekily took a sip of beer. It was a Darwin's finch obviously still "evolving" and now into tourist beer

The third thing was in the dinghy much later when we returned to the jetty. It was a sea lion, fast asleep, with her head in the bow and flippers over the transom. I think it was actually a she, still bigger than me, so thanked God, it was not one of the larger males that get very angry if you disturb them.

It was a great introduction for me but all was shattered by the harbour master who refused us any more than seventy two hours to refuel, re-water and depart. We had time to visit the research institute when we met an interesting Swiss zoologist. We saw the giant tortoises and took one long hike down the rocky coast and then we had to pay more than one hundred dollars for our clearance papers and go.

We should really have sneaked around some of the other islands but with the wind picking up in our favour we flew past Isabella Island and out into a massive empty Pacific. In front of us was a body of water stretching 3,000 miles to our next destination, the Marquesas Islands, the first islands we would encounter in French Polynesia.

This is the largest stretch of water in any part of a circumnavigation. When you get half way across, you can truly say you are 1000 miles from anywhere north, south, east or west!

Sea Loone is heavy and slow but well-organized for sailing downwind with the tradewinds. We hanked on a large genoa to each of the forestays and poled them out with the spinnaker poles. These run on individual tracks on the front of the mast. The sails were made specially from light nylon. They were sky-blue and looked very fine.

So rolling slightly we cruised down the long swells, the Aires wind vane steering us effortlessly. The mainsail, already showing a lot of wear, was folded up on the boom resting awhile under its canvas cover.

The El Niño was obviously finished. The wind was steady and the water cool from the Humboldt Current coming up the South American coast. This huge weather disturbance which had delayed our trip for six months had become world news. Yachts had spent ninety days doing the trip we were now doing.

I was still worried that this trip would be much longer than thirty days considering our two very slow Atlantic crossings. But with the wind not changing and with an extra push from the west-moving current we were eating up the miles. We hadn't touched the sails, and twenty three days later we were on the foredeck looking for our first glimpse of Fatu Hiva. I had had the sextant out a few times, but now we had the satellite navigator switched on.

A lot of the islands in French Polynesia are spectacular to see. Volcanic cones reach into the sky, huge cliffs are broken by sandy bays and surrounding reefs create quiet lagoons. Of all these islands, Fatu Hiva and the anchorage in Bay of the Virgins is the most awe-inspiring. There is no surrounding reef and not much shallow water. We have the bay to ourselves so we put out two anchors, one to the north and one to the south. Squalls of wind came out of the funnel like valley. Pillars of rock rose hundreds of feet like giant phalluses and the precipitous mountain wall in the background was pierced in one spot with light shining through from the windward side. The place was like a fairytale and a little intimidating.

A local returning from pig-hunting in his outrigger canoe welcomed us in French which I could manage but which Jean spoke well. We had caught a wahoo earlier, a mackerel type fish over twenty pounds in weight. We gave him the majority of it.

As he arrived at the boat in his outrigger canoe, he threw out all his dogs into the water. There were ten of them. We were a long way from the beach but the dogs were left to swim and manage the giant surf on the beach. He explained that the dogs often got injured by the pigs. This was his method of testing them to see if they were still any good.

Arriving in Fatu Hiva without clearing-in was against the law. First one had to go on to Hiva Oa, do the paperwork and then sail back against the wind. Fortunately for us, the local policeman was on holiday so we didn't get reported but still we only stayed for a few days, drinking in the fantastic scenery, catching freshwater prawns in the stream and eating fresh mangoes.

There was one strange incident which never happened again. I had gone walking along the reef edge at low tide, dodging the large swells and peering into the coral grottoes as the waves passed over them. There were beautiful cowrie shells some three inches across, dark brown with clear spots. I had jumped down and grabbed a few before the next wave returned. Suddenly I saw a pair of antenna sticking out of one small cave. I waited for a large swell to pass jumped down and pulled out a decent sized lobster. Unfortunately I was never able to grab a lobster as easily as this again in the Marquesas anyway.

We cleared-in to Hiva Oa with lots of pieces of paper to fill out supervised by some very serious French gendarmes. A huge mountain hung over the village with an almost vertical slope rising 1,000 feet. On a small rocky hill just outside the village was the grave of Gaugin who had spent his time here painting the colorful, charming, exotic people and their beautiful South Pacific environment. We had left behind the somberness of Fatu Hiva. Here we found smiling, friendly, people welcoming us.

From Hiva Oa we sailed north to Nuku Hiva. This is the location of main town in the Marquesas, Taeohae. It is built round a deep bay on the southeast of the island with two imposing rocky islets standing sentinel on either side of the bay. We anchored on the west side of the bay.

By now it was December already and, as it turned out, we were to spend the majority of our time in the Marquesas here, before finally leaving on April 11 the following year, 1984. The cyclone season in the southern hemisphere runs from November through April. Here in the Marquesas we were close to the equator between 9 and 10° south and normally unaffected by cyclones. Tahiti further west and south is another story so we would not move in that direction until April.

Our friends on the French yachts from Cocos had already arrived. There were two other French yachts, one very small gaff-rigged Breton-style boat; the other, was more or less a resident boat with the girl on board working as an anesthesiologist at the local hospital. There was one other yacht which was from Zimbabwe.

In the centre of the bay, waves crashed on the beach but in the eastern corner there was a dock where coasters could tie up to unload. On the west side, where we were, there was a reef. We could come in behind this and land on the beach with normally no problems.

We had stopped for a day in a beautiful bay on Tuhuata on the way to Nuku Hiva. The beach was white sand with a fringe of waving palm trees behind. It looked idyllic but we had been warned about the sandflies or no-nos on the beach. So, when we went ashore to pick limes from the lime trees behind the beach, we dressed in hats, long pants and tee-shirts. We also slathered ourselves in insect repellent and took a can of fly spray.

We rowed to the beach and leapt out and dashed across the sand into the trees. On our way we passed a couple of Americans throwing a Frisbee back and forward dressed only in swimming trunks. We collected our limes, shouted for them to get off the beach and dived into our dinghy. Half way back to the boat we took out the fly spray and zapped the no-nos that followed us out. These were the white no-nos, almost as bad as the black no-nos that live up in the mountains. They live only in the sand, no sand, no no-nos. So ten yards inland you are free of them.

The beach in Taeohae had the same problem so we never lingered on the beach especially after rain. The no-nos bite is hardly noticeable but the next day you itch like hell. If you scratch it, it gets worse and then tropical ulcers develop. We heard later that the two Americans ended up in hospital. There are no tourists in the Marquesas and that is why!

In the Galapagos the night before we left, we treated ourselves to a meal in the restaurant. There were several courses and the meal cost one dollar. Here in the Marquesas, the price could be ten times that for something much less. There was no inexpensive place to buy anything, so we were going to have to be very careful with our money here.

Limes, pamplemousse, huge delicious grapefruit-like fruit, papaya and bananas were easy to grow and often given to us. There was also plenty of seafood once you discovered how to catch it.

My problem was I still liked my potatoes and Jean spent a lot of time looking out for them. Years before, a Liverpool seaman had jumped ship here and married a local girl. Now his son, Maurice, ran one of the two stores in town. From his father he had a little English so Jean found out from him when the schooners coming up from Tahiti would be arriving.

The *Taparo* and the *Araroa* were small coasters bringing anything and everything to the islands. There were even a few cabins for passengers, or you could sleep on deck. It's 1000 miles from Tahiti and the ship stops at a few of the larger atolls in the Tuamotu's. A friend took the trip. As soon as they left Tahiti he had his place on the deck and once out at sea, the party began. The passengers drank so many bottles of Hinano beer that they ran out by the time they reached Manihi. Luckily, the ship was delivering beer to the island so the passengers disembarked, bought all the deliveries of beer from the shop and brought it back to the ship.

The potatoes arrived in a large box in Maurice's shop and Jean would sort through all of them to get my monthly supply from the crinkled rubbery mixture.

Close to where we landed on the beach, a local couple had a small house.

Justin carved bowls, tikis and other traditional items. Tikis carved in wood or stone are distorted human effigies. They can be huge and all hold a spirit within which is treated with much respect. Justin's wife Julienne had a vegetable garden. She grew lettuce in April and May for the passing American yachts. We became friends with Justin and Julienne and often met with Stephan and Guy from the other yachts, at Justin's house. Because the French spoken by the local people was so much simpler and without the argo or slang of French French, I could converse quite easily with Justin especially after a beer or two.

Amongst shell collectors, the Marquesas are well known .They have quite a number of shells which are endemic, that is to say they are only found there. Because the islands are remote even the easily found shells amongst these group had some value. The most well-known shell was Conus gaugini, named after the painter.

This shell lives in deep water. But not long before we arrived, a lot of these shells were thrown up on the beach in Tahuata when the cyclone passed through. The local chief, a woman, had closed all the beaches until she had collected all one hundred or so of the shells. She then flew to Tahiti to sell them all. This was a very silly marketing move. The value of the shells had suddenly dropped from over $1,000 each to only $300 just before we arrived.

Justin and I often went snorkeling together. He is a really big man and in the water swam like a sea lion. He knew the good spots to find shells and octopus and knew which fish to spear. Many fish were prone to carrying ciguatera poisoning and were never eaten. Without diving gear, that is scuba bottles, we weren't going to find any really rare shells but with Justin we found beautiful cask shells and I was lucky to find an area where I could find the endemic "sept droit", lambi crocata pilsbur, which was reportedly worth nearly one hundred dollars each.

There were many different types of cowrie shell to look for. Jean was really lucky to find a huge tritons trumpet. The local people call the shell a "Poo". It's still used in parts of Polynesia. Returning fisherman blow on it to advertise their arrival with fresh fish. You don't need to ask what it sounds like!

The Rhodesia boat, or was it now the Zimbabwe boat, was owned by a couple en route to Australia to find a new life. Keith was a printer and his wife had been a flight attendant. *Jobey Doe* was built in concrete like ours, though much larger. They had built it in Salisbury, now Harare. Loaded with all their possessions, they had transported the boat by road to Richards Bay in South

Africa. There they had had to sign forms to say that the boat would return within two years. The whole project had been a means to get their money out of the country. They were lucky because shortly afterwards, new laws were enacted to stop boats leaving at all.

Keith was almost as big as Justin, muscular, blond haired and another sea lion in the water. I think he missed the excitement of his time in the Rhodesian Army fighting the terrorists in their bush war so he was keen to do anything. We had sailed around to Huoome, the bay at the east end of the island and I had set the gill net on the small reef there. We caught one mullet, one lobster and a shark which made a real tangled mess of the net.

Keith was keen to dive all along the edge of the bay at night. My underwater water torch really wasn't very good. The first thing I saw was a huge shark pass in front of me. I discussed this with Keith and we decided to ignore it and start again. Eventually we found some lobsters but I had better explain the technique.

The lobsters were not the normal painted lobsters. They live in deep water. But on dark nights with no moon, they climb up the reef or the cliff to feed near the surface. They can weigh two or three kilos each and have short tails and long heavy legs. They are easy to see with a good torch as their eyes glow red. If you keep the light on them they seem to be a little mesmerized and you can swing down and grab them behind the head.

Their bodies are really spiny so you need a good thick pair of gloves. It also helps to have large hands for the bigger ones and they usually have a good hold on the rock face. It sounds quite straightforward but sometimes with the movement of the water you could be thrown all over the place as you tried to pull the bastard off and it takes a moment to work out which way is up to the surface.

By moving the base segments of their antennae, lobsters can make a loud creaking noise which attracts sharks. They do this when they are pissed off so it's really important to have a dinghy following you very closely so you can get them out of the water as quickly as possible. I know two people bitten on the arm by a shark while holding lobsters, one seriously. We ate lobster and on our return to Taeohae, sold five kg to Bob, the local hotel owner..

We had just paid our bond and applied for a three-month extension. The bond was $1780, a lot of money, which hopefully we would get back in Tahiti. We had been buying groceries and a few beers so any money for our lobsters was good.

Keith was even more keen and, when we mentioned it to Justin, he wanted to come out with us too. Justin, of course, knew a lot more about it than we did. He also had underwater lamps, basically a car headlight sealed with silicone, a long lead with small buoys to float it, and a battery in a dustbin with a flotation ring made from a car inner tube. He was a professional!

The next night, it was late January with no moon, we set off in Keith's fiberglass dinghy .There was Justin, Keith, Jean and I. We had wetsuits, weight belt, fins, electric lights batteries and dustbins so the dinghy was pretty full. It was raining as we set out towards one of the Sentinels at the entrance of the bay. Keith 8 hp outboard pushed us along reasonably well and the sea wasn't too agitated.

To find the lobsters you need a cliff face going vertically down into more than one hundred feet of water which is how it is almost everywhere. In the other places where there is a slope the ocean swells, instead of just going up and down, sweep you powerfully in and out. So we had to carefully avoid these areas or be swamped.

Justin's lights were fantastic like being in a lighted room. Jean and I alternated in the water or rowing the dinghy. Justin was a machine. One time he came up with three monsters in one dive. He had clamped one to his wetsuit under his arm, had one in one hand and managed another in the other and still held the lamp and each over a kilo in weight.

The rain started pouring down and it had a strange effect. Squat lobsters, in French called cigale, started appearing. Their antenna are two flaps and their bodies are like a trilobite or wood louse. They are not large no more than half a kilogram but much better eating.

Within two hours we had two sacks full and were on our way home. The freeboard on the dinghy was only a few inches. When we weighed the sacks we had forty four kilos.

We had made a lobster hotel under the boat from two bread trays so filled up these and then had to find customers for the rest. Justin was obviously no salesman, Keith spoke no French so it was up to Jean and I to sell the lobsters. Meanwhile we put them in the freezer on the dock for which we paid a small fee.

Bob in the hotel was again a good customer and he found some doctors and teachers and other buyers. Frank and Rose, the Americans, with the hotel upon the west side of the Bay took a few more and that night we all went out again, this time to the other Sentinel on the other side of the bay. We got no rain this time and it was all lobsters another thirty six kilos.

When I visited Bob again in the hotel he introduced me to two customs offices. Initially I had not want to talk to them but was assured they were nice people and they wanted to buy the lobsters. It appeared they had flown from Tahiti to meet a large Russian cruise ship arriving here in Nuku Hiva. They wanted to buy lobsters which they could return to Tahiti with on the cruise ship.

I agreed to meet them on the wharf the next morning. Jean and I took out a sack of lobsters from the freezer when the custom guys arrived. They started asking nasty questions How come two English people were fishing for lobsters here in French Polynesia? What was the name of our yacht? They were trying to frighten us into maybe giving them the lobsters for free. I sent Jean off to fetch Justin.

In the meantime a small crowd and two gendarmes had appeared to see what was going on. Justin arrived with a huge Polynesian scowl on his face. Before the customs officer could say anything he picked up the sack telling everyone that his lobsters were not for sale. Then he walked back with them to the deep freeze and locked them away.

The nasty little man turned out to be the Chief of Customs in Tahiti. He said he would see me there. The police and the rest of the crowd were amused. I could see a few problems ahead. We found customers for the lobsters in the end. Now the moon was waxing and so we left the lobsters in peace for a few weeks.

It was now February and we were well settled in. Occasionally we be given a piece of meat, goat or pig and we had plenty of fruit. Jean did serious bartering for fishing net and other things with the other yachts arriving. By the time the moon was gone again our lobster hotel was empty so we were planning to go out again. We had new gloves and I had a new torch and a supply of batteries.

The day we were preparing to go, we got a visit from the police. They had had a call from a French Navy ship due to arrive in the bay the next day. They wanted to put in an order for a couple of sacks of lobsters!

It was a beautiful calm night and we went to Sentinel L'Est again. This time we towed our rubber ducky behind with Justin in it plus some of the gear so we were not so worried this time about getting swamped by a rogue wave. In the next few hours we collected about 57 kg of lobster. Keith and Justin took them over to the freezer in the dark as the gendarmes had asked us to be a little discrete. The next night we went west along the coast and came back with another 40 kg, so we had enough for the Navy.

Now we had to go out and get enough for us to eat for the next month so the following night we again caught a load but the weather had now turned and the big swells coming in. The job became quite exciting riding two or three meters up and down the face of the cliff.

On the way home we suddenly realized we had lost Justin. Looking back we saw that the dinghy painter had broken with the weight of both Justin and all the lobsters. We went back the way we had come and found the rubber ducky free of its tether rocking merrily up and down with Justin there fast asleep!

We caught a few more lobsters the next month but already the season was changing and the wind turning southeast rather than northeast. This was bringing big swells into the bay and churning up the bottom ruining the visibility. All in all, he made some respectable money. We gave Justin half; then divided the rest between *Jobey Doe* and *Sea Loone*. The best day was when the Navy paid-up for 97 kg a total of 77,600 cpf (central pacific francs) or US$517.

By March, quite a few boats had arrived in Taeohae and our social life was busy. I was getting pretty good at catching octopus with a few tips from Justin and also watching the old ladies who were the real experts on the reef. Tenderized properly and cooked well, they are delicious deep-fried in a spaghetti sauce or minced into patties.

Spearfishing is not my thing and anyway so many fish carry the ciguatera poison that we didn't bother. If it were not for one yacht that arrived we may have had no fish at all. But one day, a boat called *Mirail* sailed into the bay with a massive marlin dragged up onto the aft deck. Keith helped him get it ashore and it provided meals for all the yachts for weeks. We named the proprietor "Mr. Poisson" and he was good. He sailed up to the north coast for a few days and came back with another monster fish, this time a sailfish. Amazing!

At the end of March a friend of Keith sailed in from Panama. He brought me a load of decent cigarettes I had asked for. I no longer had to smoke Gittans, French coffin-nails.

We were thinking at last of moving on, first to the Tuamotu's and then the big islands. Unfortunately the magic satellite navigator was no longer working so we were back on the sextant. It would make sailing through the Tuamotus, also called the "Dangerous Archipelago", more interesting.

Justin had promised to carve me a Marquesian tiki before I left. I had already found some little ones made by Mokio in the Valle des Artesans. Justin had made us a beautiful coconut rap. It is used for grating coconut to extract the milk. He had made it using the purple nazarina plank I had given him from Costa Rica. He had made a second one with the same wood and was asking 5000 CFP for it. I hoped he didn't want a lot of money for the tiki.

Little Roy, the tiki, arrived on the boat after a bit of bartering involving one of Jean's cakes and a shark tooth I had inlaid in black coral. We clipped Plod's feathers so he couldn't do anything silly; then, after lots of goodbyes, we left for Hakatea, a bay just west of Taeohae, before sailing on to the Tuamotus another five hundred miles to the south west.

The Bay in which Taeohae nestles is surrounded by almost vertical mountain slopes, a volcanic caldera inside a much larger caldera. Coming into Hakatea put us alongside the inside vertical cliff of the main caldera. It was spectacular. Turning to starboard inside the bay, we were completely protected from the ocean swells and were able to anchor in calm waters off the deserted white sand beach.

Once in Hakakea Bay, we took the narrow path round to the river where we met Janet and her grandmother, Caroline. They lived in a house just there and insisted on collecting a huge amount of fruit for us to take to the Tuamotus where there is nothing but coral and coconuts. Grandmother was tiny and scampers up the pamplemousse tree like a monkey and out into the thinnest branches. In no time, we had a full sack of limes, another of pamplemousse and a small one of star fruit.

Granny was then determined to carry the largest sack back along the track to the boat. It sounds as she is if she has emphysema but she arrived on the boat unharmed where she wanted to look into everything. Meanwhile Janet was having a go at rowing the rubber ducky in a straight line. She was roaring with laughter as she spun around in circles.

In the morning we were away. The cost of living in French Polynesia was a shock. The remoteness of the Marquesas made them expensive; even higher prices than in Tahiti. So for the five months or so we had spent there, Jean recorded:

Changed $900. Spent $800 + $33 Marlboro's and $10 lids. -$366 lobsters = $1,208.

Jerry's dock in Stuart, Florida

Building the sea wall, Florida

The Carenage, Grenada

Sailing down island

The lobster business, Nuku Hiva

Peccary, Costa Rica

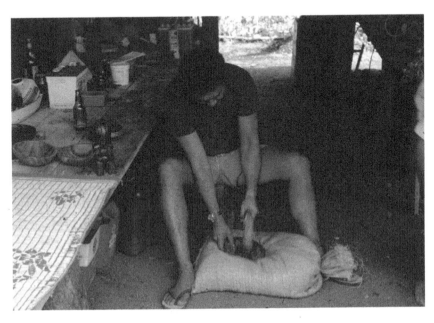

Justin adzing bowl Taeohae, Nuku Hiva

The paper mill, Sydney

Opua Regatta, New Zealand

Running down wind inside Barrier Reef, Australia

Plod on route to Bora Bora

Jean's Galah

Winging Bruce in Sydney

Jean, Joan & Fafa in Bora Bora

Tern egg collecting, Suvavor

The water baby

Lobster

Ursin Crayon

Octopus

Fairy tern, Chagos

Tracey joins Sea Loone

Tracey's blue fronted amazon

The landing St. Helena

6

THE TUAMOTUS ARE spread over a huge area of ocean. They are all low atolls and most have navigable lagoons with one or two passes. Maybe the most famous of these atolls at the time was Mururoa where the French were testing their nuclear bombs. It was far to the south in a prohibited area. We were heading for Takaroa, one of the nearest atolls to the Marquesas only 500 miles away.

The Tuamotus are called the "Dangerous Archipelago" because the islands are so low. They are difficult to see unless very close and because the ocean currents among the islands are very unpredictable. Four days from leaving Nuku Hiva we were very close to the atolls. The satellite navigator was not working and I was busy with the sextant drawing lines all over the chart. We heaved to for the night not prepared to get any closer until we had a better fix on where we were.

We spent a nervous sleepless night listening to the sound of surf breaking on the reef and imagining the boat being picked up and shattered on razor-sharp corals, but eventually dawn broke and we set sail in the direction we assumed was correct. Midmorning we saw what might have been the tops of coconut palms and at the same time met up with *Whoosh*, a small American yacht, heading in the same direction. Together we carried on and before dusk were tied up together with a third yacht on a crumbling jetty next to the village and at the entrance to the lagoon.

The whole village turned out, all one hundred of them, mainly to see Plod the parrot. . The children persisted in peering in through the cabin windows until I stuck Little Roy, the tiki, in the window. They all ran away.

Next morning, we all went to see the village chief to get permission to enter the lagoon. They were pearl farming in the lagoon so we were worried we might get tangled in their lines. There was talk of a pilot boat but eventually they agreed that we could go in without.

This was the early days in the pearl farming business. They were producing black pearls which could be worth hundreds of dollars each if perfect. They had bushes suspended in the lagoon onto which the young oysters attached themselves and grew. From the bushes, they were transferred to small cages and eventually, when over four or five inches across, they were put in individual pockets in a sheet of mesh. Here they were impregnated with the seed by a Japanese expert that visited regularly. From the seed, the pearl took over a year to form, while suspended in the deep waters of the lagoon.

The pass into the lagoon is quite frightening. The tide swished in and out at up to seven knots. The channel was narrow and bordered by steep coral walls. Just before it entered the lagoon it turned sharply to port and passed over a shallow shelf. At the turn there was is a serious whirlpool.

The technique was to go at slack water. So we spent time throwing coconut husks in the water and watch them spin away with the current. When the current finally stilled, we untied ourselves from the dock and motored into the channel. Once inside the lagoon, the next two problems are coral pillars which come to the surface from one hundred feet down and also avoiding the mooring buoys which are holding up the sheets of oysters.

We zigzagged over to the other side of the lagoon, a few miles away and anchored off the islands close to a narrow shallow pass. The lagoon was disappointing. The water was not clear and the coral not very live. But because it was all so different to the Marquesas, we were keen to explore.

At high tide water flowed in over the reef between the islands into the lagoon. The islands are called motus. They sit on the reef only a few feet above the water and usually covered in coconut trees. Motus also are found on the reefs surrounding the high island like Bora Bora. The reef was almost dry at low tide. In the pass the reef was more alive and there were lots of different shells to be found. There were also octopi. Our collection of shells was increasing dramatically and octopus became a staple diet, although I did spear a few groupers, a black and white cod-like fish.

We had been told that the same lobsters we had been catching in the Marquesas came and walked round on top of the outer reef on moonless nights. Also on the motus there were coconut crabs which came out at night. So with the new moon, we lit the Tilly lamp and set off in the dark. We crossed the island and then waded it out to the outer edge of the reef where the surf was pounding.

Sure enough we eventually saw a pair of glowing red eyes and I grabbed a huge lobster out of the water. It was the only one we found that night. We hadn't been in water more than knee deep .Now we knew they were there we returned a few nights later. As we crossed the island among the coconut palms we found a coconut crab scuttling along. He was only small we later discovered. He had a hairy abdomen and two big pincers out front. We left him alone.

We socialized with the two other yachts one of which, from Victoria, Canada, had the misfortune of getting a rat on board from the jetty we had tied to. They had a little black Belgian barge dog on board. These are apparently bred for catching rats on Belgian barges. But this particular little chap hadn't been told this, so was petrified.

We spent seventeen days fossicking around the reefs. Jean caught her first octopus but got sucker marks up her arm and a bite on her wrist. We had had eight octopus dinners, two lobster dinners and three fish dinners. Now it was time to move on. We decided to give Tahiti a miss and sail directly for Bora Bora. From there, we would leave French Polynesia. The main reason for this was to avoid the nasty customs men we had had dealings with over the lobsters.

From Takaroa we had to weave between a few more atolls before leaving the Tuamotus. First, we had to pass between Rangiroa and Aratua; then past Makatea. With only the sextant it was an interesting exercise.

On the fifth day we picked up Raiatea, Taha and then Bora Bora with its famous silhouette. The weather was still stormy with heavy thunder clouds. We arrived off the pass into Vaitape, the main village, with a huge black storm hanging to leeward. We hung around until finally I decided to head into the pass.

Fortunately I had taken a bearing, 100°M to keep in the pass. Half way the purple blackness overtook us. The wind howled and the rain came down in sheets. I couldn't see the mast, let alone the bow and there were reefs everywhere. Jean with her nose to the compass shouted the course and I steered on blindly. I was really worried about a reef which jutted out from the island which we would have to dog leg around. Finally I decided not to go any further. So we swung around and did a reciprocal course back out the pass; or hopefully out of the pass if we hadn't unknowingly been pushed sideways.

The storm passed us as abruptly as it had arrived. We found ourselves in the middle of the pass, thank God, so swung around once more motored on in.

There were a few yachts anchored off the village all in over one hundred feet of water, three times deeper than we normally contemplated anchoring in. But our nerves were still jangling so we threw in the anchor into the depths and retired below for a deserved cup of coffee. It was May 5th.

Two days later I awoke to find another yacht anchored next to us. It was white with a green stripe, flying a red ensign. It was looking very shipshape and "Bristol Fashion" as the British say. Without seeing the name, I knew it had to be *Wanderer V*, the latest yacht of Eric and Susan Hiscock, the gurus of the English-speaking yachting world. I crept out and ran up our red ensign; then, later in the morning persuaded Jean to go and say hello to them. They gave her a cup of tea.

They also told Jean that there was a much better anchorage around the back of Topua Island, a small island near the pass, in a more reasonable depth of water. So we invited three strapping lads from a Canadian yacht for a cup of coffee in order to "shanghai" them into helping us pull our anchor and chain up out of the hundred foot abyss.

Still inside the main reef not far from the village, the anchorage behind Topua was perfect. There we met Dominique a French rocket scientist on his yacht *Kurma*. He had worked in French Guyana on the Kuru rocket range and was now working for the electricity company in Bora Bora.

Within days of being in Bora Bora we realized that maybe we were going to have some visa problems. To start with, we had already been in French Polynesia for six months and needed an extension to our stay. We eventually got three more months, but not without a lot of arguing with the "police de la frontier". At the same time we realize that it may be difficult to get our huge $1,700 bond back without a trip to Tahiti.

However there was good news when we discovered that the moorings off the Oa Oa hotel in the village were available and free and also the Bora Bora yacht club occasionally had free moorings if any of its floating cottage tenants were away. So we divided our time between these two places.

I visited Dominique's power station where they were using coconut husks to make electricity. We danced in the Club Med, a small scruffy place compared with what was to come and we poked our noses into the Bora Bora Hotel, at that time, probably one of the most exotic and expensive hotels in the world. We invited the Hiscocks to tea and Jean made one of her superior cakes. It was a near disaster when Eric, as blind as a bat, nearly fell down the companionway. Susan was intrigued to know what Jean had been doing wading on the reef. When told she was looking for an octopus for dinner, she was delighted but said: "Of course Eric would never eat octopus"!

Bora Bora Yacht Club was being refurbished and a new bar was being built. One beer there was so expensive even in Happy Hour that we rarely visited but the proprietor had agreed to employ a group of South Africans to do the work. They had agreed to work for unlimited free beer. There must have been five South African boats on the mooring, including *Jobey Doe*, *Morning Star* and *Shadowfax*. I knew their ringleader who eventually sailed back to Knysna in South Africa and started the famous bar on the wharf there. His drinking alone could have made the bar-building job very expensive.

We were given directions on how to get around to the windward side of Bora Bora. It involves lining up a tall coconut tree with the northwest point. From deep water you suddenly only had seven or eight feet but it was as flat as a billiard table. Eventually you got used to skimming over sand and grass inches below the keel.

Dominique invited us to dinner. We started with boiled bonitiers, very large clams. Eaten whole, they are horrible. He followed by serving steamed land crabs; muddy and disgusting. Finally we had pen shell mussels. Raw they are delicious; but he had boiled them until they were as tough as boots. Obviously cuisine was not his "rocket" science!

On a motu in the northwest corner of Bora Bora we were introduced to Joan de Kat and Fafa. They lived in a huge fare, a traditional Polynesian house, which Joan had designed and built for a French millionaire. Joan's boat, *Mong*, was hauled up on the beach. It was a very strange yacht which obviously was never going to be sailing any further.

Joan entered a single handed TransAtlantic race years before. His catamaran broke up and he was fortunate to get rescued. He then sailed around the world on a weird pirate ship he had designed, accompanied by some friends. I never read the book about it that he wrote but Fafa said it was more about a girl in every port than sailing.

At the beginning of July, the people started preparing for the festival of July fourteenth. It was the climax of the year. A festival village was built on the wharf in Vaitape. Canoes were built for the races, and costumes were made for the dancing. All day you could hear the sound of electric planes smoothing down the hollowed out logs to make the streamlined outrigger canoes.

A small amphitheater was built opposite the police station and on the evening of the first day we went to see the dancing. We waited in the dark and then the drums started. From across the road the dancers appeared from behind the police station and made their way onto the dance floor. Lit by flaming torches held by the male dancers. I was mesmerized by the long lustrous black hair, often down past the dancers' waists, the flashing eyes and huge smiles. The swaying hips with the grass skirts were intoxicating. I was ready to jump ship and stay forever.

Fortunately for us one of Joan's friends who had sailed with him on the pirate ship, came to stay for holiday with his family. He was an important advocate in Paris. Using the telephone at the power station he agreed to help us try to retrieve the bond money from the bureaucrats in Tahiti. A lot of unintelligible, high-speed Parisian French was spoken and there was a promise to send our money to Bora Bora. Brilliant!

By November we expected to be in New Zealand and unfortunately Plod was not going to be welcomed. There was an American chartering his catamaran from the hotel Bora Bora that was really interested in taking him but finally we decided to leave him with Joan and Fafa on the motu. We had got so used to Plod messing around on the boat, screeching, flapping his wings whenever we returned from the shore and arriving in bed with us in the morning. We were going to miss him. We told Joan he was only on loan. We would come back.

Joan found us a solar panel which we fixed on the back of the boat. It instantly solved all our electricity problems. Finally, I had to rebuild the water pump on the engine and returned to the power station to make a new shaft for it. Then on August 1st, having collected our money and with letters for Bernard Moitessier, the guru of French sailing, on Suvarov Island in the northern Cook Islands, we left French Polynesia.

Suvarov Island, an isolated atoll in the northern Cook Islands, was made famous by Tom Neal who spent many years there alone. He was a real hermit and wrote a book "An Island to Myself" about his early years on the island. He had left the island only a year or two before we arrived. In those last years, he ran a post office for the Cook Island Government.

It was a silly thing, but to have a letter sent from there had some value to stamp collectors. I heard an amusing story from a sailor who had met him in the late afternoon before leaving the island. He had gone to Tom Neal's shed to post a letter. It was a few minutes past four and he was told that the post office closed at four. He was shown the door.

Having met the Hiscocks in Bora Bora, we were looking forward to meeting Moitessier, the guru of French sailing. He was in Suvarov and we had two letters for him. Unfortunately he had had problems with the coral heads in the anchorage and had left by the time we arrived, so we were disappointed.

The old coast watchers sheds where Tom Neal had lived and which dated back to the 2nd world war, was now occupied by a Scotsman his wife and a very small baby. Ron Falconer had been living for some time in the Tuamotus but had decided to try and make a life on Suvarov with his family. His small yacht, *Fleur d'Ecose* was anchored in the lagoon.

Almost hitting a wreck in the entrance to the lagoon, we eventually managed to anchor among the coral heads. There were fish everywhere but lots of sharks too. Some of them were large gray reef sharks. These have a nasty attitude and tend to take pieces of flesh off people. In fact only days before, a yacht had shot up to Pago Pago with a girl in her crew missing a large chunk of muscle out of one arm.

The reef was quite broken up but at low tide you could walk for miles. The occasional bushy islands were home to thousands of terns. The larger bushes were nesting sites for frigate birds and there were occasional red tailed tropic birds nesting under the bushes in the shade. The higher islands, all six feet out of the ocean, had palm trees and lots of holes dug by coconut crabs.

In one of his books Moitessier describes how he staked out a square in a tern colony, threw out all the terns' eggs and came back the next day to collect fresh ones. This seemed a bit harsh to us. Jean and I preferred to find where the new nests were getting built and then drop what appeared to be fresh eggs in a bucket of saltwater. If they float they are no good. Tern omelettes were pink but tasted good.

There were too many crevices and holes in the outside reef to go walking at night so over the holes and crevices which communicated with the outside ocean, we nailed down pieces of gill net using old screwdrivers, files and anything else we could find. At the same time we cut a path through the scrub around the coconut trees and then, splitting coconuts with a machete, we nailed the halves to the trees at waist height.

That day a very luxurious 65-foot Swan racing yacht arrived. That evening, the owner joined us on the crab hunt. He was an elderly German who had made his millions in the USA. The crabbing was a "doddle". We just followed the cut path using the Tilly lamp. At each tree was at least one coconut crab feeding on the nut. Some of them were enormous and I'm sure could have nipped off your hand with their claws. We had brought large buckets with lids so they got knocked into the bucket and we quickly jammed on the lid. The only problem was later. We failed to put each in a separate buckets and they started to chomp on each other.

The next morning using binoculars we could see that may be we also had some success on the reef. Sure enough as the tide receded, we waded out and had caught three large lobsters and a couple of small ones. We had dinner that night on the "Swan". Lobsters, crab, steaks and cold beer. Then, strange on a desert island in the middle of nowhere, we watched a film on their TV.

A lot of the main island was overgrown with many young coconut palms sprouting up. Finding one just the right size we chopped into its growing point, peeling away the fronds. You have to look out for small yellow scorpions which lived between the fronds. But eventually, at the center, we uncovered its heart. Destroying such a large plant for such a small return seemed immoral. But it was worth it. The heart of palm had a lovely nutty taste.

The sharks were a nuisance and made fishing difficult. There was a snapper type of fish called a sweet lip under the boat. To catch them you had to bait a hook with a piece of octopus, attach a heavy lead weight, and drop it to the bottom as fast as possible. The fish bit almost instantaneously and then you had to pull it up as fast as you could before the sharks left you with only the head. You got maybe one in ten.

Having talked to Ron on the island, we realized that we may still have a paperwork problem. Leaving Bora Bora we had got our money back but had not been given a "sortie" or clearance paper. This was again was only given in Tahiti.

Arriving in Pago Pago in American Samoa without the "sortie" would be a huge problem. Ron had set up a radio on the island and using shortwave, talked to other yachts. This was handy for him if he needed anything brought from Bora Bora and an insurance for the baby.

A yacht which had passed on the way to Bora Bora still had their clearance paper from there the previous time. It was used but easy to change. They posted it to Pago Pago for us to pick up when we arrived. The problem hopefully was solved. We stayed a little longer while Jean found some good shells and I found a glass fish float which might be worth something. They were becoming quite rare.

We left for our next stop, Pago Pago in American Samoa where we needed to buy cooking gas. Leaving though, wasn't that straightforward. At least there was no paperwork to do on a desert island but we had two anchors in the water with buoys and lines to avoid the coral heads. We got the first anchor up but had to dive into the water a few times to untangle the second one.

It was lunch time before we motored out through the pass and got the sails set. We had hoped to catch a fish in the pass but instead caught a booby bird which dived onto our lure. By the time we dragged him on board and untangled him, he wasn't very happy.

We were still taking sextant sights as the satellite navigator was only giving us a position once every few days or not at all. The weather was much warmer than Bora Bora but still with lots of heavy squall so the sailing was uncomfortable.

Pago Pago, the main port of American Samoa, is one huge fish factory processing thousands of tons of tuna brought in by big seine netters. The water is filthy and the whole place stinks. It has to be the most polluted place in the whole South Pacific but we had to do some provisioning and fill the gas bottles.

Clearing in and out we had to tie alongside the custom's wharf. Friends had checked our mail and the letter from Bora Bora had not arrived so customs were not happy. So having anchored, we had to row ashore and then be interviewed by the Chief of Customs.

On the way to his office, we passed the main post office so nipped in just in case. It was truly our lucky day, the letter had just arrived. The "sortie" already had the former names and dates blanked out so we filled in *Sea Loone* and completed the rest of the form. Then we continued on to the customs office where would-be doom and gloom turned to smiles and a warm welcome.

The two large 19 kg gas bottles went on the bus and were back on the boat refilled in not much more than an hour. The bus driver had waited for the bottles to be filled so there was no problem with gas for us for the next few months. We also bought duty-free booze and cigarettes, cheap shorts and shoes, bits for the engine, diesel fuel and food although the food was not much cheaper than in French Polynesia. The anchorage was horrible and there were a number of yachts doing much the same as us, storing up.

A boat behind us dragged onto the reef while the delivery skipper in charge was socializing in town. He actually managed to wade out, get on board and, with lots of black smoke from the engine, managed to reverse his boat off the reef.

With Mike on *Shadowfax*, I had gone to lend a hand in the rubber ducky. He drove right over us, swamping the dinghy. He then zoomed round in front of *Sea Loone* still dragging the anchor which he never attempted to pull up. He snagged our chain and again caught Mike and me between the two yachts as he crashed into us.

At last he turned his engine off after another attempt destroying the Aires steering gear on the back of *Sea Loone*. By this time I'm roaring at him, It was getting dark so I tied him behind us for the night and told him to do absolutely nothing until the morning. The stupid man was sure his anchor had come unshackled. In the morning we should have agreed with him and confiscate his anchor when we untangled it from our chain and shoved him off.

There was lots of mail for us from all over, some of it not so good. One friend who had built his boat in Cape Town was lost overboard on a delivery to Hawaii. Another lost his boat in the in northern Cook Islands. Yet another had given it all up and sold his boat for a few dollars in Christmas Island.

Samoans are large, in fact huge, and after a few beers a bit aggressive. So it was to say the least, a bit hazardous bar-hopping at night. We did however manage to meet one of the helicopter pilots from the tuna boat and have a few beers with him. The tuna boats each have a helicopter to spot the fish or the debris in the water around which the fish shoal. The tuna boats can carry up to 1,000 tons of fish, so not small. They carry a very powerful launch to pull one end of the long net while circling the fish. If fish try jumping over the net, the helicopter blows them back into the water. The tuna crew will all get paid a share of the catch. The helicopter man gets a straight $1,000 a week, come what may.

We tied alongside to clear-out and take on water before heading towards the open ocean. It took a few miles to leave behind the dirty smelly water. We were heading south for Tonga.

The weather was still really unsettled. A few boats had already ventured out and come back but the first day for us was fine. It was the next day that things started to look as if they might deteriorate. Overnight there had been a light behind us and in the morning we could see a yacht following. We assumed it was Wayward Wind that had left about the same time as us.

By mid-morning there was a purple black line of cloud bearing down on us. We were running before the wind with both poles out with the two big blue genoas on them. I took one of these down. The other yacht was coming up behind us. It also had one genoa poled out. The purple black nastiness got closer looking more and more ominous reminding me of the one that got us entering Bora Bora. I took the other sail down secured the spinnaker poles and we sat almost dead in the water waiting to see what was going to happen.

The other boat, still with the genoa still poled out disappeared into the curtain of heavy rain. It hit us like a brick wall. One of the self-steering gear lines parted so I was stuck in the cockpit steering off downwind while Jean closed up the hatch and peered out at me just as she had done in Fastnet gale. It howled and poured down and the seas quickly build up into short foaming monsters all trying to climb on board and broach the boat, turning it sideways so we would be swamped. I hung on and fought the tiller. At least the sea was warm compared with southern Ireland.

It was hours before the wind dropped enough that Jean could take over steering while I replace the broken line on the Aires steering gear. That done, I went below to dry off and drink some coffee.

The huge squall left us with little wind and a horrible lumpy sea for the next day. We had drifted west so had to harden up the sheets to make it to Vavau'u, northern Tonga.

The island is beautiful with a hilly main island and lots of small reef islands strung out to the south. The reef at some stage had lifted up so the islands are all a little higher than the atolls we were used to. They had a lot of good volcanic soil on top. The Tonga Trench running south immediately to the east of Tonga has two major plates running over each other with associated volcanic action. In fact, while we were there, one underwater volcano was producing vast quantities of floating pumice stone which covered the surface of the ocean. In places it was many meters deep and making problems for the ships engines cooling systems. The pumice eventually covered beaches from Fiji to Australia.

We arrived on the Saturday but didn't clear in until the Monday. Clearing in was an all-day process which seemed to involve feeding all the officials, providing cold beer and donating clothing, fishing tackle and anything else they saw lying around. They only got cheese and biscuits and warm Tang orange juice from us but it still took most of the day.

Unlike French Polynesia and American Samoa, Tonga is independent and poor. At least the ordinary people are poor. Within the extended families there are farmers and fishermen and so no one goes hungry. Vegetables grow quickly and plentifully in the rich soil and there are almost as many pigs in the villages as there are children, and there are plenty of children. The sea provides a huge variety of good edible fish.

Tonga is a kingdom, a real one. The king owns the land and he and his barons govern the people. What the king does not siphon off, the church's demand so the people remain poor.

A week after we arrived in Vavau'u Wayward Wind limped into the harbor. On the morning we had seen him disappear into the black squall he had been down below tuning his radio to get a weather forecast! He never saw it coming. The genoa got ripped to shreds but the big problem which had really slowed them down was that the spinnaker pole got torn off the mast leaving a huge hole in the mast itself. The mast was still standing but he had some work to do.

There was a charter company in Vavau'u, South Pacific Yacht Charters. They had numbered the many anchorages among the islands and reefs so we all cruised by numbers comparing number this with that and so on.

Jean and I spent hours diving for shells wading on the reefs at low water. Often we met local people on the reef turning over sections of the reef with steel bars collecting things to eat, urchins sea slugs and such. They destroyed the reef as they went but they had family to feed. I'm not very keen on sea urchin eggs, the taste lingers and sea slugs are tough as boots. Two girls were squirting the innards from a particular green slug into a rusty tin. This they explained was for their grandfather a sort of elixir life. I didn't fancy it.

We had a huge party one night on the Swan 65 with fourteen dinghies tied behind. I mentioned that I had all the New Zealand charts which he agreed to buy. I had got the whole portfolio from the ships warehouse in Liverpool. At four dollars each we made one hundred and seventy six dollars but were left without a single chart for ourselves to arrive, no matter.

Through our interest in shells, we met a Canadian guy, David, living in Vavau'u with his wife and child, Hanita and Barbara. He was a keen shell collector and had a business making jewellery. A lot of his business was with visiting cruise ships which would come right into the main harbour and tie up. Unfortunately for David, one of the barons who was the chief of police had organized that the regular cruise ship would now only stop at his island with facilities for them to have a beach barbecue. Only his traders would be allowed on the island. There was a near riot in the village over this and finally all vendors and traders were allowed on his island but they still had to get there.

So the day before the cruise ship came, the wife, the little girl and boxes of shells and jewellery came on board *Sea Loone*. The materials for the stall were to come in their dinghy by the inside route. We had to go all the way round.

We arrived and anchored off in the late afternoon and in a squall of wind at ten o'clock at night the dinghy arrived with the helper. The Seagull engine had given up twice. We dried him off and fed him some sandwiches.

The next morning a New Zealand destroyer arrived plus a few yachts. We were ashore helping set up the stall and Jean and I had a preview of all the other things arriving. We bought some interesting shells and two really nice turtle shells. I pointed out that the shells couldn't go back to Australia with the tourists on the ship and anyway had no value as they had already eaten all the meat. The price was reduced dramatically.

The cruise ship, Fair Winds eventually arrived. We helped them eat their barbecue, sat with the captain, a charming Italian, and drank his beer. Tony and Connie the couple with the Dutch barge dog went out to the ship with the second officer to scrounge some charts. Hanita, David's gorgeous Tongan wife, made a fair bit of money. Everybody had a good day.

What with one thing and another time slipped by. The weather became blustery again so we shot south to Tongatapu, the main island. This would be our starting point for heading to New Zealand.

Anchoring off Nuku'alofa, the capital, was not so good. Behind the main wharf, which sticks out into the lagoon, is a small area of not too deep water. But there was no real shelter from the easterly winds. Me and a neighbour chased one yacht which dragged past us unattended and managed to stop it before disaster struck on the reef.

Sometime in its past, Tonga had been invaded by Germany. More recently, Germany had provided aid to build the wharf and seawall. Maybe because of this there was a German bakery and a sausage maker in town, both of them excellent!

We were invited on the cruise ship *Oriana* (a P&O liner) coming up from Sydney. I had known the ship when she was still doing trips across the Atlantic to Liverpool in the 1960s. Tied up on the wharf in Tonga she was looking a little old.

November had arrived and with it the cyclone season. We heard that cyclones were developing already; so it was time to leave the topics and head for New Zealand.

Finances
November 1983 -- November 1984 in US dollars
Arrive Marquesas $ 5,308
Credit Debit
Taeohae Change $ 943
Lobsters $ 300 $ 300
Takaroa Outboard bracket $ 52
Bora Bora Change $ 830
Fuel, gas etc $ 120
Solar panel $ 150
$ 3,473
Pago Pago Food $ 200
Booze $ 90
Fuel, gas etc $ 140
$ 3,007
Tonga Charts $ 176
Change $ 325
Arrive New Zealand $ 2,858

7

NEW ZEALAND IS 1,000 miles south of Tonga. We were heading for the Bay of Islands close to the northern tip, at 35° south. There was talk of gales and rough seas en route but in fact our trip was uneventful.

It got colder and colder as we headed south. By the time we saw the "long white cloud" under which New Zealand was hiding, we were in pullovers and jeans. It was the first time in years the clothes had been out the cupboard. Sailing into the Bay among lots of different seabirds, we had a gorgeous black-browed albatross come to say hello and a couple of little blue penguins scooted out of our way. The rocky coast and green hills were very reminiscent of parts of Pembrokeshire or Anglesey.

We tied up to the old wooden wharf in Opua to clear with customs and immigration. We had had to get a visa for New Zealand in Tonga which seemed a bit rude considering how Britain treated New Zealanders. The customs man was very grumpy. He had just found five cases of booze undeclared on an Irish boat in front of us. We promised him we were far more honest, and gave him our shotgun to look after. But we forgot to tell him about the case of gin under the cockpit.

The next day we found a mooring off Ashby's boat yard and hitchhiked into the next village, Pahia, to do some shopping. Jean bought me a proper china teapot. Hitchhiking back, we were picked up by a guy called Ken who invited us for a cup of tea at his house overlooking the anchorage in Opua. Ken worked for the forestry and his wife, Joss, was the postmistress in Pahia. For the rest of our stay they took us under their wing. Joss was from a family that had been in the area for generations and Ken had come out from England after the war.

We were introduced to the old dog, the cat, the huge rabbit, the one eyed chicken and a family of possums that they fed each night. The possums didn't make Ken and Joss popular with the neighbours. Introduced from Australia, the possums are a disaster if you are growing fruit of any kind

It was November and we had arrived in time for my birthday. We planned to stay through the New Zealand summer, leaving in April. There were a few hundred yachts arriving to do the same thing a number of whom we had already met in the Pacific islands and become good friends with.

The $2,800 that we had was more than enough to last us for our stay. But Jean was keen to find some hotel or restaurant work. I promised I would look around a bit, but with the low wages and the work I needed to do on *Sea Loone*, I wasn't going to look too hard.

In April we planned to cross to Australia where work prospects were better and wages almost double. By that time, the piggy bank was going to be pretty empty.

Our stay started well, first meeting Ken and Joss and then contacting Eddie White my former boss at Liverpool University. Eddie now had a research station on Lake Taupo in the centre of North Island but was keen to come up to Opua to see me and the boat. He had the grand title of Director of Ecology for the Government but obviously wasn't too busy. Within days, he arrived with his secretary in a flashy Jaguar car and the four of us took the boat out among the islands for a few days.

It was still pretty cold and when I jumped in the water to dive up some scallops for tea, I nearly died. Years in the tropics had melted away any body fat. I was a bag of bones and the cold seeped in. My heart started palpitating and I came out of the water like one of those penguins onto an ice floe.

Eddie had apparently separated from his wife and was now living with Janet his secretary. They both enjoyed the few days sailing, although they had to make do with pipi's, small clams you found at low water, rather than scallops.

We sailed back to Opua where we organized a young boy to keep an eye on the boat He was on a boat we had met in Pago Pago. We piled into the Jaguar and went off on a tour of the North Island. Eddie was a bit miffed that we seemed to know more people in New Zealand than he did. We kept on bumping into other sailors sightseeing like us. But the event that really got to him happened one day on a little wooden jetty watching a fly fisherman trying for trout on the famous Lake Taupo. Talking to him he was a local but had sailed on a yacht a few years before in the Caribbean. The yacht was *Passing Through* that we had had the adventures with in Barbados and Florida.

Jean and I tried a bit of hiking around the volcanoes which overlook the Lake. The weather turned horrible and we were stuck in a hut for two days high on the mountain. Eddie took me to a small stream to tickle some trout. I had got quite good at it working with Eddie years ago. He dare not hang around while I looked; but anyway I was not successful.

We took Eddie's laser dinghy out on the lake. We drank beer in the local bar full of Maoris the largest of whom, a girl, wiped the floor with me playing pool. It was all good fun and great to be back on land for a while. But as the saying goes, fish stinks after a few days and so do house guests. We didn't want to overstay our welcome and the boat beckoned. So one morning, Eddie dropped this on the road back north and we stuck out our thumbs.

Jean found work in a hotel in Pahia. There's no public transport so she had difficulty commuting initially. But as we got to know people lifts were normally available. I started building a plywood dinghy. Rainbow Yacht Charters had room for me in their shed.

We had our gill net in the water most the time and caught a variety of fish, mostly edible but the rest went to Joss's cat. Occasionally we went with Ken and Joss to help them lay their much bigger nets and if lucky, came back with a sack full of mullet and kawai. All went into the big smoker in the garden. The local hills were covered in low bush, mainly tanika which Capt. Cook called the "tea tree". It's brilliant for hot smoking fish.

The beaches were covered with Pacific oysters, not my favorite, but on the rocks and pilings were some lovely mussels. If you went and looked at very low tides, we found huge blue-green mussels. Jean found blackberries by the bucketful down the railway track and as the weather warmed up we were given plums, grapefruits and apples.

In a small shed close to the boat yard, there was an engineering/welding business. Loethe was one of the partners. We had met him in Madeira in 1978. He was German, his boat being very recognizable with its bulbous bow. He and his wife had become New Zealand residents. At the same time, I was pile-driving in Florida he was working as an engineer for a local boat yard on six New Zealand dollars an hour, almost a logarithmic difference to my earnings.

For Jean and I, he sorted out our Aires self-steering gear, welded up the exhaust and did a few other minor jobs. We had discovered his weak point. He got paid in blackberry and apple pies.

Many years later, I met Loethe again in New Caledonia. He was retired and cruising in his lovely new yacht. One night we polished off a bottle of whiskey while he described the horrific scenes he had to watch as a boy in Hamburg. The British and Americans carpet bombed the city and he had seen the whole city in flames and bodies blasted into bits. Not quite Hiroshima but, for him, as a boy, very traumatic.

Just before New Year, I took a job at burning off the paint underneath a huge motor yacht on the railway in Ashby's yard. The fumes from the paint knocked me out. I was really ill and got an infection in my waterworks which gave me problems for the rest of my stay in New Zealand. The doctor really never isolated the problem. I took hundreds of pills and didn't get my first pint of beer for 1985 until late March!

Still, between bouts of unpleasantness, I got the dinghy finished. It was my first attempt and, as usual, I didn't bother with plans. It was not a great success. In fact, it threw me in the water on its first trial. I rebuilt another dinghy for another cruiser which involved a complicated deal centred around a long length of chain which I was given. I then had to re-galvanize it and sell half in order to pay for the other half.

Jean had met a farming couple across the river who were avid shell collectors. By this time, we had a huge collection of shells including some rare and maybe valuable ones from Nuku Hiva.

Through them, the Rigdens, we met other collectors and even one day went to a meeting of the Shell Club in Whangerai. After protracted negotiations, we sold the Conus gaugini for more than NZ$200. The rare seven-finger shells made even more. The farmers had pleaded poverty as farmers do, so they got a special deal. A few weeks later they bought an Angora lamb for more than $100,000. I wish I was that poor.

Opua is a small village with a wharf. The wharf was constructed from huge timbers and had been used for exporting timber mainly kauri logs. It was served by a single track railway coming down from Kawa Kawa. There was a local shop and a post office, some sheds used by the oyster farmers, and the Opua Cruising Club which was another wooden shed used as a hub for the visiting sailors.

The big day for Opua is usually Regatta Day but this year, before that happened, they had another big day when the *Alexander Pushkin*, the huge round the world cruise ship, came to tie up at the wharf. This was the same ship that had visited Nuku Hiva and brought the nasty customs chief to the Marquesas. It was by far the biggest ship Opua had seen in many years and the steam train came down from Kawa Kawa and onto the wharf to meet it.

The ship dwarfed the village and people came from miles around. Whoever piloted the ship must have been a nervous wreck. I doubt any ship as large as this has been since and the railway line had been closed or more like abandoned from lack of maintenance.

The Opua Regatta was more a village fête than a regatta. It was great fun. The huge Maori war canoe or waka, made a visit. There were tug-of-war competitions, rowing competitions and even a dog swimming race. The dog swimming race was Ken and Joss's speciality. Their black Labrador, Dan, had once been a great champion. But now he was a little past his prime. He made a noble effort, swam the wrong way and came last, never mind.

Jean and I shared a table on the wharf with two other sailors and displayed our shells, turtle shells and the turtle jewellery I had made. We did rather well. Ken and Joss took the nicest of the turtle shells and it still hangs in their lounge.

There was a note in the post office advertising preserving jars. Jean and I went to the address. The old house had a pantry with shelves full of lovely preserving jars. The old lady had passed away so the jars were not wanted and anyone interested could have them for free. We had to drag Joss out with her car to go and collect them. In the end, we left the quart jars with Joss. We took the two dozen pint jars and passed on more to Jamie and Marg on *Ave del Mar.*

Marge had also become good friends of Ken and Joss. Ken had a Model A Ford plus another in bits. Jamie bought another. They were very unreliable and always overheating. I preferred Joss's little Austin Mini.

My fancy Nikonos underwater camera which I had bought in the USA, had been returned to Liverpool with Brian when he left us in Costa Rica. Once it was repaired, my mother sent it out to us in New Zealand. We waited and waited but it never arrived. Eventually we contacted Whangarei, the main town. It had arrived there but they hadn't sent it on to us in Opua and after three months had sent it back to Britain by ship! That story finishes in Sydney where I heard of someone flying out from London. They were happy to bring out the camera so my mother posted it to them in London. The camera was lost in the post between Liverpool and London never to be seen again.

We occasionally bumped into Eric and Pascal. They had been in the Marquesas with us on a very small Breton sailing fishing boat. Pascal was learning to make sails, working with Claire Jones who had a small sail loft near Russell. Claire agreed a good price and made a new mainsail for us. She had to extend the floor into the garden to do the job but the result was good and only NZ$800 which was US$400 It made a major hole in our piggy bank but the old main sail just wasn't going to get us across the Tasman Sea.

January had been lovely weather but even then interspersed with windy wet fronts coming up from the Southern Ocean. By March it was getting cold and we had some howling gales out of the northeast. By the time April came, we were preparing to leave.

We had *Sea Loone* hauled out at Ashby's yard. Jean had painted the top sides and then anti-fouled the bottom. I helped but needed to spend most of my time under the engine. There was some serious corrosion on the sump from the sea water dripping down from the raw water pump I did what I could and then fitted a flexible coupling between the gearbox and the propeller shaft. This involved a bit of engineering. The engine by this time was off its beds and in the middle of the cabin. It all went together well again in the end and we were back in the water but were another NZ$800 poorer.

It's not easy leaving places like Opua; so many people to say goodbye to. Ken had finished his dovecot so we saw it put in place and he gave us a sack of fresh fruit. Lou, the customs man had agreed to pick up our shotgun from the police in Whangarei and then clear us on April 11th, together with two other boats.

We motored down to the wharf and tied up to wait for customs. Susan Hiscock saw us from their mooring across the river. She rowed over to give us some sailing magazines to read which was nice of her. Ken arrived with his dog, Dan and a load of goodies for the trip. So it was midday by the time we could leave and motor down towards Russell.

Out in the bay it was rough so we headed in among the islands to find a calm anchorage. Jean went ashore and gathered a bucket full of pipis so she cooked chowder for dinner. The next day the weather was as bad if not worse. On 14th April we set out to try and at least get to Whangaroa. We stopped for lunch behind Cavalli Island and then carried on into another little bay where we had a rotten night and nearly dragged onto the beach.

The next day we made it into Whangaroa bashing through really rough seas. We anchored in Owanga Bay the sixth anchorage since leaving. We had seen more coastline than all the last six months. It continued blowing. We might as well have been in Scotland. The sky was dull and overcast and it rained and it blew. So we waited.

In search of bread and maybe a paper, we scrambled over the hill to the Kingfisher Lodge where we were hoping to find a shop. No such luck, but we did find a telephone booth at the end of the dock. This could be used by yachts arriving and wanting clearance. A notice gave telephone number for customs in Whangarei. It was a long way for them to come.

Once when we were on the farm with the Rigdens, the telephone had rung but they had ignored it. It was a party line and they were brr/brr...not brrr/brrr/brrr. We thought to ring Ken and Joss to say how we were or rather were not progressing. I wasn't sure about winding the handle but as soon as we picked up the phone, the lady asked what number we wanted. I told her where we were and she replied that she knew exactly where we were... amazing!

On April 23 1985 we set off again. The wind had at last dropped and the forecast was SW at ten knots. We still had a few miles to go to Cape Rheinga, the northern tip of New Zealand and then we had almost 1,000 miles to go due west across the Tasman Sea to Sydney.

We motored out into a choppy sea, the wind had died to almost nothing. There was a yacht and a fishing boat nearby so we had a miserable night keeping watch. It was freezing cold.

Next day we passed the Cape. The wind had swung to the East and we passed the Three Kings Islands to the north. The sky was now brilliant blue and again we were surrounded by seabirds including the black-browed albatross and a few immature wandering albatrosses which were huge. The wind picked up and we streamed the log behind us. We were making five knots under the genoa alone. Sydney here we come!

The Tasman crossing took us only eleven days. The wind swung behind us and blew constantly, but often a little too much. We ran with the main and genoa or just the genoa. But when the genoa tore across one seam, we continued with the medium jib. A big swell built up behind us but there was also a swell coming up from the South creating a washing machine effect. Huge lumps of water reared up in all directions and we rolled and pitched like crazy. It was three days before we settled to the movement.

I spent hours watching the albatrosses which followed us. They effortlessly sped along the front of a wave, rocketed up, turned and raced back. The adult wandering albatross with an eleven foot wingspan was truly awesome.

As we approached the Australian coast, the sky cleared a little and the sun actually shone. The satellite navigator which had broken down in the Pacific and had spent months in the repair shop in Auckland was still reluctant to tell us where we were. It did indicate we were getting pushed south by a prevailing current so we altered course a little north. Then on May 4th, as the sun came up, we could see the imposing cliffs of The Heads, the entrance to Sydney Harbor.

All the previous night we had seen the glow of the city. Now, as we turn through the Heads, we could see it emerging. After 1,100 miles the wind which had blown us along, died. We motored into Watsons Bay where we had to wait for customs, immigration and quarantine. We picked up a buoy and customs and immigration soon arrived on their launch but they wouldn't come aboard before the doctor had made sure we didn't have any nasty diseases. He eventually arrived, passed us fit and then we did the rest of the paperwork. We still had to go into the city the following day to acquire a cruising permit from the Small Boat office, whatever that was.

By lunchtime we were ashore, walked over the cliffs and then sat in the garden of a pub for a well-deserved pint of beer. Australia, we had arrived!

In New Zealand we had applied for Australian visas. They allowed us six months and we could extend them for a further six. They were of course tourist visas but we had only US$960 left in the piggy bank so we would have to look for work in that year. This would hopefully give us enough to carry us back up to the islands and on to Africa. Australia and New Zealand have an agreement that their citizens can each work in the other's country. In fact Bondi Beach was known as "Little New Zealand" so we decided to be New Zealanders, if anyone asked.

First we had to finish off doing the paperwork and get our cruising permit. We had to show that we had AU$1000 per month for the six months. The girl in the office was just learning the job fortunately. I had some old bank statements. They were all for the same money which was no longer in the bank, but she added them up and then we gave her a very inflated value of the pound against the Australian dollar. The US dollars were then added to the total and the girl agreed that we were rich enough for a permit.

We had motored into the harbor and were now anchored in Rushcutters Bay just around the corner from the opera house. At the head of the bay was the Cruising Yacht Club of Australia (CYC). They were actually more into racing than cruising and so not very friendly towards us. To the left was a park with sandstone seawall and all around us were expensive looking apartment blocks and high-rise luxury flats.

Of course we were not allowed to anchor here and in fact the only place allowed was a no man's land way up the harbor. Over the next month we looked around different places but eventually realized that Rushcutters Bay was the best proposition. Occasionally, the harbor police asked us to move but as long as we didn't put washing out to dry or have wild parties, they never got serious.

In the first month we both dashed around looking for work but at the same time, lived a very busy social life. There were already a couple of foreign boats anchored in the bay including *Cygnus*, the 65-foot Swan we had coconut-crabbed with in Suvarov and *Jellicle*, Mike Bailes' Folk Boat that we knew from Opua. Within a few days, Allen Dunshae arrived from Opua. After being towed back twice into Opua, he had finally got round the north of New Zealand and aimed for Sydney. When I say aimed that's exactly what he did. Other than the compass, he had no navigation tools.

He had a French girl as crew. She admitted to having been very nervous but was relieved when they finally saw the Australian coast. The entrance to Sydney Harbor, the Heads, came up right on the bow. Brilliant, although I realized years later it had been pure luck.

When you meet sailors, especially those that have been around a while, there are always stories. So among this small group in Rushcutters Bay, we had some crackers. One evening, Jean and I went ashore to the yacht club and there, tied up in the marina, was a large steel yacht flying a Trinidad flag. Trinidad yachts were not common. I only knew of one. So when I looked at the name of this boat and saw that it was the same *Hummingbird*. The *Hummingbird* I knew was a small wooden ketch, it had to be related.

I had been given an introduction to Harold La Borde and his wife Kirailan by my friends in the Virgin Islands. I had also been given the book Harold had written. But we had never visited Trinidad so had never met. They had built a small wooden ketch in Trinidad in 1959 and sailed it to England. They arrived in Falmouth after fifty days. At the time it was an amazing feat. With the publicity and the book they became famous Trinidadian's.

After that, they built another boat and sailed around the world. Now they were taking two years off from their government jobs to do it all a third time.

Mike Bailes had been a submariner during the war. With his Navy pension he had set sail from England in the early 1950s in his wooden Folk Boat. He had spent time in the Caribbean skippering huge exotic schooners out of English Harbour. He passed into the Pacific Ocean where he had spent the last I don't know how many years.

He spoke Tongan and was on the Kings cocktail list. To be invited to the palace in Nuku'alofa was comparable with being invited to Buckingham Palace. He had also taught navigation to the Vanuatu Navy. The boom on his boat was still a tree branch cut for him in 1950 in northern Spain. His original boom had broken crossing the Bay of Biscay and the Lord of the Manor had sent his woodman out to find a replacement in the forest.

When we walked into the bar and saw Mike sitting next to a dark skinned guy it had to be Harold. They had known each other in the Caribbean. We drank a lot of beer and swapped a lot of stories

An old girlfriend of mine in Liverpool had moved to Australia, married a prawn fisherman and was living in Perth. Her brother had followed her out and was living in Sydney. We had been in touch with Colin and he had agreed to let us use his address for our mail. He and his wife entertained us, showed us around the city, and helped us in our search for employment.

Colin was involved in the wine trade and was an auctioneer. One memorable evening, he collected us from the boat and we drove down to Bondi Beach. We sat in the car watching the huge waves coming in, had fish and chips just like home, and washed it all down with a half-finished bottle of very expensive wine left from a wine tasting he had been involved with at lunchtime.

Finding work was not proving too easy. We had done a little casual work but needed a lot more. Eventually towards the end of May Jean found a job in a fish mongers in Edgecliffe, just up the road. She spent the day scaling and filleting fish and trying to work out how the complicated till worked when she served customers.

Meanwhile, I had applied for jobs welding broken containers, pile-driving, making surfboards and what sounded a really nice job making models for architects and shipbuilders. I failed. But there was a government job center down the way and there I saw a really good job advertised as a forensic scientist.

I took the card to the desk and asked for more information. The girl looked on the computer screen and made a telephone call. From the conversation I understood that the job was more or less taken. I asked if I could talk to the person but she shook her head and put the phone down. The next day, there was a job for a chemist in a paper mill but no more details. This time I changed my tactics when I handed the card over to the girl I moved my seat so I could see the screen. The company was called APM, Australian Paper Mills.

Before she could make the phone call I told her I had changed my mind and didn't think the job would suit. Then I went and found a telephone kiosk round the corner and phoned the company. I was put in touch with the chief engineer and arranged for an interview in two days time. I then shot off to the secondhand clothes shop and bought trousers, shirt, tie and a pair of beautiful handmade Italian leather shoes, all for a few dollars

APM had a huge factory on the north shore of Botany Bay. The one paper machine was half a mile long in a long building with a cloud in the roof. They had their own power station for electricity.

I met Athol McCoy, the chief engineer. He showed me around. I was to take over from a young chemical engineer graduate who was taking off on a backpacking trip around the world. He himself had only been a temporary stand-in for a sick guy. I was also only to be temporary, a job for three months.

After my experiences in America, I knew not to be bashful, so I gave Athol the story of my academic brilliance, my status as the Food & Agriculture Organization (FAO) expert on water chemistry and so on. I was shown the laboratory which didn't have anything fancy but still I was a bit rusty and nervous.

It was agreed I should start work the following Monday and, with difficulty, I persuaded Athol that it would be good if I could watch work in progress on the Friday, before Dave ,the engineer left. In fact, I spent Thursday and Friday with Dave following the routine stuff he did, in particular monitoring the boiler waters in the power station. I was fairly confident as I stepped into my laboratory on Monday morning.

So by the first week in June we were both working. The pay wasn't particularly good for either of us, but making paper was fascinating and I was going to enjoy getting into it. Jean was already involved in her job and as the owner also ran a restaurant, in the evening she had the possibility of more work there occasionally.

Commuting for me was not easy. Jean would row me to the seawall at 6.15. in the morning and I'd scramble up. I would then walk through the park and up the hill behind St. Vincent's Hospital from where I would get a bus which would eventually drop me off close to work.

My laboratory, near the power station, was in a large deserted administrative building across the street, but quite a distance from where the paper was made. Not too far from the power station, there were a lot of empty buildings and abandoned machinery. Years ago, they made a much larger range of paper. Now they only made stuff for making cardboard boxes and only used one machine.

However, as I said, the machine was impressive. The paper spun off at twenty miles an hour. The main raw material was wastepaper which was gobbled up at twenty tons per hour. The huge reels of paper were sent off to be made into cardboard boxes. I was told that the paper could be made into a box, the box filled, delivered, and emptied and returned to us as wastepaper, all within ten days!

Apart from the power plant I was involved in monitoring the composition of the stock as it went through the pulping process and mechanically testing the final product. Occasionally, they needed the paper died a certain color and I experimented to see which dyes were most suitable and least costly. I also solved other minor problems so really got quite involved.

Three months went by and I was asked to stay on for three more and then three more. I was becoming a fixture. Jean at the same time was very involved in the shop where there always seem to be some crisis or other. She had become really good at catching blue swimmer crabs under the boat using traps she had made. They went straight to the fish shop. Still very much alive and very angry, I'm surprised they didn't nip her fingers off and those of a few of the customers.

After four months, we invested in an old car, a Holden Kingswood. It cost us $1,000 but made my commuting easy and we could travel around a bit on our days off.

We had met in Australian couple in the Caribbean, Rob and Lynn. They were sailing their boat *Brolga of Kiama* around the world and were now back in Australia. They were living just north of Wollongong not far from Sydney. Their property was on the escarpment above Kiama

There is a narrow coastal plain running south from Sydney way down past Kiama. This is backed by a steep escarpment and then its dry semi-desert landscape extending inland. The escarpment is wooded and lush with streams and waterfalls. We first visited Rob traveling down by train, but with the car we could visit more easily.

I had been amazed by the birdlife in Sydney from the first day when a rainbow lorikeet had landed on the table with my first beer. Commuting through the park there was always a flock of gallah's, amazing rose- colored parrots and every day a flock of huge noisy sulphur crested cockatoos flew over the boat. I'd seen a pair of kookaburra's perched on the wind indicators at the top of a mast in the marina zooming around and around and laughing their heads off.

At Rob and Lynn's place there were lots of birds and other animals. There were king parrots, strange birds called frog mouths, bowerbirds and wallabies in the field. There was also a wombat keen on digging up the foundations of the house and a huge carpet snake living in the roof.

One weekend we borrowed a canoe and paddled down into a gorge full of red-bellied black snakes. We camped under our old mainsail but hardly got a wink of sleep from all the strange noises. On another evening, with Rob, we sat quietly on the side of the small stream and watched a duckbilled platypus that was a serious highlight for me, the zoologist!

Our small group of foreign yachts remained fairly constant. We had all found work, those that needed to. So we ate together occasionally or had a few beers after work. The scruffy steel yacht with an American flag had a New Zealand guy and his French girlfriend living on board. They had already been anchored in the bay when we first rrived. Their story is worth recording.

Mark and his mate were hitchhiking south through Central America. Bernadette and her friend were doing the same thing so they joined forces. In Ecuador, they crossed over the mountains and arrived in a small village on the headwaters of the Rio Negro which flows into the Amazon. They borrowed an ax and made a crude raft in order to float down the river to Manaus where the Rio Negro meets the Amazon.

Apparently the trip was a horror story. The wind kept blowing them into the bank and Rob caught malaria but eventually they made it to Manaus. There they found a barge they could camp on as it was towed down to the sea. Eventually they got to the coast where Mark and Bernadette were taken on as crew on a yacht sailing to Panama then on to Tahiti, French Polynesia. In Tahiti, they met a disillusioned American who, having sailed from California, wanted to go home. Mark and Bernadette agreed to deliver the boat to Sydney for him. They did it slowly, taking more than two years via numerous islands in the central Pacific before eventually arriving in Sydney. Here they were still on the boat.

The months rolled by, the weather got warm but we still had vicious fronts coming up the coast now and again. They were called Southerly Busters and were pretty well forecasted. I watched one arrive. Standing on the deck I saw the rolling line of cloud appearing over the hospital. You could see gusts being thrown up over the buildings and yet we were still facing northeast in a fair breeze. The wind hit us like a wall directly from behind. *Sea Loone* took off. By the time we had passed over the anchor and the chain pulled taut, we were probably doing three or four knots. We jerked to stop and the boat spun round into forty odd knots of wind.

A small French yacht which had just arrived, didn't stop. It just tripped its anchor and was off into the harbour heading for the zoo on the north shore. We had to chase after it

On another occasion Australia demonstrated another of its meteorological wonders. The wind switched to the west and Sydney got a superhot blast of air from the desert. The temperature soared into the 40's centigrade and a lot of the city came to a standstilll. So did our paper machine. Luckily, we never experienced the golf ball-sized hailstones which are another feature of Australian weather.

We spent Christmas with Rob and Lynn. Then they returned with us to Sydney on Boxing Day to watch the start of the Sydney-Hobart race. Among the spectator boats it was bedlam. I got an amazing photo of the yacht passing next to us with the deck full of very drunk, very well endowed ladies, waggling their bare boobs at us.

On one trip south, the engine in the car developed serious problems. We used a gallon of oil to get home, leaving a trail of black smoke. So just like the camper van in Florida, we had problems. In the end I bought a secondhand engine for $150 and paid a local garage another $250 to put it in.

Ever since leaving Plod the parrot in Bora Bora we had talked about another. I particularly fancied a sulphur crested cockatoo but we had wanted to get a baby we could train. In January we heard there was a bird available in a local pet store. When we arrived there was just one left out of a nest full of seven and so Bruce the cockatoo joined us on the boat. He was fully fledged with only a few fluffy baby feathers left. We stuffed food down his throat for a week or so but then he managed on his own. Amazingly he only made mewing noises. I had been worried that inside boat he could be too noisy. So it was whingeing Bruce. He'd fly from his perch in the early morning and landing in bed with us, turned on his back to have his stomach tickled. This is a bird with an almost three-foot wing span.

Unfortunately he only stayed with us for a couple of months. The problem was, he couldn't be left alone. He would get bored and then wandered around the boat destroying things. I made a cage but he hated it. Crashing around he lost all his tail feathers and one day would have really hurt himself.

We had to take him back to the pet shop. I rowed ashore with Bruce on Jean's shoulder but half way he took off, landing in the water. We washed him down with freshwater but still, by the time we arrived in the pet shop he was still very wet and bedraggled and had no tail. The man was horrified when he saw the state of Bruce. He was sure we had mistreated him and was wary of getting bitten. I explained the problems, picked Bruce up by one-wing and shook him. I knew he always enjoyed this. Then I put him on Jean's shoulder. An old lady was watching. She begged us to let her have him and promised to really look after him. And this is how Bruce got his new home. I was upset that we'd had to let Bruce go but, I think, looking back, Jean was a lot more upset.

Closely following this, two more things happened which may have affected Jean. Firstly, *Whoosh*, a yacht owned by an American couple we had known for a long time, arrived in Sydney. They were to have a baby and sure enough after some difficulties, a little baby daughter arrived. Then Mark and Bernadette who were planning an overland trip across China and Mongolia on the way to France, announced that Bernadette was pregnant.

Jean was adamant that she did not want children. Her mother had had serious mental health problems since Jean was born and from an early age Jean had had the responsibilities of looking after her mother, father and younger brother. Maybe this was what had drawn her to study medicine. She was sure that her mother's problems were genetic.

Anyway as the time approached to leave, Jean began to complain of feeling depressed. For her to complain of anything was unusual. I persuaded her to see a doctor about it, which she did. But nothing came of it and no more was said.

We had discovered Tom Joel's boat yard in Middle Harbor. Tom lived in a bungalow on the water's edge overlooked by millionaire homes. He had a floating dock from which he hired out aluminium dinghies and an old boat shed with a railway running up into it. The railway was far too small for us but *Whoosh* used it and we tied to the dock to get some welding done by Mick the welder from work. Then, with the mast plucked out in another yard across the way, we used Joels' yard to paint it and oil the new galvanized rigging we had bought.

I was still at work and in February had a real fright. Colin, our old friend, had a phone call from the police asking to talk to me. He contacted Jean at the fish shop and she called APM to tell me that I had to present myself at Lane Cove police station immediately.

I drove down to the police station and was given the "third degree", until eventually they explained. A car similar to mine had been parked where mine normally was in Rushcutters Bay. The driver had abducted, or attempted to abduct, a young girl. Fortunately, the description of the driver was nowhere near my good looks.

In March we had a serious problem making paper. There were complaints from the box makers of a twisting diagonally across the paper. I spent weeks on the problem, changing different factors, taking samples. I finished writing a paper on the problem explaining that the machine had to be run differently from the normal. The paper came with graphs and diagrams. Most people were not happy running differently but it worked. Still I was the upstart, a zoologist, not a paper technologist. The gurus in Melbourne got involved. It seemed a good time to leave.

Athol McCoy who had first employed me, and who had helped me enormously, was keen for me to become a permanent employee. I have never been able to explain properly to him why I could not be called out if they had an emergency. Even without a telephone he could still send a taxi but I had been adamant that I was not available. So in the last week I invited him and his wife to dinner. They had to walk across the park and clamber down into the dinghy for me to ferry them out to the boat.

So the call-out mystery was solved, taxis are not amphibious. I then pointed out the lack of stars on the flag and the "Liverpool" on the transom. I had no work permit and staying in Australia was no longer possible. Our visitors' visas were expiring.

I suppose Athol could have been annoyed that I had worked illegally but they never really asked me if I was Australian or a New Zealander. In fact he didn't care and was still keen that I stayed on and he was sure that, with APM behind me, I could easily and quickly get a work permit and even citizenship. But for Jean and I, we now had a full piggy bank and half a world to see.

The last couple of weeks in Middle Harbor was spent working on the boat. The mast was refinished, gleaming white and with shiny new rigging. The new stainless steel stanchions fabricated from pipe found in the scrapyard looked good and I had found a secondhand genoa for less than $300 to replace the old one. If it gave out again we now had seven different headsails jammed into the aft locker. None was new. In fact three were originals from our Milford Haven days, having been made in 1963. Jean often called it "sewing our way around the world", rather than "sailing around the world".

We took a day sail out through the Heads into the Tasman with Colin and his wife, but they both looked very unwell as soon as we got out into the big seas. So we scooted back into Manley and opened a bottle of wine.

May 1986 had arrived. We had spent a year in Sydney harbor I had my final pay from APM which together with holiday pay and other such things, came out to far more than we expected. We took $10,000 to the bank, deposited it for on a one-year term at 15%. The interest rate was worryingly high but it seemed like a good idea. I then cheekily filled in tax forms to reclaim some of my income tax. I didn't claim that I had children but I claimed everything else. I left the tax forms with Rob & Lynn to be sent in later in the year.

On May 6, we cleared out for New Caledonia and motored out of Middle Harbor and through the heads into the Tasman Sea.

8

Our plans were fairly open. We were going first to New Caledonia, a thousand miles to the north east; then on to Vanuatu and from there on to the Solomon Islands where we might stay through the cyclone season. From there we could either return to Australia or carry on to Papua New Guinea, along its north coast

We started much the same way as we had from New Zealand. We had lost our sea legs in the harbour, the sea outside was doing its Tasman washing machine action, and the wind was on the nose. So we sailed north a few miles and ducked into Pittwater to wait for something better.

Two days later we set off again. I wanted to get back east before heading north. So we beat our way towards New Zealand. It was cold and miserable in lumpy seas and rain squalls. The wind tried to push us back to Sydney, the current tried to push us south to Tasmania. For a week we beat to windward. We were bashing into the seas and burying the bow in the swishing waves that washed down the deck and sometimes over the cabin top.

We took a day off and dropping the head sail, hove to on just the main sail. The bouncing up and down stopped and there was no more water on the deck. Jean cooked a good meal opening one of our jars of beef stew and I laid back and read a book. The next day off beating again.

Turning north, the wind still headed us but we slowly made progress and the seas turned from grey to blue. The air temperature was rising. Two weeks out with clear skies above, I took a sight, my first for days. I put our calculated position into the satellite navigator and came out with a reliable fix. We were half way. With cloudy skies, with the log spinner regularly getting caught in the fishing line, and the Sat Nav being its usual unreliable self, we were not very precise with our navigation.

On May 22, listening to Radio Australia and later to the BBC, we heard that Cyclone Namu had caused devastation in the Solomons and a number of people had died. From the Solomons I wondered where it had gone. New Caledonia would normally be on its route and then where we were located, just to the south. We had a nervous few days but thank goodness never saw anything.

And so eventually, feeling thoroughly battered, we saw the lighthouse on the reef marking the main pass into Noumea, the capital of New Caledonia. Amidee lighthouse is a classic tower sitting on a small reef cay. We could see its tall tower gleaming white in the early morning light. Across the huge lagoon, the mainland was a bit of a surprise. It was steep and mountainous but bare. The closer you get to it, the more it looks like an enormous slag heap.

Threading through the reefs in the lagoon, we passed between two low, dry, headlands to find ourselves in the calm, enclosed harbour of Noumea. We anchored off the dilapidated concrete wharf. A three-masted brig was tied to the wharf, together with a number of work boats. It looked very much like an industrial sort of town.

Planning the trip through to Vannatu and the Solomons, we thought we would have the islands to ourselves. The yachts crossing the Pacific this season would not be arriving in this area until later in the year. However, we hadn't realized that this was a favorite cruising ground for Australian yachts and already there were a number that had crossed from Queensland and anchored in the harbour. Just like in the Caribbean, messing around in boats was becoming more and more popular.

There was nothing in Noumea to hold us so we cleared out for Vanuatu, intending to stop here and there along the coast. We headed east along the south coast beating our way through the Canal Woodin between Ile Quen and the mainland. We ducked into Prony Bay, a huge convoluted bay into which a number of rivers flowed and where there seemed to be a number of places of interest.

The whole area had once been covered by thick forest, mainly huge valuable kouri trees. The forest had disappeared and then the miners had arrived. They discovered one of the world's largest deposits of nickel. Then they also discovered copper, chromium and other heavy metals. The whole area was a treasure trove of different ores and it seemed to us every square meter had been turned over. The hillsides were basically red with blue, gray, purple and white patches where the different metals had been extracted and soil erosion had taken over

Once we were anchored we went ashore. First, we climbed up to another lighthouse high up on a hill overlooking Havana Pass. This formed the lagoon's eastern entrance through which we would pass when we left. The view of the barrier reef with the surf pounding it and the small reefy islands dotted over the lagoon sitting in turquoise water, was beautiful. We sat mesmerized for a while as we caught our breath from the climb.

What little vegetation there was, was very interesting. There was a primative pine tree with very short branches, strange flowering bushes, and in one volcanic hole in the rocky terrain, an amazing pitcher plant. It was surrounded by buzzing flies which it had attracted and wanted to eat.

Cyclone Namu had curved past New Caledonia dropping vast amounts of rain. At the top of the bay a substantial river flowed down. It's bed had been scoured by the floods and we spent hours picking up beautiful smooth round pebbles, a lot of them greenstone, a type of jade. Had we stayed much longer we'd have sunk *Sea Loone*. Later we had to jettison the majority of the stones.

We also "fossicked" around some of the old mining sites finding old railways and boilers. Everywhere had been worked out and nature was trying to reclaim the mess.

There were a number of cowrie shells which had been affected by the heavy metals in the water. Some have turned black, melanic; others were misshapen, rostrate. They were unusual and had some value to collectors so we spent time looking for them .We failed. We did however find the hot spring but it was having a cool spell so not very interesting.

Two weeks seem to fly by before we finally pulled up the anchor and headed out through Havana Pass. The ocean was fairly calm and the tide ebbing so we were out in deep water with no problems

Vanuatu is north east so we were hard on the wind again but the seas were dark blue and warm. We passed Ouvea Atoll without stopping and a few days later saw a plume of black smoke on the horizon. It had to be the very active volcano on Tanna.

June 23rd we sailed into Port Villa, the capital of Vanuatu which had until recently been the New Hebrides. Britain and France had shared the administation of the islands. They called it a condominium. There were still two Governors, two hospitals, two colleges and so on.

The cost of living with our Australian dollars, was high. The only remarkable thing I recall was a day in the market. A lady sitting on the grass, had a number of piles of black fur in front of her. When I knelt down to look, I realize there were flying foxes with furry black bodies large leathery wings. They were a local delicacy. In Tonga they are protected and only the King can eat them, like Britain with the royal swans.

Jean met an old University friend now working as a doctor in the British hospital. She gave us some advice about malaria but also explained some of her problems working as a doctor. She had recently been to Tanna, the island with the volcano. She had to take with her a couple of translators. She spoke pidgin and some words of other languages. But on even a small island like Tanna, there were a dozen languages, often completely different from each other.

We sailed north no longer having to push to windward. The large island of Malakula has a deep protected bay in the south called Port Sandwich. We anchored off the dilapidated wharf. There was nobody around. It seemed nobody lived on the coast and there were no villages behind the beach. They all lived in villages in the jungle, presumably in isolated villages, hence the languages.

We had been there for a few days, when we were joined by another yacht sailing under the Polish flag. The odd group of people on board were looking for the Little Namba's. The Big Namba's were by now famous. They lived on an island across the way.. They wore strange penis sheaths and jumped off high platforms with vines tied to their legs, an early form of bungee jumping.

The Little Namba's lived on Malakula somewhere up in the jungle. The crew hadn't had any success so far in finding them and were looking a bit worse for wear from trying to penetrate the forest.

Jean and I took the dinghy to the top of the bay, pushed our way through the mangroves and found solid ground. But there was no sign of any paths. The vegetation formed a green wall full of thorns, mosquitoes and sand flies.

On a dilapidated jetty at the entrance to the bay there was a crude sign warning of sharks. We found out later why the sign was there. The bay is a breeding ground for tiger sharks and the previous year an Australian girl had her baby snatched from her arms while she was washing her from the dinghy.

Further north we did find a village and anchored close by. When I dived in the water I found a gravel spit which had to be the perfect spot for an octopus. Sure enough, a pair of eyes was watching me over his castle wall. I dragged him up on the beach to beat him on a rock to tenderize the meat. The whole village came out to watch. I think they were a little surprised the white man could find a good dinner right on their doorstep.

Luganville, the town on Espiritu Santo has a deep water anchorage, too deep for us. So we sailed a little north and went round into Palikulo Bay. There were a couple of other yachts there already. It's a long walk from there into town so we tried hitchhiking. This worked well apart from the fact that there were virtually no cars.

Luganville is a strange little town strung out along the coast road. Everywhere there are huge rusty Nissan huts and hangers, half collapsed. It was a major staging port for the Americans during WWII in their move against the Japanese in the Solomon Islands.

Our first stop was the butchers. It'd been recommended to us by Mike Bailes in Sydney. Lo and behold, when we entered the shop there was Mike himself. We asked him where was *Jellicle* and he said he'd show us. A short walk down the road was a small bridge over a creek. There was *Jellicle* sitting in the muddy creek. When Harold la Borde met Mike in English Harbour in 1960, Mike was skippering a 133-foot schooner called *Te Vega* in and out of English Harbour, Marigot and other tight hurricane holes in the Caribbean. He obviously still had a taste for such antics.

The beef was good and cheap and for the next few days, Jean was busy with our pressure cooker. When we left Mike he was busy applying for citizenship in New Zealand. We cleared out for the Solomon Islands.

In Shark Bay, a few miles up the coast, we were invited one evening to a barbecue on the beach with an Australian couple. They had caught a good-sized coral trout and had it wrapped up in foil on the fire. It was a pleasant evening. The food was delicious and the wine flow, but then something really weird happened. A snake slithered out from under the upturned canoe that we were all sitting on and headed for the fire.

It was a sea snake and seemed mesmerized by the light the fire. They are deadly poisonous but have no fangs. So unless you let them chew you they are pretty harmless. I flicked him into the sea but he kept coming back. He was then joined by two more. Eventually, with difficulty, we moved them down the beach away from the light and they swam away.

The Banks Islands, north of the Vanuatu, but still part of it, are volcanic cones sticking up out of the ocean. They are covered in thick forest and one island has a beautiful waterfall cascading into a deep pool right on the beach. Quite a large river drops vertically down from maybe twenty feet. It was an idyllic anchorage.

A local couple had built a small palm-leaf hut close to the waterfall and had cleared a piece of ground by the river to grow sweet potatoes, taro and such like. One evening, they invited us over to eat with them as it was their national day. We arrived with a cake and a bottle of rum. They fed us with freshwater prawns and then a stew with bowls of black fur floating in it. I couldn't find any leathery wings but I'm sure we were eating fruit bat or flying fox!

A few days later, the couple had gone off down the coast and disaster struck. Sometime in the middle of the night, our dinghy and new outboard engine were stolen. We searched the coast but we were not going to find anything I was really pissed off.

There was no point in hanging around so we sped north through some really rough seas and strong winds to arrive in Graciosa Bay in the Santa Cruz islands, the first islands of the Solomons.

Throughout the Solomons there is a major problem finding shallow enough water to anchor in. It seems to be either one hundred feet deep or too shallow with live coral reef. In Graciosa Bay, we drifted off the village to clear in and then found a small shallow patch of water in a bay not far from town and opposite a mission school. We were back to rowing ashore in the Avon inflatable dinghy.

The mission school was interesting. The children came from all over the island. With no way of commuting, they boarded. But it wasn't at all like England. They were busy weaving palm fronds to lace into a framework for a new dormitory. They were digging away in the gardens which provided virtually all the food and there was a contingent of children in the kitchen cooking for the hundred or more students. I assume that some stage they took time off for lessons. There were a couple of very enthusiastic young American VSO's helping out.

Having seen customs we were given only two weeks to arrive in Honiara, the capital, to do the rest of the paperwork. So we had to keep moving and I particularly wanted to stop in Marau Sound on the south coast of Guadalcanal. Having had some contact with shell collectors in New Zealand, we got in touch with the Shell Collectors Club in Sydney and there we had met Ron Moylan. Ron had an architect's business and lived quite close to Joel's boat yard. He was a serious shell collector. His wife's family lived in Marau Sound. Marina's father was an Australian and his wife a Solomon Islander. The father ran a coastal shipping business from the sound.

Within Marau Sound, among the numerous small islands is a tiny lagoon with a very narrow entrance. We anchored within feet of the shore off one island and on the island opposite was an interesting A-frame house where an elderly English couple had decided to retire. Ignoring the flies during the day and one night an invasion of huge moths, it was a paradise. I saw my first eclectus parrots, the male iridescent green, the female bright red and purple.

There were numerous other birds including another type of cockatoo and one day, while tramping through the mangrove swamp, I saw an enormous butterfly. It was far bigger than the blue morphos of Costa Rica. I later discovered that the Solomons Island's aveoptera are among the largest butterflies in the world.

We met Ron Moylan's family one day and were told he was coming out for holiday soon. Having met Marina, we now met her sister. The two girls were stunningly beautiful with a flashing eyes and long long dark hair.

Sailing was really hazardous especially at night. Cyclone Namu had washed what seemed to be half the forest into the sea. Hitting some of these tree trunks would be like hitting a reef. We had already clobbered one on our way from Graciosa Bay. As we approach Honiara, we were passing huge floating islands of tangled vegetation. So after a sleepless night sailing up the coast of Guadalcanal we were glad to arrive.

Anchoring off the yacht club involved throwing the anchor into very deep water and then backing up to the beach and running stern lines ashore. We managed this with a little help from two local boats that we had slid between.

The Solomons, like a lot of ex-British colonies, managed to make their paperwork a nightmare to clear-in. On top of that, they wanted one hundred American dollars light dues. Barbados had a similar thing only the lighthouses didn't work. Here in the Solomons, they didn't even exist!

With the paper work done we went off to the market. Half the stalls were only selling small piles of nuts and bunches of green leaves with piles of white powder. It was betel nut and it seemed like most of the population was addicted. Eating the nut entails chewing the leaves and the powder together with the nut, then spitting them out. So there were piles of bright red spit all over the pavement. The continuous chewing dyed the teeth red which wasn't at all attractive when they smiled. The story I was told was that people trek high up in the hills to tend the crops returning each evening. Chewing the betel nut gives them the stamina to do this each day without a break for food... maybe?

From Honiara we are we sailed across to the Floridas, a small group of islands which had once housed the capital .We had to make quite a long detour because of a barrage of tree trunks in the middle of the main channel. We anchored off a boatyard that was making large tuna boats in ferro-cement.

The boatyard was funded by the United Nations through the Food and Agricultural Organization, FAO. The management were New Zealanders and seemed very successful. The finished boats were used by the tuna factory right next door. I spent the day in the boatyard watching work progress on the two boats under construction. Of course it was something I knew about and I was intrigued to see how they had done things.

So it was late in the day when I returned to *Sea Loone*. Jean had been on board all day. When I climbed on board I found her lying in the bunk. I suddenly realized that she was not just asleep. She was completely comatose! Lying alongside her was an empty bottle of sleeping pills. I didn't even know the pills existed on the boat.

Christ Almighty! What do you do? Heart pumping, I grabbed her, shook her and sat her up. Her eyes opened. She bent down and threw up. Thank God for that! She was at least alive. I forced her to drink some water and she threw up again.

I spent the whole night keeping her awake, shaking her whenever she closed her eyes. She recovered rapidly and by the morning was fit enough for me to take her ashore where I hoped to find some professional help. The manager of the boatyard was sympathetic but could offer no assistance. So we up anchored and went back to Honiara. But even there, with doctors in a hospital, what you do?

Jean by this time was fully recovered. Fortunately, she must have thrown up most of the medicine before it got absorbed into her body. She was embarrassed, and apologetic but had never mentioned her depression since Australia or shown any indication of any problems. Taking the pills honestly hadn't improve the situation and, as I explained to her, she was going to have to get some professional help. Under no circumstances could we continue sailing on the boat with her maybe trying again and me having to watch her twenty four hours a day.

As a consequence, Jean contacted her parents and arranged to fly home to get some treatment. It was far from a perfect arrangement. Jean's Dad had retired to a small village in Anglesey and Jean's mother still went backwards and forwards to the hospital with schizophrenia. But on September 10th, Jean flew home. I was to sail back to Cairns, Australia and wait for her to return when she was recovered.

Suddenly I was a lone sailor. I quickly realized how much I had depended on Jean. In fact I had been living in the lap of luxury with the cooking, the cakes, pies. the washing and cleaning the painting etc Then of course there was Jean herself. She was a beautiful strong girl with not a bad word in her head for anyone!

Sitting alone then on *Sea Loone* in Honiara, I reflected on the last few years and realized that it was, in fact, almost exactly ten years since launching the boat in Morpeth dock, Birkenhead.

A lot of water had passed under the keel since then a lot of interesting places and people. Since the disastrous first trip out to the Caribbean, we had managed to find ways of making money. We had made serious improvements to *Sea Loone* since the early days. We had a new engine, electricity from our solar panel, the satellite navigator (which at least worked now and again) and the big thing, a lot more confidence in our ability to handle everything. I desperately hoped that Jean would get herself sorted out and come back on board and carry on sailing.

Fortunately for me there were two other yachts in Honaria both with people we had met when we first arrived. On a Thursday night at the yacht club they had Scottish dancing. Watching one Scotsman and a dozen half drunk Solomon Islanders skipping around over two crossed swords was memorable! Garth and his wife Joan on the yacht *Camelot* both Canadians, and Clark a German off *Asma* were equally amazed. The far-flung British Empire still has a few odd corners to hide in.

The wooden toe rail around *Sea Loone* was made from teak but it was rather thin and a few pieces had washed away or cracked. It was a mess. In the timber yard just out of town, I bought some planks of local hardwood called vasa. The planks were six inches wide and one inch thick. Two of the planks were twenty three feet long. I bought enough to go around and provide a capping piece. The whole last cost me twenty four Aussie dollars. A lorry delivered the wood down to the beach. I lashed it together and towed it out to the boat. A bright yellow pigment leached out of the wood when newly cut but fortunately it didn't stain.

Once on board, I up anchored and sailed back out to the Florida's where I had organized to have the wood cut to size and planed. I tied alongside a concrete tuna boat and the wood was taken off to the machine shop by a string of workers. I followed, feeling a bit like Livingston in Africa. Half an hour later the string of guys returned with the wood smooth, bright yellow and gorgeous.

There was a guy fitting new windows in a large scruffy steel yacht anchored close by. It was Brian Bailey, Ron Moylan's friend and shell collector. I was invited to dinner the following day when he was to return from Honiara with his charter guest. The following morning he had the windows back in and was rolling white paint on the top sides before leaving for town. When I rode over in the evening I was introduced to the charterer. He was another keen shell collector. He owned steel mills or something in Oregon.

Apparently Brian, already a well-known shell collector had flown to South Africa on hearing that a new species of cowrie shell had been found. He found his way to the Wild Coast south of Durban. Diving at night the first time, he found the rare shell. Then the following night he found a dozen. He stopped, phoned Oregon and made a deal. He was given an open checkbook to build the fifty foot yacht we were now sitting in. Brian built the yacht in Cape Town found a wife in Mauritius and has spent years in the Solomon finding shells and chartering to shell collectors. It was quite a story that Brian told me as we drank beer and watched the guest prepare the meal. The charter guest cook was the millionaire who had paid for the boat those years ago!

When I returned to Honaria, Ron Moylan was already there having flown in from Sydney on his way to Marau Sound. He helped me find Brian's mooring which I would use before leaving. A cruise ship was due to arrive and there also was to be a festival for National Day.

With the arrival of the cruise ship people arrived from the other islands with their native crafts. Woodcarvings from the Solomons are highly prized. The ebony carvings, nusa-nusa's, masks and bowls were beautiful and valuable. Not wanting to take their wares home unsold, pieces became more reasonable in price as the last tourist returned to the ship. So I spent a little money and acquired some nice keepsakes.

The National Day was highlighted for me by a dance group from Ontong Java, a reef atoll northeast of the main islands. The people there are Polynesian, utterly different from the crinkly haired, small dark-skinned Melanesians; and apparently they had not been subjugated by the "London Bible School" and the dress code of "Mother Hubbard". They were really big people and the ladies danced in grass skirts, bare-breasted. Watching such a huge unfettered boobs was for me, amazing. Some of the local people, their fellow Solomon Islanders, probably thought it was a dance conjured up by the very devil himself!

I found some potatoes and onions and some fruit in the market and then early next morning, I set off back south to Marau Sound from where I would set out to return to Australia.

It was my first time sailing alone. No one to help me look out, no one to pass comment with, no coffee and no bloody dinner unless I got busy myself. I beat out towards Malaita and then back. By morning I was close to the north passage into Marau Sound. By tea time, I was back in Tivanapupu. Not a long trip and no problems but the next trip alone was going to be very much longer.

In Australia we had bought a huge bag of T-shirts from charity shops. I also had a whole case of inedible tinned stew and, having bought another sewing machine, had a spare old Singer. I was hoping to barter this lot for shells and maybe resell these to make enough money to replace the outboard engine which had been stolen.

Talking with the locals who passed by in their dugout canoes, it was obvious that the rare valuable shells were well known in Marau Sound as was their value. So I decided to go for large pretty shells which I could sell to the tourist shops in Cairns. These were cheap and readily available. I put the word out that the following day I would be bartering the T-shirts, sewing machine and all. The word must have passed round the whole area really quickly. In the morning around a dozen dugout canoes and one huge fibreglass canoe with an outboard engine had arrived. The latter must of had a whole village on board.

They all tied up around *Sea Loone* and I pointed out one large helmet shell and offered a T-shirt. After five minutes of deciding which T-shirt he wanted, the deal was done but then one minute later he wanted to change his mind. This wasn't going to work, so we started again. I held up one T-shirt and asked all to put in a bid. The biggest glossiest shell won.

Things went swimmingly and soon I had the cockpit full of shells, helmet shells, trumpet shells, finger shells and so on. The beef stew went as well as the T-shirts and the final item, the sewing machine, went for ten large helmet shells and three Triton trumpets. The trumpet shells were to be delivered the next day. When they arrived they were still alive. They were taken away again to be cleaned, together with a few helmet shells which didn't smell too good.

I had a few meals with Charles and Melanie, the retired couple in the A-frame and when eventually the trade winds eased off to something less than a gale, I pulled up anchor and headed out, north around Bellona Island and then west across the Coral Sea.

The first few days were rough but at least we were running under blue skies. I soaked up so much sun that I thought they might not let me into Queensland.

The fishing was good but wasteful. I caught an eighty pound yellowfin tuna and must have only eaten one pound of it. Another smaller fish I fed to a huge hammerhead shark which was following me. I took photos as it grabbed the lumps of fish. I had taken in the spinner for the Walker log while doing this and lost it when I reset it. Stupid bugger. The spinner, a six- inch long bronze finish, was almost irreplaceable. The only other one I'd seen was in a museum in Victoria, British Columbia.

There wasn't likely to be much shipping en route but there were lots of coral reefs to steer around. I tried to get as much sleep as possible, knowing that tiredness was the cause of the loss of lot of single-handed boats. In fact, the last night I slept right through the alarm, skimmed past a reef and woke in broad daylight. When I shot out on deck I could see the light for the entrance through the Great Barrier Reef less than 10 miles ahead. Two more hours sleep, and I'd have woken with a crunch.

Late in the afternoon, I motored up the channel into Cairns and anchored across the river from the town, next to *Asma* and *Camelot*. I'd clear-in tomorrow after a good night's sleep. It was October 29th. I was twelve days out from Marau Sound.

After a wonderful night of uninterrupted sleep, I pulled up anchor and motored over to the wharf to clear-in. My new timber for the toe rail was lashed on the deck away from the dock. The huge box of shells sat on the aft deck.

The officials all arrived together and I ushered them quickly below. Customs was happy that I had nothing to declare. Immigration wanted to know why I had come back and did I want to stay. He was very unfriendly. I told him that I was now en route to Africa but Australia was in the way. It didn't help.

I was more worried about a man from the Ministry of Agriculture and Fisheries (MAF). He could confiscate my new wood and all my shells. However, I had kept a sack of large coconuts and asked if they were a problem, knowing full well they were. He whipped out a huge heavy-duty plastic bag, stuffed in the coconuts and sealed it up. Then they all marched ashore without looking any further. What a relief!

Within a week, I had made a deal with the shell shop in the market and, with the money, bought a secondhand 2 hp outboard engine, to replace the one I had lost.

Clark, the German on *Asma*, had become friendly with an Austrian couple with a bakery and restaurant in town. They were building a large steel yacht and collected shells. So most days Clark and I would arrive for coffee and cakes, amazing cakes. I paid each time with a pretty new shell.

While working at the paper mill had been asked to go through the stock of chemicals in the laboratory and get rid of those no longer used. Some were quite dangerous and difficult to dispose of. Among them were two dozen small bottles containing mercury. They were carefully stored in *Sea Loone*'s bilge in case we found gold in the stream of some obscure exotic island.

As it happened but there was a minor gold rush going on somewhere north of Cairns extracting the metal from ancient defunct hot springs. I called into the tiny office of one of the companies involved and left a note to say I had the mercury and that I would be at the yacht club around lunchtime the next day. Next day, sure enough a very dirty four-wheel-drive jeep shot into the car park and with little or no discussion the mercury disappeared. I was left holding a wad of money. Counting it, I discovered I had fifty dollars too much. So I rang the bell and shouted the bar a round of drinks. It was definitely a gold rush!

By mid November, Jean was apparently fit and ready to return. She arrived on the 24th and was dragged straight off to a party at the Austrian's restaurant. They had organized a welcome home with a huge anchor shaped loaf of bread wrapped around a ham. With Clark, and Garth and Joan from *Camelot*, it was a great evening.

Jean was fine, a little pale from an English autumn but really happy to be back on board. I was back to being the pig in shit.

With the cyclone season arriving, we were all heading south to reduce the likelihood of meeting one and to find a good anchorage to stop and get some work done. I wanted to haul the boat out and seriously attack the underside. I also had to remove the engine and look again at the corrosion on the sump; one of the engine feet needed welding up. I also had the toe rail to put in place and a new dinghy to find or build. Jean had all the sails to look over and repair with the new sewing machine which, unlike the old one, could do the zig-zag stitching.

Fitzroy Island just south of Cairns was a first stop. A new resort had been built on the island and the opening day party was a riot. The bar next to the swimming pool couldn't sell beer quick enough. The wet T-shirt competition became a no T-shirt competition and the pool was overflowing. I'm not saying with what.

With the party people all ferried back to Cairns, it was a pleasant quiet anchorage. There was one prawn fishing boat using the anchorage and he agreed to take us out one night. We wanted to see what shells they dredged up with the prawns.

The *Evelyn B* was over sixty feet long with two long outriggers which spread the mouth of the net. We motored out as the sun set and Dan and his crew shot the net. As soon as it was set and dragged along the bottom, they went off to get some sleep. Two hours later they hauled up the net and emptied the cod end onto a large sorting table on the aft deck. The lads picked out the prawns and bugs and Jean and I sorted through for shells and anything else of interest.

There were two types of prawns. The larger ones were orange striped tiger prawns. These were the most valuable. The bugs or squat lobsters were much less valuable. Then there were small round scallops which they kept. For Jean and I there were lots more interesting things. A few shells, a small octopus, an arrow squid and a variety of other fish including a little anglerfish hanging his extended snout over his wide mouth as bait, even a few sea snakes.

As soon as the prawns were sorted and the net back in the water, the crew changed watch and trawled for another 2 hours. Jean and I collected the shells including the rest of the scallops, a bucket of squid and a couple of anglerfish. Then we swept the rest back into the sea. We slept a little between hauls and, as the sky brightened with the dawn, the last haul was dumped on the table and we headed back to Fitzroy Island.

We came back and motored up behind *Sea Loone*. With little wind blowing, we were able to tie off the *Evelyn B* behind her. Then with the bucket of bugs, scallops and squid and with some bacon donated by Don, Jean produced a huge breakfast come dinner.

It made an amusing picture with the trawler, wings still spread hanging on our stern. We pulled her up close and the two lads clambered up onto their bow and then we let them drift off a bit before they dropped their own anchor. Then we all caught some more sleep.

We went out a few more times and each time they came for breakfast, bringing a packet of bacon and a bucket of seafood. Quickly fried in bacon fat, the scallops were fantastic. The baby squid and the bug tails also tasted wonderful. We were eating like kings.

Clark had already sailed south and it was now time for us to leave, together with *Camelot*. We planned to spend Christmas in Bundaberg just south of the barrier reef. Towards the end of the year, the wind tends northeast rather than southeast making it easier to sail down the coast.

We day-sailed, stopping at different islands inside the reef each night. With our little black-and-white television from Sydney we classified each anchorage according to how good the reception was.

We left Fitzroy Island and sailed to Durk Island, Orpheus Island, Magnetic Island, Hook Island and Brompton Island. Then we anchored off the town of MacKay and were invited to a children's Christmas party at the sailing club.

The kids were having a frog racing competition which involve placing all of their frogs (they were actually toads) in the center of a large circle in the middle of the room. The winner was the first frog to reach the edge of the circle. No prodding was allowed. One child's frog was banned because it was actually a frog and leapt out of the ring in no time. The parents propped up the bar, drank lots of booze and putting bets on the results. It was hilarious.

From MacKay we sailed to Purdoe Island, then Middle Percy Island and then, two days later, with a fair north wind blowing, we came out from behind the Barrier Reef and sailed up the river to Bundaberg. We had leapfrogged down the coast with Garth and Joan on *Camelot*.

They were already tied up at a little marina and we decided to try our first marina stay and joined them. They had two girls on board, a French Canadian and a Norwegian. Another friend of Garth's was to join them. Above us on the high bank of the river, was the RSL Club, the Retired Servicemen's League. Sitting in the bar of the club you could see the top of *Sea Loone*'s mast. So it seemed a good idea to make sure the club were not strict on flag etiquette before I dressed *Sea Loone* with all our flags. These included the huge White Ensign from the Cayman Islands Rugby Club at the top of the mast. No problem, mate, this was Australia. No Pommie bullshit here!

Garth and Joan had seen the Scottish dancing in Honiara. Here in the Bundaberg RSL on Christmas Eve we were all introduced to square dancing or something similar. With a band playing, a huge metronome ticking, the people swirled around the room changing partners and weaving in and out. Garth, his whole crew, Jean and I were mesmerized again.

We drank a lot of beer, sampled the local rum, and welcomed in 1987. To start the New Year, *Camelot* was heading on south to Brisbane. But we had decided to head for Maryborough to start work on the boat.

Maryborough, the original capital of Queensland, is twenty miles up the Mary River. The river is badly silted up and not easy to navigate but with the tide flooding and a local chart, we managed without touching bottom. The town had seen better times. The once capital and centre for heavy industry such as locomotive building, was now a back water. No ships could navigate the river but there were a few large, steel, prawn-trawlers being refitted and an occasional timber barge at the main wharf. There were however still twenty odd pubs and a lot of customers for such a small town.

We arrived in the first week of January 1987 and stayed for three months. By that time, we had done most of the jobs on our list. We hauled the boat out in a sort of do-it-yourself boat slip where positioning the boat on the carriage was a nightmare.

Three times we hauled the boat up the steep ramp only to find it was not sitting properly. When we finally got it up and onto the level, it was still slightly askew. But diving in the thick mud soup feeling for the location of the underwater girders wasn't fun. Across the river was a far superior railway but here we only paid thirty three dollars for the key to the yard and the use of the winch; then another eight dollars a day for the facilities. Very cheap.

I decided to hire a sandblaster to clean off the old paint below the waterline. It was a big mistake. The machine was far too vicious and left me with quite a large area where the reinforcing was exposed. I was going to have to refill it with expensive epoxy filler. No matter, eventually it was all repaired and the bottom painted first with coal tar, then with an anti-foul paint. Clarke and *Asma* arrived from farther south and followed us out of the water once we had relaunched.

The local newspaper had written a small article about us and followed it with another full-page about *Sea Loone* and *Asma*. As a result of this, Jean and I were invited to stay for free in a local hotel over a long weekend. With the boat out the water, this was a nice surprise. Later, ABC radio invited us to take part in their Breakfast Show. We were becoming famous!

Volvo were demanding a huge price for sending me a new sump for the engine. In the end, a local boiler maker brazed up the corroded corner and I fiberglassed the inside with epoxy resin before replacing it. The boilermaker had a huge shed full of odd junk including a brand new engine identical to mine, still in its box. It wasn't for sale and anyway I couldn't afford it.

I bought a very ugly homemade dinghy for one hundred dollars but it was made from very expensive marine plywood. So I took it to pieces and made a much nicer dinghy with a sailing rig. We anchored in the center of the river, borrowed a generator and some electric tools, and started fitting the new toe rail around *Sea Loone.*

I had found a box of large old G-clamps at an auction and with these, slowly pulled the timber around the sides and then bolted it in place. The cap rail was not so easy but that too eventually pulled around. After sanding it, Jean gave the wood a dozen coats of fine oil and it looked beautiful.

Having seen us struggling with the toe rail in the middle of the river, one of the steel trawlers invited us to tie behind and use their electricity. We also borrowed their welder to repair the engine feet and the electrician gave us four large batteries which were being replaced, but still seemed pretty good.

Come March, the list of jobs was done. The engine was back in place and we sailed the new dinghy up and down the river, admiring our bright new toe rail. We had our piggy bank money sent up from Sydney and added it to over $1,000 tax refund money from my job at APM. We changed it all into US dollars, the bank taking a fair old bite out of it but we had received the 15% interest. The Aussie dollar hadn't dropped, so the interest plus the tax return had paid for a year in the islands, not including Jean's trip home. The work on the boat had gobbled up a good lump but we now had a few years worth of funding stacked in the piggy bank. Converted, it came to US$6,866.

Just before we left, Jean found a parrot for sale in the local flea market. It was a gallah, bright pink with a grey back. It seemed happy to sit in its cage and entertain itself, unlike Bruce. So Lady Pink moved on board. Jean was delighted.

For our leaving party, Clarke, Paddy, one of the former trawler owners and myself snagged a couple of ducks which regularly visited us. They went on the barbecue among slabs of beef and sausages for our leaving party. Joe and Jackie, a lesbian couple, who owned a steel yacht they had built themselves, joined the party. Jackie, had she known she was eating one of her pet ducks, would have murdered us and she was big enough to do it.

Paddy had gone out with my shotgun to get two "wild" cows for his freezer hold. He failed to bring anything back in the four-wheel drive truck he had borrowed. I think he got chased off by the farmer.

It was time to head north. We wended our way to back down the Mary River, anchored for the night behind Frazer Island, then then set off up the coast. It was April 9, 1987.

The next cyclone season would begin in November so we would have to be in on the African coast by then. We had a lot of miles to sail to achieve that. Firstly, it was 1000 miles to Cape York the northeast tip of Australia. Then we had more than 500 miles to Darwin along the north coast of Australia.

On the way across to Africa, we planned to stop briefly in Cocos Keeling Island and then spend a long time in Chagos, a reef archipelago in the middle of the Indian Ocean. Darwin to Chagos was 3,500 miles and then there was another 2,000 miles from there to the African coast. All in all, that meant 7,000 miles of sailing. Out of the seven months available to us, we would actually be sailing nearly half of that time.

We retraced our steps to Middle Percy Island, climbed up the hill and met Andy Martin. He had lived there for some time in a Robinson Crusoe sort of way. The Australian Government had decided he had not improved the island enough during the period of his lease and so he was being thrown off. It was a bit harsh and he had become a well-known local character.

We stayed for lunch and he gave Jean some very dirty beeswax from his hives. Jean melted and sifted the dead bees out, and dipped chunks of cheese in the wax to preserve it.

On Dunk Island, we got a very unwelcome visit from a "coastal surveillance vessel". They were two scruffy-looking characters in a tinny, a small aluminum dinghy. I showed them our paperwork but refused to allow them on board. An hour later they returned to say that they had seen a gallah on the boat. This they said was against the law as the gallah was Australian and *Sea Loone* was a foreign yacht. I suggested that they were the gallahs and told them to go away. We were told to report the parrot once we arrived in Cairns.

Within hours of arriving in Cairns, we were visited by a big gray patrol boat and had two "uniforms" with heavy clumping boots on the boat, examining Miss Pink. These are the parrots they shoot in the hundreds because they eat the crops. They agreed we can keep the parrot as long as we didn't take it out of Australian waters. This we already knew.

A few days later on the local news we heard of a family who was looking for their daughter's pet gallah which had gone walkabout. We phoned them and they were delighted to take Miss Pink as a replacement. From Cairns all the way round the coast we got dive bomb by a spotter plane at least once a day. I thought of making an oversized "Miss Pink" to sit in the cockpit when they next came past.

One lunchtime in Cairns yacht club, we listened to a table full of locals next to us trying to work out what language was being spoken. Suddenly Jean exclaimed "it's Polar Bear". And so it was. It was the crazy Finn we had met in Barbados. Together with a group of other Finns he was busy knocking down the lovely old wooden buildings of Cairns and building concrete replacements. That night we had an impromptu party at his home where, in the Finnish way, they threw away the tops to the whisky bottles, a whole case of them. We got very drunk.

Loaded with provisions, we continued north from Cairns. The weather was terrible, blowing like hell with squalls of rain.

At Low Island we met up again with the *Evelyn B*. They were having a good season and presented us with a bucket full of squat lobsters, bugs. At Hope Island, disaster struck again. Overnight, the new dinghy had disappeared; this time, at least, not with the outboard engine. I have a sneaking suspicion it was my knot but say no more. As Jean said, third time lucky. Maybe next time, the third dinghy, we might be able to keep it permanently?

We spent a few days on Lizard Island, climbed the mountain and looked over Cook's Passage where Cook, had to find a break in the Barrier Reef. He entered it to find a quiet creek (today the site of Cook Town) where he could careen his ship and stop the most serious leaks.

The wind continued blowing. A small yacht in front of us was flying a blue ensign. British yachts were unusual but the blue colour rather put me off. Blue ensigns are flown by members of Royal yacht clubs amongst others. They are posh. When eventually we thought we should visit, having seen no activity for two days, we found an elderly couple. They were waiting for the wind to die down. They were Bill and Betty and their boat was *Didycoy*. Bill apologized and change the flag for the ordinary red one. They had earned some money over the last four years doing sail repairs. You wouldn't know it looking at their sails. And then they had a leak in the hull which after a lot of work still wasn't repaired.

With the improving weather, Clark arrived on *Asma* and we continued north together with *Didycoy*. Each day, Jean or I caught fish on the way or in the anchorage with the gill net, enough to feed all three boats. In the Bathurst Bay near Cape Melville, Clark and I decided to do a bit of hunting. I took my shotgun and Clarke his small .22 rifle that he'd used on pigeons in Papua. By now, we were careful about the red and green ants which fold leaves together in the bushes to make their nests. The first time they got me I stripped off my clothes faster than you can blink and still got bitten to death.

The hunting expedition was for a pig and we found plenty of evidence of them. But never saw the actual animal. Only just in time I managed to stop Clark shooting a buffalo calf. He'd have been lucky to kill it with his gun but the mother, which he hadn't seen behind another bush, would certainly have done a job on him. We were absolutely exhausted when we got back to the beach. We were empty-handed but Jean had saved the day by catching another bucket of fish.

Once you leave Lizard Island, you leave civilization behind. There's just hundreds of miles of completely desolate coastline, long beaches, mangrove swamps and desert islands. We stopped at the Flinders Islands, Staines Island, Morris Island, and the Night Islands .Then we took a long day off in Portland Roads where a supply ship for the prawn trawlers was due to arrive. Jean and I hiked into the bush to look for the enormous palm cockatoo. We failed to see it.

We stopped in Margaret Bay where we got attacked by horse flies, then Bushy Islands and lastly, Mount Adolphus Island right opposite Cape York. Day-sailing is tiring! Anchor up and down, sails up and down, and then continuously changing course to avoid reefs. So at Mount Adolphus we took a few days off. Also, the next leg of the trip took us round Cape York through the Torres Straits. Here the tidal currents run up to ten knots each way. So it is essential to get the timing right. We needed to catch the west moving tide and ride it all away into the Gulf of Carpentaria.

We were anchored in a large protected Bay fringed by mangroves and a wide muddy reef which almost dried out at low tide. Looking to see if we could find any interesting shells, Jean and I waded across the reef.

Only a few inches of water covered the mud and broken coral. We got quite a shock when two large claws came out of the water threatening us. Unable to dig a hole in the coral and mud, a large mud crab was sitting in a shallow depression. He had raised his claws to frighten us off. It was a large male weighing maybe two kilos.

He grabbed the spear I was holding and I lifted him up and shook him into our large bucket. It was our first mud crab and that evening he made a memorable meal. Of course, he wasn't alone on the reef. In the next few days, several more went into the pot and fed the fleet.

One day, I decided to walk round the southern headland and look into the small sandy bays facing south. It was easy walking around on the smooth rock which sloped into the sea and the beaches were obviously used by nesting turtles. Their tracks up the beach were obvious. But then the huge monitor lizards or goanas had come out of the bush and had dug up the eggs.

An hour or so later I turned back and as I rounded the headland, no more than fifty feet away sat a large crocodile. It had obviously come ashore not long after I passed and was now awaiting my return. It was maybe twelve or fifteen feet long and looked hungry. But on seeing me it slithered down the sloping rock and slid back under the water.

The water was crystal clear and the creature swam down and then back up to the surface, took a breath of air, then dived again and disappeared. It all happened so quickly that I never even took a backward step.

Wading around sometimes up to our waists in water looking for crabs and shells no longer seemed a good idea. Any logs half buried in the mud suddenly looked very suspicious and needed careful scrutiny.

Two days later the tide seemed right for an early start which should get us through the straits before dark. We motored out and by the time we were in the main channel and heading for Hammond Rock, the tide had us in its grip. We were booming along.

An old castellated freighter with a tall smoke stack past us going the other way. It was the *Ivy Bank* registered in London; a Banks Line ship and a bit of a museum piece. Now heading due west, we passed Thursday Island on our port side and by three in the afternoon were abreast of Booby Island. With the tide in full flood at midday, the flow of water is awe-inspiring. But it was a relief to be through it and out in the open water before sundown.

Another two days later and we found our way into Gove Harbour on the west side in the Gulf of Carpentaria. It's a mining town with huge opencast mines for bauxite. There is also a huge chemical works to convert the bauxite into alumina and aluminum oxide, a white powder which is then exported.

We anchored off the yacht club and Clark, who had already been there a few days and had a job doing some welding, had dinner ready for us. When we had been in Maryborough, Clark had met a very pretty Australian girl, Michelle. She had a stall in the market selling leather belts that she had made. She had spent some time with us getting involved in all the boat work. Clark had obviously kept in touch with her and now he was in a hurry to finish his job here in Gove. He was meeting Michelle in Darwin and she was joining him on the boat to cross the Indian Ocean.

The yacht club in Gove is a friendly lively place and there seemed plenty of work around. But we were already late in the season and had to push on. We shot through the Hole-In-The-Wall, a narrow cleft in the rocks dividing the Wessel Islands. Then, with a good breeze, arrived in Darwin five days later on July 7th 1987.

We spent a week in Darwin, a busy week storing up for the long voyage with hopefully a few weeks on deserted islands too. We were anchored a long way out from the yacht club having been warned about the big tides. Our friends on *Contour of Cuthill* were anchored much closer but I knew they had a centerboard and drew very little water for such a large boat. A number of boats went aground not knowing this.

When a taxi refused to take our gas bottle to the filling station, a passing car stopped, took us there and brought us back for free. A boilermaker with a sign in his work place saying he could "work miracles" made a new piece of exhaust for the engine and refused to charge us. Then on our way home from that expedition, I broke a flip-flop and another car stopped and gave us a lift to the yacht club. And this was on the first day!

We celebrated with a few beers and a hamburger some of which I fed to the five foot goana which came begging. The beers were a mistake. By the time it came to leave, the tide had gone out and did we find exactly how far it had gone out? The yacht club provided trailers to trundle your dinghy across the sands. It was a long way.

We shared taxis with Clark collecting boxes of tinned goods, sacks of vegetables, twelve dozen eggs, twenty cartons of cigarettes to cater to my bad habits, bottles of gin, and rum and whiskey, from the duty-free store. *Contour* and their friends on a yacht called *Mash* had their beer delivered on a pallet, they had ordered so much. Thank God we didn't have refrigeration on the boat or we'd be doing the same.

We arrange with Clark to listen for him on our shortwave receiver and also got the frequencies for the other boats to see what they were doing and where they were. We did the paperwork and cleared out on July 15th 1987, heading first to Cocos Keeling and then on to Chagos. We had been in Australia for almost a year.

9

THE FIRST LEG took us twenty one days with a slow start and very little wind. Later the wind picked up and we surfed into Cocos Keeling and rounded up into the anchorage to find *Contour*, *Mash* and a few other boats already there.

Cocos Keeling is a quarantine Island for Australia so we were restricted to anchorages way across the lagoon from the village, we socialized, swapped some books and snorkeled around the reef but we were keen to move on. So four days later, well rested, we started on the next leg to Chagos.

The trade winds were fairly constant by now so we gobbled up the miles with our downwind sail poled out on either side. We were catching fish on two fishing lines trailed on either side, baited with colorful plastic squid, dorado, wahoo and tuna, sometimes getting so many we were throwing some back.

On the tenth day we picked up Clark on *Asma* on the radio. He had sailed straight through to Chagos and was on Egmont Island, a little visited atoll well south of the more popular Salomon Atoll. The reception on the little radio was not good so we got no details. But we decided to head for Egmont anyway.

A week later having passed by Diego Garcia where the Americans had their base, we saw the palm trees of Egmont on the horizon. We called Clark on the VHF radio but got no reply and could not see his boat anyway. Only when we came up to the reef and were sailing around to the pass did we see *Asma* careened on the beach.

The pass wasn't well defined, just a wide gap where the reef dipped below the surface. We chose somewhere in the middle and rode the swells in. Watching the depth and keeping the boat straight on the swell, I could see the bottom rising up under us. One swell carried us all the way in and the bottom fell away again. My heart beat slowed down. The lagoon was still full of isolated reefs, some coming all the way to the surface. As we turn to head for where we had seen *Asma* they came up on the radio. It was a bit late to tell us where to enter but he could give us the best route through the maze of reefs to the anchorage.

By the time we wended our way with me standing up on the bowsprit directing Jean, Clark had floated off the beach and was back on anchor. We threw our anchor behind him and Jean put the kettle on. We had completed another sixteen days on the ocean, altogether thirty-seven days sailing from Darwin.

Chagos was the last part of the British Indian Ocean Territories that had not been given independence. The Labour government of Harold Macmillan had been keen to rid themselves of any responsibility for these small, very isolated, islands. The coconut plantations were not doing well and the resident labour force, which years before had been brought from Southeast Asia, were going to be a drain on the British government.

So when the US offered to lease the main atoll, Diego Garcia, in order to build a military base there, Harold jumped at the chance. They must have been offered a lot of money because one of the stipulations of the lease was that all the people on all the islands, even Salomon one hundred miles to the north, were to be removed. They were all shipped off to Mauritius over 1,000 miles to the south. Imagine taking the whole population of the Scilly islands and dumping them on Malta. But Chagos is so remote, no one knew about this or probably even cared.

This all happened in the 1960s. By the time we arrived, there were only a few tumbled ruins and two clogged up wells. The plantation was completely overgrown and impenetrable and Diego Garcia was a hornet's nest which wasn't to be approached.

Egmont was an island paradise. We were anchored off the south end and off the most southern of five islands protected from the prevailing southeast wind by a sand spit projecting into the lagoon. The beach was steep too and on a high tide the water lapped up into the bushes. Behind the bushes, which needed a path hacked out through them, were five huge trees with open space beneath their massive spreading branches. Behind that was a jungle of coconut palms with fallen trunks, massive piles of dead fronds and rotten coconuts and new sprouting nuts trying to get established. Among it all lived a colony of rats and so many coconut crabs that they scurried about even in daylight.

On the windward side of the island the swells crashed on the outer reef which was only separated from the island by a narrow channel of water which in places you could wade across at low tide. The tide in fact rose and fell less than two metres and on the larger tides this exposed the outer reef along most of the windward side making it possible to walk along it.

Wading in the channel, it was easy to find the antenna of a lobster sticking out from under a coral shelf. The first day I speared four of these lobsters. Jean had cut down a small palm tree and we ate lobsters with palm heart salad.

A narrow sandbank joined the island to the next one north. Here there were terns nesting, crested terns and masked terns. They were not in huge numbers and seemed to be having problems with the rats. We left them in peace. A colony of frigate birds was using the bushes close by to rear their huge, fluffy, gray and very ugly hicks. No doubt the parents relied on the terns to catch the fish for them.

One very large tree hanging over the lagoon on the north we called the coconut crab hotel. The roots of the tree were undermined all around by huge holes inhabited by the largest coconut crabs I had ever seen. Their massive claws, one for crunching and one for nipping, were each bigger than my forearm. If you tapped a stick on the roof above for a while, the crab, being curious, would come out to to see what was going on. It's front two legs protrude further than the claws by only a few inches and if you were quick and brave, you could grab a leg and yank him out into the open. Once in the open, it was easy to steer the animal into a large bucket and jam the lid on.

We barbecued the crabs on the beach. The meat was a little too rich for me and had a definite coconut flavor. The four of us, Clark, Michelle, Jean and I would sit around the fire throwing bits of shell and suchlike over our shoulders. Behind us were hundreds of pairs of ruby eyes sparkling in the firelight, a complete circle of scavenging rats.

It was easy to catch fish, usually snapper or grouper, simply by baiting a hook. I put the net out on the sandbank to catch mullet which we were going to smoke, but the small sharks made life too difficult. Clark spent hours trying to catch one of the many turtles and even got his rifle out on one occasion. But he never succeeded. Naked as the day we were born, we ranged up and down the beaches and out onto the reefs. Our shell collection increased rapidly. We had buckets of shells everywhere in different stages of being cleaned.

Clark being of a nervous disposition, liked to keep moving. So a week later, with two large live coconut crabs tied down on deck and half a dozen live lobsters in his cockpit locker, they left us alone on the island.

It was ten years since we had first set sail out of the Birkenhead docks on the River Mersey. And here we were; in many ways a dream come true. As a boy, I had read "Swiss family Robinson", "Robinson Crusoe", "Coral Island" and so on. Here I had a desert island washed by tropic blue waters, fanned by a warm fragrant breeze, and a beautiful naked girl to chase along the sun drenched beach. It was perfect, well almost.

Water was becoming a problem. It had not rained since Cocos Keeling. I had cleaned out one of the wells and sank a crate into it for water to percolate. But the water was still almost as brown as beer and musty smelling. We used it for washing; but what we needed was to replenish our drinking water supply. I hung up a large sail between the palm trees to catch rain if and when it happened.

Having found a coconut crab hotel, we now found a lobster hotel. It was a large boulder sitting out on the windward corner of the outside reef. We had walked the outside reef at night with Clarke and Michelle and came back with a sack full of lobsters on the new moon. These we kept in a cage under the boat.

Now we realized that some of the lobsters which came to graze at night on the top of the reef, were hiding under the boulder during the day, rather than returning to the deep water outside the reef. Sometimes there were only a few. But at other times we would wade out at midday and there would be more than thirty, with only the occasional large swell washing over them to keep them from drying out.

This saved a lot of trouble marching around to the windward side in the pitch black of night and wading through the channel up to our waists in shark infested waters. And there really were sharks. There were lots of small black-tipped sharks which would come up and bump us, some large, maybe 5-foot as well as some large nurse sharks which were no threat, and then there were very large and dangerous tiger sharks.

These tiger sharks seemed to arrive in greater numbers once the number of turtles in the lagoon increased. Chasing a turtle I saw one shark almost beach itself, its dorsal fin and back out of the water. It was huge, maybe twelve feet long with the stripes down the side, beady eyes and a big mouth.

Lobster for dinner every other day can get boring. We had just finished the beef we had bottled in Vanuatu. We still had tinned corned beef but the turtles were looking more and more appetizing. I reasoned that if the sharks were eating them, then a few more wouldn't be missed. There were now dozens of turtles to choose from in the patch of shallow water not far from the boat.

We had my pole spear to ward off the sharks, a machete and a small kitchen knife, neither of them very sharp. The technique for catching the turtle was fairly straightforward. You sneaked up behind him while he was chewing on the bottom. Whenever he stopped and raised his head out of the water, you had to stay completely still. When you were right behind him, you dived down putting one hand over the front of the shell behind its neck and one on the aft point of the shell.

We quickly realized on the first attempt that we'd chosen too big a turtle. It must have weighed over seventy pounds. Holding him fore and aft we found we could steer him towards the beach and from the water's edge managed to drag him out of the water. We butchered him right there and it wasn't pretty. Decapitated, the muscles still spasmed, the lacrimal glands still excreted tears and having separated the shell from the plastron and removed the meat, the heart was still beating. We finished with ten kilos of meat making two meals and nine bottled jars of turtle meat!

Some days after Clark and Michele had left, another yacht hove over the horizon and came to join us. The boat was called *Zenie P. II*, an English designed plywood boat. The couple, Alvah an American and Diana a New Zealander, had spent two and a half years in Borneo building up a sailing, diving, and water sports business.

Easily bored, towards the end of his Borneo stay, Alvah had organized an expedition into the center of the Borneo jungle to seek out the few remaining rhinoceroses. Getting into the jungle had been easy. Alvah and his two helpers simply jumped out of a plane and floated down into the wildest part they could find. Unfortunately they lost one supply parachute which included the means to get out, an inflatable raft. So although Alvah was sure he found some rhino poo, the whole expedition became one of survival and getting back.

They were keen to push on towards South Africa as Alvah had another expedition in mind involving the Okavango Swamps in Botswana. So having visited the two hotels, dived the reef and eaten well, they left to sail south to Mauritius.

Left alone, we marched along one day and found a huge hawksbill turtle digging in the sand under the bushings. Obviously she had come ashore to lay her eggs. When we returned later, she was finishing covering up the hole. Then, having smoothed off the sand, she headed down the beach to the water.

We dug up two dozen of the eggs and carried them back to the boat. We had no idea how to cook them. Jean's attempt at an omelette was a disaster so we took the remaining eggs back ashore and reburied them under a bush.

At last, on September the fourteenth it rained. Clouds had been building up for a few days and with the rain came a gale out of the south. Within minutes, the rain refilled the tank and our water bottles. It threw it down and the decks steamed. No need for the genoa rain-catcher ashore. It was a huge relief; we had been down to our last jerry can.

With the rain came the mosquitoes on the island, barbecuing was no longer a good idea. With the wind and the rain, the sandspit to the north had washed away so you could no longer walk across to the next island. The windward side of the shoreline had eroded away and palm trees had been uprooted and fallen. This at least made collecting their green drinking-coconuts easy.

After our first turtle, we became more expert at choosing a turtle that would provide a meal for two plus one bottling, which is three jars in the pressure cooker. We also made sure the shell was in good condition and dark coloured. We scraped and dried the shells, then brushed them with formalin to preserve them.

Two huge manta rays then arrived in the lagoon. They swam round and round the boat. The last time we had swum with them was in the Marquesas. But the weather was changing and we saw a few finches on the island which may have been migrating as we had not seen them before.

It was October. We were happy to stay longer but the seasons were not going to wait for us. So on October 10th we threaded our way out through the coral heads and held our breath as we passed through the shallows into the deep blue beyond.

We took a couple of live lobsters with us keeping them in the cockpit locker and dousing them with water every so often. They didn't last long. We now had quite a large collection of shells, mainly cowrie shells, some of which were new to us. We also had the turtle carapaces which we still had to clean and polish and more than two dozen bottles of turtle meat.

We now decided to make our next stop at Aldabra Island famous for its giant tortoises and a flightless rail. The island, together with a few others close by, had belonged to the Indian Ocean Territories but had been ceded to the Seychelles when they were given independence. You needed a special permit from the Seychelles to visit them, so maybe we wouldn't be made very welcome.

We had to sail almost due west from longitude 71° E to 46° E, a distance of 1,500 miles. The weather was fine with only moderate winds and we took eighteen days. We passed north of Agalega Island, Providence Island and Cosmoledo Island. There were lots of sea birds around, noddys, terns and booby birds, all of which wanted to use *Sea Loone* as a resting spot at night.

They had to be dissuaded as they seem to crap their own body weight each night onto on our solar panel where it stuck like cement.

As we got closer to Africa we picked up BBC Radio Africa. We heard about the New York Stock Exchange crash and a UK winter storm that had knocked down all the old oak trees and caused major damage.

We came around the lee side of Aldabra, eighteen days out and saw another yacht anchored off the government station. It was a Swan 51 sailed by a German, Peter, and his Japanese wife, Yuki. They were very friendly and interested in our adventures. The warden on the island unfortunately wouldn't let us land. He had only just taken the job and was expecting a boatload of scientists to arrive any day; so he dared not bend the rules.

Peter had been up north to Mahe in the Seychelles and had all the paperwork. So although we stayed a couple of nights on the anchorage we had to leave without stepping ashore. However, before we left, we did see a giant tortoise through our binoculars.

We had agreed to meet Clark and Michelle in the Comores Islands a few hundred miles south west of Aldabra. They sit half way between Madagascar and the African coast in the Mozambique Channel. The only thing we knew about the islands was that they had recently been given their independence from France.

Three days out from Aldabra, we arrived off Grand Camore a forbidding sort of place with a volcano in its centre. We lost the wind as we sailed around the lee side and had to motor the last few miles to arrive at Marone, the capital.

Two freighters were anchored off the town, together with a catamaran and a Chinese junk. The bottom shelved rapidly so you had to anchor close in. The boat rolled from the gusts of wind that swept down from the volcano so not a good anchorage. As we stowed away the sails, the local mosque started blasting out its midday prayers from loudspeakers from the mosque's minarets on the beach.

Then, over on the nearby jetty, two uniformed characters indicated that we must come ashore. It was a dirty, smelly, little town with narrow streets. The latest president had come to power with the help of South African mercenaries. He seemed to spend the whole day driving back and forward across town trying to run people over with his motorcade. Everybody, included ourselves, had to flatten themselves against the wall and jump into the alleys while the motorcycles, cars with bodyguards and the presidential limousine itself, shot past. I'm sure it didn't endear him to his people and certainly not to Jean and I!

We spent two uncomfortable weeks in Marone waiting for Clark. There were however, three minor highlights. The junk next to us was on a diving expedition. Ernst Klarr, the German skipper, was quite a successful treasure hunter. The morning after we arrived, there was great excitement on his boat as a swarm of bees had taken up residence in their mainsail. Two of the crew in wetsuits and masks managed to collect the swarm and take it to a derelict lighthouse on the beach. I was impressed.

Meanwhile, the catamaran from South Africa had two long plastic tubes on the deck. They held a dismantled ultralight aeroplane with floats. When the guys put it together and flew over the town, the officials came out like another swarm of bees. The pilot was arrested as a spy from the CIA.

One of the freighters close behind us, the *Julia II* as also captained by a German. They were offloading cement into lighters and it was taking a long time. Unable to go ashore because the anchorage was so precarious, the captain was getting bored. So he paid us a visit and invited us for a barbecue on board. We met the Polish chief engineer, the German mate and the rest of the crew, mainly Filipinos. The cook served up a feast under an awning on the aft deck. It was a great evening.

They let me use the ships radio and they managed to find out where Clark was. He was on his way from Madagascar. When we invited the captain over for dinner a few days later, he pointed out that his ship was rigged with heavy duty derricks for log carrying. He didn't yet have orders for his next port of call but offered to pick us up and take us wherever it was. It was an interesting offer. As it was, he got orders as he left the anchorage. They were going to New Orleans via South Africa.

Clark eventually arrived and we set off together for Dar es Salaam, Tanzania. Grand Camore was not going to be on our list of places to revisit. In fact I was looking for to hearing about the next revolution there and wishing it success.

We had intended crossing the Mozambique Channel to Mtwara, the most southern port in Tanzania and then coasting up to Dar es Salaam. However our plans changed and we headed directly to Dar.

When Africa appeared over the horizon what we saw of the coast wasn't very impressive. There were no jungle-covered mountains, just low scrubby sand hills. Sailing up the channel into Dar es Salaam is a complicated affair, with reefs and islands to skirt around and then a narrow dogleg channel bringing you into the basin. I will never forget the last turn around a sandy spit where the fish market was established. The beach was covered with a seething mass of black Africans offloading boats on the beach. They were as tightly packed as a football crowd on a Saturday in Liverpool. It was intimidating darkest Africa.

Finding nowhere to tie up, we anchored off the customs house and rowed ashore. Crowds of people were milling around but with the luck of the devil we found another white person and latched onto her to get some directions. Her name was Lynn and her husband, Mike, was the chief pilot for the port. Mike was an ex Liverpool pilot and they lived in West Kirby only a few miles where I built *Sea Loone*. So we found out where to go to clear-in. Then Lynn directed us to sail round to the Yacht Club a few miles out of town, when we had finished the paperwork.

The boat had to be inspected and searched. We had to declare all the money we were bringing in and then change fifty dollars at the bank and bring back the receipt. Lynn had explained all this and told us that the exchange rate at the Bank was seventy four shillings to the dollar. However, on the black market it was one hundred and seventy shillings. Naturally we didn't declare everything as, clearing out of Tanzania the original amount declared had to match the money remaining less the bank receipts .

This all took some time but then we returned to the boat and sailed down the channel and round into the large bay to the east. We anchored off the Yacht Club.

This was no ordinary yacht club! It was the centre of social life for most of the foreigners living in Dar. There were a number of small yachts on moorings and a lot of dinghies ashore. The club provided a launch, day and night, to go back and forward to our boat, and the bar closed when the last member left. We were allowed free use of the club and would get a monthly bar bill as no money crossed the bar. You simply filled out chits for whatever you wanted. Every Wednesday night they laid on a fantastic barbacue with meats, fish, lobsters, curries and salads.

There were always old African hands at the bar and some amazing stories. Late one night, I sat and listened to a venerable old gentleman describe hunting down a huge bull elephant in the Sudan and shooting it with some huge elephant gun. It sounded like a story out of the previous century.

A small yacht on a mooring nearby had been brought down from Lake Victoria when the owner moved to Dar. The watchman, or ascari, who looked after the boat had come with it, sitting in the cockpit all the way on the train. He had acquired a second wife in town and was very happy. I saw the boat go sailing one weekend. The launch brought out the people. As they boarded, the ascari pulled up the sails, let go the mooring and stepped onto the launch. The owner took the tiller and the party sailed away on their jaunt. I was impressed; but that weekend, saw something even better.

At the weekend, there were dinghies sailing including some very fast catamarans. There was quite a crowd watching the sailing and the bar was very busy. The first boat home was one of the catamarans sailed by a very flamboyant member of the club. The boat rocketed towards the slipway with one hull lifting out of the water. With only yards to go, he let the sails go and stepped up to the front, jumping ashore hardly getting his feet wet and accepting his gin and tonic from the waiting barman.

He never looked behind knowing that his ascari would catch the boat before it went aground and also sort out the flapping sails. I was impressed, but still felt he could have done with a kick in the backside for his arrogance.

Clark arrived for his birthday on the 25th -and we joined the barbecue. He had got word that his mother had died on the tenth which really upset him as he been hoping to go home and see her from Dar. Unusually for Clark, after a few beers he relaxed and told us a bit about his past

His mother had died in East Germany where he had been brought up. He had represented East Germany as a boxer but was imprisoned as a political activist for publishing an underground newspaper. He had spent almost two years in solitary confinement but was part of an exchange organized by Amnesty International who knew him through the boxing. When he arrived in West Germany he became a well-known photojournalists working with GEO magazine. His hopes to see his mother in East Germany after all those years were dashed so naturally he was very upset.

Clark still wanted to return to Germany for a few weeks and I thought of maybe going home myself to see the family after eight or nine years away. We toured the airline offices and were offered a large seaman's discount by the Dutch airline, KLM, but Clarke first wanted to talk with Lufthansa, the German airline. The manager there offered us the same deal as long as we paid in dollars and not local shillings. Then when we asked for an extra baggage allowance he offered business-class for the same price. I had to pay $580 for a return ticket to Manchester via Frankfurt.

This was a really good deal so Clark and I booked a flight for a week's time. Then we returned to the yacht club to tell the girls they would be on their own for a week or two. In fact there were a couple of other visiting yachts to socialize with and we had met Lynn again there. Lynn and her husband Mike and their young kids lived nearby. We also met John Buffett and his wife Betty. He had an electrical contracting business in town and there was an interesting Norwegian who somehow worked with the government. So no problems.

We left on November 28. Clark would be away for only two weeks. I would be back just before Christmas. I had managed to contact my mother and organized to stay with my sister who would come and collect me from Manchester Airport.

In business-class we were pampered. Clark told the pretty flight attendant that we were great adventurers on the ocean and we sampled a fair amount of German white wine. Arriving in Frankfurt in the early morning I had to wait till the afternoon to carry on. However Clark was being met by some friends so I joined them for a few hours. When we arrived at Clark's friend's house there was a huge German breakfast waiting for us and a bubble bath which I dived straight into. Then lunch time we spent in the Christmas fair in the city eating sweet chestnuts and all sorts of other interesting things. The half timbered houses, cobbled streets and the festive decorations plus the very cool breeze was a massive change from my years in the tropics.

Business-class to Manchester was crowded after Clark and I had had the whole cabin on the flight to Frankfurt almost to ourselves, but they served potted shrimp which I hadn't had for years. They were delicious. When I arrived in Manchester I collected my luggage and followed the little green arrows, I was suddenly faced with the family; Diana, my sister and her husband, Paul and the children, Colin and Nicola.

It was a quite a shock. Di and Paul were much the same, but the kids were no longer kids. They were huge! I had been sending small T-shirts to Colin, the ten-year-old. But he was bigger than I was and played serious rugby! Nicola had developed in other ways. She was a young lady.

I spent three weeks at home. A lot had changed but I had the chance to meet old friends. A surprise party for me in the local pub brought people from all over England. Many of them had been involved with building the boat especially the cementing day. It was Sue from school days, Sue who fed the crowd on cementing day, who had organized the pub party.

December 20th found me back at the airport with a box full of bits for the boat and groceries not to be found in Dar. I also had a parcel of black pudding; a present for the manager of Lufthansa in Dar.

I had a few hours wait, sampling German beer, in Frankfurt airport. When we finally arrived in the departure lounge I was seated with some very well-dressed Germans. I was my normal scruffy self in jeans and with my cardboard box as hand luggage. I went for a pee and when I returned, the lounge was empty. A very angry stewardess found me and rushed me to the plane. But when I presented my business class ticket and a box full of sausage for the manager, she became a little more friendly. The posh Germans were all going on holiday; they were somewhere in the back of the plane. I was in business-class.

Before arriving in Dar es Salaam, the plane did a half turn around Mount Kenya and then around Mt. Kilimanjaro. Rising up from the veldt tipped with snow, the mountains are beautiful and having seen the one I could stroll across the plane and see the other. A short while later, we descended back to reality and a rotten customs officer who confiscated my Christmas holly. I shook the red berries off before I passed it over.

While I was away, Jean had been busy painting and varnishing. The boat looked like a picture. Jean was looking good herself, bronzed and fit compared with all those pasty white people wintering in England.

Clarke and Michelle were keen to spend Christmas out on one of the islands away from the milling crowds. We chose Inner Sinda Island and sailed out with all our Christmas goodies including a large live muscovy duck in our cockpit. On Christmas Eve a fleet of fishing boats arrived and had a noisy party. Then on Christmas Day, we were invaded by Japanese tourists. In the morning, I had to give the duck the coup de grace then clean and pluck it. It did tasted good that evening but some of it was a little tough. The next day Clark was not well. I hope it wasn't the duck's revenge! All in all, not a great Christmas.

Clark, with engine problems returned to Dar. Jean and I set out for Mafia Island down the coast. But with all the fishermen using explosives for fishing, the reefs were ruined, dead and covered in algae over large areas, so a few days later we also returned to Dar

Back in the yacht club, Clark had arranged to do a slide show. It was well advertised and Clark did a very professional job. The slideshow was of his trip from the Red Sea to China following the route of Sinbad the Sailor. The photographs were great. Michelle had been coached into doing a dialogue and it all went down very well.

With some misgivings, I followed with a slideshow of our time in Chagos using pictures I had had processed while home. Much to my surprise, and Clarks, it also went down well.

Jean and I were keen to travel inland on a little safari but it could prove rather expensive. However while working on this, John Buffett suggested we join him on a trip he had to make to Arusha where he had some work being done. On the way, we could stop in a small game park, stay one night and see some of the wildlife.

The car was a well-used Peugeot 404. We had three spare wheels. We used all of them. The road was busy with a lot of heavy goods traffic coming down from Uganda, which normally would have gone to Mombasa in Kenya. For some reason or other the port of Mombasa was not operating. The road was really torn up with potholes. You could almost loose a bus in one. So we wove back and forwards to avoid the worst. We bounced around in the swirling dust and heat, eventually arriving at the small Game Park through which the road passed.

We used up our Swahili words claiming residence in Tanzania as tourists had to pay a huge daily fee. Then we were shown a small round cottage, a "rondavel", for our night's stay. By the time we had showered off the grime, we were ready for a cold beer and a meal in the restaurant. It was circular again and had a huge baobab tree as its centre post.

Open grassland with the occasional thorn tree stretched away for miles in front of us and there were the animals, zebras, antelope, and, in the distance, some obvious giraffes. The sun was rapidly heading for the western horizon. It really was a unique African experience, you seemed to see miles and miles across the veldt. It was like being on top of the big ocean swell and being able to see the curve of the earth.

A tiny hut sat alone out on the grass. It was the toilet and before the meal arrived, Jean walked across to use it. Later as we were eating, an elephant walked by passing close to us. It went across to the little hut and snaked its trunk inside. Jean pointed with her hand, speechless, imagining what could have happened a quarter of an hour earlier.

John had a friend working in the game park studying the baboons. After dinner we were invited to coffee at his place only a short walk away he was a young American working for an American university professor and head found a job while hitchhiking through Tanzania almost two years earlier. He spent his day following a troop of baboons around the bush noting down their behavior patterns. Initially he had a guard, an askari, who would accompanying him. But in the end they were all too frightened. So now he walked alone and the baboons accepted him.

He had some good stories as we sat around the open fire outside his hut. The most amusing was yet another elephant story.

In the early days he invited two old friends from New York to come and visit. They were city people so a long way out of their depth. The first night, after a meal, they spread the sleeping bags on the floor in the main room. In the centre of the room was a dining table with the remains of some food. A passing elephant smelt the food and tried to reach it with his trunk through the window. Pushing further and further he found the table but woke the visitors. The girls screamed when she saw what appeared to be this huge snake. The elephant threw up its head in surprise but its tusks were embedded in the wall of the hut, so it lifted the whole roof off. What a welcome to Africa!

We heard lions roaring that night and set off early to try to find them. Bumping down a small track, we found a magnificent male lion stretched out on the road in front of us. I was in the back of the car and keen to get out and take a photo. But fortunately John dissuaded me. Just then, out of nowhere, a large lioness materialized behind the car and sauntered around past my door. I did get some nice pictures, but from inside the car.

We saw so many different animals but the car was taking a beating. We had changed two wheels and one of the brake shoes had seized up so we had to carry on to Arusha. It was a wonderful introduction to African wildlife, a great beginning.

We completed the trip with only one more puncture and even though the brakes weren't working so well, had no major accidents.

Back in Dar we made more plans. There was a huge, little visited game park south down the coast in the Rufigi Delta famous for a German pocket battleship that hid there in the 1st World War. Then there was Mount Kilimanjaro. Our Norwegian friend, Magna, knew people living on the lower slopes of Kilimanjaro. He planned to take us to visit them in his aeroplane but unfortunately the machine was in Nairobi being repaired. So that plan was put on hold.

In town there was a lot of native art for sale and I became very interested in the carvings of the Makonda people. They carved ebony wood Into classic elephants and other animals, figureheads and also strange nightmarish creations. Apparently the original carvings were done in ivory and were often very erotic. We took a trip to meet an old Russian who, before nationalization, owned a major tanzarite mine. He had an interesting collection of some of these earlier carvings and we also saw beautiful examples of tanzarite, a turquoise-blue precious stone with unfortunately a rather ordinary name.

Talking with a couple anchored nearby, we learn they were heading north to pass through the Red Sea. They were planning to buy a large collection of Makonda carvings and resell them to the French Navy in Djibouti. We decided to join forces and travel out to the big market established near the University on the north coast.

We arrived by bus and spent all day with the hundreds of dealers and carvers. We did some hard bargaining, walking away, coming back; but finishing up with some beautiful pieces. We found a Land Rover to bring everything back and, as we loaded it, we were still doing last minute deals. We had a stack of walking sticks with two snakes winding up to the handle. We also had elephants and a beautiful rhinoceros which I still have. We had stick or skeleton people and the ladies busts with intricate hairstyles, letter openers and so on.

The couple we were with had bought, among other things, a massive piece of ebony carved into hundreds of little people climbing on top of each other. It took two of us to lift it. Fortunately, they had a very big Taiwanese ketch it could never have fitted in *Sea Loone*.

And so we had plans to go on safari again. We also made vague plans to head out from Dar es Salaam to the Seychelles later in the year. There we would pick up the southwest monsoon and returned to Egmont Island in Chagos where we would spend the whole season before moving on to South Africa and back into the Atlantic.

We were busy and life was interesting so what happened next is difficult to comprehend and extremely difficult for me to write down.

10

I WENT ASHORE that evening for a few beers at the bar taking the dinghy as it was easier than raise the launch crew. Jean, not unusually, stayed on board. I returned not so late to find nobody on board.

I thought this strange because Jean had no transport and we never swam around at night. I began to panic and rowed around the anchorage calling her name. When I returned to the boat it hit me like a bomb. On the aft deck were Jean's glasses without them she was virtually blind. I shot down below remembering seeing the forward floor open. The large heavy weight used with the anchor was missing. There was nothing else, no note, nothing. But I knew where Jean was and it totally freaked me out. She was only twenty feet away under the boat!

I only recall bits of what happened after that. I found Mike, the pilot, and John. Then, first thing in the morning, two divers from the local dive club brought Jean up. She was naked. She had cut her wrists and tied herself to the weight. We wrapped her in a blanket and she was taken away in the back of a pick-up to find some refrigeration.

Meanwhile I was a mess. I couldn't stop crying. I couldn't understand and of course I blamed myself. Over the next couple of days, without much help from me, the wheels started turning. I went with the truck to recover Jean's body and deliver it to the hospital for a post mortem. It seemed like a thousand Africans swarmed around the truck when we arrived and I remember wanting to kill every one of them for their morbid curiosity.

John took me to the police station for an interview with the Chief of Police. He was sympathetic. He accepted that it was suicide and also accepted that I had the right to deal with the burial. But then of course the British Government stepped in, sending some idiot from the Embassy. In typical British fashion, he did not agree with our "common law" relationship and insisted that everything be done through Jean's father in the UK.

John eventually succeeded in quietening down the man so that, once the death certificate was finally made out, I could go ahead with the burial. But this was not going to be easy. There was no Church of England in Dar, no protestant priest, no church, no cemetery and no crematorium. I didn't know where to turn. Jean's dad was very accommodating but would really have liked to have some sort of small service for Jean.

Then, out of the blue, an Indian lady came to the rescue. She was John's business partner. She said she'd be happy to arrange an Indian burial which would involve a funeral pyre. I insisted that there should be a coffin. So a carpenter was found to make one and I provide an ebony urn for the ashes. I would take it to sea and scatter the ashes on the ocean.

The Indian family invited me to lunch at their home to go over the details. Without their help and support, I would have been lost. When I finally received the death certificate, the remains were collected from the hospital and the following day, at the Indian burial site, we stood as a small, sad group, me, Mike and Lynn, John, Magna and someone from the Embassy.

The funeral pyre was enormous with the coffin perched on top. Someone climbed a ladder and poured black oil over everything. Then it was set alight.

How long we were supposed to stay and watch this, I don't know. The fire burnt ferociously and I could see the coffin blackening and burning. I could also see what was about to happen. The coffin was about to fall open. I made a rapid exit. It was another nightmare.

Afterwards, we had a small wake at Mike and Lynn's house, although my Indian saviours were a little nervous in a European household.

The last little episode in the nightmare happened a few days later with the delivery of the ashes. The urn was delivered full but there was also a large clear plastic bag with more ashes and charred bones. I dug a hole in Mike's flower bed and buried the excess.

All this time, Clark and Michelle had been sailing down the coast. They missed the funeral although I think they may have known about it but couldn't handle it.

It was out of the question for me to stay in Dar es Salaam Too many ghosts; too many eyes. So I went down to the Dhow Harbour and for only one hundred shillings, less than one dollar, got coastal clearance for Mtwara, the most southerly port on the Tanzanian coast. I was in fact going to head direct for Richards Bay, South Africa down the Mozambique Channel .It was the middle of the cyclone season. I really didn't care and wasn't looking much farther ahead than *Sea Loone*'s bow.

A week out in the middle of the ocean and with blue skies and a deep blue ocean , a light breeze pushing me south, I scattered Jean's ashes on the surface of the water. My pilot fish shot out from under the boat to see what was happening, having no interest, they shot back into the shade. The ashes were left behind in the gentle wake. I listened to some silly sentimental music and cried my heart out. I felt very sorry for myself one minute, then wondered if it was all my fault the next.

Dar es Salaam is seven degrees south of the equator; Richards Bay twenty nine degrees south. I had more than 1,300 miles to sail. In the mood I was in and without Jean to record anything, nothing much got written down.

The days passed. It was when I was off Maputo, Mozambique, with some 300 miles to go, that things got a little worrisome. Huge swells stared to develop. Eventually they got so big that I was losing the wind in the valleys and then being knocked over on the tops. It had to be a cyclone creating this; but where was it and which way was it moving?

The barometer wasn't doing anything dramatic so I assumed the cyclone was moving away. The swells decreased but the wind howled and moved to the northeast. Adding the strong Agulhas Current to the wind, we were tearing along in seas that were coming right over the boat. Battling to get the storm jib on the foredeck in the middle of the night was no fun!

After three days of this, battered and bruised, I came into the coast off Cape St. Lucia. The barometer had been dropping dramatically and it was going to be a race to get into Richards Bay before the southerly change caught me and blew me back to Mozambique.

With only twenty miles to go, the wind died and I motored into the buoyed channel. I had never been more relieved to get into calm water. I had arrived safely.

The dredged channel leads into a huge busy port with a massive coal-loading berth and container berths. It was busy! I was met by a small warship and escorted into the small boat harbour where the crew helped me tie up and wait for the officials. The whole harbour was inside a huge security fence with no access to the public.

Quarantine and customs were quickly dealt with but I had to stay where I was until next morning before immigration arrived. There was no problem and the navy ship returned to escort me to the yacht club. I borrowed two crew to help me tie up when I arrived. They were nice lads doing their military service but couldn't tie a knot for love nor money. So here I was tied up to the wharf at the Zululand Yacht Club. I had some thinking to do!

The yacht club was in a creek on the north side of the harbour, separated from the ocean by huge sand hills. There were maybe a dozen foreign yachts tied up three-deep against the wharf. Other boats were tied to a rickety jetty and others still, tied stern-to on the far bank. Some of the yachts had been there a while others, some of which I knew, had arrived in November and would stay for a year. The best time to sail around the Cape was mid-summer, December or January. So I would also be staying until November or so.

The yacht club was lively with a busy bar and a small restaurant. There was a primitive trailer, slipway and winch to haul boats out. There was a small village within walking distance with a shop and a post office. A short bus ride from there was a new shopping center and an early morning bus could take you to the big city of Durban and get you back in the evening.

I spent the first days propping up the bar drinking away my sorrows and being unsociable. But that was only going to cause me more problems so I had to get a grip.

Dick, the New Zealander on *Contour* and Alvah on *Zenie P. II* were both on safari as were a few others, but some had found work and Paul, a German on a large steel yacht, had a job with Bell Equipment, a large factory in town. He got an interview for me with one of the engineers who was looking for a boilermaker.

Andre, the engineer, was an Afrikaner. He was designing tools and equipment to facilitate some of the work in the factory. My job would be to make these things. The factory made heavy earth moving machinery and forestry equipment. There were very successful and busy, partly because of the restrictions on imports for the mines because of apartheid.

I was given some space in a quiet corner of the factory. It had a bench, welding machine and burning gear, the last of which I wasn't sure how to use. I had explained to Andre that I could easily understand his drawings and shouldn't have any problem making things up but I wasn't actually a boilermaker. We agreed to give it a week's trial and then we would both decide whether to carry on. The pay was so poor I wasn't very enthusiastic.

The weeks went by and although I wasn't earning much money, I was at least keeping myself busy and out of the bar. Andre spent a lot of his time drawing the architectural plans for houses needing local planning permits, nothing to do with Bell Equipment. A lot of the designs and drawings he gave me turned out to be impractical and my efforts finished in the waste skip.

In the end, I was allowed to have a go myself and had fun making jigs for welding. I also designed a mobile machine for pressing bushings into axles and then reaming them out with the same tool.

From the first day, I had been given a helper. He was a Zulu and he knew his way around the factory, spoke English, and was an enormous help. Besides him I had another group of Zulus to dig foundations for some new machinery, and a group on the far side of the factory, removing a huge concrete engine bed.

Initially, I hounded them all to get the work done. They would slow down and stop altogether if I didn't keep an eye on them. There was always a crowd of men outside in the street if I needed more workers. I simply walked out there and pointed to one or two likely lads and if I wasn't happy with them it was just as easy to put them back on the street

On pay day, I had to go to the accounts office and pick up the wage envelopes for all the men and hand them out. This was Friday afternoon. The amount of money they were getting was printed on the envelope.

I was only getting nine rand an hour, approximately four dollars – hardly worth getting out of bed for. But the Zulus that I had been pushing and shouting at were getting a small fraction of that. I was embarrassed. I handed out the wages. They had a few hours to go before knocking off but I told them all to piss off early and never hounded or hassled them again. If the bosses wanted the work to go faster, I simply went out in the street and got more men.

The biggest job I had was making up some massive rails for a gantry crane to be installed in the factory in Johannesburg. I was then flown up there to put the rails in place. Nobody told me how cold it would be. The first morning there was frost on the steel beams. They also never told me that nobody spoke much English. Andre came with me and disappeared to see his family for the whole week. Still, I found a special mobile crane I could hire and got the beams up and bolted together.

While I was up in the roof doing this, a black guy staggered in underneath me and fell down with a knife in his back. Apparently, it was the anniversary of some riots in which a lot of people had been killed and the guy should not have been working. The poor bugger died right there.

Back in Richards Bay I made some extra money selling some of the Makonda carvings and the shells, sea shells and turtle shells. I exchanged two turtle shells for a small dinghy which I put my sailing rig on. I wondered how long this third one would last me.

There was a steel barge anchored out in the creek and I moved *Sea Loone* out and tied alongside. I had to use the dinghy to get ashore but at least out there the tide didn't affect me. A few weeks later another cement yacht joined me on the barge and we both emptied out our boats to clean up and paint the interiors.

The other boat was called *Ouais Ouais*, a gaff rigged ketch. On board were Frank, an American and Elise, French Canadian and a trained artist. I had to make a non-contamination line across the barge as they had a huge infestation of cockroaches in their gear.

I learned a lot from them. They made jewellery from anything they picked up on the travels and they had a boatload of amazing stuff. Elise did scrimshaw on whales' teeth if she could find them. They made earrings and bangles, bracelets out of shells, coral and so on and they made good money. I had made a few small things like the turtles on Bora Bora but they had taken the whole thing to a much higher level and sold to shops and galleries in large quantities, a full-time occupation.

Meanwhile, Alvah and Diana arrived back from their safari. They had bought a Land Rover and done a lot of work on it before leaving. They had taken a canoe with them for when they arrived at the Okavango Swamps. But Alvah was not happy. He had been restricted from going where he wanted and had to camp in the designated sites. They were not supposed to leave the vehicle nor have a campfire. The canoe had also been a problem; but he'd covered huge area I'm sure they saw lots of game and amazing scenery.

I had to give them my news about Jean. Ad similarly, had to tell Dick from *Contour* when he returned, not so pleasant.

Dick had his own news. While in Chagos, *Contour* and *Mash* had swapped wives so Dick was now with Jane and Christopher and James had a new mother which they seemed very happy with. *Mash* was apparently not far away, in Durban.

Dick and family had taken a camper-van all over the place. Dick was as mad as Alvah and at one point had come face-to-face with a huge bull elephant. It charged him but before he fled, he took the most amazing photo of the elephant with its ears spread and it trunk in the air, barreling towards him. Apparently, there was a large tree to dodge around and the elephant turned away.

Tony Soars, one of the members of the club, had a sports fishing boat he had sold and had to deliver down the coast to East London. Tony was a huge man, an ex-Londoner and a really friendly helpful person. Together with another club member, the three of us set off, first to Durban and then, weather permitting, down the Wild Coast to East London. There was no autopilot so we had to steer the whole way and the boat tended to broach as you motored down the swells. We spent the day in Durban and then carried on. Luckily, with good weather, the whole trip was easy.

Meanwhile, I had put up notices in the yacht clubs that we passed saying I was looking for crew. It went something like:

Crew wanted for Caribbean. Must be:
- **A girl**
- **Have a non-South African passport (because Brazil and most of the Caribbean islands refuse entry to South Africans)**
- **Be less than 5'4" (the spare bunk is a bit short)**
- **Must have no sailing experience (I don't need to be told how to run the boat)**
- **Have some money, including enough for flight home (otherwise if push came to shove I'd have to pay)**

I got two replies. The first was a girl member of the Royal Natal yacht club who crewed for the racing boats in the harbour. She worked as a representative traveling all over Natal so one day turned up at Richards Bay. She arrived dressed for work in skirt, stockings and high heeled shoes but was game enough to jump in the dinghy and get rowed out to the barge.

It wasn't a good idea on her part to stand on *Sea Loone*'s foredeck and tell me this was where she normally did her thing when racing in Durban harbour. Nobody goes on my foredeck in anything more than a strong breeze, not if I can help it. Anyway I told her I'd get in touch when I was coming south.

The second reply was a letter enclosing a picture of a pretty young blonde girl, Tracey Smith. She lived in Durban, had traveled around Australia and was keen to travel some more. She was born in Liverpool – amazing! Her parents came to South Africa when she was ten years of age. She was now twenty four. She knew nothing about sailing, had a British passport and was 5'-2". She was trying to save money teaching aerobics during the day and waitressing at night.

She sounded too good to be true. But the thought occurred to me that, if she saw *Sea Loone* with half its innards on the barge and still needing a paint job outside, then she wouldn't be impressed. So I put her off coming to Richards Bay. I told her I would be in Durban in November.

It was the sort of incentive I needed to work on the boat. A young lad called Plastic who seemed to spend most of his time hanging around the yacht club, promised me a hand to get the boat out of the water, grind off the bottom and paint it with antifouling. I couldn't afford to pay him but Plastic worked like a Trojan. With a new coat of coal tar epoxy primer on the bottom and a good coat of anti-foul the boat went back in the water. On the barge, I painted the top sides sanded down the toe rail and oiled it and then put the interior back together. The boat hadn't looked better in a long time.

Plastic wanted a captains sailing ticket which required him to have spent days at sea on the ocean, so he came with me to Durban and he filled in his log for a week at sea which I signed. He was such an enthusiastic sailor that I wished I could have done more for him. We had only actually sailed over night to Durban.

Durban's International jetty, a scruffy wooden structure was next to the Point Yacht Club with the Royal Natal Yacht Club across the road. The jetty was chockablock, four or five deep in boats all heading south. There was one smaller boat up front and another about the same size as *Sea Loone* which I tied alongside. It belonged to a single handed Swede and the boat was a bit scruffy. All the other yachts were much larger and luxurious looking.

I telephoned Tracey and she promised she would come down to the jetty as soon as she finished work, around teatime. Dick and Jane were also tied to the jetty so I had them looking out for me in case I missed her. No problem, she was as pretty as a picture and vivacious with it. She looked around the boat and didn't look horrified at how small it was. The Swede came up trumps inviting us on his equally small boat. I then introduced her to Dick and Jane and whoever else was around. After that we set off to find a bar and discuss the whole thing over a few drinks.

I explained that sailing down the coast to Cape would probably be very rough and not a good introduction to sailing. Maybe it would be better to meet the boat in Cape Town and start sailing from there. Tracey would have nothing of it. She would leave on *Sea Loone* with me.

I explained that we would spend some time in Brazil and then, when we arrived in the Caribbean, we would have to find work. She saw no problem with that. What little money Tracey had managed to save would be well gone and the US$400 I had left, would only just keep us until we found work. I did however have lots of shells and some carvings. These would bring in some reasonable money.

So in a couple of hours it was agreed. I had a crew and she would be moving on board in a matter of days. Meanwhile Tracey had to leave and get to the restaurant to do her evening shift which ended well after midnight.

I slept that night with a smile on my face thinking that maybe there was a life worth living. I must have been deeply asleep. I woke to found a very naked, very curvaceous body in my bed. Like any sailor, I took full advantage.

The following evening Tracey's mum and dad came down to meet me and see the boat. Tracey's dad was a ship's agent and her mum worked for a large store in town. Her mum was only a couple of years older than me so naturally we talked a lot about Liverpool in the 60s, the clubs and the bands. We finished off a bottle of gin before going out for meal. Then we returned to the jetty as we had been invited to a party on a huge Australian yacht which had just arrived. By this time, we were all very merry.

Tracey was happy to get away from the subject of Liverpool, a place she hardly remembered. Meanwhile, her mum was telling everybody how wonderful *Sea Loone* was. There was an impressive mixture of nationalities and the whole thing went down perfectly.

Tracey moved on board and over the next two weeks reorganize the galley and the clothes storage. A couple of large boxes arrived which were the contents of her bottom drawer. It was stuff apparently put away for when she settled down and got married. A month later, most of it went to the flea market in Cape Town.

While in Durban, I met a young guy Hans Klarr. His father, Ernst was the owner of the junk I had met in Grand Comore. Hans, his brother and his sister, had been brought up on the junk sailing from Vietnam. He had just come down from Madagascar with a small catamaran. He and a few other boats did a regular tour around from South Africa to Madagascar to the Comores and back, trading goods in between and doing really well. He spoke of the wildlife, the birds, orchids, the lemures and reptiles of Madagascar. I wish I hadn't missed it but with not much left in the piggy bank I couldn't turn back. Next time, maybe?

Tracey and I left Durban on November 30th. The wind dropped to a flat calm and we sat out there for more than a day. By the time we got past Port

Shepstone the seas started building up and we were motor-sailing south.

So far, Tracey was having no problems. We picked up the current which pushed our speed up to seven knots then past nine knots at one point, all on a pitch black night. I was hand steering and getting tired so Tracey took over while I lay down for a short break. She was to call me if any ship was getting close.

An hour or so later she woke me and right there coming up astern was a huge ship. I grabbed the tiller and we shot off at right angles. The ship steamed past. My heart was thumping but Tracey was unperturbed and I got my head back down for another hour. The following morning beating into big seas we were not making much headway through the water but the current was sweeping us along and by midday we were heading into East London. We were soon tied up to the wooden wharf at the back of the harbour.

So we had done the worst leg, the wild coast. Although it was a pretty miserable sail, Tracy had actually enjoyed it. The next jump down the coast was to Port Elizabeth so we waited for the next front to go by. I remember finding a pretty yellow orchid with a small chameleon perched on it and I remember a shower stall we found in the middle of a derelict building site where we spent a bit of time together.

The trip to Port Elizabeth went without a hitch and we tied up alongside a trawler in the main harbour. With the boat secure, we hitchhiked down to Knysna where *Contour* was anchored. We spent a night with Dick and Jane and the boys and then borrowed their tent to carry on to Oudtshoorn to see ostriches and the Kango Caves which Tracey wanted to see.

Hitchhiking was quite easy and we arrived at the caves which were worth seeing. On the way back we camped by a small stream one night and then in Oudtshoorn visited one of the many ostrich farms. The young ones tried to eat my camera as I photographed them. There were fresh ostrich eggs available and I really should have taken one back for breakfast with Dick and Jane.

We returned the tent, checked on the boat in Port Elizabeth, and set off to return to Durban to spend Christmas and New Year with Tracey's mum and dad. So we had a family Christmas and then a monster party at their friends house on the Bluff for New Year.

The first day of 1989 we spent mainly in bed, recovering. But the next day we were on the road again. In only twelve hours we hitched 550 miles to get back on board *Sea Loone*.

It took a day to scrub the black manganese dust off the boat from the loading wharf across the harbour and a few days to wait for another break in the weather. Then we were off again.

The coast was tending due west and we were already 34° South, so it was cool. We still had the Agulhas Current behind us and with an easterly wind we could move fast.

We ducked into Mossel Bay to miss the next front coming along from the southwest. It was a fishing port with a large Afrikaans population. There were lots of "whites only" signs which we hadn't seen before.

One of the fishing boats had a crew of Cape Coloureds, friendly smiling people one of whom had a glass or two whisky with us on the boat. They were fishing for squid and the next day we were given a month's supply. We had sea lions playing around and under the boat to amuse us. One young one floated out from under the wharf to drift alongside us, fast asleep.

From Mossel Bay with a good break in the weather, we could easily make it to Cape Town. We had to round the most southern point of Africa, Cape Agulhas and then around the Cape of Good Hope into Haut Bay underneath Table Mountain.

It all went well as far as Cape Agulhas. We saw some penguins and a black browed albatross came by. The wind then started picking up and moving around. We were flying along with one of the blue nylon downwind sails poled out. The forecast was for 60 knot winds in the opposite direction, dead against us. So we were pushing it! I finally decided to take the sail down and put something much smaller up. As I released the halyard the sail blew to smithereens. One minute it was there; the next, just a few torn blue ribbons.

We kept going with a small jib and rounded the Cape of Good Hope. We were now in the Atlantic and had only a few miles to go to Haut Bay. It was already dark when the change came. We hove to with a fully reefed mainsail. It howled and the seas started building up. Table Mountain was highlighted in the moonlight. As dawn broke, we hoisted the storm jib and beat into the coast. It took two tacks and the engine, but just after lunch we arrived.

Inside the harbour wall was a sort of floating marina. Dick and Jane were there to catch our lines and tie us up.

The exchange rate was about two rand to the US dollar and we had to pay the yacht club ten rand a week and five rand per day for the marina. The marina pontoons were not attached to the side so we still needed the dinghy, but nobody was complaining. The sea lions had the use of the pontoons for free and Dick's lads speared sardines and fed them to them.

We took a few trips around with Dick and Jane. We got into trouble on the first trip by train to Simons Town and False Bay. We had bought the cheapest tickets and we were in the best compartment. So we were thrown off. The second trip out, we went wine tasting to Groot Constantia. We bought tickets for the tasting but Tracey and Jane got caught helping themselves to the two spare jugs on the bar. Jane's jug contain only water but Tracey's jug of red wine was actually the slops from tastings.

Dick and I laughed and the girl at the bar explained that the tickets were for the university students who visited. We could have as many samples as we liked. We took full advantage and left quite drunk. Staggered down the hill we noticed the sign for the Brazilian Embassy so we brazenly called in there to see about our Brazilian visas. Thank God Brazilian people are so charming.

In Simons Town and Haut Bay there were businesses polishing and cutting semiprecious stones and exotic minerals. Tracy and I spent hours sorting through mountains of polished, tumbled stone, amethysts, tiger's eyes, carnelions and so on. The equivalent of forty dollars bought us four kilos. In Cape Town I found jewellery supplies and bought hooks and eyes, all silver-plated and very cheap. Made up into necklaces and earrings, the stones, I reckoned, would be very salable.

The wind could certainly blow. It went on for days and sometimes it could be freezing cold. We wanted to go on around to Cape Town harbour to do some provisioning before leaving. So on one flat calm day, together with *Contour*, we motored around. We passed the sea lion colony and chased the penguins and sunfish, some of which were huge. Tracey on the bow directed me towards another huge sunfish and I actually ran up on its back but it was no sunfish, it was an absolutely huge great white shark.

Tracy took an amazing photo of just its head immediately beneath her on the bow with its beady eyes and gills slits. When I touched it, it swam forwards and then I saw it. As you can imagine I turned the boat away. I reckoned that one sweep of its tail could seriously damage our rudder.

We tied up at the Royal Cape Yacht Club amongst the forest of other masts. Table Mountain loomed over us with the tablecloth rolling off its edge most days. So of course the next trip with Dick and Jane was up on the cable car to the top.

Ever since falling out of a tree as a lad, I have had problems with heights. Dick found the most nasty precipitous path around the lip of the mountain. I followed and then froze. We were on a narrow ledge which dropped vertically to the city below. I could feel gravity pulling me to the edge. So Dick, Jane and Tracey strolled casually along; I followed on my hands and knees.

Stocking up to leave was easy in Cape Town. The supermarket had a large trailer which they could use to deliver everything to the yacht club. The duty-free shop would deliver the booze. For the vegetables from a wholesaler down on the docks, we needed a taxi; but there were some fantastic bargains.

We bought nearly two hundred tins of meat and vegetables, two cases of whisky for Brazil, a load of dried fruit from a farmers co-operative, a sack of butternut squash for a few rand, a box of small apples, five kg of grapes for one rand, sacks of potatoes and onions. Loaded up," Sea Loone" squatted down in the water.

We had spent six hundred and fifty rand in the supermarket alone. I had used all the money saved from Richards Bay and Tracey had used up all her money but we had food to last half a year or more, so money well spent. I was back to using my piggy bank money.

11

ON FEBRUARY 15, 1989, we cleared out. Tracey presented her South African passport. It's known as a "green mamba" because it always bites and sure enough we had an extra office to go to for a South African to leave on a foreign flagged vessel. It delayed us but finally we motored out into the ocean into a thick fog bank. A mile further out and we broke out into blue sky and blue sea but not much wind.

Three days on and the wind had been picking up. We were running at night with the genoa, broad reaching down the swells. We were outside the shipping lanes and I was dozing down below. The swells were getting bigger and bigger. I must have been asleep for a while and woke up to the boat being picked up by a huge swell. The stern kept lifting and suddenly a loud gurgling noise meant that we were surfing down the front of a wave.

Fortunately we didn't broach, but kept straight ahead. Otherwise we might have rolled over horribly. I shot out into the cockpit, let go the sheet and then went up to the mast and dropped the headsail. Half an hour later we had the small jib up and were moving along steadily. *Sea Loone* had never made any attempt to surf before. It gave me quite a fright!

We were heading for St. Helena, a dot in the middle of the South Atlantic. Each day the weather got warmer and Tracey burned her bum as we headed back into the tropics. A couple of calm days and we jumped over the side and swam with small tuna and dolphin fish. Later we had a huge shoal of tuna under the boat and a marlin some ten feet long, its beak almost touching the self steering paddle.

We caught a lot of fish. One huge tuna split some of the teak planking and bent the compass bracket in its death throes. Fortunately, I had put the compass down below when I saw what was on the hook.

On March 2, we had a little celebration as we crossed the longitude for Liverpool. I had circumnavigated the world! Three days later we arrived at St. Helena.

St. Helena had been Napoleon's prison island and an important coaling station for the steamships heading around the Cape. It was now no more than a sleepy village. The Royal Mail ship *St. Helena* called every six weeks, traveling from Southampton to Cape Town and back. The only other visitors were yachts.

We dropped the anchor in deep water and ran stern lines to a mooring. We then pumped up the rubber ducky to go ashore. The customs and quarantine man had been out to see us and Dick and Jane who had already arrived, came over to say hello. Tracey was keen to get ashore. She had a back pack full of washing as there was a place right on the wharf to do it.

Since leaving Durban we had not had much need for a dinghy as we were normally tied alongside. So it was a novelty to Tracey. Unfortunately, St. Helena needs a bit of experience as it's famous for its rollers.

The landing place is a vertical rock wall. There is a ladder nailed to it and at the top, a platform with an overhead beam from which a few ropes dangle. The sea rose and fell, so at the top of the swell you could step onto the platform and grab the rope if you needed to steady yourself; or step off onto the top rung of the ladder which had two handrails. When the swell dropped, it did so dramatically maybe ten feet, and on big days much more.

So I was going to drop Tracey off and come back a little later after doing some work sorting out in the boat.

We rowed across and I turned the dinghy round and backed up to the ladder. I said I'd shout "now" when the swell was at its top and Tracey could step off onto the ladder. Unfortunately, she dithered when I shouted "now". The swell dropped and she stepped off onto the ladder at the bottom. I could only row away and watch, together with a small group of locals on the wharf.

The swell came back up and Tracey disappeared. Then she reappeared climbing up the ladder looking very wet with water pouring out of the back pack and her clothes. I fell off my seat into the bottom of the dinghy roaring with laughter and the locals joined in. Poor old Tracey arrived on the platform spitting blood, set to murder me. But when she saw the audience laughing, she eventually saw the funny side and started laughing herself.

To come ashore with the rubber ducky was quite easy with a bit of practice. You rowed in, jumped out holding a long painter, and then slid the dinghy onto the platform with the next swell. On a big swell you could row on to the platform and simply step out as the water receded.

Just up the hill on the way to town, was "Ann's Place", a restaurant, bar, meeting place, mail drop, information centre and everything else you could think of for visiting yachties. We became good friends because of the new onion law. There was a new ban on the import of onions on the mail ship. The islanders were told they had to grow their own. So when we arrived there were no onions and running a restaurant without onions was not easy.

Ann's husband was the quarantine officer. But when I mentioned I had a whole spare sack of onions on the boat we came to an agreement. She got the onions and the husband turned a blind eye .In return when we left we got a sack of fresh vegetables to take with us. It was worth its weight in gold as they were difficult, or impossible to find.

The local people speak a strange olde-worlde English which isn't too easy to understand. They live in one tight little valley facing the anchorage. There are fortifications everywhere from the time they brought Napoleon to the island. The coast is desert dry but we were told there is some greenery higher up; and even a forest on the mountaintop. So we had to make another excursion.

First we visited the mansion where Napoleon had lived and met the tortoise, one of the giant tortoises brought from Aldabra. The tortoise was supposed to have known Napoleon.

The next place to visit was the third green on the golf course. A PhD student from England was studying the wire bird. An endemic wading bird, it is found nowhere else. With very few left they usually hang about the third green. Sure enough there were two of them pecking around right there.

Having ticked off one of the world's rarest birds, we took a footpath up to Diana's Peak and sure enough we entered a lichen-covered forest. We even found a banana tree with a bunch of bananas which we appropriated.

We had to pay a landing fee of twenty six pounds when we arrived. I had met a German guy and his New Zealand girlfriend in Cape Town on a very small boat called *Notos*. He was on his way back to the Virgin Islands to work again for the Moorings Charter Company. I was hoping to meet him and talk more about work in the Caribbean. Unfortunately, their budget was even worse than ours and they had refused to pay the landing fee and carried on sailing.

By the end of the second week we had squeezed all we could from our twenty six pounds. Ann came up with a sack of cucumbers, carrots, tomatoes, Chinese cabbage and bananas in payment for the onions and we set off for Salvador, Bahia de Todos Santos, Brazil.

On March 23rd, Tracey had her birthday complete with birthday cake and a few candles. She was twenty-five. Apart from problems with a persistent itchy rash on her arms, she was well into life on the ocean waves. Having given up smoking on New Year's Day, I had continuous problems with mouth ulcers, something I knew was going to happen. And then I had to see the doctor in St. Helena for another more personal problem, which he put down to "over indulgence". Ah well!

St. Helena to Salvador was a very uneventful trip. Maybe the most interesting event was when Tracy was cooking, a flying fish arrived and narrowly missed going directly into the frying pan. I had a large squid do that once. The satellite navigator had been in hospital again in Durban but was now sick yet again and I had to drag the sextant out. I hadn't managed to find a 1989 Almanac in Cape Town, so was using a 1985 Almanac I had kept.

As we entered Bahia, we saw the city of Salvador covering the hills to the north. We passed the naval station and turned into the harbour. A large fort, Forte da Santa Marcola, sat in the middle of the harbour and yachts seemed to be anchored all around it. There were dozens of French yachts, mainly steel and looking rather rusty. We found a space for ourselves and threw in the anchor. *Contour* with its centerboard and shallow draft was further in.

The city crowded down to the water's edge, noisy and busy. The centre of town looked down on us from a steep escarpment and there was an escalator lift arrangements just like you'd find in Lisbon. I find Portuguese a difficult language to understand but my bit of Spanish helped and the people were very friendly anyway. The Port Captain offered us coffee before starting the paperwork and it turned out that most business starts with coffee, even sometimes buying just the simplest thing. I'm a coffee addict so had no problem with that custom.

It was important to be streetwise. Jane had already lost her gold necklace in the market. Dick had taken off after the thief but lost him when he dived in the harbour and swam across to the other side.

There was some slick money changing going on in the streets. With hyperinflation, the different notes available were confusing, old crusado's, new crusado's and so on. There was a black market so there was no occasion to go to the bank. We finally used a coffin-maker's shop which offered the best deal. The inflation created difficulties. For example, something in the supermarket would disappear from the shelves only to reappear the next day at half as much again as the original price. Or maybe it wouldn't reappear for weeks.

One day Tracey and I saw chocolate at a very reasonable price, a whole shelf of it. So we went up on the escalator and crossed the Cathedral Square to the money changer to change the dollars. Half an hour later, we returned to buy the chocolate. It had all gone. But we then had to find something else to buy with the money and quickly, before it inflated. We later found the Dick and Jane had bought most of that chocolate!

In Cape Town we had been told to bring whisky to Brazil, in particular Johnny Walker, where we could resell it for lots of money. We found the posh yacht club just out of town but when we inquired, we discovered that we had brought the red label and not the black label which everyone wanted. Anyway, we did find a buyer and anchored off the club for a day to row the two cases ashore.

Just down the coast from Salvador, there was a boat builders, making huge seventy foot racing yachts using local timber. We sailed down with *Contour* to Morro de Sao Paulo, a lovely little touristic village on a peninsula at the entrance to a wide river. The next day we followed Dick and Jane up the river. Our depth sounder was not working so we were relying on them to keep in the channel. We left the main river and motored through a mangrove swamp to arrive in a small basin where the boat builders occupied a huge shed on the beach. It wasn't very deep but the English guy managing the place said there would be no problems anchored where we were.

There were two massive hulls under construction laminated from the sheets of local mahogany which was sawn from huge baulks of timber in the yard. The hulls, when completed, would be launched and towed to Salvador. From here they were shipped off to Italy where the keels, mast, rigging etc. were added.

Just after sunset, we touched bottom. The tide had dropped and then continued dropping. We heeled over until the water was lapping on the deck and spurting up through the sink. Dick and Jane came over. *Contour* of course was upright with the centerboard up but we were over at 45° and they enjoyed taking photographs. I slept the night in the bookcase. Fortunately when the tide turned *Sea Loone* lifted back upright without a problem.

Going back down the river we hit a sandbank and for a while the current pinned us against it. *Contour* circled around, found a deeper channel and the current spat us out of the river into deep water.

Back in Salvador we agree to anchor off a yacht club way in the back of the Bay. From there we would take it in turns to make a trip inland. Tracey and I took the eldest lad, Christopher, with us first while Dick, Jane and James looked after *Sea Loone*. They were going to build a new dinghy to accommodate the growing family, Christopher was already taller than me.

Tracy and I now had a small tent. Chris brought his own tent and we set off. I had found out that there was a rare parrot, Spinx's Macaw to be found not too far inland. According to my parrot book, the macaw lived in the forest on the banks of the Rio San Francisco. Looking on the map, we found a town on the river some 300 miles inland. It was called Xique Xique. With such a strange name we decided that it would be our first stop. From there, we would make our way up the river.

We arrived at the huge bus terminal in Salvador and found the bus to Xique Xique. We stowed our backpacks and sat down. There were a few passengers already on board including two nuns. Some minutes later they all got off again including the nuns and the bus started to move. They were all out there push starting the bus. It didn't boost our confidence but in fact, we kept going all night and in the morning arrived at Xique Xique.

We got off the bus and were faced with a huge concrete wall with steps going up it. On the other side was the river. There was not much water flowing and lots of strange river boats pulled up on the muddy shoreline. Communicating wasn't easy but we finally found one boat which was going up the river in the morning and he was happy to take us wherever he was going.

As we clambered back over the wall into town, a fisherman passed us with a basket of fish. I noticed one of them had to be a piranha, a big one. We followed him into the fish shop and I persuaded them to cut the head off the fish and sell it to me. In fact they gave it to me. I still have the top and bottom jaw with the big triangular teeth which mesh together so perfectly.

We camped the night on a swampy piece of ground by the river and daybreak we were back at the beach. Our boat now had four other passengers, young cows to be delivered on the way. The boat was long and narrow with a small cabin in the front for the crew and a solid roof all the way to the stern.

We took up residence in the back and the cows in the middle. The smiling crew disappeared into the little cabin and we set off winding our way around mud banks. There was no sign of any riverine forest so not much chance of seeing our macaw. Smudges of smoke upriver gave us some indication of what had happened to the forest.

At lunchtime we stopped to offload the cattle which were unceremoniously tipped into the shallow water. We took the opportunity to have a little swim in the muddy water just to cool off. There were little fish in the water, tiny things that nibbled our skin but Chris, further out in the river, must have had a more serious nip. He thought of that piranha head in my bag and literally levitated back to the river bank!

The river trip was not really very interesting although the crew were charming and even brought us food they had cooked up in the little cabin. We were dropped in another small riverside town and stayed in a small hotel for only a few dollars including a massive breakfast with the family in the morning. We never did find any forest just an occasional huge tree left untouched which showed how it might have been.

Further up the river we turn back catching a bus heading towards the coast. We came into an interesting mountainous area and a sign indicating a national park and an old diamond mining town, Lensois. So we jumped off the bus and hitchhiked down the side road to the town.

It was a picturesque little town perched on a rocky fast flowing river. We found an office for the National Park. A huge area had been designated as parkland which I suppose looked good to any outsider but in fact, apart from drawing a few lines on a map, nothing else that been done.

We followed one of the rivers which went up into the hills and made camp. The exposed rock in the riverbed was like a coarse granite that smoothed to a slippery sheen. The next day as we climbed up, we found lots of these natural waterslides often dropping into deep pools .It was great fun swooping down each one.

Higher up we left the river and follow the cliff face in which we thought we had seen a cave mouth. Sure enough, a cave with a huge gaping entrance disappeared steeply into the ground. This was hard rock not limestone and must have been a volcanic blowhole or a strange fault in the rock. People had been here before us. We found stubs of candles on the floor which we collected and making sure we had enough to get back out, we set off into the dark gaping hole.

Ahead of us was a roaring noise of fast flowing water. We had gone quite a long way in and the way ahead was getting narrower and lower. Then in front of us was a river. It went from right to left and dropped down into what looked like a bottomless pit which was where all the noise was coming from. We couldn't go any further and with only a few stubs of candle left, we couldn't hang around or we'd be groping in the dark, literally.

We found where the river came out below the cave mouth welling up into a pool. The rest of the day was spent slithering down the river like otters, until we got back to the tents.

Back in Salvador Dick had made a really ugly dinghy but it would carry all four of them. Dick was well over 6 foot and Christopher was catching him up. We sent them off together to try the water slides while we boat-watched.

In the city, I had managed to get an address of a man who sold parrots. Tracy and I went up into town past the money changers coffin shop into a really rough area of old dilapidated tenements. The building we were looking for was grey concrete streaked with mold, the odd weed growing out of cracks. The stairs were filthy and it was dark and smelly as we climbed to the top floor.

When we banged on the door we were let into a room filled with large cages full of parrots, lots of them. There were half a dozen different species. The popular parrot in the old sailing ship days, was a blue fronted Amazon and that's what we came away with. We called him Lorro. For Tracey and Lorro it was love at first sight. Sitting on Tracey's shoulder, Lorro would preen Tracey's eyelashes, fluff its feathers to have its head scratched and do little mating dances. Any female visitor got much the same treatment. But the damn bird hated me. It would even fly into bed in the morning and try and peck me out of it.

Having met Lorro, Jane had persuaded Dick to find another so they retraced our steps and came back with another blue fronted Amazon. Fortunately for them, their's wasn't sexist. Of course, Dick was sure he could manage Lorro so one evening he sat next to the perch and spoke with a squeaky high-pitched voice. Sure enough Lorro marched along the bookshelf and landed on his shoulder all set to preen his facial hair of which he had plenty. Unfortunately, Dick laughed at his success; but it was a ho-ho-ho not a hee-hee-hee. Imediately Lorro realized his mistake and gave Dick a painfull peck on the ear....ha-ha-ha!

Tracey got a letter from her sister in London saying that she was getting married and enclosing a wedding invitation. She had to go but the airfare was going to be a killer. At the Air France office in Salvador I was offered the usual 30% seaman's discount. But we decided to sail up the coast to Natal and maybe get a cheaper deal there. It was already the end of May.

Sailing up the coast was miserable. With ships and fishing boats we had to keep a good watch and there were lots of rain squall often with strong winds. Still it was only 500 miles, not too far.

We arrived off Natal and hove-to for the night. It was a new moon and spring tide, so the next morning, passing between the entrance wall and the reef marker, we had to fight a tidal rip and overfalls. We eventually motored up river opposite the yacht club just down from the town, and threw in the anchor.

I had been wanting to clean the bottom and put on some more antifouling paint. In the Caribbean hauling out was expensive. Here I could use the tide and tomorrow was going to be the best day. So after a quick night's sleep, early in the morning we put *Sea Loone* up against the wall in the yacht club and dried her out.

An old mariner who worked around the yacht club came to help us. Together we scraped off the weed and barnacles as the tide dropped. Then we washed the salt off with a hose. By midday we had a coat of anti-fouling paint that I had bought in Cape Town, painted on. The only panicky bit, was when the boat, which I thought was sitting on hard sand, broke through and started sinking into mud.

Fortunately, we had some spare tires as the side of the boat slid down the wall. After sinking down a foot or so, it stopped and we could go and get a beer while he waited for the tide to rise again. Just like that, a clean bottom for a minimal cost of only fifty dollars for the anti-fouling plus a few dollars for our boatman.

It was now five months into 1989 and five months of purgatory for me with my mouth ulcers from giving up smoking at New Year. Sometimes with the damn things on my tongue, I couldn't talk and on my lips, it was really painful to eat. Worse, it made me really grumpy which didn't please Tracey; so naturally I gave in and bought a packet of cigarettes. I can honestly say next day the ulcers were gone. I was a lot happier and even though Tracey hated the habit, she was happier also.

We found a travel agents that understood the seaman's discount business and they contacted the Brazilian airline Varig who were happy to offer the discount. They were also happy for me to pay in Brazilian money so we could exchange my dollars on the black market. As a result, from $1,500 we got down to $500. Having attended the wedding in London, Tracy would have to find work there to be able to afford the airfare to join me back on the boat.

On the ship's wharf was a small restaurant with a clean toilet, a very unusual thing. One Friday lunch time we were tucking into a meagre meal of chicken, beans, rice and spaghetti which only cost a few dollars and of course a cold beer. There was a large group taking up much of the rest to the restaurant and they invited us to join them. They all worked in the offshore oil business.

Plates and plates of different food arrived, each of which we had to try and of course the beer flowed. The guy who invited us over spoke English. He had worked in the USA. It was Friday and it was normal for them to finish at midday. So they spent the afternoon eating and drinking in this or some other restaurant. The next day, Saturday, our friend Paolo said he would pick us up to take us to the beach.

The beach just out of town was a long stretch of rather dirty sand, the ocean was brown from the river waters which were dragged along the coast by the then north flowing current. At the back of the beach was a continuous row of restaurants, each with tables, chairs and umbrellas. Paolo had his favorite restaurant so we settled under an umbrella.

The beach was a little drab but the people were amazing and some of the girls were drop dead gorgeous. It was difficult at one stage to follow a conversation or drink my beer and nibble my prawns when only a few yards away were two identical twins. They were playing some sort of beach tennis wearing thongs and string bras trying to contain two pairs of very large bouncy boobs.

Having done the beach, Paolo was keen to take us to a cherascaria. We arrived at what appeared to be a very posh restaurant. We were salty and sandy from the beach. Paolo was still wearing his swimming costume. The waiters were all wearing dicky bows but nobody seemed to mind.

In the centre of the restaurant was a huge salad bar which you could visit whenever you wanted. At the table a succession of waiters arrived carrying pieces of meat spit on a sword and a carving knife. With the point of the sword on your plate you could then indicate which piece of meat you wanted carved off if any. They brought different cuts of beef, pork and chicken. More and more arrived. You could eat until you burst!

We met Paolo's wife. They visited the boat and we had more meals together. It was through Paolo's wife that we got involved with bikinis. Tracy and I had talked about buying some bikinis to re-sell in the Caribbean. We thought maybe we should invest quite a lot of whatever was left in the piggy bank

Somehow, Paolo's wife had a contact, two guys that came up from Sao Paolo with a van full of low-priced bikinis, presumably old stock or whatever. She arranged for us to meet them.

We didn't want the "dental floss" which is what Brazilians called string bikinis, and a lot of even normal bikinis were really too skimpy for the Caribbean. Fortunately, what we were shown were reasonably conservative.

We spend a half day with a huge pile emptied on to a table tennis table, deciding which to take.

Unfortunately the large, medium and small in Brazilian translated into medium, small and tiny in American. So we weren't going to be able to satisfy the majority of buyers in the Caribbean. Never mind, the material was good Lycra and the workmanship was excellent. There were a variety of designs and colors. The price was three dollars each. They would normally sell for ten times that price. We decided we couldn't lose and bought two hundred bikinis.

By this time it was approaching the wedding date and Tracey had to fly to London. Hopefully she would be back in November by which time I would be in the Caribbean. Dick, Jane and James had been and gone also. Christopher had flown home to New Zealand to start a boat building apprenticeship.

There was still an English boat anchored in the River, *Thagati*. George, the skipper, was another Liverpudlian so naturally we spent a few hours together in different bars around town. I was keen to see what shells I could collect from fisherman. There was a warehouse where most of these shells were landed, but George and I became friendly with the lobster diving boats. Whenever we saw one coming up the river, we were given first choice from whatever shells they had found. As the weeks passed, I slowly amassed another good shell collection.

In my wanderings I had gone across the river to walk on the deserted northern beach. The tide line was covered in weed and shells as well as small flat sea urchins called sand dollars. A lot of these were alive and I realized that the whole beach was full of them if you dug into the sand. I took a bagful back to the boat to see what I could do with them.

Dropping the sand dollars in bleach, colouring them with fabric dye and then dunking them in a thin epoxy resin, I produced a reasonably strong object as a pendant or, paired, as earrings. A lot of the sand dollars were too large and some just wouldn't bleach white. Once bleached, they were also very fragile but I had reckoned that the process might work. I returned to the beach and collected another bucket full. George having watched, came along and collected another bucket full for himself to play with.

One day in town I bashed my ankle. It was only really a scratch but in a few days it had developed into a nasty tropical ulcer. My ankle swelled up and I couldn't put any weight on my foot .George came to the rescue and half carried me to the local clinic. Then he set off with a prescription written on a scrap of paper and came back with ampoules of penicillin, needles and syringes.

Meanwhile the nurse from hell was digging into my ankle. There was a volcanic hole going down to the bone. She was cleaning it out and pouring in betadine. I got a huge ampoule of penicillin jabbed into my bum and with my ankle bound up, George got me back to the boat.

The antibiotics started working immediately and five days later I returned to the clinic for a second treatment. The volcanic hole was definitely a lot smaller and the swelling had calmed down. A week later I was walking fairly normally and back in the bar drinking beer.

In the bar, a small group of street boys came to see me. They would go for cigarettes if I need them but also they sold me seahorses which they found somewhere locally. I had agreed a price with them but one day, one of them came with three and wanted more money. I told him I wasn't interested. Obviously he didn't want to lose face so he stalked off. Half an hour later the same three seahorses arrived with another boy .They were the normal price and the deal was done. They were great lads and, given the chance, I'm sure they would take over the world.

By mid-August 1989 my ankle was looking good. I stocked up with vast quantities of fruit and vegetables from the market. I knew that at the next stop, French Guyana, food was going to be expensive.

For trading, I had two hundred bikinis, fifty kilos of Brazilian ground coffee. sixteen triton shells, sixteen hawk winged conchs, one goliath conch, five helmet shells, six angular tritons, six volutes and about four hundred sand dollars, all from Natal. George had decided his shells and sand dollars were too smelly, so I had all his, as well as mine.

On August 15th I shot out of the river on the ebb tide and soon found myself off the north eastern point of South America. Here, a shallow bank extends out into the ocean. It was nighttime and everywhere around me I could see the lights of the local fishing boats. It was difficult to gauge how large the boats were or how far away they were. I got a shock when one dim light ahead suddenly seemed to get a lot closer. I steered to pass it .Suddenly, it was a small rowing boat passing within yards of me. The fishermen with hand lines and a paraffin lamp wished me a good evening.

A sharp left hand turn in the morning and I was heading west towards the Caribbean. A few days later I was two hundred miles off the mouth of the Amazon and crossing the equator again back into the North Atlantic. Even that far out, there were huge upsurges and overfalls from the river.

With Tracey gone, Lorro, the parrot, was becoming a little more friendly toward me. He got used to the boat movement but was frightened when the noddys, little brown terns came to roost at night. They'd sometimes land on the self-steering vane which sent Sea Loone off in circles.

I spent much of my time cleaning shells and playing with the sand dollars. The scab on my ankle came away cleanly with no more infection, thank goodness.

Off French Guyana a strong current runs along the coast and I had to start the engine to make sure I didn't get swept past Iles de Salute as we approached. I arrived just at dusk and anchored off the eastern island of St. Joseph. There were a few yachts anchored and two Venezuelan fishing boats.

After a good night's sleep, I re-anchored closer in with a stern anchor out for the tide change. There were three French yachts, a Brazilian yacht and a Swiss yacht. The Venezuelans were shark fisherman.

Iles de Salute's common name is Devil's Island, the infamous French penal colony off the coast of French Guyana. Once ashore I walked around some of the ruins. The cells had gratings in the ceiling where the guards patrolled. The main building had a single raised train rail in a large circle to which presumably prisoners were attached to exercise. It was all straight out of the book "Papillon" which I had read.

The main island across a narrow channel, Isle Royale, had the old administrative buildings and also a brand-new tracking station. Kourou across on the mainland, was the base for the European rocket range. When launched, the rockets flew directly over the islands but unfortunately this never happened while I was there.

A few days later, a customs launch arrived and cleared me into French Guyana with no problems. At the weekend, a fleet of yachts came out from the Kourou River and anchored around me and also almost on top of me. The storm on the Saturday night made one boat dragged and hit me and the others all dragged into each other, typical French sailing bedlam!

The following day I found my stern line broken and my anchor lost, probably from another French yacht which had anchored on top of my line. Fortunately the guys on the Brazilian yacht were brilliant free divers who earned their living from spear fishing for massive grouper fish. To my great relief, they eventually found my anchor in the muddy water. It was my back-up anchor, a CQR which I was very fond of as it only weighed twenty five pounds.

I was getting bored, so decided to go into Kourou. I followed one of the French yachts. There were a few markers but the way into the river wasn't obvious. As the water got shallower, the swells picked up and started picking us up and surging the boat forward, all a bit worrying. But once in the river, the water again became deep enough.

Anchoring off the islands hadn't been easy. In the Kourou River it was much more difficult. There was a really strong tidal flow in and out. The anchor either dragged through the mud or huge areas of mud would shift with your anchor embedded in it. I eventually anchored but when the tide changed, a huge concrete yacht was threatening to come down on me. But before that happened another fifty foot fibreglass yacht which looked brand new dragged into me and caught my anchor chain between its rudder and keel.

The river was full of yachts, mainly French, and all working with the rocket range. Fortunately, the French yachtsman just loves messing around with anchors and dragging them into each other. They have their own design of anchor which seems to guarantee anchoring problems. Anyway, some help arrived and I put out a second anchor, slacked off the first, and managed to get it out from under the other boat.

There was no one on board the rogue yacht and it continued on, dragging up the river. It was going to have major problems when it arrived at the road bridge over the river. But another Frenchman found a spare anchor and managed to stop it before that happened. Weeks later the boat was impounded and the crew arrested. It had been stolen from a charter company in the Caribbean.

The town of Kourou was a scruffy concrete place and everything was expensive. In some ways, this was to my advantage. I had an excess of onions and potatoes which I gave away, but I sold some of the ground coffee and even found some girls interested in bikinis. But I had to take care as customs were used to people coming from Brazil and wanted to stamp out any such trade.

There was good money to be earned in Kourou with the rocket range but people in town were not nice. It was hot and humid and in the rainy season with the river in flood, it must have been much worse. I certainly wasn't tempted to stay.

A yacht I had met in Durban, *Genebelle*, had arrived here and they were recovering from a long trip. Conrad's girlfriend, Mary, was Australian but he was South African. That first major ocean crossing from Cape Town to

Salvador went well enough but with a South African passport, Conrad was not welcome. He was told to leave Brazil immediately. They only had time to take on water and a little food and then had another long passage ahead to French Guyana.

On a little expedition across the river, I caught a large iguana by digging him out of his hole. Back on the boat he escaped under the cockpit and I had a hell of a job finding him. A German, Holger, on a nearby catamaran had a lovely painted boa constrictor so I gave him the iguana for supper.

I had met Holger together with a lot of the other sailors at the pavement bar in town. With things so expensive, the Chinese shopkeeper had put two planks outside on the pavement and here we all sat drinking beer out of his fridge.

Holger had had some problems after arriving in Kourou and asked me to come and look at his boat to see what could be done. It was a thirty foot catamaran built in England which Holger had bought in Gibraltar.

Arriving off Isle de Salut, Holger had miscalculated the current and had had to really push the boat to windward in shorts steep seas and lots of wind. One of the rudders had broken but something much more serious and happened to the boat. The whole thing was now a parallelogram one hull slightly in front of the other.

There was nothing we could do. In the end poor old Holger abandoned the boat there in the river and flew back to Taiwan where he ran a school teaching English. Hopefully he would eventually recoup some of his losses and set off again.

The barometer dropped and there was talk of a big hurricane in the Caribbean. In fact, it turned out to be Hurricane Hugo which ripped through Guadalupe, devastated the Virgin Islands and sank more than a thousand yachts.

It was now mid-September 1989 and with the hurricane season not over before the end of October, there was no great rush to carry on. Still, I had itchy feet.

I had tried crocodile hunting up the river by dinghy at night but saw nothing. I did find a humming bird's nest completely with the bird sitting on it. The nest was minute, sitting on a branch, and could only have been about an inch across. I'd have liked to see the eggs but didn't want to disturb the parent bird.

Down across the river was a dredged creek. I took *Sea Loone* in there out of the current and dived in to scrape off the growth of barnacles. I had cleared out in town for Grenada, the southernmost island in the Caribbean chain. Grenada was near enough to the Equator to be reasonably free of tropical storms and hurricanes.

When I left, the current swept along at more than three knots through the shallow water. That night I got mixed up in a fleet of prawn trawlers and had to stay awake all night dodging them. The next day I headed out away from the coast into deep water. It was maybe 600 miles to Grenada, downwind and down current. The satellite navigator wasn't interested in working but at the naval base in Salvador I had bought a Brazilian Almanac for 1989. It was laid out the same way as the British Almanac so the language was no problem.

The first sight had put me a long way from where I thought I was. When I took it more seriously the next day I got the same discrepancy. I then realized that I had edged so far north to get away from the trawlers and coastal shipping and that I was now in the equatorial counter current. I had allowed myself two knots in the right direction, I in fact had one knot current against me. Well the rules of navigation say you have to believe the book. We passed close to Tobago but I never saw it during the night. Later I picked up lights ahead which had to be Grenada, so I dropped the jib, flattened the mainsail and hove to, "hobby-horsing" into the waves for the rest of the night.

At dawn Grenada was right there and I turned and swept along its south coast. Around midday, I rounded into Prickly Bay. The water was crystal clear for the first time since St. Helene. At the top of the bay opposite the boat yard, I kicked the anchor in and laid back in calm water.

Grenada to Grenada marked my real circumnavigation! Then, contemplating that achievement, I stripped off and plunged into the lovely sparkling water.

Book Three

Period: 1989-2000

1

OCTOBER 8TH 1989 was a Sunday and customs in Grenada charge overtime. So I stayed on board tidying up before rowing ashore in the evening to find a bar for a celebratory cold beer. The sailing season was still a month away, so there were only a few boats in the bay. At the bar I found only one boring Englishmen who had just arrived from the Canary Islands. Still, beggars can't be choosers so I drank a few beers with him.

In the morning I cleared-in at the little office in the boat yard and borrowed a little local money to get to town to collect my mail, change my money, and visit the market.

The mail was waiting for me in the yacht club in St. George's and I strolled around the harbour to the Nutmeg, my favorite cafe, overlooking the carenage. There, with a cup of coffee, I started on my mail.

I left Traccy's letter for last. It was just as well. It was awful! She had got back for the wedding which had gone off without a problem but immediately after, Tracey's dad had dropped down dead. It was a disaster of huge proportions. The house I knew in Durban had been rented but coming to England, they had let it go and everything was in storage.

To pay for the trip and the wedding her dad had cashed in his life insurance so Tracey's mum was left with nothing, not even a place to live. Fortunately, her mom did have a job to go back to and had good friends living on the Bluff in Durban. Tracey had to fly back to Durban to help out in whatever way she could.

Tracy was then going to fly back to London and work as long as she could before flying back to the boat. It seemed to me that to do all this in the couple of months available wasn't going to be easy. She would be lucky to get enough money together simply to buy an air ticket. Well, I tried phoning Durban and wrote a letter to London. I'd stay in Grenada for a month or so and then head north.

The last time I was in Grenada was just before the Americans invaded. The army had paraded on the cricket pitch and the Cubans were building the airfield. The south coast, including Prickly Bay, were then off-limits to yachts and there were stories of a submarine base being built a few bays along from Prickly Bay.

The Cubans of course had now left. Maggy Thatcher, the British prime minister had thanked the Americans but told them that she didn't want Grenada back. So the US was stuck with finishing off the airport which was a great boost to tourism and must have cost the US a lot of money.

There were a few new hotels on Grand Anse but nothing else had really changed. The carenage was really busy; people smiling, the market full of fruit and vegetables and spices. I loved it.

After a few days in Prickly Bay, I dodged round the reefs and anchored off Hog Island just to the east. It was a jewel of an anchorage, totally protected with a lovely sandy beach on the corner of the island where the yachties got together on a Sunday and had a communal barbecue. It was a place to come and hide away during the hurricane season, relax, and prepare for another season working on the islands up north.

There was some particular shells called flamingo tongues with a fancy Latin name, cyphoma giboso, that I wanted to collect. They are small pink and shiny and would join my jewellery stock. While snorkeling around looking for them I could find the odd lobster or octopus for dinner. I found the shells and had cleaned and polished all the other shells by this time, I had also fine-tuned the manufacture of sand dollar earrings in every color you can imagine.

In French Guyana I had sold a few bikinis for the equivalent of twenty-five dollars. I sold a few more on Hog Island. One very voluptuous French lady came to the boat and wanted my opinion on the different bikinis. She was determined to try on each one to find the smallest and skimpiest and I was the judge!

With money coming in, I soon had a kitty of a few hundred East Caribbean dollars; so the US$400 dollars left in the piggy bank could rest undisturbed.

On November 1st, I sailed around to St. George's and anchored off the yacht club in the lagoon. The next day I met Bruce and Lorna, friends from Richards Bay on the yacht *Tantrum*. Bruce had run a sailing school in Durban and was looking for work, skippering. They were heading north to St. Martin where there is quite a population of South Africans working. They were in Cape Town at the same time as Alvah and told me a strange story.

Alvah saw a man fall off the pontoon into the water at the yacht club. The man got stuck under the pontoon and Alvah dived into the freezing water to pull him out but the man had a death grip on something. By the time he had him out of the water, the man was well gone. The ambulance took forever to arrive and by the time the man got to the hospital, he was pronounced dead.

The man was an American and I knew him as Orran. He had something to do with an organization like the CIA. He had once mentioned the Bay of Pigs, the Cuban invasion fiasco, and when Alvah had tried to resuscitate him, he noticed several bullet wound scars through his body.

I had met Orran briefly in Durban but knew him from years before when I was in Golfito, Costa Rica. At that time Orran and his wife were crewing on an old man's yacht parked off Whitey's hotel. On one particular windy rainy night, the old man fell overboard and drowned. The old man had had a number of heart attacks and the couple were waiting for him to die.

At least this was what Whitey thought. The drowning story had a number of holes in it and Whitey was adamant that the old boy had been knocked off. It would be interesting to hear what Whitey would have to say now when he heard about bullet scarred Orran's untimely demise in South Africa.

I set off north in the company of *Tantrum* and made it in daylight, with one tack, to Tyrrell Bay, Carriacou. Passing the infamous rock, Kick,um Jenny, I caught a huge barracuda. I can't eat barracuda, it gives me the screaming abdabs but I kept it for Bruce and whoever else in Tyrrell Bay.

The next day was rough but the day after, I set off again past Bequia without stopping and the following day made it to Marigot Harbour in St. Lucia. I arrived in time for happy hour in the Hurricane Hole hotel where there was a letter from Tracey. I also met the manager of the Moorings Charter Base now operating from Marigot Harbour. I had known him in the early days in the Virgin Islands. When I mentioned the exotic bikinis he promised he would have a word with his boutique lady.

Tracey was coming back, flying into St Lucia on November 19th. I had given her a huge shopping list so she was going to be loaded down.

Still with *Tantrum*, I sailed on up to Rodney Bay and into the lagoon. It was happy hour again so I rowed over to the A-frame, one of the bars at the water's edge. I had been listening to amazing news on the BBC as we sailed up the coast. When I landed in the bar, there was a lone German drinking a beer. I asked him if he had heard the news. He hadn't; so I said, "The Berlin wall came down today!"

He didn't believe me and thought I was trying to be funny. He got angry. Fortunately the next customer was another German who confirmed my story. They were both on holiday, the first from West Germany with relatives in the

East. He could have apologized but just then, Bruce and Laura came in and we left the Germans crying on each others shoulders.

The airport in St Lucia was right on the other side of the island. The road was apparently not very good and taxis were very expensive. I had to go back to Marigot Harbour anyway so I decided to beat along the south coast and anchor in a small bay quite close to the airport.

My friend in the "Moorings" had spoken with his boutique manageress who was enthusiastic about my Brazilian bikinis. She picked out fifty at twenty American dollars each. She would pay me cash when I called in on the way back from the airport. So in one fell swoop I had got my investment back, made four hundred dollars, and still had nearly one hundred and fifty bikinis to go. Things were looking up.

I beat down to the southeast corner of St Lucia and anchored in Vieux Forte Bay off a large banana wharf. The next morning I found a taxi to take me to the airport. It seemed deserted when I got there. The few people I did find there had never heard of Dan Air, the airline Tracey was flying with. I was beginning to wonder if I was in the right airport or even on the right island.

At the last minute more people arrived and one person that did actually work for the airline. Some other airline did most of the groundwork for Dan Air as they didn't come here very often. The plane arrived and taxied up to the terminal building. Steps were pushed up to the plane and people spilled out onto the runway. They were nearly all local people so Tracey's long blond hair was going to stick out but I didn't see her.

The flow of passengers finished and the crew came out. There at last was Tracey. One of the crew was carrying a large box, my new outboard engine. Another had my new pillows...and so on. Tracy had avoided excess baggage by involving the crew and the other passengers. They were all smiles. Customs waved us through, dazzled by another Tracey smile and shortly afterwards, we were motoring back to the banana wharf in a taxi.

Tracey was really happy to be back on the boat. In fact, maybe as happy as I was that she was back. It took two trips with the dinghy but finally we had everything back on board. As soon as she had sat down, Lorro arrived to perch on her shoulder and gently nibbled her ear. A minute later he looked up at me and tried to take a piece out of my hand. All those weeks of slowly getting closer and we were back to square one, the bastard!

The next morning we set off back around the island. Tracey, of course, had not been in the Caribbean before. We passed under The Pitons, the two spectacular peaks on the south west corner of St Lucia and then sailed into Marigot Harbour. It's one of the most beautiful natural harbours imaginable. We sailed into the pool through the narrow channel with steep hills on either side. It's a natural hurricane hole.

With the new Moorings Charter Company docks, it was quite crowded now and there was even a fancy pirate ship replica anchored in the middle, waiting to take a bunch of tourists on a booze-cruise back to town.

The money from the boutique lady was waiting for me and we had a few beers. There was a letter from Pete and Barbara in the BVI, British Virgin Islands, offering a job demolishing a hurricane damaged dock. It was a start but first I wanted to see some people in St. Martin and see if there was anything bigger. I also wanted Tracey to see English Harbour in Antigua, another amazing natural harbor.

We headed north as quickly as possible. In Rodney Bay we picked up Bruce who had just delivered a boat from Martinique and needed a ride back to Fort de France. Bruce is a big man. When we went to winch the dinghy out of the water he leaned over and just picked it up and plonked it on the foredeck.

We didn't have much time to stop in Dominica or Guadeloupe, just anchoring for the night. In English Harbour, the big boats were arriving from the Mediterranean. *Sea Loone* and *Tantrum*, anchored behind each other, were midgets. Alongside me was an old "J" class classic boat from the 1920's, having been recently refurbished at a cost of millions of dollars by an American woman. The mast was the tallest single strut in the world. The boat was a dream.

The boat anchored in front of us again was huge. It was owned by the barbeque manufacturers, Weber. That night that they put on a party to which we were invited as neighbours. All the huge fancy charter yachts had just crossed the Atlantic to start their season in the Caribbean. Our neighbour came up with a huge ice chest of beer, cases of wine they had won in their ocean crossing and fish they had caught, grilled by the chef. It all made for a great party.

It was easy to get trapped in English Harbour. There was always something going on. We hadn't cleared-in as harbour fees had escalated from last time to something ridiculous. So the morning the Port Captain was to do his rounds, our two small boats slipped out and set sail for St. Barts.

St. Barthelemy, or St. Barts as it is normally called, is now a French island, although it was Swedish a couple of times. It is a tax haven due to some agreement the last time Sweden gave the island back to France. There are a few Swedes left on the island. The rest are mainly descendants of French pirates and smugglers.

The island is small with steep hills. It has some beautiful beaches but virtually no arable land; so there were never any plantations and slaves. The main town, Gustavia, was a trading port known as a good place to pick up a case of Barbados rum for a dollar a bottle. But it was developing into a rich man's holiday paradise. Expensive villas were being built looking down over the beautiful beaches.

We only stopped briefly to meet up again with Gordie Murray who we last saw, with his Peruvian wife, when we all sailed out of Bayona in northern Spain. Since then he had sailed back to Milford Haven and then out to the Caribbean. He now had a sewing business in Gustavia making canopies and awnings and such like. They had two children, a girl and a boy. It made me realize the passing years.

This was the area where hurricane Hugo had passed through and Gordie and had had his boat in the lagoon in St. Martin. Tangled up with other boats, it had been driven ashore damaging the rudder and destroying a lot of the bow but it was all back together now. There were maybe 1,000 yachts destroyed and damaged in the area and many more in the Virgins and Culebra Island. The stories were horrendous.

There was nothing for us in St. Barts so we sailed over to St. Martin and anchored off Phillipsburg, a really busy duty-free port with huge wharfs for the cruise ships which arrived every day. I found my contact in the offices of Sun Sail, a huge bare-boat charter company like the Moorings. In fact I think they were already organizing to merge the two companies.

There was talk of me building a small dinghy dock there in the harbour for the company, but they were offering nothing beyond that. The harbour was dirty and always busy with traffic so not very comfortable. The town was full of tourists off the cruise ships.

So the choice between staying in St. Martin or carry on to the Virgin Islands to do the job there was straightforward. I knew that in the Virgin Islands was a perfect quiet anchorage in clear water surrounded by reefs and little islands which would delight Tracey.

I would get a thousand dollars for the demolition job and felt sure that Tracey would find something to occupy herself. I also felt that I would be offered more work after the demolition job. So I telephoned Peter Bailey and said we would be leaving the next day for the Virgin Islands and that we would be able to start the job as soon as we arrived.

We cleared into Virgin Gorda and found Charlie and Janette still there. We had crossed the Atlantic together in 1978 and Charlie now had a thriving outboard engine repair shop on the island. They had taken time off to circumnavigate on *Quark* their 32-foot sloop but we had never bumped into each other. Jeanette was skippering the Rockefeller's private yacht which they kept at their resort just up the coast.

We had a few beers together before shooting over to Great Camanoe where the Bailey's now had a house and where we would find the broken down dock. Peter had been the general foreman on a big marina development close to Road Town, but was now managing a large section of Camanoe Island. There were a dozen or so expensive private homes there. He had built his own home on the island and had a busy job maintaining the homes, roads, dock, and other infrastructure for the owners, none of whom lived permanently on the island. Their son Bill was now living with them and added another helping hand.

The dock job was fairly straightforward. Tracy had done a diving course so she helped out and we borrowed some diving tanks. It was all so shallow however that they weren't really necessary for most of the work. The concrete beams were separated and then we dragged them away so that they were not a hazard to any passing boats.

We had a fantastic English Christmas dinner at the Bailey's house looking down on the boats. By the time the dock job was finished, Tracey was running the office on Marina Cay. This was the little island close by, on which there was a defunct hotel, a busy bar and restaurant and a fuel, ice and water dock. We had moved *Sea Loone* over to Marina Cay where Peter had a mooring we could use.

Tracey could row back and forwards to the restaurant with the rubber ducky and I motored over to Camanoe where I did all sorts of odd jobs on people's homes. I also spent a fair bit of time repairing the fiberglass whalers people used to commute to the main island.

Camanoe Island had been quite lucky in Hurricane Hugo although one or two places had been devastated. I had to demolish the roof of one home. The roof including the concrete ring beam that it was attached to had blown off and landed in the bush several yards away. Another very modern place had been built on a rocky exposed spur. It was almost all glass and had imploded. I carried away barrow loads of glassy crystals which were all that remained of the place.

I had kept in touch with my cousin ever since my medical problems in New Zealand. He was doing some sort of research still at Oxford and had already qualified as a surgeon. He was coming out with his girlfriend to stay with us for a fortnight. I explained that we were going to have to work some of the time while they visited, but that there was plenty for them to do to keep them occupied.

They flew into Beef Island just across the way and I took the Marina Cay whaler to pick them up. There is a small scruffy dock for the use of Marina Cay and the people on Camanoe Island and a footpath through the bush to the airport terminal.

The last time I saw John, perhaps in fact the only time, he was maybe two years old; so I wasn't sure if I'd recognize him. As it was, he was the only white man. Everyone else was at least slightly tanned. John and his girlfriend were deadly white from a winter in England. He had a Somerset accent which amused me and his girlfriend was obviously Scottish.

We tramped down the path. The first view of the turquoise water around the islands stopped them dead. Then when we zoomed out skirting the reefs on the Boston whaler, they were speechless. It was late in the day and the charter boats were arriving racing each other to the moorings. We tied up to *Sea Loone* and unloaded their luggage. John was adamant, he was jumping in. He dug out his mask and fins and disappeared over the side and headed for the reef just to windward.

We were left with his girlfriend. It was dusk before he got back wreathed in smiles. I don't know about his girlfriend but John wasn't going to need looking after. There were boats he could use, a windsurfer from Marina Cay, miles of reef to explore, a taxi boat to the mainland if he wanted, and James at the bar to make the best piña coladas every happy hour

As our neighbour we had a lovely wooden yacht called *Tumbleweed*. The skipper Fritz Seyforth had chartered his boat up and down the Caribbean in the early days. He now had a small office in the old building on top of Marina Cay .He wrote books of the Caribbean, amusing pirate stories and charter boat stories.

He had the books printed in St. John's and distributed around the Virgin Islands. They were popular with the charter guests and kept Fritz busy and in rum money.

There were maybe twenty moorings around us protected from the swell by Marina Cay reef. These belonged to the restaurant and had to be paid for each night. It was our evenings entertainment to watch the holidaymakers try to pick the moorings up. Often with Capt. Bligh at the helm and a very frazzled wife hanging over the bow with the boat hook.

In between jobs, I cleaned out a room next to Fritz on the island and started making sea urchin earrings. I had two tables to layout pairs of urchins and dipped, dyed and painted them with resin. The finished product were pinned on boards, all the colors of the rainbow. I even made display stands for shops.

Tracy in the meantime took the rubber ducky around the moorings each evening with a basket of shells. She found it really hard initially. Some of the charter people could be really rude and Tracy would come back in tears. At other times she would be invited on board and plied with drinks. If she did really well she would come back to refill the basket handing over a fistful of dollars before she rowed away again.

She disappeared on board one large yacht and didn't come back till dark. The guy was so impressed he had taken the whole basket. Some of the big exotic shells were selling for fifty dollars or more so we were making hundreds of dollars.

The sand dollars and bikinis went to some shops in town and to a gallery in Trellis Bay. We decided to do a little tour around so sailed first over to Virgin Gorda where I sold the Makonda chess set for five hundred dollars. This was a good start. I then put the earrings in the boutique in the Marina. We sailed on down to Norman Island, a popular anchorage for the bareboat charterers, and Tracey again rowed around with the shells.

The next morning the customs launch arrived in the bay and came directly to us. We were under arrest!

We had to follow the launch back to Road Town and anchor off the Customs House. We were taken ashore and in our absence the boat was rummaged. Tracy had written some rather damning comments in her diary and then there was a note that I had sold a preserved coconut crab to a marine biologist for the twenty dollars. Fortunately on the way back to the harbour, even with a guard on board, Tracy had managed to destroy all the receipts we had for the shells, bikinis and so on. The chief customs officer was a posh Englishman sent out to fight the war on drugs. He obviously hadn't found any drugs at all since he'd arrived in the islands, so was going to take it out on us selling sea shells.

Apparently a really despicable English guy living on a boat in Norman Island with his old mother, had radioed customs to say Tracey was going around the other boats selling drugs. He ran a private parcel service between the American and British Virgin Islands so was obviously trying to score points. I should have gone back and sunk his bloody boat, mother and all!

The final outcome was that customs estimated that with the shells bikinis etc. we had a cargo on board valued at one thousand dollars. As we had not declared it, we would have to pay 100% duty. They wanted one thousand dollars. If we did not pay immediately, we would go to jail for the night and be in court in the morning. This would mean that *Sea Loone*, unguarded, would probably be stripped overnight. Then immigration people would some to court in the morning and there would be maybe bigger problems.

So we gave them one thousand dollars which was all the money we had made since leaving Marina Cay. I asked if we were then obliged to leave the country and they said, "No not at all, everything is now correct."

We returned to Marina Cay pretty shook up. However within an hour of us picking up our mooring Peter came over. He wanted me to come over to Camanoe and meet the marine contractor.

When we first arrived, the final work was being done on the small marina on the island. It had been dug out to a depth of five or 6 feet and had a cement wall all around and then they had dug a channel through to the sea flooding it. The final job was to put in finger piers all around for the sports fishing boats and whalers to tie up to. This involved driving wood pilings but with all the repair work from Hurricane Hugo, there was no barge or crane available. The contractor, a local guy, was not going to get his final half payment on the job until the piling and finger piers were finished.

The bottom was sand and broken coral so not too easy to get a piling into but the man was desperate. I agreed to attempt to do the job but I pointed out that I just had big problems in customs and didn't want more problems with immigration. No problem, he said, his brother was Chief of Immigration.

So it was agreed that I would have a go putting in the piling and, if I succeeded, he would pay me fifteen thousand dollars. I would divide the money between Peter, who would provide his work boat and other equipment, Bill who would be the labour, and myself. The contractor had to come up with the piling, fastenings and a suitable petrol-driven pump, hoses, and piping.

I was promised a work permit but would have to leave the country and return. So I had to do a short trip to St. Thomas in the US Virgin Islands. I made a list of things needed for the contractor and Tracey and I sailed away the next day.

Coming back into Road Town tongue-in-cheek I asked the customs officer if I should write "in ballast" on the form or list all my shells and bikinis. Next stop the Immigration Department. I requested a permit but they laughed at me. I'd be lucky to get an extension on my visitor's visa, they said. Then my friend, the contractor, walked in and, bang bang, work permit stamped in the passport.

Next day back to Camanoe, the pump had already arrived plus a lorry load of timber to construct a tower on the deck of the workboat and an outrigger to tie it to the dock to stop it falling over. Bill and I nailed all this together and attached one of my halyard winches to pull the piling upright. The three inch outflow from the pump was reduced to one and a half and attached by a long hose to a 20-foot galvanized pipe.

We dragged one of the pilings over from where they had been stored, sharpened the bottom with the chainsaw, drilled the other end for the lifting crane and threw it into the water. We winched the piling up alongside the tower and nailed a cross bar to the top. Then with the pump going full bore and the galvanized pipe clamped to the piling, we lowered it to the bottom and started to screw it backwards and forwards.

It worked its way down and finally stopped some five feet into the bottom. We washed the muck back around it and moved away. It looked good. Another twenty odd to go and we would have fifteen thousand dollars. In fact, the first few pilings were the best penetration we managed but we did eventually get them all in and the contractor's work was complete. He was more than happy because he would now get paid and we had made some pretty easy money.

I made some drawings for putting walkways onto the pilings and would do that job too when we came back up from Grenada in November. That would be like icing on the cake.

Easter was the end of the sailing season and charter boating slowed down. June was the start of the hurricane season. So May was a good time to start heading off down island.

The first leg from Virgin Gorda to St. Martin is dead to windward, due east. It can be a bitch but we managed it overnight and motored into Simpson's Lagoon when the bridge opened the next morning. We had friends tied stern-to to a scruffy island, Snoopy Island, just inside the lagoon so we dropped our anchor and backed alongside them with our stern lines tied into the bushes. They had been working in Road Town but had got better work offered to them here.

We had a few drinks ashore and they casually mentioned that their friend was coming from Road Town next day for a few days holiday. He was the No. 2 Customs Officer. If he was anything like his boss, I thought, I'd push him overboard.

It turned out he was quite a different character and was himself having problems with his boss, who didn't think he should drink and socialize in the local bars in Tortola. Right, he might have met a drug dealer.

Well drunk that night, we had a rat come to join us climbing up the stern ropes. It had jumped from their boat to mine but, like lightning, I had my hatches closed. The bloody thing then shot back and disappeared down their forward hatch. It took them two days to get rid of it by which time it had chewed a lot of wires and hoses.

I had found a good place for my jewellery, a really fancy boutique which had another shop in Paris. I was wholesaling the earrings for ten dollars a pair. If a shop took one each of each color it was a hundred dollars; but of course you need more than just one of each. You also need big and small sizes. So the sale got bigger and bigger.

This particular shop took all I had but also requested black. I had never thought of black. But I went back and found some Indian ink to dip them in. So the next day I delivered black ones.

By the time we got to Grenada, I had a string of outlets in almost every island. But I was going to need more sand dollars. I could dive up sand dollars in Portsmouth, Dominica. I knew exactly where they were but also knew they were all too big.

From Bequia, we went across to Mustique where I sold my earrings to a very enthusiastic lady. This was Princess Margaret's island so maybe she would buy a pair of my earrings, I don't know.

Unfortunately, someone had written an article about Hog Island in an American yachting magazine and after hurricane Hugo more people were coming south. As a result, the anchorage there was full of fancy yachts, mainly Americans from the Virgin Islands and most with retired people living aboard. It was definitely not a good market for skimpy Brazilian bikinis.

There was great interest in hunting lobsters but nobody was really any good at it. I actually speared one lobster under one of the yachts and Tracey had to make sure no one was watching before I heaved it into the dinghy. No point in letting them know there were more in the anchorage than on the outside reefs.

There were no big hurricanes that season, only a small depression came our way and then fizzled out. October we started north again and restocked the shops on the way. The shells had nearly all been sold, the urchins running out and a lot of bikinis sold in the French islands, Martinique and the Saints. Another good season in the Virgin Islands and the piggy bank would be full and we could think of moving on.

The Caribbean was changing rapidly and becoming crowded and expensive. Most of the islands now required yachts to buy cruising permits and short-term visas. There were hundreds of private yachts and thousands of charter yacht moorings were taking over the anchorages. Finding an anchorage to yourself was a thing of the past. It was still a good place to find work and make money, but having done so, I wanted to return to the Pacific to spend it.

Back in the Virgin Islands, I found Peter and Bill had finished building the finger docks in my absence. I wasn't very happy about that but held my tongue. Tracey went back to work in the office on Marina Cay. The couple managing the island were happy to sit back and let her do most of the work. She got on well with the restaurant and kitchen staff who came over on the ferry every morning.

I rebuilt the island's work boat and then drew out a design for a dinghy dock between the restaurant and the fuel dock. I had the idea of using the old concrete beams from the dock we had demolished a year ago. I could use plastic pipes filled with reinforcing bars and concrete as the pilings. I priced it all out and the owners agreed that I should go ahead. The beams I brought over towing each at high speed behind the whaler then I dragged them up onto the beach. Each beam had a 6 inch hole at each end which got a pipe slotted into it. Reinforcing bars were added and the pipes filled with cement for a few feet

I made seven of these structures and then I borrowed the gardener and we got them dragged out into position. I then managed to let the beams into the bottom a little. The water was only four or five feet deep. The plastic pipes were quite strong so by the time I had bolted on the cross beams and the longitudinals the whole structure was quite rigid. I decided to carry on and got Fritz to come and help me to nail down the decking. Filling the pipes with cement was then really easy using a wheelbarrow to bring the mix out from the beach. Though I say it myself, it looked pretty good and I got paid one thousand dollars for my efforts.

I had found some small round sea urchins to replace the sand dollars. This seemed to work just as well as the originals. They lived on the reef under the rocks and were easy to collect. So the factory was back in business and I had cucumbers and a row of tomatoes also doing pretty well outside my factory.

On Thursday nights, the restaurant closed and Tracey, Fritz and I ran a beach barbecue. Tracey ran the bar and collected the money and Fritz and I barbecued. Fritz was the expert and did the chicken and ribs, I did the fish. Fritz's instructions to me were to burn it with lots of flames and throw things around. It worked. We were really popular. My fish got splattered with lemon butter and flames shot up. Fritz had the occasional half chicken actually catch fire. These got given away as extras to any really greedy customer. This was a good move as the tip always escalated.

We normally had around thirty customers but once had seventy and had to move back into the restaurant and fire up the big grill. We were always left with food for half the week. We got paid; the tips were usually much more and we had a lot of fun.

Our two boats *Sea Loone* and *Tumbleweed* were obviously quite different from the visiting charter boats and we regularly got people coming over offering us the leftover food from their charters. This was sometimes a huge amount of food as the people had spent their whole time in bars and restaurants. Fritz would send over what he didn't want and we would send him all the peanut butter and other strange American products. Fritz would send people over to see the jewellery and the shells from all over the world and Tracey in return would send visitors to Fritz for a signed copy of one of his books. We were a good team.

Tracey had two friends come over from London and I had Phil Hicks arriving. He had done so much work on the boat originally and then at the last minute had decided not to come with us in 1978. Everybody enjoyed themselves; it was that sort of a place.

Unfortunately, Lorro the parrot got sick, stopped eating, slowly wilted and died. Tracey was heartbroken and even I missed the cantankerous creature, a little.

The owners of Marina Cay were very rich Jewish people from New York. Anyway, they had their boat anchored off the island, a huge aluminum yacht with a massive circular bed taking up the front of the boat.

I helped the skipper take the boat down to St. Thomas to get some work done on it and while there, bought Tracey's birthday present. When the yacht returned after a few weeks, the present was in a large box on the foredeck. Tracey was at first excited but, when she opened it, the thrill evaporated. It was a complete new toilet for the boat. Well she had been complaining about the old one.

By Easter, we had reached our target of $20,000 and had enough to fly home before we set off for Panama. Bernt and Jeanette who had passed us without being able to afford to stop in St Helena, had sailed directly on to the Virgin Islands where they had started work with the Moorings Charter Co. Hurricane Hugo had seriously battered their small boat, flattening the mast on the water a few times. In fact they were lucky not to lose their lives.

They ran a big sixty-foot charter boat for two seasons while their boat was up on the hard. They had planned to leave at the same time as us heading back to New Zealand, Jeanette's home. At the last minute, they decided to do one more year so that they had enough to buy property in New Zealand when they arrived back. So they very generously emptied out a vast amount of food from their boat and gave it all to us. They stocked the charter boat each trip with expensive tins of ham, salmon, mussels and suchlike and of course anything not used was theirs so in one more season they could easily replace what they had given us. What a bonus.

In May, we left *Sea Loone* on the mooring, with Fritz keeping an eye on her, and flew home via Puerto Rico and Barbados. I sat in the smoking section at the back while Tracey, up front, chatted up a West Indies cricketer.

We flew into London and were met by Tracey's sister. From there we went up to Liverpool and stayed a few days with my mother. Tracey then went off to Northumberland and I went down to Bristol and stayed with my uncle. From there my cousin picked me up and drove me to Oxford. Tracy met me there in Oxford and then it was back to London where Tracey's sister took us back to the airport. So it was bit of a whirlwind visit but Tracey saw a bit of Liverpool and we had a few really nice days in the Lake District with Paul and Diane, my sister.

Back in Marina Cay we threw a massive beach party before we left. People came from all over. Fritz and I burnt chicken and fish at the barbecue and Tracey, now an expert at making rum punches, made up gallons and gallons. I also made a huge pot of conch chowder which was so good it disappeared in five minutes. It was a good party.

We jumped from island to island saying goodbye to people. Bruce and Lorna were working in St. Martin. Gordie was still busy in St. Barts. We were meeting John my cousin, in St. Vincent and arrived just in time. Together we cruised around the Grenadines from Bequia down to Carriacou. We still had the two dinghies plus a windsurfer which Tracey was battling to tame.

Anchored in Hog Island, the three of us climbed the mountain ridge up to the point where you could see the whole eastern coast of Grenada. We got drenched by a big rain squall and the path through the jungle became slippery mud. We finally dropped down to the waterfall where we stripped off and dived into the cold water. With our pockets full of nutmegs, we finally got down to the coast road and caught a bus back to town and then on to Clark's Court Bay. John was good company and I was sad to see him fly away home.

By now, Hog Island had become a small village. Many yachts had come down from the north for the summer; others had found work locally. One English guy had found a job teaching in the north of the island. He had a long commute every morning using the minibuses. He was late one day getting the first bus into town and missing his connection. He was one very lucky man because on the way up the west coast that minibus and all the occupants were obliterated by a huge boulder which fell onto the road.

His wife had just had a baby and its effect on Tracey were worrying. One evening, Tracey even brought the baby to *Sea Loone* to babysit while they went for a night out. I hoped she'd not forgotten to take her pills. *Sea Loone* was not going to become a family boat.

It was time to get moving not that there was really a time schedule. We had a whole year before I intended crossing the Pacific to the Marquesas but it was still over 1000 miles from Grenada to the Panama Canal and there was plenty to do on the way.

The first stop was on rocky deserted islands, Los Testigos. I had bought a hookah diving compressor while we were in the Virgin Islands. It consisted of a small petrol driven compressor which sat in an inflated inner tube. Two hoses provided air to a depth of thirty feet. for two divers. The compressor got dragged along by the diver.

Testigos proved the first chance to use it to find shells. There was a large cowrie shell that I particularly wanted to find. I did actually find it, but only one.

The next stop was Margarita Island; a large duty-free island where we cleared-in before moving on to some other interesting little sister islands. Unfortunately, Tracy really gashed herself when we went diving for mussels so we had to make a quick run to find a doctor in Puerto La Cruz. There she could get some stitches and fortunately there was no infection. It healed up quickly.

Puerto La Cruz had a reputation as a den of thieves. Sure enough, our dinghy and outboard disappeared overnight even though we had locked it to the boat. This was the dinghy from Richards Bay so the third one had lasted all of two years.

We had met up again with Bruce and Lorna who were going to sail down to Los Rocas before turning back beating up to St. Martin for the next season. We arranged to meet them in Los Rocas which turned out to be quite handy for us. We found a nice little anchorage all to ourselves, a place I'd discovered when I visited ten years before. Those days there were conch, huge ones, all over the sandy bottom and huge sponges full of lobster. Well now the conch been harvested but there were still a few lobsters.

One morning I was looking for octopus. I found a big one in only six feet of water but was having problems trying to hook him out of his hole. I had one hand on the ground and was pulling with the other when the double tuna hook tore out of the octopus and buried itself in the base of my thumb I came to the surface and couldn't really see how I was going to get the hook out.

Just at that moment, Bruce and Lorna came sailing into the anchorage. I waved and shouted and Bruce quickly anchored. Then he jumped in and swam across to me. I asked him to just tear the hook out while I held my thumb with the other hand.

Bruce is a big man and he gave a good yank but the hook didn't come out. He started to turn a sort of green color while I shouted obscenities at him. At the second attempt, the hook tore out making a bit of a mess of my hand. I had to apologize to Bruce for shouting at him and then went and bandaged up my hand. I went back and got the bloody octopus and then back on the boat poured myself a large tot of rum. We all had octopus spaghetti that night.

Soon after wards, we left Bruce and Lorna in Los Rocas and sailed to Curaçao in the Dutch Antilles. Spanish Waters is a large lagoon with a narrow entrance, very protected. We anchored near a curious little bar on the edge of the mangroves. They provided different services for the passing yachts and sold cold beer.

A huge hardware store in town had some beautiful Brazilian plywood and also a lot of the other materials I needed to build another dinghy. So I decided to do it again. There was nowhere suitable to build it so I built a makeshift platform on the coral behind the bar. At high tide it almost floated.

It turned out to be a really good dinghy. I made it in two parts then bolted them together. The front half neatly fitted in the back when stored on deck. It was long, over eleven feet and being plywood, was quite light.

Curacao was also a good place to buy outboard motors so I bought a new a new 2 hp engine and I was offered an almost new 5 hp Yamaha at a price I couldn't refuse. Amazingly, the dinghy with both me and Tracey in it would get up on a plane with the five hp which was a big bonus.

The stretch of sea between the ABC islands, Aruba, Bonaire and Curaçao and Panama is always rough and windy. Half way to San Blas, the second and last of my two nylon downwind sails blew itself into tatters. Considering they had been made for me in Florida in 1980, they had done well.

I knew that, this time, San Blas was going to be a lot more popular with yachts than my last visit so we headed well south into the Gulf of Darien hoping to avoid them. The problem was the charts. One area was not charted at all and some of the American charts were very inaccurate.

We found our way in among the islands taking it very cautiously. Initially it was rough and windy but it later improved. A small French yacht was anchored behind the first islands where we found shelter. The boat was called *Virus*. Philippe, a single-handed doctor, was also making his way slowly to the Panama Canal. He joined us in our diving expeditions and we became expert at catching the huge spider crabs which lurked under the dead coral slabs.

Tracey was keen on meeting the Kuna people in their villages and wanted to find some of their molas to buy. Molas were multicolored designs stitched together from different colored pieces of cloth, like quilts. It was important how the design was cut out and it was no longer easy to find really good examples. Tracy would have bought them all.

As Christmas approached, I wanted to return to Nargana village where I might find my Kuna friend, Jamie Filos. We anchored off the village and went ashore. We no longer needed to be interviewed by the chief and we soon found Jamie and his family. He no longer lived on one of the outer islands. His baby was now a boy of ten and they had two more children. Jamie was the leader of the village band. So that evening we were invited ashore to a concert they would put on for us. We would need to bring a bottle of rum to lubricate the players and a packet of cigarettes would also be good.

The three of us, Philippe myself and Tracey, were led through the village to a building with a veranda at the front where the band was sitting with their drums. There were three chairs in the middle of the street for us.

I handed over the rum and cigarettes and Philippe produced a small tape recorder. The music was a bit discordant and the singing was more like shouting but they were all very enthusiastic. Philippe's tape recorder was a huge success when he played their efforts back to them.

I wanted to make a little trip up into the Kuna Yala, the jungle mountains which rose up from the mangrove coast just across from the island. I had been in touch with Joan de Katt in Bora Bora and they would really like to have a mate for Plod, my green Mealy Amazon parrot. Maybe we would see one.

Jamie came along as our guide. We took the new dinghy which easily carried the four of us and motored up the coast before cutting into the mangroves and following a small river inland. It went quite a long way before the water became too shallow. At that point, we started out on foot, following a narrow path up into the jungle.

After an hour or so the path petered out and Jamie admitted he was lost. Fortunately for us, Philippe and I had sort of marked our trail or maybe we would have really become lost. By the time we got back to the dinghy we had seen a few parrots squawking as they flew over us and there were lots of dragon like lizards, butterflies and a few orchids.

Jamie apparently had never spent much time on the mainland but had a relative who was a hunter so we repeated the journey with him. He got a little further, and arrived at a small banana plantation but we never really got up into the jungle proper.

We joined a number of other yachties for Christmas. Tracey decked the boat out with all the flags including the huge white ensign which went to the top of the mast. 1990 was our fourth Christmas together.

New Year found us in Puerto Bello where some effort had been made to preserve the ruins of the old forts. Capt. Morgan was a popular figure now. We found a bar in town with a pool table which was good as it poured with rain most of the time as usual. It was supposed to be the wettest place in the Americas.

2

THERE WERE ALL sorts of problems in the Canal Zone when we arrived. The Americans had invaded, Noriega had been toppled, and Panama was broke. In Colon, rubbish was piling up in the streets, and the shops all had armed guards with shotguns and machine guns.

The yachties went about in groups but spent most the time at the yacht club. A container full of small arms had just been hijacked on the docks which wasn't going to improve matters.

I still had my Panama Canal registration for *Sea Loone* so we didn't need to go through the clearing-in rigmarole again. In fact, they found *Sea Loone*'s papers in the files and we were told we could pass through the following day. Normally there are long delays and we did have to organize line handlers, lines and extra fenders. Still, a week or so later we had everything organized and transited the canal. Our engine still didn't have neutral which worried our pilot so as we were going to pass through the locks with two other yachts. We all rafted together with *Sea Loone* in the middle. It was perfect for us. We didn't have to do anything, not even run the engine.

We popped out the other side, untangled ourselves from the other boats, and motored down to the yacht club. There we anchored across the channel. The yacht club itself were trying to force us to use and pay for moorings they had put down but they were expensive. So all the yachts simply anchored off. The manager then persuaded the immigration officer to visit all the yachts and collect the passports. I wasn't on the boat at the time but Tracey was intimidated and gave away our passports. These were all now with the manager of the yacht club who wasn't going to give them back until we agreed to pay for moorings.

This was unacceptable behavior by anyone's standards; so at teatime, we all descended on the manager's office. I threatened him with the British government, intervention with gunboats, international repercussions and so on. He was a worried man by the time I had finished. He found our passports and handed them back. I then held up the passports for the other boat people to see. There was a bit of a stampede and then we retired to the yacht club bar for a celebratory drink.

While Tracey and I were working in the Virgin Islands, I had kept in touch with Alvah and Diana as well as with Clark and Michelle. Alvah had gone from Cape Town to Rio de Janeiro and then turned south sailing down the coast of Argentina to Cape Horn where he spent some time. He had then sailed up the west coast of South America.

Clark and Michelle meanwhile had sailed from Dar es Salaam to Germany via the Red Sea. They had traveled all over Germany with their film show and had managed to find sponsorship to build a new yacht to sail the Northwest Passage from the Atlantic into the Pacific round the north of Canada.

So one boat was going to pass around the bottom, braving Cape Horn in mid winter. Another was going to sail around the north into the Pacific, a feat rarely accompished. The last was *Sea Loone* making another trip through the canal with the only ice seen in the glass of rum and coke. We had all agreed to meet again at Whiteys place, the Jungle Club, in Golfito, Costa Rica.

Of course I had the easy trip via the canal but we were running late and by this time, Clark had managed to sail the Northwest Passage. He then sailed on down from Alaska stopping only briefly in Golfito. He then carried on down to Cape Horn and the Antarctic before completing a circumnavigation of the New World.

I had not heard from Alvah but thought he may be in Golfito by now. So we left Panama and sailed north round Punta Mala. This time we had no problems and stopped in Bahia Honda on the coast opposite Isla Coiba. Here I knew there was a shell I was looking for.

Coming up the coast, I was really shocked. Where once there had been heavy jungle all along the coast, now there was nothing. The forest had been cut and burned and turned into grassland for cattle or so I was told. But the tussock grass I saw didn't look very edible and there was serious soil erosion all over.

We anchored where once howler monkeys kept us awake at night and in the morning I went diving. When I came back there was Alvah drinking coffee with Tracey. Their boat was anchored behind the little island in the middle of the bay and we had not seen them.

They had been in Golfito for a while, staying at Whitey's place. Whitey no longer had the hotel but had moved over to the island opposite Golfito and opened the "Jungle Club". Alvah and Diana were heading back down to the canal and returning to Florida. They had plans to get a new boat in steel and, like Clark, sail the Northwest Passage.

Alvah told me that Clark had managed to get a "piggyback" ride over one section of the passage where the ice had blocked them. A huge Canadian nuclear-powered icebreaker had picked them out of the water. So Alvah was going to do it better. He didn't but the book he wrote about it is worth reading.

The locals on the island brewed up chicha for us, a fermented drink from pounded maize. We drank and talked and, next morning, suffered terrible hangovers. This was the island where Jean and I had seen them digging huge holes and in fact grave-robbing. They were still finding things. One guy had just come back from Panama after a week of debauchery having sold a gold breastplate he had found. He must have got a minute fraction of its true value.

We were told one day that somebody had found some good things not too far away from where we were, so together with a French guy who was anchored with us, we navigated up one of the small rivers in my dinghy and then walked a fair way inland till we came to a small *finca or* farm.

The guy was a good salesman. He had lunch prepared for us before he showed us his finds. Apart from a load of quite nice adze heads, he had three attractive pieces, a classic round pot on three legs formed into crocodiles, an unusually long thin pot which had a glaze on it with snakes intertwined, and the piece de resistance, a piece that looked a bit like a flatiron with tiger heads on each end of the handle. It was made from a hard stone, like jade, and was beautifully crafted.

There was no point in us fighting over the pieces so we drew lots and then negotiated the price with the farmer. Unfortunately, the French guy got the good piece paying some fifty dollars. We got the snake pot and Alvah and Diana, the crocodile pot. I'd love to know what exactly the stone implement was for and what it was worth.

One day, we went iguana hunting with some of the guys off the island. We took Alvah's boat, *Zeny P* out to one of the islands just outside the bay. We towed a canoe full of dogs behind us. It was the season for iguanas to come to the beach and bury the eggs. The dogs chased the iguanas up into the small trees and bushes and the hunters took them alive. We got three including a female full of eggs, and had a party in the village that night.

Alvah brought the music and pots of chicha arrived. The iguanas were barbecued. There wasn't a lot of meat on them but it tasted like chicken. The eggs from the female were strung up and smoked. Maybe this was the way to go with turtle eggs?

I had not found the shell I was looking for, a very large beautiful olive that lived in the sand. Down the coast, about a mile or two offshore, we had passed some spikey rocks which seemed to have a sandbar at one end. Alvah and I took the dinghy to explore it. He wanted to spear some snapper and I was going to find the shell.

When we eventually got there we were surprised by a tall skinny guy suddenly appearing on one of the rock pinnacles. He was crying out to us for water. Alvah was keen to get closer. The man by now was wringing his hands and calling on God to help him. Unfortunately for him, the people on the island had already told us some stories.

Isla Coiba, a few miles further out to sea, was the site of a large Panamanian prison for the really bad offenders. It's a big island with no other people living there. The prison guards had not been paid for months so they had all upped and left. Some of the prisoners had built rafts and managed to get to the mainland. There they had robbed and murdered the isolated farmers along the coast. Obviously, here was another. And he was clearly desperate.

The locals were not going to thank us if we took him ashore and I didn't want some desperado in the dinghy. The mainland was maybe two miles away with plenty of sharks and some lovely black and yellow sea snakes reputed to be deadly poisonous. We left him there. He never attempted to swim out to us so I went looking for the shell. I never found it but Alvah came back with a big red snapper that would feed the four us.

Alvah left "Lost Loone" Bay as he had called our anchorage, and they headed for Panama. A few days later they were replaced by Philippe on *Virus*.

I already realized that there was something in the wind so I was not surprised when Tracey told me she was leaving me and going off with Philippe. I had no plans to get married and definitely did not want babies. Also Tracey knew that *Sea Loone* was sixty four sixty fourths mine. Tracey, of course, wanted babies but I wanted to be sure they were on Philippe's menu as well.

I told Tracy I wanted to talk with Philippe and that she should go over to *Virus* and send him to me. Tracey looked a bit worried and when Philippe arrived he looked a bit sheepish but anyway he admitted he wanted to marry and have babies. He had already been offered a job in French Polynesia so he could support a family.

I demanded that Tracey stayed on *Sea Loone* until we arrived in Golfito. It was probably going to be a fairly windless few miles and she could help steer when we had to motor. Philippe could join us a few days later and Tracy could jump ship.

Whitey had known we were on our way. As we came round the point, he took his rifle and fired a few shots over our heads. Silly bugger gave me quite a fright!

There were a number of yachts anchored at his Jungle Club. Some we knew from the canal, others were Americans sailing down from California. We anchored amongst them.

Whitey and Barbara had bought a piece of land intending to grow vanilla, but it hadn't worked out mainly because he couldn't find suitable labour for the rather fiddly business of pollinating the flowers and pruning the bunches of pods. So they had organized a sort of yacht service, bar, restaurant etc for the passing yachts. They also provided security from the thieving locals. They had a lovely little bit of jungle up behind the main building. They served cold beer and Barbara cooked and baked bread.

Whitey and Alvah had got on well. It was good explaining to Whitey who it was that Alvah had tried to save from drowning in Cape Town. Of course Whitey reckoned Orran had got his desserts.

A few days later, Philippe arrived and tied alongside *Sea Loone*. We started transplanting Tracey's stuff. *Virus* was an aluminum yacht. She was quite light so started to settle in the water as we worked. The boats around us were trying to work out what was happening and tongues were wagging already.

Philippe had a plywood box which he described as a dinghy. Tracey didn't agree so Philippe arranged with one of the yachts to buy his inflatable. The man wanted one thousand dollars, which seemed quite a good deal. With all the gossip going on, Tracey and Philippe decided to go on a short cruise around the Golfo Dulce as a sort of honeymoon while things settled down. A deal was struck whereby Philippe promised to buy the dinghy as soon as he got back.

So I knew about this and was surprised to see somebody else using the dinghy. The other person had bought the dinghy and would be getting the money in the next day or so. When I cornered the original owner, he said more or less "first-come first served". But he agreed that as yet he didn't have the money. So I went back to *Sea Loone*, collected one thousand dollars and took it over. Then I collected the dinghy and tied it behind my boat. I was just following the rules.

When Tracey and Philippe returned I explained what had happened and asked them to do me a favour. I had already settled up with Tracey. There never had been any major work done or money spent on *Sea Loone* while we had been together, so I divided up our kitty which still stood at around twenty thousand dollars. One share for Tracey one for me and one for the boat. So Tracy had almost 7,000 dollars as a nest egg. The favor I wanted was that they should pay for the dinghy but pretend it was a going away present from me to Tracey. That would confuse a few people and get tongues wagging again. It worked a treat.

I planned to be staying in Golfito for more than six months leaving in October to spend the southern cyclone season in the Marquesas. There was plenty to do. Firstly, I wanted to go over to the Corcavado National Park. It was on the other side of the Golfo Dulce on the Ossa Peninsula. Alvah had spent some time there looking for big cats especially the tiger, puma or whatever name you want to call it. He was really enthusiastic about the area and had given me the detailed map.

Philippe and Tracey were keen to come too. Whitey would keep an eye on the boats so we were able to take a very cheap short flight on a small, four-seater plane to the other side of the Gulf. From there it took two days walking to get into the Park carrying all our food and tents. It was hard work but we arrived in an area of swamps and uncut forests on steep hillsides. The trees were so huge and the canopy so dense that there was virtually no undergrowth; so it was easy to move around. There were lots of animals around, three species of monkeys including huge troops of the noisy howler monkeys, toucans with their huge beaks, flocks of red, blue, and gold macaws and lots of smaller birds, all the way down to the minute hummingbirds.

We stopped at the government research station which had a small airfield running down to the beach. There were a few friendly scientists, a local family serving some food and a roof for us to camp under. There were no tourists. The path we came in on, without the map, would have been difficult to follow and there was no accommodation. I particularly wanted to see a tapir. They were not uncommon but we never saw one.

We tramped down to a swampy lagoon behind the beach where we saw prints on the sand which had to be a tiger. There were also some big crocodiles floating in the open water like dead logs.

There was huge surf pounding on the beach. At high tide, the waves came right up to the jungle edge. We intended to return along this beach which turned out to be really hard work. When the tide ebbed it left the steep black sand beach into which your feet sank. Occasionally a stream flowed across the beach and we could stop and cool off.

The first night a troop of monkeys arrived in the tree above us and started throwing sticks at us. We had to move the tents before they found a larger branch to chuck at us.

Not too far out of the Park, we came to an old gold mining site with a small airfield and a few people around. We found that for not much more than we had originally paid, we could get the little plane from Golfito to come and pick us up. An hour later we were flying back over the Golfo Dulce with a little detour over the "Jungle Club" to take a photograph.

I was so impressed with Corcavado that I wrote to my friend Guy in Liverpool and suggested he came out with all his cameras. Guy and Sue were still living on the Wirral close to where I built the boat. Guy was working in Manchester, still an accountant but his real interest was photography, animal photography.

A few months later he arrived. He only had two weeks before he had to be back in the office. A friend of mine, Mark, who had spent months in the jungle in Guyana, was coming with us.

After only one night on the boat, Guy found himself on the small airplane we had chartered and we flew directly into the park. So we didn't have to carry food, camping gear or cameras on our backs, at least not until we left.

We set up camp in the research station. I had my little orange tent, Guy a large mosquito net and Mark a clever arrangement of hammock-and-net slung under the roof. The plane charter cost one hundred dollars. Well worth it when I remembered the long trek in. We had a huge loaf of bread that Barbara made specially in the Jungle Club and we had tins and rice. But after a few meals thrown together on an open fire, Guy decided that we get the local family to feed us, which was fine with me and Mark although I thought my jungle culinary expertise was exceptional.

We built hides for Guy and left him with his cameras to take pictures. We went out at night looking for the brightly colored tree frogs. We spent days looking for a tapir and still never saw one. A huge flock of macaws came one day and destroyed a bush full of guava's right in front of us. A pair of toucans reached into a hole in a tree and pulled out a small parakeet. They tore it in half and ate it and there is me thinking they only eat fruit. I found a beetle sitting on the trunk of a tree and had to run back to the research station to get a kill jar to put it in. The beetle is now in the natural history museum in San Jose. It is only two and a half inches long but has antennae more than two feet long!

Time past quickly and having described the walk out along the beach, Guy was persuaded to get the plane to come back for us. It gave us an extra couple of days in the park but we got a little worried when the plane was delayed by thunderstorms over the park. We did get out in time and Guy had a night at Whitey's where he "shouted" the whole bar. He got back on the plane to San Jose not the least bit sunburned but covered in bites and scratches and needing another two-week holiday to recover.

An Australian yacht arrived with two zoologists and a surfer. We made a trip out to Pavones where Holly wanted to try the surf break. I was hoping to meet up with Winfried Zigan and maybe go pig hunting again. I had heard he had been shot off his property further up Punta Barica and was now living in Pavones. Unfortunately he was away and Pavones had become a really popular surfing venue. It was no longer just the one little finca where I had borrowed the horse to ride to Winfried's place.

The other girl on the boat was Australia's bat expert. With the vampires and fish-eating bats in Golfito, this had to be a good place for her. One evening we set out some mist nets and retired to Whitey's bar for a few beers. In a short time, we caught three different bats. We brought them into the bar to look them over and they were amazingly different to each other. One bat was a nectar eater. Ann took some sugar and the bat extended a long tongue to taste it. The second bat was an insect eater and fairly standard. The third had suckers on its feet. Apparently it didn't look for a dark cave for the day but found a large leaf in the jungle and using the suckers to curl the leaf around itself.

One of the Californian yachts asked Whitey where he could plug in his electric toothbrush and another complained when he found a terciapelo, a very poisonous snake, in the shower. He didn't actually complain, he shrieked. Whitey pointed out that this was not the City Club it was the Jungle Club.

Barbara cooked up a big dinner at the weekend and we all went ashore for the evening. There were always two large tables; one full of Californians, the ladies wearing all their war paint, and then the other lot, us.

One day I had been into Golfito and met a very vivacious lady in one of the bars. She knew Whitey and was very enthusiastic when I offered to take her over to the "Jungle Club" for dinner. I discovered she had really gone overboard when I collected her with the dinghy, high heels, fishnet tights, bare midriff and a bra that was pushing up a storm!

By the time we arrived at Whitey's the tables were full. My friend strolled over and introduced herself to Whitey. He had known her mother when she was still in business. She then saw the table for the Californians and went to each of the men and explained in broken English where she worked, she didn't need to explain her line of work. The wives looked daggers but that was nothing to when I sat her next to Tracey. Tracey was, as they say in Liverpool, gob smacked. Whitey behind his bar couldn't stop laughing. Tracey said you can't but I did, and it was a great night!

There were some serious problems with my dinghy. It was not even a year old and the plywood was delaminating and coming apart. A large mushroom poked its way out of the transom. My lovely Brazilian plywood must have been glued together with flour and water.

I found a scruffy workshop in Golfito where they did some fiberglass work. They were happy for me to buy materials from them and build a new dinghy in their yard. I was losing count but I think this would be the fifth dinghy. I gave the old dinghy to the restaurant I used in town as my dock when I came ashore. I didn't expect it to last much longer. The new dinghy was fiberglass and not going to rot but it wasn't anywhere as good as the old one.

Whitey was getting more and more upset with the Californian yachts and felt he needed a holiday. They had not had a holiday for many years so they packed their bags and were gone. I was left in charge. The bar and restaurant were closed unless I felt like inviting people. In fact I really didn't have to do anything other than shoo away anybody I didn't like, or that Whitey might not have liked.

I took a walk each morning up into the jungle behind the house. I had sugared traps out for the big blue morpho butterflies. I visited a couple of big tarantula spiders which had their burrows near the path. I often saw a three toed sloth in the trees and I caught a small boa constrictor which I kept for a while. There was always something new to see.

After three months, I had had to take a long bus trip up to San Jose to extend my visa. After six months had elapsed I had to take a trip across the border back into Panama and stayed in David for a couple of days.

The small town on the border was a good place to stock up with food and with cheap booze and cigarettes for the trip out to the Marquesas. Horses were still an important means of transport in Costa Rica and I considered buying a horse saddle to sell in the Marquesas where the saddles were primitive or not used at all.

I took the bus back to the border town and bought tins of food, packets of biscuits, boxes of ground coffee. Then I bought cartons of cigarettes and twelve cases of rum. Surprisingly, the rum was labeled, Ron Marquesa which was fortuitous as I was intending to sell it in the Marquesas,

My last stop was the saddle shop. Whitey was back from his holiday and had given me the basic vocabulary for saddles and so on. I chose one saddle then the reins, the bit, the stirrups, the bit round the tail, the belt under the belly, the rug... and so on. The girl helping me realized I didn't know the front of the horse from the back. She kept bringing all the bits and pieces I needed. It made quite an impressive pile. The saddle was a work of art, polished leather with tassels and fancy stitching. The stirrups were like leather half-shoes.

I asked the girls to tally it all up and it came to just over one hundred dollars. This seemed ridiculously cheap so I asked her for another one the same. The girl was dumbstruck but happily put together another pile.

By this time I had a lot of goods around the town which had to be brought to Golfito. So I organized a small lorry to pick everything up and deliver it to the dock in Golfito the next morning. The lorry arrived and I loaded two dinghies to bring everything back to the boat. I had found some small Jerry cans which would each take a case of rum so transferred ten cases of rum into these. All I had to do then was visit the weekend market for vegetables, fruit and eggs

I had chased all over the place looking for a mate for Plod the parrot and, at the last minute, Whiteys gardener found another mealy amazon. This one was named the Lorita and quickly made herself at home on *Sea Loone*.

With the boat well loaded down, and having said all my goodbyes, I set off on the long trip to the Marquesas, just me and the parrot.

Sailing alone is so utterly different from having someone else aboard I must admit, I find it a lot more relaxing. Certainly there were no more worries about the safety of the crew but also mealtimes, keeping watch, sleeping arrangements and so on all become totally arbitrary. And of course *Sea Loone* was so much bigger with so much empty space.

Leaving the Golfo Dulce, I headed south to the Galapagos Islands and the equator. With contrary winds and current, it was two weeks later and I had drifted a lot further west than I intended and still had not crossed the equator. With the boat heeled over all the time and tacking into the wind, I already had goose barnacles attached way above the waterline.

By the time I reached the tradewinds south of the equator, the crop of huge barnacles was seriously slowing me down. To make matters worse, when I tried to run it, the engine would not start, not that I had enough diesel to motor even a small fraction of the thousands of miles still to go.

The Marquesas eventually hove over the horizon. I had read all my stock of books, done all the crossword puzzle and all the jigsaw puzzles. I was getting bored. The engine was still refusing to work so arriving off Taeohae, Nuku Hiva, I had to beat into the bay. A small dinghy came out and offered me a tow, but by that time I had more or less made it. I anchored on the west side of the bay opposite Justin's place. It had been fifty-three days since I had left Golfito.

Justin and Julienne prepared a welcome feast for me. A long table was piled with food and there was a whole roast piglet at the end. Julienne had made a garland of the elang-elang and tiara-tahiti. The latter are like frangipani but with a much stronger perfume. It felt like coming home.

Since I had been away, Justin had taken the job of caretaking in the school which was just along the beach road. The job had made an enormous difference as it was a French government job and very well-paid. He even got paid holidays and had twice traveled to France. So now he lived in a huge house they had built. It had a large gardens sloping down to the beach road in which he had young pamplmousse trees and a mango tree producing massive gorgeous mangoes.

He had a Land Rover, an aluminum dinghy and a few outboards, weed eaters and other machinery. Life was honestly treating them well. The only problem was that Justin had found religion. He had become a born-again Christian of some sort. A large room in the house had been designed for church meetings. There was no beer drinking and any contact with people outside the church was frowned upon.

I had arrived just after Justin's daughter's wedding. The wedding had seriously loosened the hold church had on Justin as they had stipulated that only church members could be invited. Justin had not agreed and had a big Polynesian blow out. I arrived to drive in the wedge a little further.

At the post office I met Stephen Spengler again. We had been in Golfito, Cocos and the Galapagos Islands together, ten years before. He had stayed and settled down in Taeohae. His boat had got so rusty he had taken it out and sunk it. He now lived with a very vivacious local girl, Flarice, in a little house in the village.

Flarice had been the cook for the Governor General, so he was being well looked after. He now had quite a large fishing boat anchored in the bay and had been experimenting with long lining around the islands. There had been some talk of extending the airfield over on the west coast of the island in order to export large tuna for the Japanese market, but nothing had come of it.

I had Christmas dinner together with Stephan and Flarice. We had a green lipped mussels and oysters flown in from New Zealand. The Marquesas were not Third World, even though they are so remote.

I dug out the diving machine and went diving for shells. The first day, just snorkeling, I found a number of large cask shells. When I showed them to Justin, he wanted to know where I had found them. He hadn't dived in years, but the next day we were out together again and found more shells as well as an octopus to take home for dinner.

There were a number of quite rare shells worth collecting and these I could only find at night when they came out from their hiding places. So I would take the dinghy out around the coast and anchor under the towering cliffs. I would then float the compressor and, leaving a paraffin light in the dinghy, jump in. I could only go down thirty feet so there were only a few places I could dive. Normally the cliffs continued straight down to around one hundred feet. In a few places, there were small coral reefs. But mainly it was just rocks and sand. There were a few cones I collected, a very small cowrie shell and others.

With my friend in Sydney who I knew would take all I could find, I was making a little money every night; and, like gold prospecting, there was always a chance of finding something really valuable. There were shells there worth more than a thousand dollars!

Sharks often gave me a bit of a fright. I'd pick them up in the beam of my light as they cruised past. I tried to ignore them. One night I was concentrating on the sandy bottom looking for cone trails, when something banged me on the head. I had swum into a cave without knowing it. Another time, I came back to the surface and into a solid mass of stinging jellyfish. Then there was the time the paraffin light went out on the dinghy and with no moon, I had a difficult job finding it.

The people anchored next to me were also keen shell collectors. Odile was an anaesthetist at the hospital and Alain, her husband, had built a small motorboat to use for diving around the coast. We had met ten years before. We took the dredge I had made in Golfito and dragged it around a bit, but without bringing up anything interesting. However, by using scuba gear they could drive dive down much deeper than I could, so were finding much more. Still I was getting enough excitement in the shallows for my liking.

My jungle partner, Marc, arrived together with his friend on a Spanish yacht and then Philippe arrived with Tracey. Philippe was to start work as Chief Medical Doctor for the Maquesas. He had a difficult job ahead of him organizing the completion of the new hospital in Taeohae.

Justin was persuaded to dig out his dive lights that we used for lobstering and, using his aluminum dinghy and my rubber ducky, we went night-diving for lobsters. While I had been away, the coasters coming from Tahiti had got more sophisticated with refrigerated containers. The local people had decimated the lobster population to feed the hotels and restaurants in the big islands.

As long as it was near the new moon, with maybe six people in the water with torches and Justin's two dustbins and car headlights, we could still fill a sack with lobsters and cigale, slipper lobsters. There were in fact two species of lobsters and three species of slipper lobsters. One of the latter was as big as a dinner plate. The following day I would go for octopus and others would troll for tuna and then go spear fishing. Other times, someone might spear the crabs on the rocky shoreline or find huge murex shells while diving.

The lobsters were boiled, the octopus beaten, boiled up with coconut milk and a little curry powder, the small fish had the side sliced and were marinated, the tuna was left as raw sashimi. Justin had an electric rap for grating coconuts and there was always a huge pile of nuts behind the house. The gratings were squeezed to make the fresh coconut milk. Cooking bananas were boiled, as was the taro, manioc, sweet potato and rice. If we had a fire for a barbecue, the bread fruit was thrown whole onto the fire.

In the evening when everything had been prepared and was placed out on the long table on Justin's veranda, he would shout "Kai Kai" and we would all dig in. Only Stephan insisted on a knife and fork. The rest dug in Polynesian style, hands only. Bottles of cold Hinano beer washed it all down.

There were usually around ten of us. Philippe and Traecy, Stephan and Flarice, Mark and his mate and their wives. Flarice would open up the big cigales for Stephan and then wipe her hands on her new Parisien Dior dress before delving into some other delicacy. The table in the end would be a total mess. There would be food bits scattered everywhere and at the head of the table totally satiated, would sit Justin, fast asleep.

Justin had been brought up in Huomi, the valley to the east of Typee Vai where Melville had lived. One weekend, Philippe, Tracey and I decided to go there and see where he had lived; and then carry on to see the large stone tikis up in the main valley.

Walking up the narrow road from the beach we passed an elderly couple in the garden of their house. They said hello and asked where we were going and then we carried on. We found Justin's old house and the people next door asked if we needed any fruit or anything. We were given two large paw-paw's and some beans. Then two youngsters took us to a huge mango tree. One of them, the boy, climbed the tree and shook down huge mangoes. The girl skillfully caught them in her pareo.

By the time they had found two large regimes of bananas and cut them down, the people decided it was lunch time. So we were invited onto the veranda and served freshwater eel in coconut milk. It was delicious. Lunch over and too late to carry on to see the tikis, we decided to return to the beach but there was far too much to carry even for the three of us. So a Land Rover was brought out and we drove back to the beach in style. The dinghy almost sinking under its load we got back to the yachts. It's difficult for us to accept the generosity of the Polynesian people and not offer something in return. In fact this would be very impolite but there was more to come.

The next morning we went ashore again to find the stone tikis but when we got to the old couples house the lady demanded to know what happened to us the previous day. She had made a huge Kai Kai for when we came back down the road. But they of course hadn't seen us pass because we were in the Land Rover. So we spent another pleasant day with these couple and sat down to another amazing meal .The wife was a retired schoolmistress, the husband an expert at making Maquesian beer. Behind the house was a small plantation of pineapples. The skins of the pineapple are boiled up with sugar and the left to foment for a week or so. The result is a sort of sparkling wine which is delicious.

On Sundays, the young men in the valley are invited to play boules in the road outside the house and drink the beer. A lot of money is on the games and everybody gets a little drunk. The old guy had had some problems with the Catholic Church so was happy to lead the boys astray.

On the third day we got to see the tikis. The path had been cleared and the site tidied up; so the stone platforms associated with the ceremonial site were exposed. It was interesting to stand there and speculate on the human sacrifices and maybe human kai kai's that might have taken place.

Stefan took his fishing boat around to Hakatea. Flarice is related to Daniel who has the bay named after himself by the passing yachts. We had a big party with him and walked up to the waterfall passing his pig traps which unfortunately were empty. The thousand foot waterfall was as impressive as ever. The French government had spent a huge amount of money to eradicate the sand flies which were making life miserable on the islands. That walk up the valley was perfect. But two years later, according to Tracey the sand flies were back and even worse.

Time flew by and in April the yachts started arriving from Panama so I wanted to move on. But first I wanted to stop in Tahuata, one of the islands to the south and dive up some more shells hopefully.

Saying goodbye was hard. I felt very at home in Taeohae but I'm a rolling stone. In Tahuata, I found a tight corner where I could anchor under the huge cliffs with a bolder scree disappearing into the water. It looked good for finding my little cowries. That night, sure enough, I did well. I found six good ones which equated to one hundred and twenty dollars.

It wasn't a good place to anchor but in the morning, two American yachts came around the corner and anchored right next to me. The girl on the nearest boat started scrubbing the foredeck with a broom once they were anchored. Lorita, the parrot, seeing a boat so close by, decided to visit. She had never tried this before and with clipped wings, I was surprised she did so well. The bird almost made the foredeck, but not quite. She hit the side of the boat and fell into the water. The girl holding the broom watched all this. The bird was drowning but the girl just carried on scrubbing the deck.

I dived into the dinghy, rowed across and rescued Lorita before she sank. I lifted the soggy mess into the dinghy. Naturally, I asked the girl why she hadn't rescued the parrot with her broom. It would have been so easy. She said she thought it was a seagull. I must visit California one day and see the green seagulls. So much for the round-the-world sailors of 1993!

I spent a day in the main village where the shop tried to sell me bags of flour which were more weevils than flour. I then moved on to Hanamoenoa, the bay with the beautiful sand beach and the killer sand flies. It was popular, with half a dozen yachts anchored. I didn't see anybody on the beach so the word must have got around.

I was invited to dinner with Glenn and his boat full of pretty girls. The boat, *Blue Drifter*, was from Cape Town. They had visited Marina Cay where Tracey had helped them out with shower tokens. Then I'd seen them briefly again in Golfito. I had to take my hat off to Glenn to manage four gorgeous girls over all those miles.

That night he did me a great favor by rescuing my dinghy. I have anchored the dinghy off the point and gone night diving for shells. When I swam back to the point the dinghy was gone. I could just see it drifting off out to sea. With the compressor and long hose I wasn't going to be able to catch it up. Fortunately, I managed to attract Glenn's attention by flashing SOS at him with my torch.

On May 4th I left Tahuata. I had a meeting arranged with Joan de Katt in the Tuamotu's. There I was to hand over Lorita the parrot and we'd sail on together to Bora Bora.

As I approached Takaroa, the satellite navigator took another holiday. It was just typical of it to choose the most treacherous piece of water to fail me. The Tuamotu's on the English charts are named the Dangerous Archipelago. I motored up to the village in Takaroa. There were obvious huge changes since last time. A lot of money been made from pearl farming. There were now houses all over the island and as I approached two airplanes landed on an airfield which was also new. At the entrance to the Pass was a huge sign in English saying "No entry". So no problem, I sailed away!

Rangiroa is a huge atoll and my sextant sights were off or the current was doing something strange. . I arrived at the wrong end of the atoll and by the time I got to the pass, the tide was changing. In Nuku Hiva I had got the engine working again and pushing into the pass didn't do it any good but I made it and anchored for the night. Joan was somewhere in the lagoon so I did a little sailing around myself. But in fact we didn't meet up until a few days later. Joan had bought a new boat which I didn't know; so in fact he found me.

We had dinner on his boat and I brought along Lorita. Joan had put up a large branch of wood for her in the main cabin. She seemed happy with it so Joan busied himself making a large pan of spaghetti. He offered a good-sized bowl of it to Lorita. I told him I thought it was not a good idea but he went ahead. It was late anyway and Lorita was more into sleeping than eating. I returned the next morning for breakfast and sure enough, Lorita had plastered spaghetti all over the cabin.

Joan had promised to find me a second solar panel similar to the one I had got from him last time. A new power station had been built in the north of Taha, the large island next to Raiatia so there should be loads of redundant solar panels. We would go and see.

We arranged to meet again at the east pass into the lagoon and then sail around the north side inside the reef. So four days later we met again but had no luck with the solar panels. The local mayor had snaffled the lot. We had dinner with some friends of Joan and carried on to Bora Bora the next day.

The pass into the lagoon in Bora Bora is on the lee side of the island. As I approached I went to start the engine and it didn't want to know. Fortunately it was slack water in the pass so I managed to sail through easily enough and sailed around to the Bora Bora yacht club.

There were a few yachts on the moorings but one mooring was free and, as the water is over eighty feet deep here, I sailed over and grabbed it.

The problem with the engine was the injector pump which had been liberally sprayed with saltwater from a leaking saltwater pump. I had taken the pump out in Nuku Hiva and, using small cramps, had managed to free up the three little pistons. Unfortunately, this time they wouldn't move.

The pump is a complicated delicate piece of machinery which is repaired in specialist workshops. I foolishly removed the retaining spring holding it all together. It sprang apart, bits flying everywhere. I was left with a pile of pistons, springs, spacers and so on which had I had no idea how to put back together.

I took the lot to a helpful German guy in the village who repaired outboard engines. And he sent it to the specialists in Tahiti. I had visions of a massive bill. A French friend had paid nearly $1,000 to rebuild the injector pump on his engine in the same place and Volvo engines were known to be far more expensive.

A week later, the pump was returned in working order, no parts needed and a bill for only three hundred dollars. I made a new shaft for the sea water pump which had created the problem and put it all back together with new seals. The engine worked again and I could leave the yacht club and weave my way through the reefs to anchor off Joan and Fafa's fare on the windward side.

When I arrived Lorita the maybe female parrot had already been introduced to Plod the maybe male in Joan and Fafa's fare. Plod had had half a tree to live on intside the house but it had not been love at first sight. Lorita had chased him off and taken over the roost. Anther perch had to be made for him across the room. So much for all the searching around Costa Rica to find him a lover! We actually had no idea which sex either of them was.

Fafa was busy making pareos. She painted them with gaudy fish, flowers and so forth. The Bora Bora Hotel, still a very exclusive place, was selling her pareo's in their boutique. Joan had a small workshop overlooking the ocean where he carved wood. Joan being Joan, his specialty was breasts and penises. I'm not sure he sold any.

Joan's new yacht, a fifty-odd foot steel sloop with a huge centerboard, had belonged to a fleet of yachts which had arrived in Bora Bora some years before as part of a religious cult called "Extra Terreste". They had taken over a section of a motu just south of Joan's motu and built a small village to accommodate the followers.

The leader of the sect, a Moroccan, I believe, had direct contact with flying saucers which were preparing to arrive. In the centre of the village was a circular landing platform which the leader had been told by the space travelers to build. Only couples were allowed to join the sect and at least initially, the wives had to be given to the leader for his own personal use. It was bizarre, but popular with rich people, and the sect was thriving. But by the time I arrived, they had all moved away and gone back to the south of France.

Joan had bought a very cheap boat from them and when we visited the derelict village, we found they had left behind a large number of solar panels. Many of them were damaged but I found a good one for myself, and Joan found a couple more. There were no spaceships or little green men but a good yacht and a few solar panels made us both happy.

Joan and Fafa had a number of rich and influential friends in France and in Bora Bora, among them Paul Emile Victor, the apparently famous French arctic explorer. He was a flag-waving, pompous man and he and I didn't get on. More useful to me was Joan's friend the Island's Governor General in Tahiti. So using Joan's name, I wrote to him to ask about extending my visa for French Polynesia.

I received a personal letter in reply saying basically that if I sent my passport to Papeete it would probably take so long that I might want to leave before my passport was returned. Therefore, why didn't I simply enjoy my stay and not bother with any paperwork.

A few weeks later, anchored off the motu, a large inflatable boat arrived alongside. I came up to find that a customs officer had boarded and was standing uninvited in my cockpit. He was another small aggressive little man with lots of stripes on his uniform. He demanded to see my passport. I was livid and told him that the next time he had better not set foot on my vessel without an invitation to come aboard. This was not France. This was a British registered ship.

He spluttered and his face glowered. When I gave him my passport he took off in another tirade of French telling me I'd overstayed and was in big trouble. I loved it. I let him finish and then produced my letter from the Governor. The change in him was chameleon-like. In an instant, he went from nasty aggressive to friendly and fawning!

It was now July and the whole island was busy preparing for the "Quatorze" festival. A big village was built on the wharf and an impressive arena for the dancing. Lots of tourists arrived for the week and everything was much more organized than the last time. For instance, the pirogues, or native war canoes, were now fiberglass probably because there were no longer any trees of sufficient size left.

Joan, Fafa and I commuted to the village in their aluminum dinghy each week to have lunch with Coco the doctor. It was a long boozy affair and afterwards with the weeks groceries we returned to the quiet life on the motu.

I had a few yachts visit. *Blue Drifter* came with Glenn and his four girls as did Andy Ball, whom I had met briefly in St. Barts where he had worked. Andy had built his yacht *Balize* in a shed on the Dock Road in Birkenhead, not far from where I had launched *Sea Loone*. His workmates in Liverpool had referred to his boat, when he was building it, as Bally's Boat; hence the name *Balize*.

Andy arrived just on the new moon which was the time to go out on the outer lip of the reef at night to catch lobsters. There were not as many as in the Tuamotus and the reef was a bit broken up so I'm sure he was a little nervous. But he never forgot that night. He probably still has dreams of being sucked down into one of the huge gaping holes in the reef as the swells receded and then being gobbled up by an enormous shark or seized by a giant octopus.

Joan flew off to the South of France where Paul Emile Victor had organized an art exhibition for Bora Bora artists. I don't know how well Joan's phallic sculptures went down. The only native Polynesian artist had had to be almost kidnapped and dragged onto the plane to go to France,

I rebuilt Fafa's frames for painting the pareos. I doubled up the cloth so that she was making two each time. The second was a little dull but she was able to sell them to a less fancy establishment than the Bora Bora hotel. For myself, I collected a lot of huge purple sea urchins off the reef and was carving the spines into small tikis and making little turtles which I sold to the Japanese hotel at the entrance to the pass.

Waking up each morning anchored in a calm lagoon in only eight feet of crystal clear water with a backdrop of the volcanic peak of Bora Bora, was idyllic. Still, time and the seasons marched on and I was soon having to think of leaving.

Phil Hicks who had spent a lot of time helping me build the boat and who had originally wanted to join me when we first left Liverpool, now wrote to say he would like to join me in Bora Bora and could he sail with me to New Zealand?

His meteoric rise from shop salesman to University graduate, to business consultant to business owner had come to an abrupt end. I didn't ask for the details but was happy to have him along ignoring the normal stipulation of a return ticket. I felt I owed Phil a lot.

And so Phil arrived in Bora Bora bringing me a new electronic navigator, a GPS, which I had bought in Liverpool. He also brought a huge amount of luggage including silly things like a bag of rice from his kitchen. The excess luggage between Tahiti in Bora Bora on the airplane had almost crippled him physically and financially.

He settled in up forward without any problems, except for one night when the large gecko I'd brought on board to control the cockroaches, jumped onto his chest from the bookshelf. I really should have warned him about that.

After lots of goodbyes to all my friends in Bora Bora, Phil and I set off for Tonga. I wanted to stop at Beverage Reef, a reef in the middle of nowhere with an anchorage in its lagoon and a few wrecks to explore.

With the new GPS navigation was now a doddle. No more waiting around for fixes. The new machine gave your position continuously, accurate to maybe one hundred yards. Not only that but, by putting in your destination, the machine told you exactly which way to steer, following a little line across the screen I could click the string on the Aires selfsteering gear and watch the course change. Navigation had become a video game!

The trade winds picked up into a maramu or reenforced trades. The wind was blowing more than thiirty knots which saw us surfing down the ocean swells. Because of this, I decided to give Beverage Reef a miss and turned for Vavau'u, the northern islands of Tonga. We rounded the northern tip and motored up the channel to tie up at the wharf in Nieafu. There were immediate obvious changes since last time I was here. The population doubled and it showed. In fact, with so many children around, it looked as if they would double again in the next few years. The number of yachts had more than doubled and so had the number of officials that clambered on the boat.

The chief of customs, a huge gross individual, decided that my paperwork was inadequate. I argued, not a good thing to do. I was finally told my clearance papers from Bora Bora were no good. All clearance papers should be in English and mine was of course in French. We were told to leave.

We went to the market for some fresh vegetables, collected some water and left. We sailed back down the channel and anchored off a small island round the corner. Over the next few days, we visited a few more anchorages before heading south to the main island, Tongatapu.

In one spot, I met Ivan Wakelam again. We had spent some time together in Tahuata in the Marquesas. He had been anchored off the main village and got trapped there. He had repaired a few outboard engines and then been given a television to repair. This had happened when, in typical Marquesian fashion, a family argument had ended with the TV being thrown through the window ending up in the stream below the house. Ivan had got the thing working again and after that was regarded as the Island's miracle worker. He was not allowed to leave, not allowed to sleep on his boat and was fed huge amounts of food.

Ivan's parents had come to visit from New Zealand and so I met Henry and Yanik Wakelam. Their boat was in New Zealand. They had acquired New Zealand citizenship and bought a piece of land near Keri Keri. Henry had sailed many many years and was a great friend of Moitessier. Yanik had sailed a Nicolson-32 solo around the world, years ago. I promised to visit them when we got to the Bay of Islands.

When Phil and I arrived in Nuku'alofa, we cleared in with no problem. A new wharf had been built and a fishing harbour carved out of the coral reef. We anchored opposite the fish market with our stern tied to the seawall inside the harbour, a huge improvement on anchoring in deep water off the old Queen Shalloti's wharf.

We had a good three weeks or so before leaving for New Zealand and I intended to use the time selecting and buying a load of jewellery made from bone, shell and black coral. The most popular items were dolphins, whales, turtles and such like, carved out of cow bone or sometimes whalebone or black coral. Also popular were the native fishhooks. These varied; sometimes in bone with wood shanks and fancy lashings, and sometimes a work of art with complex hooks and swirls. All these were hung on black string to make pendants.

Besides carving these tiny items, there were woodcarvings and of every size including huge octopuses carved from tree stumps and full-size dolphins and marlins. This was all men's work, the women wove baskets of many different sorts. Some were bowls woven so tight they held water. Others made tapa cloth, the ancient clothing material beaten from tree bark. The women were organized into cooperatives. Phil got quite excited about their work and disappeared into town to see what business he could do with them.

I spend a few days talking to the carvers. There were a few around the harbour and in the market. Finally, I had to choose who I was going to do business with. It was an easy choice in the end. Steven Fehoko. He was a brilliant carver, an artist, but also a good businessman. He had a group of boys working for him doing really nice work. Apart from that we had a connection. His brother was Tongan Bill who had been Mike Baile's crew in the early days when he was sailing his folk-boat around the Pacific. Since that time Bill had acquired his own boat, sailed around the world and made a name for himself.

Steven had a small house perched on the coral reef a few miles out of town. When the boys were working it was a factory. Some were cutting basic shapes, others carving the details, and others sanding and polishing. I ordered maybe fifty dolphins, whales and so and within a couple of days the finished items started to arrive. I wasn't happy with the strings and the way they were attached so did without. Besides I was going to make earrings with some. So business began.

In the evening, I rowed across to the local bar, popular with the resident palangi white men. I didn't want to discuss with them what I was doing but was seriously warned against dealing with the local Tongans who had a terrible reputation for ripping everybody off. They did make me a little nervous as

Stephen wanted a fair amount of money up front to pay for materials and wages, every time I saw him he always needed a little bit more.

Still, the order was completed. Steven and I sat on the cabin floor and went through the piles of pieces and I paid up the small amount still owing. I promised I would be back in six months to maybe do some more business. I had spent more than a thousand dollars in the end.

Meanwhile Phil had been busy talking business talk with the women's cooperative. He tried to organize an interview with the Princess, the head of the cooperative but she was as usual having fun in California. His grand plan was to send the container full of basket work to London. Through Phil's contacts, they would have an exhibition in Harrods selling the basket work and promoting all things Tongan. The one thing Polynesia's are good at is talking so Phil was busy and I saw very little of him.

Drinking beer in the bar at night was great fun. A Swedish brewery had gone into partnership with the King to build a small brewery in town. In the bar I met the designer, builder and managing brewmaster of the Royal Beer Company Limited, Andrew Klystera. I also met his crazy noisy Tongan girlfriend. We would all drink the night away and with Andrew's magic checkbook the brewery would pay the bill.

On Thursdays, Andrew's office in the brewery was the meeting place for the local businessman. The beer was lifted from conveyor belts, before the pasteurizing plant, straight into the office fridge. The problems of doing business in Tonga were a major topic of conversation. The stories were highly amusing and sometimes heartbreaking I began to realize how well I had done so far with Steven.

At the end of October, we set sail for New Zealand. Phil's plans had come to nothing but I suppose it had kept him occupied.

A few hundred miles south of Tonga are two reefs. We stopped and stayed a few days in South Minerva and I dragged out the diving machine so we could look around in the water. Unfortunately Phil was a bit too buoyant.

Disaster struck on the third day there. I woke up to find that the dinghy had disappeared complete with engine and oars. No excuses this time I had tied off the dinghy on the aft rail. The knot had come undone.

With a huge tide overnight the dinghy would have cleared the reef and would now be off across the ocean to Australia. I didn't want to count how many dinghies I had lost by now.

The rest of the trip south was uneventful. The mainsail which was about to complete its circumnavigation, started to fall apart. Even half a litre of contact adhesive couldn't keep it totally together. It certainly didn't look very pretty as we sailed up the channel to Opua.

3

KEN AND JOSS were waiting for us on the wharf, taking our lines as we tied up. Colleen, the postmistress, ran down the wharf from the post office calling my name. There were letters. I was home!

The paperwork was soon finished. Just as I was preparing to cast off and motor up the river to anchor little Alan arrived in his dinghy. I had not seen Alan Dunshae since his last effort to leave Sydney. He had been having the same problems that he'd had leaving Opua and had been towed back into the harbour having almost surfed onto Bondi Beach. He now told me the rest of the saga.

A young American guy had joined Alan for his second attempt to leave Sydney and sail back to New Zealand. They spent weeks at sea and got thoroughly lost. Finally land appeared, what looked like the sandhills of the northern point of North Island.

When they got close, they realize it was not sand, it was snow! They were somewhere off the west coast of South Island. A fishing boat towed them into port. Weeks later, Alan set off again to go up the coast to finally get back to the Bay of Islands. He lost sight of land and when he found it again he was towed into another harbour even further down the coast.

Alan gave up. He sold the boat and returned overland to Opua. A few years passed and Alan decided to visit Mark and Bernadette, the couple in Sydney who had done the Amazon trip. They now had a baby and were living in France.

From France, Alan went to Holland with the idea of buying another Dutch boat. He bought a lifeboat which had had a keel added and had been decked over and rigged to sail. He found another little French girl and they set off together but this time with a satellite navigator. He crossed the Atlantic and sailed to the Caribbean. Them via the Panama Canal he sailed across the Pacific arriving in Raratonga in the Cook Islands. All this with no problem.

Instead of heading for Tonga, and then going down to New Zealand he now decided to go direct. Miles from anywhere, heading south, he hit bad weather. The boat turned upside down and stayed that way. Alan dived down and up to the surface, then returned for his crew. They sat on the keel until another large wave came and flipped the boat over again. They managed to bail the water out but the satnav no longer worked. They were lost again.

Weeks later the long white cloud, New Zealand, appeared in front of them and they managed to sail into the Bay of Islands. Alan turned and pointed out the boat tied up to a mooring not far away. He never went sailing again.

Back up the river above Ashby's boat yard, I made my plans. First the jewellery had to be sold, then I needed a new mainsail and a new dinghy and outboard. I went out and bought a car, a Datsun Sunny for nine hundred New Zealand dollars. That is about five hundred American dollars. It was one of the thousands of secondhand cars brought in from Japan and was perfect.

Ken and Joss had invited Phil to use their basement flat so he moved ashore. I zoomed around everywhere and successfully found outlets for the jewellery. On one of these trips I invited Phil along. I was going across on the ferry to Russel to see if I could find a shop there interested in my wares.

Phil wandered around and then I suggested we go for a lunchtime pint in the pub. He didn't want to go which seemed very strange to me. He then admitted he didn't have enough money to buy a beer. I was flabbergasted. I knew he didn't have a lot of money, and wasn't rich, but was surprised that he had absolutely nothing and no job. Having brought him into the country, I was responsible.

I bought him a beer and lent him fifty dollars; then and asked him if he wanted me to find him work. Glenn on *Drifter* was putting up some fencing down the road and there were also fruit picking jobs in Keri Keri. But Phil had other irons in the fire and was talking business with some people in Pahia. Sometime later he moved to Pahia and was managing a restaurant there. Ken being an old socialist and union leader was happy to see him leave.

With the jewellery going well (I even had Colleen selling stuff at the post office) I turned to the next problem. I telephoned Claire Jones the girl that had made the mainsail and asked her to visit as a sail she had made "was no good". She was horrified when I showed the sail. But then I explained that, over the last ten years or more, it had sailed me around the world; so I wanted another the same. She smiled!

The other problem was the dinghy. I wanted to build a new one in fiberglass so I went looking for somewhere I could buy resin and fiberglass in bulk at a proper price. So one day I found myself turning down a farm lane near Keri Keri looking for a fibreglass factory I had heard about.

I found the factory, a big old barn tucked away in a steep-sided, overgrown, valley on a kiwi fruit farm. Ian, the owner, manager and sole employee, had sold out his large factory in Wellington and bought a kiwi fruit farm. His interest was still in messing around with odd jobs in fiberglass, particularly designing and making very sophisticated rowing skiffs for him to use in the annual Keri Keri river race. This took up most of his time.

When I explained what I wanted to do, not only did he offer me the materials at cost but also suggested I use a corner of the factory. Glenn had shown interest in the dinghy project also. No problem, Glenn and I started a daily commute from Opua to build two dinghies.

By the time Glenn arrived in *Blue Drifter*, his girl crew had been reduced to one. Catherine, a Cape Town girl. She was a doctor of medicine. Having worked in South Africa and England as a doctor, only a cursory examination was required before she was allowed to work in New Zealand. As luck would have it, a medical practice became available in Pahia. There were no problems with work permits and the owner of the medical centre was a lovely lady.

In the secondhand emporium in Keri Keri, I bought a huge shop window glass. It was broken but was perfect for my purposes. With Ian's chopper gun we could spray up sheets of fiberglass to suit on the sheet of glass, stitch the sheets together to form the dinghies, and then put them back under the chopper gun to build up the fiberglass to a suitable thickness. I cut mine in half, each with a bulkhead, so that one half fitted inside the other, similar to the dinghy I had built in Curaçao. I then added a maststep and centre-board so that it became a sailing dinghy. When both the dinghies were finished, we hung them from a roof beam and weighed them to work out the cost of materials. It did not amount to much more than one hundred New Zealand dollars each. By this time we were great friends with Ian and his wife. He always had some interesting project or idea to discuss.

I also discovered that Henry and Yanik Wakelam lived just down the road. Henry, like Ian, was also into all sorts of projects and at the time had just perfected his latest machine for cracking macadamia nuts. It worked well without crushing the meat inside the very hard, round shell. Phil tried to help with the patenting of the design before marketing it. I'm not sure what happened.

With the jewellery selling so well, I began to consider the possibility of returning to French Polynesia with it. I was sure it would go down well and

I could easily double my profit because it was such an expensive place. I also had the crazy idea of taking a mould off Little Roy, my Marquesian tiki, and making resin and stone copies.

I bought some very expensive molding silicone and went back to Ian's factory to see what I could do. Ian had a vacuum chamber which was handy to remove the bubbles in the silicone and to save on materials, I made an outside fiberglass mold. I made two. They worked well with two halves bolted together and open at the base. I poured a slurry of resin and fine black road grit into the molds, shaking the mixture down. Once cured, the resulting tiki had to have the mold line ground away and then the whole thing lightly sanded to remove the surface resin and expose the rock.

They came out amazingly good. In fact they were so good that I sold a load to the yachties in Opua through Colleen's post office. I then made an expedition to Auckland where, together with more jewellery, there was a brisk demand from the shops.

There was an arty Bohemian set in Pahia. Among them was a German guy, Dieter, who did bone carvings. He was also very good with gold. I had seen gold and black coral tikis in all the shops in French Polynesia. I was convinced we could do better if Dieter inlaid gold into the tikis made by Steven. Dieter was also good at weaving string and had the polishing equipment I needed. So I proposed to him that he join me on a little trip to Tahiti via Tonga, he might enjoy the adventure and could make some money as well. Dieter had not sailed before so had no idea what beating a few thousand miles to windward was going to be like .It was going to be horrible probably.

I had cards printed in English and French to go with the stone tikis and made small wooden plinths for them to sit on. I filled the bilge with black road-grit and bottles of resin. Then I bought a mile of cord for the pendants, loads of sandpaper and all the other bits and pieces.

By April, I was pretty organized. I hauled *Sea Loone* out and applied new anti-fouling paint, bought a new outboard engine and set up the new mainsail from Clare. I drove the car up to Ian's farm and put it up on bricks for the six months or so I would be away. Then we had our last barbecue. I had been in touch with Steven in Tonga and hoped that he would get started on my order for jewellery before I arrived.

So the first week in May 1994, Dieter moved on board and we cleared for Tonga. Fully provisioned for all the time we'd be away and with a bilge full of black rock for my tikis, we were pretty loaded down, but luckily the wind turned to the southeast and we flew along. We reached the Kermadecs and were still going like a train and I anticipated us arriving in way less than the ten days we had planned. But of course such thoughts are a recipe for disaster; and so it happened.

With a loud bang the front section of the crane at the top of the mast tore off releasing both forestays. We had been reaching in big seas and all that was holding up the mast was an old jib made in nineteen sixty-three and a rope halliard. The mast was already bending and shaking alarmingly.

I grabbed the spare halliard and ran it up forward and as I tensioned it up, the sail split. All this time, I was shouting to Dieter to bring the boat off the wind and slack the main. It took a while to sort out the mess on the foredeck and remove the forestays and torn sail.

With both halliards tensioned up, the mast stopped shaking and we turned to reach to the north again with the reefed main sail but moving very slowly. I slumped into the saloon exhausted and Dieter, very agitated, complained that I shouldn't have shouted at him. One more word and he would have been swimming the rest of the way.

We crabbed slowly north not daring to put up a head sail. When we eventually saw Tonga. We were a bit downwind but we motored up and finally arrived in the fishing harbour. Dieter was still a bit shaken up, but prepared to carry on.

Steven had already got some stuff made and with an injection of my money, went into full production. I had some other designs to try out as well including some "new and improved" black coral tikis

With difficulty I managed to remove the mast crane with the mast still in place. I found a really good German engineer who made me a mild steel replacement. With this in place, and looking much more reliable than the original, and with Steven arriving with the last order of jewellery, we were ready to go.

The last night with Andrew and the rest of the palangis in the pub didn't help but it was going to be a while before the next cold beer.

We caught the tide going out to the east passage and hardened up the sheets to beat more than 1,500 miles to windward to Tahiti. This is a boat that at best can tack through 120° and can get stopped dead by every third or fourth wave. So this would translate into 3,000 miles at three knots or more than forty days' sailing. But in fact, with a continuous passage of fronts coming up from the south, changes in the wind from south to east to northeast and back to south, makes the course a lot more direct as we took advantage. It was already June 1994 and we really had to be in Tahiti before July 14, the beginning of Haeva, the peak of the tourist season.

Initially we beat northeast with not too many big seas. We were making good progress. The wind swung east and we tacked south. We passed close by Raratonga without seeing it. With the new GPS, it was easy to see how well we were doing and when it might be best to put in a tack. I wanted to keep south of Tahiti on the run in, just in case the strong southeast trades, maramu, came in. So we headed towards the Australs. On only one day did the wind and seas get too much and force us heave too. The rest of the time we made good progress.

We arrived in Tahiti on July 7, 1994. I was really pleased. We had no major problems and Dieter was still in good condition.

I had never sailed into Tahiti before so it was all new for me. We motored into Papeete Harbour and anchored downtown with a stern-line on the beach. The Immigration Department wanted me to pay the bond but I knew that Philippe was passing through Papeete the following day. I had asked him to sponsor me. So the next day we met and chatted and when I introduced Philippe to the immigration official as the Chief Medical Officer for the Marquesas, we even got a cup of coffee.

Dieter was invited to an exhibition of artisanary and got quite involved, not that it made us any money. Meanwhile I ran around the shops and hotels but didn't really get anywhere. I expected to do better out of town in the tourist places, so we sailed across to Moorea. I rented a motor scooter and circumnavigated the island, calling in at all the hotels and boutiques. It took me all day and I had no success at all.

I was getting worried. Dieter and I visited a French goldsmith to see what he made. We priced out the cost of buying gold wire and doing the inlays. It all looked too expensive and certainly a disaster if we didn't sell anything. Meanwhile Dieter was busy making strings and fittings as well as polishing and preparing. I stirred resin and rock and popped out the tikis to be sanded and oiled.

Having failed with the expensive motor scooter, I hitch-hiked back to the northwest corner of the island where Club Med had been established. There

I poked around some more and, on the water's edge, found a very expensive exotic gallery. It was stocked with a lot of Marquesian carvings and other items, at huge prices. The owner, a tall, blonde haired, bare chested guy wearing a pareo, was talking with two very rich looking Germans.

The whole thing was a little intimidating. I went to slink out but was called back and asked my business. When I explained what I had, the Frenchman, full of charm, invited me to wait in the garden until he had finished with his German clients.

I sat looking out at the turquoise lagoon resting my tired feet. When the man returned, he had a bottle of wine in one hand and two glasses in the other. In my normal way, I dumped a huge pile of stuff on the table and slurped the good red wine while he sorted through the pile. It took him a while and nothing was said other than his inquiries about the materials I had used.

When he finished, there were two unequal piles. He pointed to the larger pile and said he would take that. I tried not to show my surprise but failed badly. There had been no talk of money but the list I had given him gave him a basic idea.

When we finally added it up, it all came to around US$5,000. By the time we had polished off the wine, some minion had reappeared with the money in cash. Amazing how things were suddenly looking up!

In Cook's Bay, a Dutchman had a huge place full of carvings of all sorts. He took half a dozen of my stone tikis. I charged him more or less fifty dollars each, which was pure unadulterated profit. After that we couldn't go wrong. In Huahini an American hippy surfer bought a load. He was a nice man. In Raiatea I sold more and again a few tikis.

We sailed across to Bora Bora and picked up a mooring at the yacht club. In the morning I went to town to see Bebe with his boutique next to the wharf. We already knew each other well. Bebe was behind the counter. He was busy but asked to see what I had. I opened up a sample bag of the jewellery and planted a stone tiki on the counter.

An elderly Japanese man grabbed the tiki to show his wife, talking incessantly and turning the tiki round and round. Bebe whispered to me "how much?" and I indicated to him that US$100 would see us all right. Meanwhile two Italian girls had dived into the jewellery. It was bedlam. More and more people came into the shop.

I suggested to Bebe that I should go for a cup of coffee and come back in an hour when it should be quieter. I scooped up the jewellery, left the Japanese with the tiki and went across the road for a coffee. While I drank my coffee, I rewrote the price list adding on a fair bit more. I knew Bebe was a shark, but then maybe I had become one, too? There was no question that Bebe wasn't going to invest in some of my inventory.

Having offloaded a pile more jewellery and a number of tikis with Bebe, we sailed around the north of the island to see Joan and Fafa on the motu. I wanted to see how the parrots were getting on. Joan was away in France. The parrots were still not friends with Lorita still lording it in the huge tree perch and Plod in the far corner.

Fafa had been busy but was off to stay in Taha for a few weeks. So Dieter moved ashore to look after the house and I sailed around to the village again and then on to the Bora Bora Hotel.

A friend of Fafa's, Marie Claire, had a place just past the hotel on the beach. She had financed the first boat by making complicated wire puzzles which she still made plus other things. A lot of tourists wandered past along the beach so her little gallery worked well and she was keen to sell my stuff as well as her own.

I had one really strange ugly tiki which had made experimenting with a cement-resin mix. We nailed it on to a boulder at the bottom of the garden. It frightened locals but certainly attracted the passing visitors.

Back in the village I had two orders from Fafa's Post Office Box. One was for a load of jewellery to go to Raiatea. The other was for a dozen stone tikis to go to the Dutchman in Moorea. I also had more tikis to make for people here in Bora Bora.

I took a mooring again off the yacht club and started moulding tikis. I could make four a day and use the angle grinder to remove the molding line. But the overall sanding was time-consuming and boring. There were a number of cruising yachts around me so I chose one large scruffy concrete yacht and asked if they want to work for me.

They were South Africans and upset that I should think they needed money. Never mind. I went to the yacht next door, a Danish boat but he and his girlfriend were about to leave. I was offering ten dollars an hour for sanding two tikis per hour, sand paper provided. It seemed like quite a good deal to me.

After two rejections, I returned to the boat to pop out the next two tikis and make another batch. While doing this, the Danish guy rode over and having talked with his girlfriend, was happy to delay leaving for a day. He left with a box full of tikis and sandpaper.

Two days later I had a dozen stone tikis parceled up in a strong cardboard box and on the aeroplane to Moorea. I drank a few beers with the Danes just before they cleared out for Tonga and paid them off in dollars.

By the time I had completed the order for Moorea, I had run out of rock, the bilge was empty and I couldn't find any suitable materials on the island. I had three shops and a hotel selling my goodies but there was nothing more I could do. So when Fafa returned home, I collected Dieter from the motu, said goodbye to the parrots and set off for Tonga.

This time the weather was not so rough so we stopped in Beverage Reef. The pass into the lagoon is fairly straightforward and we anchored close to a large trawler stranded on the windward reef. The wreck was quite recent so I helped myself to some stainless steel strip for the dinghy keel and removed two windows from the bridge. The trawler was maybe one hundred feet long and had been built in Florida from fiberglass. Some hero had already sawed through the massive shaft and taken the propeller.

Dieter was nervous about sharks and not keen on snorkeling. In Beverage there was good reason. There were a number of gray reef sharks and they were very aggressive and territorial. I always swam close to the reef dragging the dinghy behind me. I knew too many stories about sharks removing pieces of people.

I introduced Dieter to catching lobsters by walking on the outside reef at night. So when we left to finish our trip to Tonga, we had a cockpit full of them. We thought we could perhaps sell them when we arrived. Over the coming days, however much we looked after them, they died. We ate lobster every night until we were sick of it.

Arriving off the fishing harbour in Nuku'alofa, the engine started giving trouble. Under sail, and with a little help, we managed to anchor and get a stern line ashore. When we looked at the engine, we discovered that the engine oil had turned to mayonnaise. It was water and oil mixed again. No matter, we had arrived and not long after finishing with the officials, a truck arrived from the Royal Beer Company with a case of beer for us. A quick trip across to the fish market for a bucket of ice, and we were happily boozing it up in the cockpit.

Dieter was in a hurry now to get back to New Zealand to renew his residence permit. I think he was also a little nervous about heading south again after our previous problems. So with the help and my seaman's forms and ship's papers we managed to get a seaman's discount for Dieter for an air ticket with a 30% reduction back to Auckland.

Back in the pub, I thanked Andrew for the case of beer and got all the news. He had been to Europe with a girlfriend and she now had gold jewelry, a fancy French dress and Andrew had even bought her a little car. She had crashed the car in the first week. She also still ran off with her boyfriends for days at a time. But it was good fun and Andrew was forever forgiving.

My jewellery was more or less all sold, so Steven and the boys had work to do. I had shown Steven some whales teeth I had acquired in Durban, South Africa. He said he would do something with them and made some lovely scrimshaw scenes. One, featuring a Tongan sailing catamaran, was particularly good. I had another quite large whales tooth with its tip broken off and suggested he rounded the top into the head of an octopus. He stopped me talking, snatched the tooth away and said he'd see what he could do.

A few days later he arrived with a huge Polynesian smile on his face as he presented me with the carved tooth. An octopus sat there on a rock with just one tentacle turned to show its suckers. It was truly a work of art.

Each Sunday, a car or taxi or truck would arrive with a huge plate of food from Steven. His family cooked in a "hungi" using heated stones in a pit. They were huge pieces of manioc, taro, sweet potato and sometimes breadfruit, goat or fish. I always had to invite a few of my neighbours to eat it all.

Apart from drinking vast quantities of beer in the pub, I occasionally went astray and finished up in some nightclub. One morning I woke up with the goalkeeper from the Tonga ladies football team. After another night out, I finished up with a New Zealand tuna fisherman, a Tongan girl who had worked on the Reeperbahn in Hamburg, a delightful young thing, maybe her daughter, and a dwarf.

The New Zealander on the yacht next to me who was married to a Samoan lady, had not been annoyed by the noise from my boat, but was amazed to see in the early hours, a large naked Tongan girl squat over the side for a pee, take a beer from the icebox in my cockpit, remove the lid with her teeth and disappear again below.

I'm claiming memory loss for the whole night. Thank God there wasn't the normal conservative American yacht next door. Apparitions like that can cause heart attacks, or so I'm told.

It was time to leave for New Zealand before I got into any more trouble. Steven had asked me to pay him the total amount for the jewellery order only when he had completed everything. So on the final day we went through the order and I paid him. He had arrived with another guy in a truck. Had I paid Steven bit by bit in the normal way, the family would have spent it all as soon as I gave it him. When you have money, you cannot refuse requests from family members.

I rowed him ashore and, at the dock wall, he handed the money over to the guy with the truck. Steven had bought the truck. It was a good move. I also pestered him to try and hide away some money so that he could make up orders for me before I arrived, maybe he could hide away what he had left.

Leaving the harbour was not so easy, I no longer had crew. I had filled the engine with new oil which would give me only minutes of use before it was mayonnaise again. I would need that few minutes in New Zealand, so I left under sail.

A friend helped me raise the anchor the last little bit when the boat had to fall off on the right tack. Then, as I turned out of the narrow entrance, he jumped in his dinghy and waved me away. I zigzagged between the reefs and anchored again for the night, before the final pass into the ocean. In the morning, by the time I had got my anchor up again and started for the pass, my back was killing me. It was time to spend some of my ill-gotten gains on an anchor winch, an electric one.

I had no problems passing the Kermadecs this time and no stops in Minerva Reef. I managed to sail up within yards of the wharf in Opua and then motored very briefly to arrive alongside.

Customs and immigration came on board the boat and we completed the paperwork. Then a young guy arrived from the NZ Ministry of Ag. and Fish (MAF). New Zealand had always been very strict on the importation of plant and animal species and always confiscated all fresh fruit and vegetables, meat, eggs and a long list of other items.

I had expected it; so invited the man to go through the boat with me and see if there was anything that might be a problem. We went through the containers under the cockpit and in the lockers under the bunks and put the few remaining vegetables in a large plastic bag. I was then presented with the form to sign which I did and then the bloody man then said he was going to search the boat, which I thought we had just done.

In the small lock under the sink, the man found a sealed packet of popcorn. He acted as though this was a major hazard to New Zealand's corn harvest this year. I was presented with another form in which I had to explain why I had brought in the goods and I was told this would go to the head office and a decision on whether to bring court proceedings against me would then be made.

My friend Catherine, the doctor, had found popcorn in Tonga and had given me the packet as a present. I had thrown it under the sink and forgotten about it. Trying to write this down, I was seething. But then I was told to stop writing. The man had been sitting looking at the offending packet and he had suddenly realized it was a product of New Zealand.

The next day I contacted MAF to complain of my treatment. The sympathetic person I spoke to told me the same guy had upset the crew on a huge stern trawler just back from Antarctica. They had thrown him in Auckland Harbor. He was about to get the sack that week.

I wasn't sure how Dieter was going to portray his trip on his return to NZ. At times I had given him a bit of a hard time. So when I saw him in the Opua Cruising Club that night I thought he might have been putting out stories about Capt. Bligh of the *Sea Loone*. But my fears proved groundless. Dieter hugged me and almost kissed me. We had tamed the wild ocean together, found sunken treasure, and were home to tell the tale.

Andrew's Royal Beer didn't have much to commend it, so it was good to be drinking a good pint of Tueys with the boat safely anchored up the river. Luckily someone had offered to tow me there from the wharf.

As always on the first day back in Opua, I rowed ashore, walk down the old railway line and then up the steep path which brought me into Ken and Joss's garden. The swamp next to Ashby's boat yard had been filled in and business properties had been built there but sitting out on the veranda with a cup of tea and homemade biscuits the view across the river was still the same, unspoilt and beautiful. Any developments below us were obscured by the trees on the steep slope.

Ken and Joss's garden was still a menagerie. But they had had to give up feeding the possums. There was still a lot of friction with some of the neighbors over the issue. They still had a few hives at the bottom of the garden and more up in the forest, but they were no longer allowed to sell the honey. The bureaucrats had decided that a sterile stainless steel room was required and licenses, permits and so on.

Ken had experimented with making mead and the first batch was really good. He then put all his eggs in one basket, brewing up a huge batch in a massive wooden barrel. The result was not good but fortunately Ken had a friend with a still, so the mead was distilled into pure alcohol.

A specialist shop in Whangarei selling brewing and distilling equipment, also sold small bottles of essences to add to the alcohol. These were additives to make anything from whisky and rum to rare liqueurs. Having found all the correct empty bottles, Ken had a cellar full of every drink you could imagine; and the constant low humming and buzzing at the bottom the garden ensured an ongoing supply.

I collected my car from Ian's kiwi fruit farm and took it to the garage to get its road worthiness test. The mechanic had agreed six months earlier to pass me twice as the car hadn't been anywhere since the last test.

The next month was a horror story of taking *Sea Loone*'s engine to pieces. I had to remove the wet liners in the cylinders, clean out the whole cooling system which was clogged with the stony deposit, and get it all back together again.

The 3-cylinder Volvo engine was saltwater cooled with separate heads. This made things easier and big jobs could be done without removing the whole engine. But parts were expensive and sometimes not available. Fortunately, there was a similar engine, a two-cylinder in pieces nearby. This provided a new head bolt which had broken when removing it. I hate engines. I hate working on them so when everything was back together and working, I was much relieved

I had been around all the shops selling my stuff, my outlets I suppose you could call them. They had all taken more. With the engine finished I now had time to look for a few more customers and made a trip to Auckland and down to Kati Kati on the Coramandel Peninsula. I stayed a few days with Dick and Jane from *Contour of Cut Hill* whom I had last seen in Brazil.

Dick and Jane had sold the boat and, having looked around, had bought back into a kiwi fruit farm not far from where they had started years before. Kiwi fruit was no longer the big-money business it had been, so farms were cheap and of course Dick knew the business. Chris the eldest son was finishing his apprenticeship and busy building boats and James, the youngest, was studying engineering at Auckland University.

The farm was in a beautiful spot with a river at the bottom of the hills, some forest, and beside kiwi fruit, had avocado trees. It obviously wasn't a very stressful life, with tennis in the summer and skiing in the winter.

About this time, the New Zealand government passed a new law. Of their own volition, New Zealand had taken on the responsibility for search and rescue of vessels in the South Pacific Ocean out as far as the Cook Islands and down into the Roaring Forties. It was like Liverpool taking on the same role for the whole of the North Atlantic except that Liverpool had more people and more money.

With two Orion airplanes and a small Navy, New Zealand was busy. The ocean races around the world were for ever getting into trouble and more and more cruising yachts were shouting for help. The new law required that all foreign yachts leaving New Zealand have to comply with their own yacht safety regulations. This involved inspection by officials and a long list of safety equipment including, at the top, an EPERB. This is a sort of radio transmitter which sends out distress signals to the passing airplanes. It is waterproof and floats. The list also included a galvanized bucket (I don't know why galvanized) together with life rafts, life jackets, rocket flares and many other things.

Many yachts had all of these things. Others, like myself, had none of them, not even the bucket. But this was not the main problem. New Zealand have no right to control any foreign vessel visiting its waters and so began a lengthy public debate and a lot of angry words on the radio, television and in papers.

Out of the blue, I had a letter from Philippe in Nuku Hiva. Much had happened since I left. Tracey had got very involved in para punting or parasailing, jumping off mountains with a parachute. The parachute was more like a wing and you could stay in the air for hours. She had one time landed in the top of the tall palm tree and another time nearly got blown away over the ocean.

Another enthusiast was a Marquesian with two young children and a wife who had run off with a French naval officer. Tracy moved in with the local guy. Philippe was heartbroken and also very upset to find that, through all his effort to make babies, Tracey had been taking precautions.

Tracey now had two children to look after. It then gets complicated. The wife came back to Taeohae and moved in with Philippe. She was a strikingly beautiful Marquesian girl, he says. So now I read in the letter, Philippe is coming to Auckland for holiday with his new girlfriend, soon to be wife, and they would bringing the children who would normally still be living with Tracey and the husband.

I drove down to Auckland and stayed the night with the four of them. They were in a backpacker's hostel so we all shared the same room. Once the girlfriend got to realize I wasn't on anybody's side, we had a good time and I drove them around in the car.

The best part was breakfast. The breakfast was included in the price of the stay. There was a large selection of cereals, toast, marmalade and then bacon, eggs, sausages etc. - a huge spread. There were backpackers from all over the world taking breakfast but they all stopped and stared as the Marquesian kids set upon the food. First the cereal was mixed with a cup of coffee and then scooped up by hand into the mouth. It's very messy picking things up, mixing them, and then filling the mouth. But I laughed and then explained, or tried to explain, where they were from and that back home this was normal.

The end of the story was that, within the year, both Philippe and Tracey were married to new people and both had new babies on the way.

My Liverpool friend, Andy Ball had had *Balize* hauled out in a huge new boat yard in Whangarei. He had cut the transom off *Balize* and was extending it by a few feet. He was also cutting off the bilge keels and making a single center keel with two fancy wings on the bottom of the keel made from the old bilge keel. The boat was steel so none of this was a problem for Andy.

I got a message from him that he had found an anchor winch suitable for *Sea Loone* so I motored down to see him.

The anchor winch was on a huge German motor sailer hauled out close to Andy. It had a huge deck house with sliding doors and a set of stairs constructed to get from the dock up on deck. There was even a doorbell. Obviously they were going to be there for a while.

I rang the bell and a very gruff German invited me on deck. The anchor winch was still in place so we went to look on the foredeck. It was surprisingly small for such a huge boat and was rigged for ten mm. chain which was what I used. It was all stainless steel with a drum on either side. It was perfect.

The German demanded NZ$900. I offered him seven but wanted the chain included. He was changing to a much bigger winch and a huge chain so I'd suggested the chain was no use to him. He grumbled a bit but agreed, and a few days later I returned and collected to winch and two hundred feet of very presentable chain. The winch was small but very heavy and the electric motor which drove it was huge and powerful. All I had to do now was tear up *Sea Loone's* foredeck and install it.

A week later, and Andy called me again. I had to go and see the German once more. Apparently he had a spare electric motor for the winch. I climbed the stairs again and rang the doorbell. I asked for the motor. I was told it cost over a US$1,000. I explained that it was no use to him. There was some words in German and I walked away with a spare motor.

Sometime later I saw the German's new anchor winch, heavy chain and huge anchors. Together they were probably worth one hundred times our small deal.

In Ian's factory on the kiwifruit farm, I made a gantry to go on the back of *Sea Loone* to support the solar panels. Glenn was also there embedding light-emitting diodes (LED's) into resin to make lights for inside and outside the boat. They were a clever new idea at the time and there was a lot of interest.

I hauled *Sea Loone* out on the railway in Opua, first getting the mast plucked out by a local pile-driving barge. The mast crane I had made in Tonga seemed more than adequate, so I simply had it galvanized and put it back. At the same time, I had the fore and aft chain plates removed and galvanized together with the two anchors. I then tore off the old stern rail and fitted the gantry. Up on the foredeck I re-bedded the cat head and bollard and fitted the lovely anchor winch. After a coat of paint top and bottom, we were set to sail away again.

I often spent evenings drinking beer in the Road Runner, a large pub between Opua and Pahia. My drinking partner was Uve, a German from Hamburg with a wife and a boat both called Inez. After work, the pub would be crowded with workers, half of them Maoris. There was a good "crack" as they say in Ireland.

Sweetie Pie, a lovely Maori lady, sold my jewellery in the pub in a very casual way. This really annoyed Uve and sometimes surprised him when he saw how much money Sweetie Pie shoved in my hand now and again. I still had a few sand dollar earrings which I had given to Sweetie Pie. One evening a huge Maori guy came over with a large black sand dollar earring. Its mate was broken but how much did I want for the one. I gave it to him but I'd love to have had a photo of him with the earring, the long hair and the facial tattoos.

Uve's wife, Inez, was determined to find me crew to go up to the islands with. The first one she introduced me to was a pretty young American girl. Unfortunately she was a vegetarian. I suggested as a trial that she should come out to the boat and make an acceptable meal from whatever vegetables and such like she found aboard.

It was a disaster. She boiled rice and then chopped up and fried up whatever vegetables, cabbage, onions etc. were there. But then she found a packet of lentils and, without soaking or boiling them, threw them in with the frying vegetables. At least she agreed that the whole thing was inedible so we went ashore to eat in Pahia.

One Friday evening after a day's work on the boat, now back in the water, the Cruising Club was full. Inez introduce me to a buxom German girl. All I wanted was to put down a few beers and get a night sleep. But Inez wasn't to be put off.

To be truthful, Inez was a really beautiful woman herself and, but for Uve, I'd have dragged her off to *Sea Loone*, tired or not tired. The next girl was French. Inez pointed her out standing alone in the corner sipping a beer. Inez knew I spoke a little French, so I was obliged to at least talk to her.

Yes, she said, she wanted to sail up to the islands. Young, attractive, lovely eyes. I weakened. I explained the boat was small compared with the modern cruising yachts and rather primitive. But if she was really interested, the best thing to do was to come out to *Sea Loone* the following morning and then we could talk.

The next morning, Laurence was waiting for me on the dock. The boat was a mess. I was cleaning out under the bunks before going out to stock up on food and such like, which would be stored there. Laurence looked around. She wasn't the least put off and the next thing I knew she was mopping out one of the lockers.

She had lived in New Caledonia and worked as a sales representative. She knew my business and was sure she could help. It was all too good to be true.

We stopped for coffee. The whole time she had been wearing a thin anorak with deep pockets. When I said okay she could come, she smiled and said that there was a small problem. She was not alone. My thoughts raced! Boyfriend? No. baby, I suddenly thought? But just then she reached into her pocket and pulled out a rat! It explored around a bit and then disappeared back into her pocket.

I could see problems. Not insurmountable perhaps especially as the advantage of a sales girl in Noumea balanced things out. When the anorak came off and the dark curly hair fell over her shoulders; and when her very well developed boobies thrust out and those eyes looked at me, she could have been the pied piper!

My plans were to sail back up to Tonga, do some final business with Steven, then sail on to Fiji, New Caledonia and then to Australia. Glenn was staying on. Andy Ball had been grabbed by the owner of the shipyard to teach apprentice engineers. So I found myself saying goodbye to Ken and Joss and a host of other people.

We had a huge party in the Opua Cruising Club. The boat was stored up and Laurence was settled in. The only nasty thing to happen was that my Datsun Sunny was stolen the day before I had it sold. Months later I heard that some Maoris had driven it off a cliff for fun!

The yachts that had been trapped in New Zealand by the new law were an embarrassment for the government. I had a man arrive to inspect the boat, some local yachtsman. He was nervous but I allowed him to sit in my cockpit. I pointed out a large cardboard box sitting on the cabin floor below. There was an EPERB with lifejackets, flares, and so on in the box. All the poor man wanted was for me to sign the form. He would give me my certificate and leave. As he jumped in his dinghy I asked him if he was going to the large ketch anchored down river from me, if so he could return the box. The same box had done a tour of a number of boats.

We had fair weather leaving and Laurence managed well even with the huge ocean swells which was coming up from the south. The rat was altogether too adventurous and got lost for a few days up forward. After that he was restricted to a large bucket.

In Minerva Reef we met up with Uve and Inez and went diving. So we ate lobster and snapper and lay around in the warm sunshine. Leaving New Zealand it had been really cold. One absolutely huge lobster I gave to Charlie and Jeanette on *Quark*. They had also come from New Zealand where they now spend a lot of time. They had been forced out of their business in Virgin Gorda in the B.V.I. by the local mafia. They anchored behind me. I had to apologize for the lack of legs on the lobster. We had had them for lunch.

We tied back up in the fishing harbour in Nuku'alofa. Steven had lots of things already made for me. He now had transport, the house had grown a bit and my order this time would pay for some furniture.

Andrew, the brewmaster, had been in hospital. He had finally decided the girlfriend had gone too far running off with her boyfriends all the time. Together with her friend, the girlfriend had returned to the house and smashed all they could find including computers and a very expensive electronic organ.

When Andrew appeared, they attacked him and he ended up in hospital with broken ribs.

When the new girlfriend moved into the house, the whole family arrived. When they weren't allowed in the house they camped in the garden. It was a week before they all went home. The new girlfriend as Andrew said was good around the house but on a night out was pretty boring compared with the old hellcat.

After no more than a week in Nuku'alofa, Laurence fell in love with a young Fijian boy working on a building site. Never mind, at least she took the rat with her. I'd miss those big blue eyes. Actually they weren't blue and I wasn't thinking about eyes but I'd miss them.

I had a huge amount off stuff made by Steven. New Caledonia had to be a good market and then there was Australia. When all was made I promised to try and keep in touch but couldn't really see how we could do business from the other side of the world.

At the last minute I was persuaded to give a young American a lift to Fiji. I charged him a daily rate but like the American vegetarian he couldn't boil an egg and he couldn't sail the boat. I wasn't going to cook for him the whole way so the whole thing was disastrous.

It is not a long trip Tonga to Fiji so in Suva the crew left the boat and I continued around the coast to Musket Cove, a popular yachting anchorage. The yacht club gives free life membership and provides a good bar with cold Fiji bitter beer. Uve was there with Inez so we propped up the bar a few nights before I carried on to New Caledonia. The people, the culture and the kava drinking didn't interest me. It was a bit rude but I was keen to get to New Caledonia, see old friends and maybe do some business.

The stretch of water between Fiji and New Caledonia was rough. It blew and blew. Waves climbed over the boat, sometimes whole seas would wash over the cabin top but we sped along and in no time we surfed through Havannah Pass into the lagoon and then on to Noumea.

Noumea was changing, growing. Next to the market a small marina had been built and in the bay next door another half constructed had run out of money. It was now known as the squats and was full of yachts tied onto rickety docks and living there for free. I tied up in the new marina in order to clear in. The officials arrived promptly and I had a night there before going out to anchor.

Surfing through the pass I had caught two good sized tuna, one a yellow fin. The one soon disappeared amongst boats. The yellow fin I took over to a Danish friend of mine I had spent some time with in New Zealand and when I presented it he invited me for dinner.

I washed down the boat, filled the water tanks and had a shower using up gallons of water while I had the opportunity. Then I strolled along the dock to Peter's boat *Galatea* for dinner. We had Japanese sushi with all the trimmings even rice wine in little bowls.

Peter had been involved in hang gliding in the early days and helped its development. He had flown across the Alps and other mountain chains. I was really envious of the time he went to fly the Andes in South America. They had watched the huge bearded vultures and when they found thermals had joined them. I could picture myself silently drifting over spectacular scenery with the birds alongside. He had a hang gliding school on Lake Como and was one of these annoying Europeans that spoke all the languages. It was a really pleasant civilized evening after being thrown all over the place for more than a week.

In the morning I motored round to anchor off the squats. New Caledonia is one of those places where sailors swallow the anchor, here especially the French sailors. In the squats I found a friend I had passed through the canal with in 1983. He was busy eviscerating his boat which was rusting away and putting the interior into a new fibreglass hull he had tied alongside.

Another boat was *Stormbringer*, I had met Nano and his wife and daughter in the Marquesas. He had helped me get the engine working again and we had shared an interest in shell collecting. He was already well established in Noumea, the little girl in school, his wife with a stall in the market and Nano with a factory producing fibreglass boats of different sorts. The wife was keen on selling my jewellery in the market and I promised to help Nano lay up a large new mold he had in the factory.

So within days I became a worker in Nano's factory, organizing laying up a large speed boat mold. The language was a problem but I learned a lot of new words. Laurence had been from Marseille so had taught me some really rude expletives which seemed to work.

Some weeks later Laurence arrived in Noumea together with her Fijian boyfriend. In my head I now thought of her as the "Rat Lady". She had arrived on a large yacht from Fiji without mentioning the rat. It had been discovered a few days out to sea in the locker of one of the crew. The skipper had not been amused but the rat had been sneaked in and was now presumably getting good French cheese. The Fijian lad was having major problems with French immigration but at least they weren't throwing him out.

Laurence, as she had promised to do, took my jewellery around town. She was not too successful but she did try. Meanwhile an English guy I knew in the marina needed a boat watcher while he went home so I introduced the rat lady without mentioning the rat and they now had somewhere free to stay.

Each morning I had coffee on Nano's boat and then we commuted into work across town in the industrial area. Coming home in the evening we would normally stop for a few beers in a scruffy bar down town. I hadn't worked for wages or commuted like this for years. It was easy and the job interesting but the time flew by too quickly.

It was soon November and I was offered the use of a large luxurious yacht in the marina to celebrate my half century. I bought a load of beer and wine, the ladies prepared loads of food and I had a memorable party. I couldn't believe that I got to this amazing old age and that I was celebrating in French on the other side of the world.

I had some good neighbours in the bay including two yachts much the same as *Sea Loone*. *Black Sheep* was built in fibreglass and Antonio, the owner, an Italian was a real charmer. His gorgeous girlfriend was a friend of Rat Lady. *Danae* was a steel yacht and French, Jean Paul, a dedicated party person and his wife Cecile working as a midwife in the local hospital. Cecile had worked in Taeohae so we had a lot of mutual friends.

By the end of November I had to decide whether to stay for the cyclone season or head south and west for Sydney. I had had enough of commuting and in my dotage I had fallen in love with a gorgeous little bar maid in the bar we stopped at each evening. I had been rejected, got drunk and blotted my copybook. Time to leave.

4

I SAILED DIRECTLY for Sydney with a fair wind on the beam and as I got further south the current picked up and helped me along. A cruise ship passed on the way to Sydney and then days later passed again heading back to Noumea.

Sydney now provided a small dock near the submarine base for yachts to clear in which made everything really easy. I tied alongside and went up to the office to fill the forms. The girl from customs asked about New Zealand and their new law. With many boats now boycotting New Zealand she was going to have a lot more business.

While she filled in the forms for me I used her telephone to phone Tom Joel at his boatyard in Middle Harbour. I was surprised he was still in business in fact I was a bit surprised he was still alive. He remembered *Sea Loone* and had a mooring I could use. I couldn't believe how well things were going. By lunch time I had been cleared in and was motoring round to Middle Harbour to my mooring.

I found the mooring of the boatyard and on the mooring next door was a huge catamaran *Fallado* with a couple on board I knew from the islands. Helmut was German and his wife a local Australian. They were just off into town and offered to drop me at the supermarket. It was all a bit of a rush but worth doing so I rowed ashore and we climbed the steep steps to the road where they had their car parked. Five minutes later they dropped me outside a huge busy supermarket on Military Road.

The vast number of people rushing back and forwards, the noise, the hustle. I got quite panicky and then having collected some basic food I really needed to get back to the boat and calm down. I suddenly realized that I had no address for the boatyard and I knew that the steps which came up the cliff between two expensive old properties finished on a suburban street with a small gate and no sign. With difficulty I found a taxi, the driver, as ever, was a recent immigrant. We cruised the suburbs for some time before I finally found the gate. Those groceries were expensive in the end but I was happy to get back to the boat.

It didn't take me long to realize that my jewellery business was not going to be a great success in Sydney. I looked around to see if I could get some work. That was also not going to happen. Australia was still strict with illegal workers, but now they concentrated on the employers and fined them huge amounts of money if they were discovered employing foreigners. So now even the most casual worker had to prove he was a dinky di, true blue Australian.

A walk up the steps then up the steep road brought me to Military Road and right there was a huge pub. There were all sorts of bars, from the public bar where I spent my time, a huge pool bar with a dozen pool tables, a piano bar, a cocktail bar, a bar with poker machines set into the bar and a night club. Bored with nothing much to do I spent a fair bit of time in the public bar drinking beer with the locals and playing the odd game of pool. Helmut joined me occasionally and soon learned to play pool better than I did.

The group of locals I got friendly with were interesting. They were all in their twenties and mainly self-employed as electricians, plumbers and so on. On Saturday nights they sometimes went to a different pub and usually finished off in some sort of fracas, but normally they propped up the bar here in the pub and played the odd game of pool or darts. I had to ask them in the end what they did about girls.

The explanation was simple. To get where they wanted to get with an Australian girl would take at least a few nights out, a few meals and a lot of meaningless conversation. Then when they succeeded the girl was normally amateurish and if you continued would soon claim half your property. The problem was solved, normally on Thursday nights, with a trip to the local whorehouse full of gorgeous girls from Thailand and the Philippines who knew each and every way of how to please. They didn't need feedings, didn't need conversation and charged a set fee.

I was beginning to realize why my jewellery didn't sell. If a piece cost the equivalent of a few beers, an Australian would buy the beers. They were proud to have no couth. I made a last desperate trip across Sydney and down to the surf beaches to sell my stuff. I walked for miles along Bondi Beach and so on. I sold nothing at all.

It was evening when I got back to the pub. I sat at the bar glugging down a few beers and struck up a conversation with my neighbour. Surprisingly he was a professor of zoology at Sydney University so we could have talked zoology but he and his girlfriend were really interested in the jewellery. They finished off spending fifty dollars with me.

I had signed up for the darts competition and got dragged away to play. I won so I claimed another fifty dollars. My rotten day finished up with a jolly drunken conversation with the professor and still a few dollars stuffed in my pocket as I navigated down the hill.

I telephoned Ron Moylan, my shell collecting friend who lived not too far away, Ron still had his architecture office and was still very involved with shells. Over the years I had sent him quite a lot of shells which he had sold for me in Australia and with other collectors all over the world.

Ron came down to see me at Tom Joel's and arrived together with Brian Bailey, who I hadn't seen since the Solomon Island years ago. He still had his big steel yacht. His shell collecting had taken a strange turn. He had bought an abalone concession way down the south coast of South Island, New Zealand.

They could only be collected by free diving, the water was freezing and only occasionally calmed down enough to dive at all. Still fit as fiddle and hyperactive and also fifty years of age he was diving up tens of thousands of dollars worth each season. He deserved every dollar. I've jumped in the water a few times in the north of North Island and near froze the family jewels off.

As soon as April came, I prepared to head north. It was slow going against the current. I passed Brisbane and headed into Tin Can Bay crossing the bar at the south end of Frazer Island. The leading markers weren't obvious and when I called the coast guard on my new VHF radio they told me they had been scrapped. They gave me way points for the GPS instead. So if you didn't have a GPS you were stuffed.

I rowed ashore and found the small yacht club in Tin Can Bay. The two guys in the bought me a beer when I told them I had come up direct from Sydney. I got another beer for sailing from England. By the time they had the story of sailing around the world a few times I had more beer than I could handle and as more people arrived so did more beer.

Clark and Michelle who I had failed to meet in Golfito, Costa Rica, completed their circumnavigation of the Americas. The boat had been sold and they returned to Chile were they bought a ranch in the mountains behind Valdivia. Clark took people horseback riding, hunting and fishing, but sadly the two split up and Michelle was back in Australia staying with her parents.

The parents lived in Gympie not far from Tin Can Bay. So I telephoned and it was Michelle who answered the phone. We arranged to meet on the sandpit facing Frazer Island in a few days' time. I anchored close to spit and Michelle arrived in a four wheel drive. She had brought lunch so we rowed out to the boat and reminisced. We had last been together in Dar es Salaam at the time of Jean's death. A sad time but a lot of water had passed under the bridge since then or should I say a lot of water passed under our keels.

Anchored off a deserted sandpit was so reminiscent of being anchored in deserted Egmont Island, in the middle of the Indian Ocean where the four of us, Clark, Michelle, Jean and I had such a good time.

I saw Michelle again when she visited me in Maryborough which was where I went next, motoring up the Mary River. The local newspaper wrote another article about me. I thought maybe I could find a crew to help me sail *Sea Loone* up inside the Barrier Reef but no one came forward. I loaded up the boat with five shopping trolleys full of food and headed north.

My plans were to cross the Indian Ocean as soon as possible leaving from Darwin. If I wanted to spend some time in Madagascar or Tanzania before going down to South Africa for the cyclone season I was going to have to hurry. I had already covered more than five hundred miles from Sydney to Cape York where I could turn west was another thousands miles. From Cape York to Darwin another seven hundred miles before heading into the Indian Ocean and a trip of over three thousand miles to Madagascar. Add on another thousand miles to South Africa and there was nearly six thousand miles of sailing to be done before November.

Once inside the Barrier Reef I day sailed stopping at islands each night. In one anchorage I met a Danish guy with a yacht called *Sea Goon*. I had caught a tuna during the day so I was invited to pass the fish over to the Dane's charter guests and come for dinner. He had four pretty young backpackers on his boat each paying him twenty dollars a day. They cooked a fine meal while the captain and I sat drinking beer. *Sea Goon* wasn't much bigger than *Sea Loone* so it was all a bit crowded but great fun. The following day I caught another fish and *Sea Goon* arrived in the next island soon after me, so we repeated the evening.

When I arrived in Cairns, the last town of any sort before Cape York I put up little notices in the yacht club and the backpacker hotels looking for crew. With another person on board we could do a few trips over night instead of day hopping. So a crew would speed up our progress.

I found a young Italian, tall, good looking but with no experience of sailing. He went off and bought more pasta, olive oil and other Italian necessities and we headed for Lizard Island.

The first two days the crew was horribly sick but mercifully recovered and then started cooking and eating vast quantities of food. No problem, he was an excellent cook and was soon capable of sailing the boat.

We took a day off on Lizard Island and climbed the mountain to see Cooks Passage and then carried on north. We stopped in Mount Adolphus Island and went swimming. The crew soon got the hang of snorkelling so I pointed out a lobster hiding under a rock in quite shallow water. I gave him the pole spear and told him what to do. That evening he ate his own lobster and I'm sure enjoyed every little bit of it.

We shot round Cape York, flew past Thursday Island and sailed into Gove on the far side of the Gulf of Carpenteria. The local radio put out regular calls for anyone leaving town for Darwin to take my crew, so a few days later he was away, but first he cooked me a special meal from his part of Italy with pine nuts he had found in town and then cleaned and polished the galley. I think he had a good trip.

I sent my passport to Darwin. I needed the six month extension on the visa. While I waited I found some work. Conrad and Mary on *Genebelle* were in Gove. Conrad from Durban had been thrown out of Brazil. They had worked in St. Martin. Mary was Australian so they were staying a while. The little Jack Russell dog had been quarantined and Conrad was doing the paperwork with immigration. Conrad was doing boat work and had a speedboat which needed a new transom. The woodwork inside the fibreglass was rotten. It was a job he didn't want so I took over. With that boat repaired there were others, in fact there was quite a lot of fibreglass work available and with time passing rapidly it made me think of changing my plans.

When my passport was returned instead of extending my visa they had given me another new visa. It was a mistake but it was well stuck in my passport and it said on it that I could extend again for another six months.

I set off for Darwin with two of the bar maids from the yacht club. One of them, Kathryn, was a marine biologist, had a master's degree, and had worked on a few projects for the Australian government. We timed it well to catch the tide and pass through the Hole in the Wall in the Wessel Islands and on the lee side anchored for a day in calm water under a line of low cliffs. There were lots of rock wallabies jumping around on the cliffs. In the water it was difficult to see much further than six feet which made it difficult to spear lobster. They were too close by the time you saw them to bring the end of the spear around so you had to back up. We climbed the hills and walked the long beach to the west and found a deep pool in the mangroves full of snapper which were just the right size for the frying pan.

A week later we arrived in Darwin and anchored amongst a load of other yachts off the yacht club. Kathryn's mother was coming up to Darwin to meet her and then they were all off down to Perth. I got cleaned up and went to the immigration department. The girl agreed that the new visa in effect gave me another year but I would have to leave the country and come back after the first six months. A short trip to Timor and back would do that. Still the girl pointed out that it wouldn't work because customs would only give a cruising permit for one year, but she agreed that if I could get permission from customs then immigration wouldn't get in my way.

I walked across town to the customs building. The chief of customs seemed a friendly person. I explained that I wanted to return to Gove and experience a wet season in Arnemland. The problem I was told was that once the cruising permit ended then the boat had to remain in one port and would be under supervision of the customs officer in that port. If the customs officer didn't want this responsibility then I could not stay.

Fair enough, we telephoned Gove. I had drunk a few beers with the officer there in the yacht club. I explained who was speaking and what I wanted to do. He replied by assuring me there would be a few cold beers waiting for me when I returned. I contacted Conrad in Gove and told him I was on my way back and would do all the fibreglass jobs once I got back.

I had some 500 miles to beat back to Gove against the winds and the current. The coast was poorly charted and full, I knew, of banks, reefs and rip tides. The water was murky brown. The tides were big, maybe seven metres, so I could use them to get back east. I hugged the coast, ducking in here and there making pretty good progress. It was often difficult to differentiate between areas of breaking reef and churning rip tides. The coast, mile after mile of it, was completely deserted. Once back off the Wessel Islands, I motored through the Hole in the Wall and on to Gove. Sure enough, a cold beer was waiting for me as well as a couple more speedboats with rotten transoms!

I took on a sort of silent partner, a New Zealand guy with a welding business. He provided a place for me to work and ordered the materials on the barge from Darwin. It went well. I had a large sports fishing catamaran which had major structural problems. It belonged to the owners of the big pub in town so there was plenty of money available. This was just as well because the more I got into it, the more problems I found.

When the jobs finally petered out, I bought a small cabin cruiser which needed serious repairs. I rebuilt it and got the huge outboard engine working. I expected to make a good profit but nobody wanted it. It would have been too expensive to send to Darwin where I knew I could get a good price for it. In the end I didn't make a loss but the whole project had been a bit of a waste of time. Well, you can't win them all.

With the cyclone season approaching, I welded up a huge anchor using Ken, the welder's, equipment and a lorry chassis I had found in the town dump. I also scrounged up some massive chain. I dumped all this in the water next to the boat and felt a bit more secure. In fact the only problem we had the whole season was a tropical storm that came through on Christmas Day. Nobody could get ashore to the yacht club where we had a big party planned. My chicken was in the deep freeze ashore so I sat on the boat with a bottle of red wine while the wind shrieked and howled and the rain poured down.

It was amazing to see the changes as soon as the rains arrived. The land turned green, there were streams and pools and even a few flowers. I always wondered whether, if the sheep, cattle, and kangaroos didn't graze and the aboriginals stopped burning off the vegetation in the dry season, perhaps a full rain forest would appear. The change was dramatic.

In the New Year 1997, I took a small plane to Darwin and the following day through to Timor where I had to stay for three days before a plane flew back. I could then get another visa extension.

In Darwin, I stayed on a friend's boat for the night and drank a few beers in a small yacht club up the Creek. There I met three baramundee fishermen who were catching the same plane to Timor, going on the annual off-season holidays.

Baramundee fishing is done from small aluminum dinghies, tinnys, in among the mangrove swamps and river estuaries. The fisherman live on a mother ship anchored off. The fish are big and valuable so in a good season the fishermen make lots of money. But after months in the middle of nowhere they need a holiday.

These guys were new Australians, Eastern Europeans. They picked me up in the morning and went to a pub near the airport where we started drinking. We continued drinking on the plane for the short trip to Timor and when we arrived we were waved through customs and immigration. They had been here before.

They were staying out of town and I had to join them. A driver and car were waiting for us. So within minutes of landing we were motoring up the road to some sort of hotel. It wasn't really a hotel. It was a swimming pool with rooms all around and a bar, and then there were girls!

I spent three nights drinking, carousing and floating around in the pool. The car then brought me back to the airport and reality. In no time, I was back in Gove in the middle of nowhere.

Mary, Conrad's partner, was now running the yacht club bar and she had an aboriginal friend who took us into the bush and mangrove swamps. We spent a fair bit of time catching mud crabs and became pretty good at it. We would wade up to our waists in mud and water in the mangroves. Looking back, I can't believe we weren't gobbled up by the crocodiles.

I had been offered a job with the local crocodile farm which I would have taken if I wasn't already involved in the fibreglass business. The job involved collecting eggs. They used a helicopter to find the nests in the mangroves. Two people were then dropped as close as possible. One collected the eggs. This involved carefully putting them in a prepared box without turning them over. The other used a hefty stick to protect the collector from the mother who usually hung around the nest. Whacking the crocodile on the nose apparently put the mother off attacking.

In the farm itself they had a few captive crocodiles. One was called Stumpy. He had one leg missing in front and he had his own enclosure with a pool of water. I had gone along at feeding time. I saw Stumpy explode out of the water, charge across the enclosure and lunge up the corrugated iron wall to take the lump of horse meat hanging fifteen feet up in the air. So I wasn't too sure about the stick on the nose being much of a deterrent.

At the end of the collecting season when I was preparing to leave, the egg collectors had gone further afield than normal and found a big nest. The huge female appeared and when the guard banged her on the nose, the stick broke. He was left with a 6-inch stump. I'm glad I didn't take that job.

The ships coming in to pick up the bauxite and alumina often used the local supermarket to stock up on a few things on board. So the owner of the shop had a fair amount of US dollars. He agreed to exchange my Australian dollars at the median rate which at the time was around US eighty cents for one Aussy dollar. I finished off with US$10,000 which I was very happy with.

I wanted to leave as early as possible in the season so this time I was not going to stop in Darwin. I ordered a lot of goodies from Darwin to be delivered on the barge. Then I dried the boat out on the grid using the big tides to clean and paint on the new anti-fouling. Mary and I went on our last crab hunt with the aboriginal girl and we fed half the yacht club with our haul of crabs at my going away party.

Finally I cleared out and sailed back through the Hole in the Wall, anchoring just on the other side for a day before the long jump to Chagos, 3,900 miles away. In the morning, I went ashore with a fishing line to walk across the long sand beach to the pool in the mangroves to catch some snapper for tea.

Between Gove and Darwin there is nobody so I was quite naked apart from flip-flops. The tide was going out and as I walked along the beach, I came across some footprints in the sand. They headed inland and the tide had only just dropped a little from where they started. So they were recent. It had to be a huge crocodile. The tracks were heading for a low cliff which seemed rather strange.

I followed the tracks and as I got close to the cliff I could see that there was a break in the rock like a big sloping fault. I climbed the last steep sandbank at the high tide mark and looked down on a small stream percolating through the break and a deep pool with the cliff overhanging it.

A picture of Stumpy rocketing out of his pool flashed through my mind. I was standing there bollock naked. I turned and ran. I got my snapper for supper and the next day set off due west.

The water was murky brown for days in the Arafura Sea but then gradually cleared to become that deep blue crystal clear water of the open ocean. I headed for Christmas Island but within a day's sail, I was buzzed by one of those annoying Australian patrol planes. With two sails poled out I edged in towards the anchorage. There was a ship loading phosphate which made a cloud of white dust across the bay.

I envisioned a cold beer but then also the pile of paperwork I would need to complete just to stop for a day. I gave the self-steering a couple of clicks to clear the far point and carried on. I still had 2,000 miles to go to Chagos.

The trade winds picked up and two weeks later with the wind slightly on the beam angling down big seas, the tiller broke off. The two cheeks which fit over the square at the head of the rudder shaft had torn off. Made in heavy stainless steel, I had thought the whole tiller arrangement unbreakable. I had no spare and there was no way I could make a temporary repair to take the strain especially in these big seas. The boat was still sailing more or less the right way even though the rudder was sweeping left and right.

So with a few careful adjustments to the sails, I found I could steer. The course wasn't exactly straight but good enough. I was going to have to stop in Diego Garcia, the American naval base, to get the tiller repaired. I hoped they weren't going to turn me away.

I still had 500 miles to go so I spent the time making a temporary tiller which I could use in the lee of the islands or in the lagoon out of the huge swells. We did really well and when I got close enough called up the naval base on the VHF radio. I was directed to a point outside the entrance to the lagoon and was met by huge military launch manned by Americans. I was surprised to see that the two guys who jumped on board to inspect the damage were British Marines. They had to decide if I really had a problem. Of course there obviously was a problem so I fitted on the temporary tiller and we motored into the lagoon.

There were over two thousand Americans on the base manning the huge airfield and looking after some huge military ships on anchor in the lagoon. There was a small force of British Marines and a handful of British policemen, very strange. The Marines had their own small dock where I tied up. The tiller was whisked off to get welded.

One Marine was to be my escort everywhere and first we had to go and see the British commander. I think he was a rear admiral. He had a pointy beard and lots of stripes on his uniform.

I had arrived in the early morning and he now told me that the repair would be done by lunchtime so I would then have to leave. I pointed out to him that I had just done nearly 4,000 miles of sailing alone on the ocean for more than fifty days. I needed a night's sleep. I'm sure he didn't have a clue about what that trip involved especially the last 500 miles with no steering. He grudgingly allowed that I could stay the night but would have to be out first thing in the morning.

My escort was delighted. He organized for all my laundry to be taken away, diesel arrived, oil and a huge box of special army rations. They wanted to give me more but I couldn't think and I was losing my voice from lack of use over the last few weeks. We had hamburgers for lunch and then went back to the marine's accommodation to drink a few beers. I wasn't allowed to do any tour of the base but it was Friday and Friday night, I was told, was a good party night.

There was a surprisingly large number of American girls on the island, all single as no married couples were based there. We started in a typical dark American bar. It was huge with only a couple of customers. Apparently the American commander was a born-again Christian and had banned smoking in the bar. He probably would've liked to have also banned drinking. The drinkers were all in the alleyway behind the bar puffing away on their cigarettes.

My escort apologized for the place but assured me that in an hour or so they open their own bar which would be much better. There were fifty Marines on the island, rotated at intervals. Over the years they had built a bar on the beach which became a nightclub with a dance floor. There was also a boutique selling T-shirts, caps and so on, all with the badge of the British Indian Ocean Territories or whatever they now called it. These marines were good businessmen.

It was a popular place to go and of course you could smoke. The only problem for the Americans was learning the bar etiquette. They could not say to the marine serving behind the bar "gimme me a beer". They had to say "please" and then "thank you", or they got no beer and also maybe thrown out.

The Marines shouted all my beers and I had a great evening staggering back to the boat in the early hours.

At seven in the morning the Marines were back. The tiller was back in place and I had to leave. They jumped off the boat as I exited the lagoon and waved me away. I was going back to Egmont Island. It was an overnight trip so in the morning of the following day, I motored over the shallow pass, then through the reef, to anchor where I had last anchored ten years before.

I was surprised to find that there was another boat there. It was called "Jonathan" with a Frenchman and his girlfriend, an Italian Kenyan. They had spent some time in Salomon Island in the north where there were lots of yachts. The island it seemed had been turned into a sort of holiday resort by the yachties. Thank God they hadn't found Egmont.

In fact as I wandered around the island, I saw no changes at all. Even the birds were roosting and nesting in the same places and the rock out on the windward reef, still had loads of lobsters hiding under it.

I invited the neighbours to a lobster dinner. They hadn't seen, let alone caught, a lobster their whole time in Chagos. So they were surprised when they got one each for dinner from the cage under my boat. In fact, there was a week's supply in the cage.

They were on their way to Thailand in a week or so. I gave them a few quick lessons in lobster catching, walking the outside reef at night, enticing coconut crabs out of the holes, hooking octopus and so on. They had found a big stone oven among the ruins of the village so we stoked it with wood until it was red-hot. It made really good bread. Then we built two smokers on the beach and I set out the gill net to catch mullet. They left with bread, biscuits and smoked fish for the long trip north and east across the equator.

I stayed on for a few more weeks doing my Robinson Crusoe thing before setting off for Madagascar. The self-steering paddle broke off on the way so again I had to balance the sails to go the right way. At least this time I still had the rudder.

There are some huge shallow banks to pass over on the way and I caught tuna and dorado whenever I needed. I hadn't tried again to keep lobsters alive in the cockpit and the coconut crabs were too rich for me.

The northern point of Madagascar is really windy. Diego Suarez is a huge natural harbour with a fairly narrow entrance just south of Cape d'Ambre, the northern tip. I surfed through the entrance and anchored off Antsiranana, which is quite a large port. There were no yachts; just one small sports fishing boat and some huge rusty sunken ships scattered around which had been sunk by the British during World War II.

I had a visa I had acquired in Sydney so cleared in with no problems. When I changed some money in the bank, I walked out with hundreds of thousands of Malagasy francs; so felt really rich.

There was a watchman on the sports fishing boat. He found me a guard for the evening and I set off into town to find a cold beer and maybe some company. Most of the buildings were in really poor repair, in fact some could be called derelict ruins but still had people living in them. There were plenty of bars to choose so I found one which looked presentable for my first beer

The "Three Horses" beer came in a large bottle. It was wonderfully cold and slipped down with no effort at all. The only other customers were two Frenchmen who were obviously discussing business but then five gorgeous girls came in together with another Frenchman and sat at one of the tables.

One of the girls came over to the bar to order drinks. She was wearing a very short red T-shirt and when she leaned over the bar, the lower half of two very large breasts were exposed. Any moment I expected two nipples to pop out. I was mesmerized. The girl turned to me and smiled, then took her drinks back to the table.

Maybe I was a little biased, having spent months in the Australian bush, on a desert island, and bobbing around alone on the ocean, but it did seem a bit unfair that this one man should be accompanied by five beautiful girls. I decided to finish my beer and find another bar and maybe some unattached beauties.

As I walked past the table to leave, the girl with the T-shirt jumped up and asked where I was going. She said she wanted to buy me a beer. I suppose that was the moment when I fell in love with Madagascar.

It took a few moments to find my voice and naturally accepted the offer of another beer. The Frenchman turned out to be Belgian and was married to one of the girls. They were on holiday from Belgium and the other girls were all friends of his wife.

Before I left to return to the boat, I had invited them for drinks on the boat the following evening. Naturally I didn't go home alone. The red T-shirt and the wearer, Pamela, came with me. In the morning, the boobs that had played peekaboo all evening were now made to counter rotate by subtle shoulder movements and then were even more amazing put in reverse. Naturally the T-shirt had been discarded for the demonstration.

After a late breakfast, Pamela went off to town with my shopping list , beer, red wine, rum, Coca Cola and hopefully some ice. Late afternoon she returned with everything including even some change. Then at sunset the Belgian arrived with his wife and a girlfriend. I collected them with the dinghy from the broken down the wharf.

He had a shoe shop in Belgium and knew nothing about boats or sailing so was intrigued by the lifestyle on *Sea Loone*. As we talked, the guard from the sports fishing boat ferried out three more girls to join the party.

In the end there were eleven girls, the Belgian and myself. But unfortunately the wife was feeling a little seasick. It was difficult to imagine in a flat calm harbour but they had to leave. That left me with ten girls to entertain all dressed in the most provocative gear with all sorts of bits hanging out everywhere.

I brought out some of my old jewellery, a few sand dollars and the polished stones from Cape Town. That kept them happy for a while and there was plenty of booze. Then one of the girls wearing an amazing clingy sort of dress with a large brass ring on a zip all the way down the front asked if I had a video camera. She said they wanted to do some exotic dancing for me. I didn't have the camera but it didn't put them off. The music blared and a lot got bared, ha! ha!

Much later I ferried dinghy loads of exotica back to the wharf as they sang "matelo! matelo!" to the sound of the oars. I drifted into sleep cushioned by Pamela.

The following day one of the girls arrived on the wharf with a small four-wheel-drive and took us back to her apartment in town. Her patron, a Parisian, came once or twice a year but provided everything in between. Another girl had a small boutique and again was provided for by an absent Frenchman.

So it was their dream to find a foreign sponsor. It meant that the local young men were of no interest and that "butterflies", the men that go from girl to girl are ostracized. But it did not mean that the girls had to be faithful to the sponsor. In fact, as soon as the Le Patron was back on the plane, the girl was out dancing in the disco. How do you say it... "what's sauce for the goose is sauce for the gander" and "when the cat's away the mice will play".

I spent another week in Diego Suarez, sometimes dancing in the night club till early morning. But the security for the boat was a worry and in fact, one of my guards stole all my cockpit cushions. There were much worse stories than that. So I decided to move on. I was tempted to take the lovely Pamela with me but the sea outside was really rough before turning round the North Cape. We had a last meal ashore and a last demonstration of whirling boobs.

The tide rips in and out of the entrance to Diego and with the huge ocean swells and ebbing tide, there are massive overfalls which can create problems for large ships, let alone for small yachts. I anchored close behind the pass and early next morning beat out into the channel with the beginning of the ebb. I just cleared the northern reef in one tack before loosening the sheets and fleeing up the coast the few miles to Cape d, Ambre.

Once around the corner in calm water though still with lots of current and wind, the boat gobbled up the miles. Ten miles and another turn sharp to port brought us inside the reefs and heading southwest. The sun was dropping and the wind still howling when I came up in the lee of Nosy Hara, a strange volcanic lump with huge vertical cliffs.

Just as it got dark, I threw the anchor in under the cliffs and just off the reef. It had been a long exhilarating day.

I slept like a log and was woken by a strange crying noise like a small baby having a tantrum. The sun was just peeking over the virtual cliffs in front of me, the boat was still in the shade. Behind me the sea was already bathed in bright sunlight bringing out every shade of blue flecked by the wind which was still blowing strongly. More rocky islands were scattered around together with many of the normal types of sandy reef islands covered in bushes and fringed with golden beaches.

The crying sound was coming from a huge house-sized boulder underneath the cliff. Amongst an untidy pile of twigs on top of the boulder stood an almost fully-fledged fish eagle! The bird obviously wanted feeding. As I was making my coffee, one of the parent birds arrive clutching a good-sized fish and the baby stopped whinging.

The eagles were untroubled by my presence the whole time I was there. It was a delight to watch them soaring back and forwards along the cliff face sometimes diving with wings almost completely closed at a tremendous speed and then opening up and spreading their flight feathers to rise up effortlessly back into the heavens.

A cliff sided valley cutting into the island was filled with trees and tangled vegetation and had a dried-up stream emptying onto the beach. As I tried to penetrate the bush, two small rufous coloured birds hovered in front of me. They had enormous long tails and fluttered around so close you could almost reach out and touch them. They were paradise flycatchers, well named I thought.

I found an octopus while wading around the reef at low tide and hooked him out for dinner. There were signs the turtles had been hauling out on the beach to lay their eggs but I left the eggs in peace.

One of the caves in the cliff had been used by local fishermen, but I saw nobody. I tried to find a way up the cliffs but I was no rock climber. Way back up the valley I found a stream flowing. It was just a small trickle, but I got attacked by mosquitoes for my pains. As always, there are some drawbacks to a paradise.

After four days I carried on south, carefully navigating around the reefs and then around Cape San Sebastian and on to Nosy Be. From the cape south, the wind dropped dramatically. As I came around the south coast of Nosy Be to find Hellsville, the main town, it was glassy calm so I had to start the engine in order to motor in the last few miles.

Nosy Be is the center for what little tourism there is in Madagascar and Hellsville is a busy small port. There is a slipway and two wharfs at right angles that provide reasonably deep water for small coasters. The large ships anchor off and use barges to ferry in cargo and containers. With small boats bringing people, market goods, and building materials from the mainland, the wharf and slipway are a seething mass of people and goods.

Further into the harbour, the tide leaves the boats aground in the mud. Here the outrigger canoes and sailing dhows come and go with the tide. In the middle of the harbour, the yachts anchor and row ashore but finding a secure place to leave the dinghy was a major problem.

When I anchored, I saw four or five yachts anchored in the harbour, including a huge Wharram catamaran. As I bagged the head sails and put on the mainsail cover, the skipper of the catamaran rowed over. It was Plastic, the young lad who had helped me paint *Sea Loone* in Richards Bay and sailed with me to Durban in 1988. In the ten years or so he had grown into a big man. He now had all his seaman's papers and had been in Kenya and the Seychelles chartering the catamaran, or at least trying to. He had recognized *Sea Loone* immediately.

It was good to speak English again and get the lowdown on what was going on in Nosy Be. I knew that outboard engines were worth their weight in gold and were stolen day or night at every opportunity. So everybody rowed their dinghies. Apart from stealing outboards, everything was calm. But tying up the dinghy was fraught with difficulties. Every metre of the wharf was in use and boats were coming and going continuously.

It took some time but eventually I got the dinghy problem sorted. There were half a dozen local boys all around ten years of age hanging around the wharf. They would look after your dinghy for a price. In the daytime I agreed to pay them with sweets and in the evening maybe something more. I became known as "Monsieur Bon Bon" and we got on pretty well. They had to move the dinghy around from time to time and I let them operate a bit of a taxi service as long as I wasn't inconvenienced.

Hellsville was an old French colonial town. Despite the buildings being in ruins and services being almost non-existent, the town was still full of life. The market was fantastic. There were a few restaurants, cafés and lots of bars; and late at night two or three nightclubs opened up and throbbed through until the early hours.

A night out in Hellsville, what a name for town, would be to have a few beers in the local taxi bar, wander up into town and have a few more in the Port a Rouge, then maybe make it to one of the nightclubs. It would take most of the next day to recover but then one hair of the dog and you were away again.

This was a recipe for disaster so I determined to spend just the weekends in town and then go sailing the rest of the week. So I sailed over to Nosi Komba just a few hours away, climbed the mountain and fed the lemurs with bananas.

I then went north again and spent time in Nosi Mitsio, a lovely island with a great anchorage and superb fishing. I could literally trawl around with the dinghy and come back with a pan size fish in ten minutes maximum.

I went out to Russian Bay and dived up octopus and waded knee-deep in mud in the mangroves for mud crabs, big ones. Then I would come back to town and party.

I met Antonio, my Italian friend on *Black Sheep*. We had last been together in New Caledonia and through his girlfriend there had news of the "Rat Lady". She had gone back to New Zealand without the rat or the Fijian boyfriend but was about to have his child. From rat to "rug rat", ha! ha!

Antonio had an Italian friend Stefano living in Nosy Komba. Stefano lived in an old colonial house on the beach next to a small village. He had taken it upon himself to improve the village's standard of living and had started by first putting in a good water supply from a spring up on the mountain.

He then persuaded doctors and dentists from Reunion to visit the village, bring medicines and provide the expertise. With the help of the village he had built two cottages for the visitors to stay in and was building more. A school was also in the planning stages. He was treated in the village a bit like a god. I wondered how it was all going to end.

Time passed rapidly. I only had a three-month visa, so by early September I would have to leave. Hellsville had treated me well. I even woke up one morning with a girl in my bed. She was pretty but extremely avaricious. But of course the rules said you cannot be a butterfly so whenever I went out at night you could be sure she would arrive.

It was good enough but the last night, having done all my paperwork to leave in the morning, I had told the young lady that I was going out on my own and had said all my goodbyes. I drank beer in the Port a Rouge before deciding to have a last beer in the night club down in the harbour.

Standing up on the balcony looking down at the dancers, I suddenly noticed that there was a stunningly beautiful girl standing next to me. I turned to say hello and immediately a glass of beer was poured over my head and a fist landed in my face, breaking my glasses. Unknown to me, the girlfriend had been lurking behind me.

Well I had been warned. I wiped the beer out of my eyes picked up the remains of my glasses and turned again to the pretty girl. I pointed out that this was not a good time to introduce myself but I suggested that if she was on the wharf at nine o'clock in the morning maybe we could go for a sail.

I left, returned to the boat and slept well. But in the morning I thought maybe I ought to look on the wharf. After all, it had been my suggestion. Sure enough, there she was, dressed to kill it and clutching a small sack of goodies. She really was gorgeous.

I hove the anchor up and we sailed gently out of the harbor on the morning breeze, the self-steering keeping us in the right direction. Cathy, that was her name, lay on the cabin top in a swimsuit which was more netting than material, her long braids spread out around her. Irresistible! We were oblivious to the cruise ship we were passing and maybe got some applause.

We had two days together in Russian Bay seeing no one. The sack Cathy had brought contained more diaphanous pieces of clothing which were paraded around the deck. Then I had to take her home. I dropped her off on the wharf and turned out to sea. Next stop, Mayotte in the Comoro Islands.

Mayotte is French, having separated from the other islands. It was quite different to Grand Comore where I had been ten years before. It had a surrounding reef and good anchorages inside the lagoon. Typical of most French territories, the place was expensive. So with no reason to stay, I carried on to Tanzania. However, before I left, I met a Frenchman I knew in Nosy Be. He had come to get a new pair of glasses. He didn't have to tell me how the last were broken. Butterfly!

Mtwara is the most southerly port in Tanzania close to Cabo Delgado and the border with Mozambique. There is a lot of current in the dog-leg channel into the huge inner harbour and it's not easy to anchor off the commercial wharf to clear customs and immigration. I paid the fifty dollars American to immigration, and customs waved me away. Then I carried on into the harbour.

I finally found a spot to anchor in a mangrove creek a mile or so on past the wharfs.

There was a landing place used by the little ferryboat which cross the creek. From there I could walk into town. Clark and Michelle had been in Mtwara when we were last in Dar es Salaam. They had met the local priest, Father Alfonse, a German, and had bought some teak planks and some Makonda carvings similar to those I had found in Dar and sold in the Caribbean. So I made some inquiries.

The word got around and a Land Rover came to pick me up to take me to the priest. Apart from running the church, the priest also ran the school, the hospital, the petrol station, timber yard and who knows what else. Each month he sent a container of Makonda carvings to Europe. We met in a dark office surrounded by filing cabinets and mounds of paperwork.

First I asked if I could buy some teak to do some repairs on the boat. He told me they had no teak in Mtwara. Not a good start. I said I was interested in buying some carvings but was told me that because the Europe container was nowhere near being full, no carvings were available. This was the end of the interview and the Land Rover took me back to the creek or at least, as close as it could get.

People had shown a lot of interest in the Makonda carvings I had bought in Dar es Salem ten years before and I was hoping to do some good business in Mtwara. But obviously the priest wasn't going to help. In fact probably quite the opposite. The few pieces I saw for sale in town were pretty awful, things didn't look good.

Help arrived the next morning on a bicycle. His name was Majida Sadalla and he described himself as a ship's agent. He was from the Makonda tribe and spoke little or no English; but with my Swahili phrase book and lots of hand waving and drawings on scraps of paper, we managed to communicate. Majeda was the coach of the local football team, very small and very fit which was very useful.

We made our first trip with me riding on the back of a borrowed bicycle. There were footpaths and bike paths everywhere. As we passed small settlements I gave the royal wave to two old ladies sitting in their porches.

At one stage we could hear drums beating. In Swahili "Habari" is a greeting. It also means "news". So I tapped Majida on the shoulder and pointed saying "Habari". He laughed and we wobbled a bit. Further on, we came to a big village of native huts with a large square of beaten earth in the middle. As we peddled across, I saw a huge cauldron being heated on the fire by a group of women. I tapped Majida on the shoulder again and asked him if it was for me. Again he understood and we wobbled some more and nearly fell off.

We had agreed that as my agent Majida would get 10% of any money I spent on carvings or on any other stuff that I liked, or that he found. That first trip we didn't come up with very much but my man was going to beat the drums and we would do some more field trips.

He understood that I didn't want the tourist rubbish or the really poorly finished carvings. Ebony is really hard to smooth and there was no sandpaper available. They use broken pieces of glass but it was more time-consuming than the original carving. On the boat I still had a few well finished pieces from Dar es Salaam so could point out the differences.

Once the news was out, Majida came to the boat early each morning and people arrived on the beach with carvings. Majida would go through them and then bring them out to the boat where we would drink coffee and choose what we wanted. Sometimes the price was too high but in most cases the pricing was straightforward. I bought statues, skinny bent statues called skeletons, families which were tiers of people climbing on top of each other, all three dimensional from one small log of ebony, busts of ladies with complicated hairstyles, a few elephants and other odd pieces.

One day we crossed the creek with the dinghy and walked through the bush. The carvers usually were found in the shade of a large mango tree. They were spread out over a wide area of scrubby land and salt flats. One old guy brought out three superb pieces including a bust of an old man and a squatting pipe smoker which now lives in my sister's lounge in England.

Over the weeks I built up quite a nice collection and spent enough money to keep my agent happy. Before I left, we went to Majida's house where he said he had a lot of "makome" which he was sure I would want to buy. I had no idea what it was. His house was larger than most and had a tin roof. There were a few wives around, at least I think they were wives. The large room was quite bare inside with no chairs or furniture. We sat on the floor and Majida brought out sacks of "makome".

They were shells. Some were really nice; large tiger cowries and red casks, some big harp shells and a couple of tritons. I bought all the good ones.

I promised that I would be back next year and buy more carvings if the quality was good. I then caught the ebbing tide and got swept out to sea. I had cleared for Richards Bay South Africa more than 1,000 miles south.

A day's sail from Mtwara brought me to Cabo Delgado. Here the west-flowing current sweeping across the Indian Ocean divides to go both north and south. Off South Africa, this becomes the Agulhas Current; but inside the Mozambique Channel, the current plays games. Watching the GPS I could see where the boat was heading but occasionally steering south or south west, we would actually be going more than 45° to port or starboard. Initially I stayed off the Mozambique coast but then headed into towards Maputo to hug the coast for the last 200 miles before Richards Bay.

Here the Agulhas current is strong pushing south and exceptionally strong on the edge of the continental shelf. At regular intervals south westerly fronts coming up the coast which can produce storm-force winds. Against the current this can cause the formation of the famous short breaking sometimes forty foot seas which can overwhelm ships and yachts alike. I already knew of a ship that had serious cracks in the hull last time I was arriving and I had some photos of bridge-wings torn off and bows stove in.

I kept in close to shore near a long line of high sand dunes but the wind turned from east to north east which indicated a front arriving. As the wind increased I sped along at over seven knots surfing down the waves.

There were whales all around me and I was hoping that they kept out of my way as they played about, occasionally breaching and waving their flukes in the air. Eventually I shot into the channel between the sand dunes and found myself in the calm waters of Richards Bay.

I was instructed to follow the buoyed channel and turn in to the small boat harbour where I would be met by the officials. I had been here before, last time escorted by a gunboat. Now the boat harbour was no longer inside the security area and was open to the public. There was a small marina, office blocks, a bar, a restaurant, and a few shops.

I tied up on a concrete wharf opposite a floating restaurant bar and between two other yachts. Totally enclosed in this harbour within a harbour, it was flat calm. I staggered about the bit for the first few hours getting my land legs back and then collapsed in my bunk to sleep the night away. I was fast asleep when the front I had been racing arrived with howling wind and rain.

My pile driving barge

The dinghy dock I built

Happy hour, Marina Cays

Christmas, Caribbean

Jamie & family, Nagana Village

Tracey feeling very tall

We meet up with Alvah & Diana, Panama

Barbara & Whitey at Jungle Club, Golfito

In the jungle,
Costa Rica

At anchor Taeohae, Nuku Hiva

Diving for shells with Justin

Tracey & her aerobic class, Taeohae

The "rat lady"

Mud crabbing in Arnemland
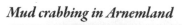

Salt water crocodiles, Gove

Outrigger canoe, Madagascar

Maria on the bow...

and from the stern

Fiona tenderising octopus

Fiona & Kathryn (Fiona's birthday) Madagascar

Becalmed off Capetown

A beach & a party, Brazil

5

RICHARDS BAY WAS by now a major stopping place for yachts sailing around the world or "on the milk run" as we now called it. There were a number of yachts in the small boat harbour, more in the marina next door, and more again around in the Zululand Yacht Club which had built the floating pontoons for yachts to tie up to.

I had kept in touch with Tony Soars whose motor launch I had helped take down the coast to East London years ago. He had sold his furniture shop and was now selling secondhand cars. He promised to come down and take me to the new shopping mall. The cupboards were bare. Tony was always a big man standing well over 6 feet. He was now huge.

He cruised up alongside the boat in a massive old open-topped American limousine. It had huge fins at the back and chrome everywhere. His giant frame filled the driving seat.

Climbing in beside him, I was given the Grand Tour including the new improved yacht club and the mall, before stopping in at Tony's house for a substantial lunch. Speaking English, eating good food and drinking cold beer felt good. I'd had nothing like it for eight months, apart from one day in Diego Garcia with the marines.

I settled into a quiet, easy life sorting the boat out, socializing with my neighbours and drinking a few beers in the Slipway Bar, a fancy stainless steel and glass affair perched overlooking the marina. The barmaid, Nylene, was as pretty as a picture and I soon had her selling my Polynesian jewelry. I also sold some of the Makonda carvings for a reasonable profit to a local tourist shop. The rest I boxed up and got sent down to Glenn on *Blue Drifter* who was now home in Cape Town. He promised to store everything until I came south. I was now set on returning to Madagascar and then going back to Mtwara.

I had been in the harbour a week or more before somebody pointed out there was another Liverpool yacht was tied up not far from me. It was Bernie MacDonald, the diver who had come over to Birkenhead docks to help me put my rudder back after it had corroded just months after first launching. I had never seen his boat but knew that he completed it a year or so after I left Liverpool.

He had then sailed around the world and returned to Liverpool to a hero's welcome. His boat was put on display in the new Maritime Museum. He was now on his second go-round, with his wife and daughter. The boat which he had built in steel from a scrapped gasometer was now very rusty and run down and they were running out of money.

Plastic's father was building a second huge Wharran catamaran the same as the one I had seen in Nosi Be. It was all financed by a Dutchman who owned, among other things, a large hotel on the Kenyan coast. The boat was being built close by in a huge shed and I managed to get Bernie, who was an electrician by trade, the job of putting in the electrical system..

Bernie was a great talker and his teenage daughter talked continuously. Amazingly enough, although they had been on the boat for more than fifteen years and had been almost twice around the world, they had only ever stopped in a very few places. The daughter had not learned one word in a foreign language. It seemed a long way to go nowhere.

As they had done the previous time, they left Richards Bay and sailed directly home, no Cape Town, no St. Helena, no Brazil. Worse, the daughter didn't return a book I lent her which, as you can see, annoyed me.

Together with a few other yachties, we hired a car and took a trip up to one of the game parks, Hluhluwe. Although it does not cover a large area, it is amazingly good with a huge variety of animals, antelope, zebra, buffalo and so on; plus lots of birds big and small. I mentioned this trip to my sister and she was quite keen to come out and visit. Friends of hers had lived in Durban and had also talked about the place. So I was going to get family visitors, the first since my mother's abortive trip to Florida in 1980.

Tony had been to see me a number of times and I had had a huge boozy Christmas Day with him and the family. He now found a place for Di and Paul to stay and promised to organize a special trip to the game park. They hired a car in Durban where they had arrived by plane and spent nearly two weeks around the Richards Bay area.

Every evening we ate huge restaurant meals apparently at a fraction of the price in Britain. My stomach had difficulty handling the huge amount of meat. But the highlight of the whole visit was our first trip to the game park. Tony picked us up early in the morning with his huge American four-wheel-drive and we headed north. The sun was still only just rising as we passed through the gates of the park and Tony drove up into the hills to stop at a picnic site looking down into a steep gorge with a river flowing through.

Since the first few minutes, Di had been shouting "Look, Look!" at the zebras, springbok and so on. Now Tony opened the back of the truck and brought out a full Safari breakfast. Spread out on the table was a huge feast of cold meats and so on all to be washed down by the mandatory champagne and orange juice. We were surrounded as we ate, by views of animals, birds, and even a crocodile cruising in the river. It was a magic moment in time!

From Richards Bay it was possible to catch a very early bus back to Durban, spend the day in town and get back in the late afternoon. I did this a couple of times looking for things like a 1998 Nautical Almanac. I also had in the back of my mind an idea to buy something which could be sold on as a little business for a girlfriend in Nosy Be.

Clothing was the obvious choice and there were businesses run by Indians in Durban making very cheap goods. I finished off meeting a Yorkshire couple with an exotic underwear store. They promised me trade prices even though I didn't want to spend too much money the first time around. The fact was that I had doubts I'd get even my original investment back. But I felt sure I'd have fun trying. I spent one hundred dollars. For that I got a huge variety of tops and bottoms and in betweens, and they hardly took up any room at all!

One of the regulars at the Slipway Bar was a welder. He had his own small-business welding stainless steel. He had been part owner of a large concrete boat and had been back and forwards to Tulear in the south of Madagascar, trading whiskey. At one time he worked there welding a pipeline. I had to stop there on the way north.

The Slipway Bar did in fact have a slipway next to it. It had a handrail on one side which was useful on the day when I came in on the high tide and tied up *Sea Loone* to dry out and scrape and paint the bottom. With the painting finished, the bar was right there to provide cold beer while I waited for the tide to rise and slide me back into the deep water.

I loaded up with food in the mall, took on two cases of Johnny Walker whisky from the ships chandlers duty free and was ready to leave. It was the end of April 1998. I shipped out on the back of a south wester heading away from the coast and out of the south-flowing current as quickly as possible. After a few days of messing around, the south easterly winds picked up and I got moving. By May 7th I was anchored off the dock in Tulear protected from the ocean by a huge reef which I had had to navigate around.

I had to ferry all the officials out to the boat. There were five of them including a doctor. They all had a piece of paper that needed filling in and signing. Later, I had to go to the dock office and pay harbour fees. The doctor gave me a leaflet which stated that there was no AIDS in Madagascar, pretty unbelievable when just across the way in Zululand maybe 30% of the indigenous population was infected.

Tulear has a long causeway out to the harbour wharf where the water is just deep enough to take small ships. To get to town is a very long walk or take a rickshaw. I felt very uncomfortable sitting in a comfortable seat smoking a cigarette while a guy pulled me along. Initially he ran but as the perspiration on his back increased, his speed decreased to a walk. I could imagine a British colonial gentleman shouting at him to go faster.

I'd hardly settled in when the wind started to pick up. It blew out of the north which put my stern to the wharf where a large fishing boat was tied up. In the shallow water, the seas picked up quickly and with the wharf behind me I decided to put out a second anchor. Not a good decision. The wind really started to blow and my bow started dipping into the seas. Water cascaded down the deck as the bow reared up in the air and then buried itself in the next wave. Behind me the steel fishing boat was trying to climb onto the quay; then falling back in the water and making a terrible racket which I could hear above the screaming of the wind.

At that moment my short bowsprit or cathead broke away taking with it the bow roller. The second anchor had chain then rope but the rope was now wearing on the broken timber. To make matters dramatically worse we now start dragging backwards towards the trawler.

I had to get out of there. I winched in the rope on the second anchor once I had transferred the main chain to the bollard. Then motoring forward I handballed the chain in whenever there was slack and I wasn't knee deep in water. When the anchor eventually came loose from the bottom, I had to really go for it and get the last few feet up and the anchor onto the deck as quickly as possible. In the meantime the bow fell off and we were drifting sideways and backwards until the main chain came taut again. If the main anchor then got torn out of the bottom we'd continue rapidly to join the trawler.

While the main chain was slack, I managed to get it back on the gypsy of the anchor winch. The anchor held momentarily. The chain jerked bar tight and the boat swung back into the wind. I was now winning. With the engine revved up, the winch brought in the main chain each time the bow dropped off a wave. As the boat reared up I stopped the winch and then started it again as the bow dipped. We were slowly moving forwards away from the trawler which was now horribly close.

As soon as the anchor broke out I took the tiller and edged the boat ever so slightly to port. We crabbed sideways until the trawler and wharf were no longer behind me. I kept going until I was half way to the reef and then let the anchor go again. With all the chain down, I attached two hundred feet of nylon warp and let all that go. I made it fast on the bollard. We were no longer dragging and any way there is a quarter of a mile of open water behind me, shallow with a sandy bottom for me to plough before I have to do anything more. Every muscle was aching and my back was killing me. Before I could even make a cup of coffee, I lay down unmoving, horizontal for half an hour. I was knackered!

With the trade winds blowing anywhere from the south through to the north east, I would have been sheltered by the land or the wharf. With a southwester coming through, the outer reef gave good protection. But a gale from the north was something new to me, it left us completely open and was nearly the end of *Sea Loone.*

Surprisingly, the trawler was still floating the next morning when the wind died down. The wharf itself had as many gouges as the boat.

I bought bread and some vegetables on the wharf and then, with the wind back where it should be, set off north for Cape St. Andre and then on to Majunga for a couple of days. Tulear was not the port for me.

Majunga is a large town inside the mouth of a big shallow river. It has the same problems as Hellsville, many boats in a small space making it really difficult to find a place to tie up the dinghy.

One thing worth seeing was a type of outrigger canoe with a dhow rig. They sail across the wind and across the estuary and could really move. One which passed had a girl nonchalantly standing up on the windward outrigger holding the one piece of rigging and flying along.

In Hellsville I offloaded a case of whisky with the "Moulin Rouge", one of the nightclubs, and promise the other to a hotel on Nosi Sakatea. A few weeks later there was a pool competition in the bar above the nightclub. I won back one of my bottles of whisky. I gave it back to the owner in return for a cold beer.

I had met the lovely Cathy again. She had something to tell me and invited me to lunch. It was good. Two other girls were also cooking on their little charcoal burners outside their tiny houses so we had a mixture of beef, prawns and fish with the ubiquitous rice.

Cathy's news was that she was pregnant. She was not showing so obviously it was nothing to do with me. Apparently, an Italian tourist had done the deed and had not been heard of again. What could I do about it? She didn't want the baby and I certainly didn't want the baby. With our relationship extending over only a few days in Russian Bay half a year ago, she realized that I wasn't going to get involved. The last I saw of her, she was heading for the hospital clutching a small amount of money I had given her, in search of an abortion.

Antonio on *Black Sheep* had spent the cyclone season in Madagascar and had had to weather one bad blow. Peter the Dane who had also been in Noumea arrived, so Antonio could use his Italian. Then Guido arrived, a Swiss, but Italian Swiss. So the three of them could waffle away throwing their arms around. They all had dinner on my boat and still couldn't help relapsing into Italian. We sailed around a bit together. Guido had sailed round Cape Horn but was a hopeless sailor and his boat loved dragging anchors.

Antonio spent a lot of his time in Ambatoloaka, a resort run mainly by Italians. Peter and Guido had no interest in local nightlife so in Hellsville I often spend time drinking in the Port à Rouge, alone, well sort of alone. I met three girls whom I later called the three musketeers. One girl was great fun but not available. Another would occasionally come out with me and Antonio. The third, Maria, became my girlfriend. Pretty, always smiling and easy to please, we got on perfectly. I had my table in the bar and the three girls would join me and share my beer. They were full of gossip and knew everything that was going on.

I had met Mike in the harbour. He was German, not so old, tall, goodlooking, with a beautiful boat. It was over fifty feet long, flush decked with lovely lines and sloop rigged. It sailed like a dream. Quite often Mike would come to the Port à Rouge for a drink. He would always stand in the same corner, drinking Coca-Cola and chasing it with the local rum. The girls were intrigued by him but he wouldn't join us. Not only was he very shy, he was really put off by the more ardent bar girls who rubbed up against him and felt him where they shouldn't. However from talking with him, I knew he wanted to find a serious girlfriend to join him on the boat.

I had been teaching the Three Musketeers English on *Sea Loone*. Progress was not too rapid but when the occasional foreigner came into the bar, they would try their best. Normally a girl would say "give me a beer", much as an American would; but then say nothing more. So when the girl politely asks "Please may I have a beer?" and then says "Thank you" when presented with it, the Vasa or foreigner was left speechless.

The girls decided to find Mike a girlfriend. The girl was instructed to try and be very coy and not the least bit pushy. It's not easy for a Malgash, but it worked first time. The girl was invited to go sailing for a few days on Mike's boat, *Duala*.

As soon as they got back we got the news and the news was not good. The girl had a baby and had brought it along but this had not been the problem. The problem had been not enough water, lousy soap, no shampoo, rotten cooking facilities and the bed was far too small. She was not going again! This was from a girl who lived in a thatched garden shed not even worth a tenth of a percent of the yacht *Duala*. I laughed.

When I spoke to Mike, he already knew the problems. I explained that whenever Maria came back to the boat the first thing she did was shower in the cockpit with ten litres of water, smelly soap and shampoo. She then looked in the oven expecting some leftover meat, a piece of cake, or whatever and then there was a large bed to eat in, play in and finally sleep in.

As a sort of ex-racing boat, *Duala* had navy style pipe berths, no water tanks to talk about and two pump up paraffin stoves to cook on. The main part of the boat was taken up by a huge industrial sewing machine which never got used. Mike was as poor as a church mouse and lived in fried bananas. His love life was not looking up.

Meanwhile my business deal with the sexy underwear was not proving profitable but when the English lessons in the *Sea Loone* bed got boring, we could always resort to a fashion show. So we had some fun and the sack of frilly bits-and-bobs soon evaporated.

My three month visa evaporated as well and I was going to have to leave. Whether I could squeeze another trip out of my piggy bank was doubtful. I had to spend a lot in Tanzania, money that wouldn't come back to me until probably the Caribbean.

I had still spent only weekends in Hellsville so my relationship with Maria wasn't really serious. But I would miss her and maybe she would miss me just a little.

In Mayotte I went to the dentist. My teeth, all of them, were a disaster. So before they all rotted out, something had to be done. The dentist had been in private practice in Reunion but had come to Mayotte as a Government dentist. There was no charge for the work but materials had to be paid for. We came to an arrangement whereby I would pay $1,000 for four stainless steel crowns on the remaining molars, two up and two down.

Each molar would have root canal treatment and the crowns would be made in the Reunion. The whole thing was to take no more than a week. There was no x-ray machine available and not much in the way of painkilling injections. The root canal drilling was very painful, then squaring off teeth for the crown equally awful, a week of agony! The crowns arrived from Reunion a few days later and got hammered into place. I'm not sure the money ever reached the French government but I had some teeth to chew with.

Before I left, Mike arrived for a few days on *Duala*. He was planning to return to Nosi Bé for another three months. He had had stomach pains and fainting fits so the hospital did some tests. He was diagnosed as suffering from malnutrition. I invited him to dinner on *Sea Loone* as part of the treatment.

When I arrived back in Mtwara, Tanzania, the tide was beginning to ebb. I cleared customs and didn't want to hang around for the immigration with the boat anchored in the channel. I promised I'd see them later and moved up into the creek.

By the time I anchored, Majida, my agent, was already waiting on the beach for me. The jungle drums are just as good as telephones. I rowed ashore and as I stepped on land the immigration man came barreling down the path on a bicycle. I had his fifty dollars and some more money that needed changing in the bank before it closed. So we did the paperwork there and then. I handed over the fifty dollars and then borrowed his bicycle to get to the bank. Majida pedaled and I did the Raj thing on the back.

Changing money in the bank in Tanzania was long-winded but we finally finished just as the bank was closing, and just as the Immigration man arrived to collect his bicycle. Everybody was happy.

In the morning, Majida came out to the boat. I had discovered that the previous yacht the year before had been Mike on *Duala* who had bought some shells. Hence the reason Majida had been so insistent about makome – shells.

I asked Majida how the ships' agent business was doing and how many yachts had been in Mtwara since I was last here. The answer was none. I was the last boat. As far as I was concerned, this was good.

The word was out and early each morning there were people for Majida to see, and each day we also went out. I numbered each of the so-called factories, mango trees, we visited and tried to organize the carvers there to carve some whales out of ebony. I drew what I wanted and showed pictures. The results were less than spectacular. I don't think I managed to sell any. Never mind, I bought a lot of other carvings and had some nice walking sticks made.

Other things started arriving. One morning Majida opened up a sack on the boat to reveal a complete lion skin but it was so rotten from mane to tail plume. It was useless. In the end I agreed to buy the claws which I thought I could do something with. The next day a leopard skin arrived equally tatty. Again I bought the claws and the two canine teeth, also needing dentistry.

A twenty foot long boa constrictor skin arrived in not too bad condition and the next day Majida wanted me to come ashore to see something he said was really good.

In a woven basket there was an armour-plated ball. It was a rare pangolin, the African equivalent to an American armadillo. It was alive but refused to uncurl. I was told it was very good to eat. After a lot of argument I paid out the equivalent of ten dollars, a small fortune, and took the pangolin back to the boat. I had no idea what to do with it. I tried photographing it but, curled up, it was boring. At sunset it was still curled up but as soon as it got dark, it uncurled and was on the move. With a pointy head, long tail and huge front claws, it was maybe three feet long.

Once on the move, it was unstoppable and the huge claws, presumably used to tearing open termite nests, were doing a good job on the interior of *Sea Loone*. I managed to get the creature in the dinghy and started rowing for the far side of the creek where the pangolin would have more chance of escaping. At one stage it climbed up and fell in the water. I only just managed to grab it before it sank. Finally, I got it to the shore and with no backward look and no "thank you for saving me from the pot", it trundled off into the undergrowth.

I reckon I got a few karma points for that little adventure but in the morning, when I had told Majida I had set the animal free, I lost a lot of bartering points even though I explained to him how rare and special the animal was, and how his children might never see one. Anyway he made six hundred shillings out of it.

The last thing to arrive was a sack of ivory. I refused to even look at it. But for Majida this was serious business and the man came back every day on his bicycle. They were medium-sized tusks each cut into three pieces. The tip of one was missing so there were five pieces in total, each maybe a foot long. Majida wanted his 10% and I was persuaded that the animal had died accidentally, not been poached. I just imagine what I could make with them and then I paid up the money, one hundred dollars. So much for my karma points.

Loaded down with my makonda, I paid off my agent and left again for South Africa. This time, three hundred miles south, I broke the journey and stopped in Pemba, Mozambique. I anchored off a big timber yard close to the harbour and then went through a lot of paperwork and money clearing in.

For twenty years there had been a war in Mozambique. Now that it was over there were still landmines everywhere and for a few dollars you could buy an AK-47 and all the ammunition. For all that time, the forest had been unmolested. Now they were catching up rapidly. Huge piles of logs were waiting to be exported with more arriving daily from the interior.

Every day a huge seine net was rowed out, a dozen muscled rowers chanting. The ends were brought to the beach and then slowly pulled in by dozens of helpers. They were after the shoaling tuna in the bay but were happy to sell me the odd prawns caught in the net and one day, a big flat fish.

One of the guys I spoke to on the beach had a salt pond on the landward side of the lagoon where he evaporated seawater. He was proud to tell me that he added iodine to the salt before he sold. But far more interesting to me was that he had one of his workers eaten by lions the previous week.

I found some makonda carvings in Pemba, quite different to those in Mtwara. Unfortunately, like everything else I found in Pemba, they were very expensive. I bought some fruit and vegetables and then carried on south.

Again I sailed into Richards Bay without any weather coming up from the south to upset me. I found the same spot to tie up at in the small boat harbour. Tied up behind me was the same South African boat owned by a local couple. Alma, the wife, had moved on board. There were obviously problems with the marriage. They had two children, the youngest leaving school that year. I got coffee most mornings.

They grew sugar cane on Nosy Bé, all of which was used to make rum. The rum was popular in South Africa so I had bought two Jerry cans of the stronger variety in fact it was so strong that Chinaman in the store where I ordered it, demanded I pick it up on the day it came in. It was a fire risk!

I sold half a jerry can's worth to a friend in the Slipway Bar. He had a backpackers lodge down the coast where they were having a big party that weekend. I was more than doubling my money.

The following week my friend complained that the rum had been far too strong and some people had got very drunk. . For the next party I sold him the superior refined rum which was not quite so strong. It went down much better but was still too strong.

For the third order I sold him my "super superior aged" rum which went down perfectly. Naturally I had to ask more money for it but it went down so well that he bought all my remaining stock. I don't need to tell you that I had refilled the first half-empty jerry can from the water tap to produce the "superior" rum; then did it again for the "aged special"!

I brought back some ebony wood for the local gunsmith. He wanted to use it for inlays in the stocks of some of his rebuilt rifles. Unfortunately, I hadn't found any old German guns in Mtwara from when it was Tanganyika, German East Africa. I got a bag full of hippopotamus teeth in exchange. The ivory from hippos in the Nile had been very popular in the days of the Roman Empire.

Danish Peter had now arrived and was in the marina next door. More worldly than me, he was using the local tourist information office to send emails. It was all new to me and I was dragged in to sign up on something called "Hotmail". In fact I got my messages typed and sent by the secretary in the office and she printed out any replies so I wasn't really becoming completely e-literate. Still I could see the huge advantages for keeping in touch with other boat people.

Relying on my mother to send on my mail to me once or twice a year, didn't work well and I had lost contact with many good friends. Quite often she would open the letters and not send the envelopes which sometimes had the return addressee on them. Quite often my mail just disappeared.

When I counted up what was left in the piggy bank, there was nowhere near enough left to return to Madagascar. In fact it would only just get me to the Caribbean with a bit to spare, while I sold off some stuff or found some work.

Using the Internet, I contacted Kathryn, my crew from Gove to Darwin, Australia. She replied that had just completed a contract as a marine biologist with the Government and she and her friend, another marine biologist, were thinking of taking off to go surfing in Indonesia. I suggested they find some work around Nosy Bé. There was a problem with coral bleaching in the Indian Ocean. Maybe they could find some grant money, stay on the boat, and finance me and *Sea Loone* for another season there.

Meanwhile Peter who was also planning to go back to Madagascar, was getting bored with life in Richards Bay. He was going to hire a car and make a tour around South Africa. He invited me along to keep him company, all expenses paid. Naturally, I jumped at the chance.

We motored due west to Kimberly and on into the Kalahari then down the Orange River to the coast at Port Nolloth. A friend of Glenn lived here. He was a diamond diver. The harbour was very poorly protected by a reef of rocks and the diamond diving boats were on massive chain moorings.

On the few days in the year when the sea was reasonably calm, the boats would go out and suck up the sand and gravel among the rocks on the sea bottom. The diver, using an airline from the boat, had to maneuver the huge suction tube into holes in crevices. It sounded like really hard work and, because the current here swept up the coast from Antarctica, the water was freezing.

The harbour master showed us a picture on his wall. It was a picture of his table with the results of one day's diving. There had to be a whole bucket full of diamonds. They went from brown to gold to light yellow to almost clear. Polished on the seabed they glistened and some were as big as my fingernail. They surely must have been worth a fortune. The picture was a few years old and now the diamonds were more difficult to find, but still...

That evening we drank beer in the local bar. The races were mixed and the whole atmosphere seemed more relaxed than in Zululand. One young diver who operated a pump off the beach had been out that day and told me the water had been particularly cold. It runs around 10°C. In Afrikaans he called it "leo cop cold" which translates into "lions head cold". This describes his private parts shriveled up by the freezing water to show just a little nose surrounded by a circle of short-and-curlies.

We had been invited to stay with Glenn ex-*Blue Drifter* when we arrived in Cape Town so we drove round to Noordhoek where he had his house. Huge gates led onto a private road which ran up under Table Mountain which hung above us.

Glenn's house was located among a number of other expensive looking residences. He had designed and built the place himself with a huge Dutch thatched roof. It looked out across the ocean. It was magnificent. Peter and I settled into the flat above the double garage.

The first day out we toured the vineyards, coming back with a case of wine and more. Peter was going to make his favorite Italian dish that evening, Fluiti di Mari. So we stopped in Hout Bay at the fish market.

Peter had not met Glenn before and I had not met his wife or the baby girl but we all got on well together. We got on so well that all the wine disappeared and we had to go back up into the mountains to find more.

Finally when we left, we followed the road right up the East Coast back to Richards Bay. The trip around had been really interesting and we both really enjoyed ourselves. In fact, Peter was already thinking of going again.

When I collected my emails from the tourist office there was a reply from Kathryn to say that they were really interested in joining me and had made some inquiries about doing marine surveys in the north west of Madagascar.

The agreement was to pay me $1,000 for six months on board *Sea Loone*, spending three months in Madagascar; then sailing across to Mozambique and spending some time inside the reefs in the north before finally arriving in Richards Bay, South Africa. The cost of food, fuel and such like would all be shared. I expected to return no richer or poorer than when I left.

Meanwhile, Peter came to me with his next plan. We would fly to Windhoek, Namibia, hire a four-wheel-drive truck and make a tour of the whole country. So we did just that. From Windhoek we went down to the famous red sand dunes and sat on one of the ridges as the sun came up. It was magical.

From there, we went up the coast, first to Walvis Bay where we watched the clouds of pink flamingos. Then on to Swakopmund where Peter spent time with the hotelier sampling his South African wine collection while I sampled the good Windhoek beer in the bars in town.

We then drove up over miles of parched rocky hills with spectacular views to Etosha Pan where we stayed in the Game Lodge. There we saw a huge amount of game including the desert elephants, lions and, one day, a little honey badger.

In the Kalahari, Peter had wanted to see an Aardvark, probably because it's the first thing in the dictionary. We tried to find one again at night in Etosha but never saw the strange animal. He did come away with a nice antelope skull which was sitting out on the salt plan not far from where we had seen a pride of lions. When he dashed out to get it, I had never seen him run so fast. I spent a bit of time looking for stone plants which Glenn had talked about. Standing in a rocky desert which extends to the high-rise and under a blazing sun temperatures that would burst a thermometer, examining each rock in case it's a plant, isn't my vocation. I never found one.

Back in Richards Bay it was time to start preparing for the trip north. Alma, who had been looking after my boat again, was also sailing up to Madagascar in a rusty old German boat from Port Elizabeth. Meanwhile Plastic, who had sailed his huge catamaran down to Richards Bay, was also returning north, still looking for charter work. In fact Plastic left before me in April and got into a nasty gale which caused a lot of damage. He lost some of his safety equipment so his father gave me the replacement stuff, plus glue and screws to re-do the deck, to be delivered to Plastic in Nosy Bé.

I took on lots of food to help feed the girls when they arrived from Australia, more whisky and bottles of Ricard pastis ordered by the hotel in Sakatia. I got away on May 13 heading directly for Nosy Bé where the girls would be flying in. There is supposed to be a north-setting current running up the west coast of Madagascar so I headed across to that side of the Mozambique Channel. All was going well until I was approaching Europa Island to the west of Tulear.

The trade winds from the south east had been picking up for days. They were now really pumping. I was broad reaching and the huge swells were picking me up and pushing me along. A few breaking tops had tried climbing into the cockpit so I had the drop boards in and the hatch pulled over. This was fortunate because the wave of the day picked up the whole boat and threw it over. We didn't roll but went way past the horizontal.

Everything flew everywhere and even with hatches closed a lot of water came below. When we came upright the cockpit was full and slowly draining. I dashed out to help straighten up to the next wave and found the aft hatch had been torn off and was miraculously lying on the side deck up by the mast. It's big and heavy and I grabbed it, and dragged it back jamming it over the gaping hole. Fortunately the eight or nine bagged sails in the aft locker had stopped too much water getting in.

With the hatch lashed down, I then spent a few hours in the cockpit nursing the Aries wind vane but no more monster waves arrived although we still got picked up and pushed along by a few monsters. When I was happy that I could leave the wind vane to steer alone, I went back below to see the damage and bail out the bilges. Amazingly, nothing was broken. The main problem was that all the tinned food in the lockers under the bunks had got coated in a mixture of salt water and margarine which had escaped its thin plastic containers in the bilge. The mixture had also covered the spare chain and other things. There was nothing I could do before I arrived so I left the sticky gooey mess till next we anchored.

The wind eased and the rest of the trip was without problems. I stopped first in Sakatea and offloaded all the whisky and pastis. I was offered dinner together with a group of South African sports fishermen who were guests, which was rather nice.

From there I went to Nosy Komba and anchored as close as possible to Stefano's place in order to use his fresh water supply to sort out the horrible mess under the bunks and in the bilge. Mixing margarine and saltwater produces a disgusting, sticky, plastic mess which is unaffected by washing- up liquid or diesel. I wonder what it does to your stomach. I found it could be removed with petrol so piled up the hundred or more tins on the beach and clean off each with petrol soaked rags. Some of the labels had completely disappeared so these were now mystery cans. The others had to be marked with a felt pen. It was a long sticky job.

I threw the anchor chain over the side but it still came back sticky. I used up all my petrol, all my rags and all my old shirts, plus gallons and gallons of fresh water. After two solid days things were as good as I could get them and I set off for Hellsville to clear in.

Kaskazi, Plastic's catamaran, was in Hellsville so I handed over the stuff I had brought up from Richards Bay and begged a couple of dozen of the largest stainless screws to repair the aft hatch on *Sea Loone*.

The day the girls were due to arrive, I had told my boat boys to look out for two Australian vasa or white people. By the early evening I began to tour the town to try and find them. All to no avail. I assumed they had been delayed. They had been surfing in Indonesia and had, I think, flown from there to Singapore before heading towards Africa.

The next day I went ashore and sat and drank coffee in the roadside café. It was a spot where everybody wandered past at some time or other. Sure enough, I was on my second cup of coffee when the two girls strolled past with their Malgash "guide". I called them over and asked them if they were looking for me.

Kathryn was her usual happy self, a bit overweight maybe but that wouldn't last long. Fiona was blonde, blue-eyed and pretty. She was also pretty big and strong. I hoped they weren't going to gang up on me. I was no match for either of them.

Not having seen the boat in the harbour, they had stayed the night in a local cheap hotel. They didn't know I was "Mr. Bon Bon". Unfortunately even their guide knew me only by that name. Anyway, they went off back to the hotel to collect their gear and would then come back to the café.

When they arrived in a taxi, with two surfboards on the roof, two huge backpacks in the back we had to borrow an extra dinghy to get everything to the boat. God knows where it was all going to be stored.

In the end, Fiona lived and slept up forward with the backpacks. Kathryn slept on the saloon floor and I kept my bunk in the saloon above her. If a big sea threw me out of the bunk, I was going to have a wonderfully soft landing. The surfboards stayed on deck where they were joined by the diving hookah with its inflated rubber ring and coils of air hose. The rubber ducky got inflated and thrown into the water, so we had two dinghies. It wasn't perfect but it worked.

They had been in touch with a number of people who were keen for them to do a coral survey in different places around the area. Nobody had come up with any money but a scientist in the Seychelles had given them some useful information. Another here in Madagascar was going to send them some useful taxonomy books from Antanarivo and maybe come for a visit.

Kathryn actually specialized in marine botany, sea grasses, seaweeds and so on. Fiona was the expert on corals and had done similar surveys before. We had hoped to get a permit to visit Aldabra and would have sailed up there with Danish Peter. But they never came up with the goods.

I had brought some clothes and materials for Maria which she was happy with. I explained that two girls were coming from Australia to stay on the boat, but were not girlfriends. It all went down very well and on the Saturday night Kathryn and Fiona found partners for the night leaving Maria and I with the boat to ourselves. This set the pattern for our weekends in Hellsville.

On the Monday, we found material to make metre squares for the survey and headed out for Nosy Mitsio, thirty miles north where we would choose our first sight. We anchored off a sandy beach with a rocky headland to the left and a large area of reefs.

I had been here before and could troll for fish for tea with ease and catch octopus off the rocks. The girls took the Avon inflatable (the rubber ducky) and spent hours on the reef with the hookah counting and identifying the corals and the associated fish.

A little over a mile away, a massive volcanic plug rises out of the water may be 1,000 feet high. With almost vertical sides all the way around, there is just a small piece of flat land under the cliffs where you can land and a shallow sand spit on which you can anchor.

A fissure in the cliff face allowed us to climb up and, not without a lot of difficulty, reach its flat top. A few trees and aloes managed to grow on the black basaltic rock but mainly the rock was bare. Standing on the edge of the cliff face, the view was spectacular. *Sea Loone* anchored on the little patch of sand directly below us, looked like a tiny toy boat. The whole of Mitsio was laid out before us. We could see the mainland to the east, the rain forest on Nosy Bé, and the bulk of Nosy Komba to the south.

Close to the sand spit in shallow water was an area of smooth rocks and pebbles. As soon as I saw it I thought of octopus. Sure enough there were lots of them, some really huge, peering out from their holes over their castle walls. We caught two of them with the hook and spear and Fiona took them ashore to beat them on a rock and then bash the upper part of the tentacles with a hammer. That night, we ate well.

The first survey took quite a while perfecting the technique and identifying all the species. Then we had days off to climb the mountain or take the hookah to find lobster or whatever. Then it was back to Hellsville. A number of yachts had arrived and in the early evenings we socialized on the foredeck with our rum-and-lime recipe. Other yachties and the crew's boyfriends brought beer. Later in the evening we would find a table at the Port à Rouge and Maria and the musketeers would arrive. Even later, Kathryn and Fiona would be away and Maria and I would row back to *Sea Loone*.

We did four different survey sites from the boat and the girls did two more on the north coast of Nosy Bé. When the biologist came down from Antanarivo, they used a local work boat. In between, we had weeks just cruising around Nosy Komba where Stefano became very enamored with Fiona. We also went to Russian Bay, where Catherine demonstrated her skill at finding mud crabs in the mangroves. Farther north past Nosy Mitsio we anchored in a bay on the mainland. I had photographs of people in the village there taken the year before. When I showed them the whole village arrived passing them around and around. They were so excited. The chief collected all the pictures together to return them to me. He was speechless when I said no they were for them to keep.

In the bay we exchange containers and bottles for mud crabs, a live chicken and eggs which quite often had half grown chicks in when we cracked them open.

Back in Nosy Bé the last time, the lime season was over and our rum recipe had to change to squeezed oranges. I said my goodbyes to Maria and the girls to their friends. The last night the three of us went bar-hopping and dancing. I vaguely remember being on Kathryn's back, legless I think is the word, as we stopped in the Port à Rouge for a final beer. They were a good crew, shoveling me into the dinghy to get me back to *Sea Loone*.

We headed north to try and visit Nosy Hara before going west to Mayotte but the wind was howling and we failed miserably. Half way to Mayotte the GPS stopped working. It was made by Garmin and unknown to me, they had all stopped. It was something to do with the millennium change over. It was really annoying because last time I met Ernst Klar, Hans's father, he had given me the coordinates of where he found his major treasure, a horde of silver. He promised me he had cleaned it out but we were going to make sure. Without the GPS, finding this spot on the ocean was going to be impossible, nothing showed above water.

When the girls saw me drawing lines back and forward and up and down and taking sights with the sextant, they weren't too sure I was going to find Mayotte. There was no wind for two days and the current pushed us all over the place. They were quite relieved when the island showed up over the horizon. The GPS was fixed by some millennium know-it-all who pressed buttons and inserted dates and numbers and such like to get it going again.

When I cleared in, there was a letter for me from my sister. Not long after her trip to South Africa she was diagnosed with breast cancer. She had to have major surgery and then chemotherapy; but had recovered. Now she had cervical cancer and had to have another major operation to remove all her "ladies bits". I suddenly realized the letter was months old. Maybe the poor girl was dead? I had to wait until evening to telephone and I was a nervous wreck.

The girls brought out the rum and calmed me down. When eventually I managed to get through on the telephone, it was my sister who answered. She sounded perfectly healthy. The operation had been no problem and they told her the prognosis was good. She laughed and joked. I wasn't so amused more drained!

Ernst Klar was on the island with his daughter. Danish Peter had arrived with Antonio on *Black Sheep* and also Guido the Swiss. So we all got together to drink a few beers before we scattered to the winds once more.

By now Kathryn was looking pretty trim but the two girls ate a huge amount of food. So sailing for weeks without a place to resupply was going to require us to really stock up. We had a sail bag full of French bread cut up and dried in the sun. We had kilos of pasta and bags of flour but not much left of the tinned goods. Still, the girls made huge doughy pizzas with the oddest fillings, no cheese but plenty of tomato sauce. We also had some huge pumpkins.

We headed for Cabo Delgado and then behind the reef which extended more than one hundred miles south. There were islands and channels between the inner reefs all protected by the main seaward barrier reef. Some of the islands had small fishing communities. Others were deserted and covered in thin bush.

One small island we anchored off had the remains of a coconut plantation and a population of more than one hundred people. The girls were surrounded by twenty small children and who then followed by them wherever they went.

Behind the beach were rows of drying racks on which the small fish were spread out. The fishermen were going out each day by canoe with their fishing nets to the surrounding reef flats. The women supervised the splitting and drying of the fish.

What amazed us was that the island was completely dry. Only a few bushes remained plus the sorry looking coconut palms. The people lived and slept under the drying racks. There were no huts and no building materials. The dried fish were exchanged for water, rice and presumably charcoal when the trading dhows arrived. When you saw the pot bellies of the children it was obvious that there were some problems with their diet.

We had a handful of one dollar bills which we could use to buy fish and lobsters. In fact, one dollar bill would buy a canoe full of fish, lobsters and shells. But because we had no refrigeration,, we could only take just what we would eat that day. On one occasion the girls were presented with a large red snapper as a present. I collected a sackful of small pretty oyster shells which I thought I could use for my jewelry-making and also cleaned up a huge triton shell which I found in a guy's canoe.

Navigating through the reefs needed some care. The water was sometimes not so clear, so we took it very slowly. For three days we had to hide behind the reef as the wind howled from out of the south. Finally we arrived at Pemba where the barrier reef had finished and we anchored off the timber yard in the enclosed bay. The officials gouged as much money out of us as they could and Kathryn and Fiona went off to the market to buy some much-needed fresh produce.

In the whole time we spend inside the barrier reef, we saw only sailing boats and no sign of any foreigners. The people in the islands were obviously very very poor and living a hard life as fishermen. We felt embarrassingly rich and fortunate among them. There didn't seem to be any way their lives were going to improve; in fact, quite the opposite as fish stocks diminished.

Now that we were on the African mainland, the girls decided they'd like to make a little trip inland to see the country. So they took a bus which would take them across the border into Malawi. I wanted to buy some wood for new window frames and had other things to do on the boat.

A few days after they left, the wind picked up during the night and really started blowing from the southwest. It was blowing on shore and at low tide my stern was almost in the breakers. The beach was really steep so the anchor was in deep water. As the seas picked up in the bow started burying itself in the waves, I prepared to get out.

The seas were so short and steep, the chain was trying to jump off the gypsy. I had the engine moving us slowly ahead and foot by foot the chain was coming in. I don't know exactly how it happened but trying to keep the chain from jumping I managed to trap my hand between the chain and the gypsy.

Fortunately the bow dropped into a deep trough and I ripped my hand out before the strain came on to my fingers and turned them to mincemeat. Still, the skin was badly torn with blood pouring everywhere. The deck turned red but with the chain only halfway up I had to keep going or finish on the beach. The torchlight picked up the red smears of blood everywhere; but the bones were intact and the hand worked fine.

The anchor broke out and I motored out of the bay en route for the other side of town. There I found an anchorage off a little hotel in the lea and calm water. I bandaged up my hand roughly, poured Betadine into it and slept till dawn. But the next morning it took me an hour to clean the blood up from the foredeck.

I left a note with the timber yard to say where *Sea Loone* was so the girls could find me again. Then I went off looking for a television with a satellite dish. The next weekend England were playing South Africa in the Rugby World Cup and I would dearly like to watch it.

I was lucky to meet a lady with a cottage on the beach near the hotel. She was happy to let me watch her television. Amazingly enough, she came from St. Helena in the South Atlantic. Her Scottish husband was building roads up north somewhere. Naturally, she knew the people that I knew on St Helena and was very happy to meet someone that had actually been there

On the day of the match, the girls came back; so they came along to watch the game as well. But when we arrived at the cottage we were told that we had been invited to a cottage further along where a party had been arranged to watch the game. So we picked up our beers and moved down the road.

The party people were all Afrikaners so obviously dedicated South African rugby supporters. I told the girls that if they didn't support England they'd be sleeping on the beach. And so the game began. The girls overdid it a bit when England showed any form, shouting and clapping. I had to explain this wasn't Aussie rules it was more staid. Although South Africa kicked the ball too much for my liking, they won.

The whole time the other watchers were talking in Afrikaans and very obviously making very disparaging remarks about England and the English. It wasn't very pleasant and Kathryn and Fiona picked up on it. The womenfolk had made a load of food and we drank our beer. The atmosphere didn't improve. In fact they were being bloody rude, so the girls decided to do something about it.

They chose a piece of music and jumped on the table and did a "Ziggy Zumba". They danced and stripped off their clothes, throwing them to me. The chatter stopped, the men round-eyed, the women shocked! As more got revealed, the deeper the silence spread among them. Retaining their knickers but with boobs flying they jumped off the table and fled into the garden where I returned their clothes. We didn't stay much longer and left plenty for them to chatter about, ha, ha!

From Pemba we were going to sail direct to Richards Bay. The girls realized that we would quite likely to hit some bad weather and were a little nervous. But the boat was well prepared and we set off. As it turned out, most of the time we had too little wind, not too much. Flat becalmed one day the girls jumped into the water with the dolphin fish, dorados.

The fish were really inquisitive and came right up. It was frustrating as the rubber on the spear gun was perished, so we could not catch one for dinner. While they played on one side of the boat I slid over the other side, swam under the boat and tweaked their bums as I came up. I got into a lot of trouble over that!

Farther south, the wind picked up and after passing Maputo we were in the south-going current and booming along. The wind clocked around to the north east as we approached Richards Bay and we roared along. We shot into the harbour in the dark and, by midnight, were tied up in the Small Boat Harbour.

The floating restaurant opposite was cleaning up after some function and sold us each a cold beer to celebrate our arrival and the completion of the cruise. As we drank the beer the south west change came through. Had we still been out there, it would have brought us a gale of cold air and misery. Instead, we were tied alongside, the boat completely still so no need to stand watch. The wind whistled in the rigging as we slept.

After a week of pottering around Richards Bay, Kathryn and Fiona left the boat to head down towards Cape Town. They had Glenn's address down there and would be welcome to visit. They loaded their backpacks and surfboards into the back of a pickup truck which would take them as far as Durban and we all waved frantically as they disappeared down the road.

6

THE BOAT FELT pretty empty without the girls, but the space they left soon got filled. My main sail was torn and patched and really needed replacing. Guido, the Swiss, had given me a large heavy genoa he had used rounding Cape Horn. I had cut it down but not used it much as it was so heavy to handle. I determined to make a new mainsail out of it.

With some help from Mike on *Duala* who had escaped the attentions of the girls from the Port à Rouge, I cut the sail to shape. I had to replace the piece I had already cut off as a head sail. I stapled everything together including the reefing patches for the reef points. Then I sent the whole lot to be sewn up in the sail loft in Durban. The sewing cost me fifty rand plus more for some large eyelets. But I finished off with quite a presentable mainsail. The sail loft also beefed up the small jib which was now thirty-five years old and a bit frayed. The sail maker was impressed by such a museum piece and did a really good job.

The French yachts arrived, two of which I knew well. Jean Paul and Cecile on their small steel boat and Nano and Mino who had been in Mayotte for some time looking for a new mast for their small boat. They had been rolled when trying to leave Diego Suarez. Picked up by a large breaking wave the mast had hit the bottom and then broken as they went through 360°.

The third boat belonged to a crazy French drunkard who described himself as a poet. They hired themselves a car and I went along as their guide on my second visit to the Hluhluwe Game Park where we had been when my sister visited. They couldn't fail to be impressed by the Park and all the animals we saw and, on the way home, we side-tracked to St. Lucie to see the hippopotamuses. The day finish with drinking lots of beer and playing pool in a dark cellar bar somewhere close to the boat harbour.

Back in the Pacific in the Marquesas, Tracey had had a baby with her Marquesian boyfriend whom she had married. The baby, a little girl, was now more than a year old and Tracey had brought her to Durban to see her grandmother. So one day in the boat harbour, the three of them arrived to see me and *Sea Loone*. The baby was a pretty little girl but I have to admit that there was no pangs of regret for not fathering something similar myself.

The New Year 2000 was approaching rapidly with talk about the millennium bug, Y2K. My GPS had already packed up once and if the whole system collapsed, I would actually be quite pleased. I doubt there was now one per cent of the yachting fleet that could do without GPS. I'd have the world to myself again!

Of course, nothing happened. Even the Slipway Bar which got hosed down with a four inch jet of water from the fire hydrant at midnight, survived. It kept serving drinks till dawn and even Mino survived when I picked her up in a fit of drunken enthusiasm and dropped her on her head, poor girl.

It was January 2000. The hangover forgotten, it was time to head south. I had slipped the boat again and painted on two coats of anti-fouling from a large drum given to me as a Christmas present by a ship in the harbour. My final trip to the mall to collect vegetables was unforgettable.

Tony had driven me to the mall in his huge four-wheel-drive. As we loaded my goodies into the car, shooting broke out across the car park. It escalated into a firefight. A guy next to me pulled out a gun and started firing and then an army vehicle drove up, flaps on its sides dropped down and machine guns poked out. A delivery lorry veered off the road and headed for a clump of trees across the field.

Tony and I roared out of the car park. The whole incident was apparently started by one guy holding up the cashier in a small restaurant. Too many guns and too much violence! It was a good time to leave.

In Durban, the old wooden International jetty had been demolished leaving only a small floating pontoon for the fleet of foreign yachts to raft up to. The Royal Natal Yacht Club had also moved to a small building on the dockside; so the old colonial snooker room was lost as well as the squash courts.

The antique shop down the road still had some small whale teeth, leftovers from the whaling station on the bluff. I exchanged my old brass Walker Patent Log for the teeth. I had lost the fish for the log a long time ago and anyway the GPS now told me all I needed to know.

Denis, a dedicated supporter of the Slipway Bar in Richards Bay, was in Durban, staying in his flat on Point Road. He invited me for a night out which involved a lot of beer in a number of bars and finished with me finding myself in a Jacuzzi in a house of ill repute. It was a going away present from Dennis and very enjoyable.

I passed the Wild Coast on the way to East London without any bad weather but got bashed about a bit before I reached Port Elizabeth. Once in the harbour, there was a big marina belonging to the yacht club where I found a place to tie up.

Alma, who had been my neighbour in the Small Boat Harbour living on the boat behind me, had now moved to Port Elizabeth. She had returned from her trip to Nosy Bé with Hans, the German where I had met with them, but her husband in Richards Bay had found an Eastern European girl on the Internet and had brought her to South Africa. She was now living in the house. That evening, drinking a few beers with Alma in the Yacht Club, she introduced me to a member who had a slip in the Marina that I could use for free. It turned out to be a very lucky thing.

The following day I moved to the free slip which put me next to Mike's boat, *Duala*. Mike had come down to Port Elizabeth to haul out his boat. The next day we were awoken early by a huge explosion somewhere down the dock. Mike and I ran down to where I had originally been tied up. Next to the slip was a large concrete yacht with the whole deck and cabin top blown off. The mast lay across where I had been tied up.

The boat still floated and we dived into the wreckage to see if anybody was on board. We found no one and minutes later the bomb squad arrived and shooed us away. The owners fortunately had gone off to town shopping, but the boat was a complete loss. Even the concrete hull was crazed in places. It had been a gas explosion from a leaking propane tank. I'm sure it would have seriously damaged *Sea Loone* had I been there, only a few feet away.

Alma was busy painting her silk scarves and working in a craft shop in town. We spent a week together and enjoyed each other's company before I moved on westwards for the Cape.

In Mossel Bay, I met a guy from Johannesburg who had built a really small plywood Wharram catamaran and was intend sailing it to the Caribbean. He had only a small cuddy on deck in which to eat and sleep. It didn't provide much protection and he had already had to bailout the two hulls and dry out all his belongings.

We met again off Cape Agulhas. Despite its reputation for big winds and seas, we were sitting there becalmed. It was so mirror-calm and airless that he swam over for a cup of coffee, leaving his boat to drift for a while.

That night I drifted in towards the coast with the current but then the wind suddenly picked up. I had the mainsail up to stop the boat rolling and was now shooting off downwind with the sail let right out. As I came into False Bay heading for Simonstown, the wind came directly behind me. It was howling more than fifty knots and the sea was covered in flying foam. I was really worried about gybing. If the boom went over, it would surely break the boom and tear the sail to shreds.

It was now six o'clock in the morning as I surfed past the Naval Base and prepared to come into the marina. I rounded up and drop the sail and with the engine going full blast, just managed to make headway against the wind up into the marina.

I had to shout and blow the horn to wake someone to help me get into a slip. Fortunately, a bleary eyed gent came to help and I rammed the boat into the dock and threw him a bow line. The wind screamed through the rigging of all the boats but the sea was flat calm. The wind kept going for another day. I hate to think what sort of seas had built up off Cape Agulhas by then.

With *Sea Loone* happily secured in the marina, I phoned Glenn in Noordhoek which was only just over the hill. It was great to see him again. Kathryn and Fiona had stayed with him for some time. They had bought a garden shed which they had moved into and had found work in the local pub over the New Year.

I had seen them fleetingly in Port Elizabeth. They were going north in a Volkswagen dormobile and we had a quick lunchtime picnic in the local park together with Alma. They managed to drive up through Botswana and eventually arrived in Tanzania before they ran out of money and steam. Then they flew home to Australia.

Glenn was busy campaigning for local conservation issues and was getting more and more involved in his opposition to genetic engineering and the multinational companies that were exploiting it. He was eventually to be invited to speak at the United Nations on the issue, so he was no lightweight.

Glenn's friend, Neutron Dave, had also returned to Cape Town with his growing family. He had built a place on a steep hillside also in Noordhoek. He had sold the boat but was still playing music and had a number of places in Cape Town where he played regularly.

Not having heard him play since New Zealand, I persuaded a local guy living in the Marina to drive into town one evening with a group of us visitors to see Dave play. There were five of us including the mad French poet who had become more and more of a pain in the bum. Since Richards Bay he had become louder and more aggressive whenever he went out drinking. We had a good night, and met a number of locals, including some pretty girls.

Neutron Dave has always provided great entertainment, a real professional. But then the bloody frog got drunk and objectionable; so we called it a day and started the drive back from the city to Simonstown.

Half way home, close to Cape Flats, we stopped for a last beer and lost the Frenchman. We had finished our beers and couldn't find him anywhere. So being all fed up with his antics, we jumped in the car and drove back to the marina leaving him to walk the rest of the way.

At lunchtime the next day, the Frenchman reappeared. He had recently bought an expensive pair of locally-made shoes. He was now barefoot with a torn shirt and stripped of all his money and his watch. He had been waylaid by two black guys from the notorious Cape Flats. They had stripped him naked. Then, with him lying on the floor between them, had discussed killing him.

He must have sobered up a bit and persuaded them that he was a Frenchman, a foreigner, and a great supporter of Nelson Mandela. They put away the knife and returned his shirts and trousers before they walked away. He was a very lucky man.

Just past the naval station in Simons Town, in a small rocky cove overlooked by suburban homes, a large colony of penguins had moved in. They nested in the bushes just above the beach ignoring the local people. Occasionally a penguin would wander down the street stopping traffic and the locals weren't too pleased about their gardens being dug up or the strong smell of Penguin guano on the breeze. But they had become a great tourist attraction. So when a friend said he'd never seen a penguin while we were imbibing a few beers in the pub, I promised to rectify that on the way home.

In the dark, with only a couple of cigarette lighters, we found our way onto the beach where I immediately nearly tripped over a pair of penguins. I called over my friend in in the glow of our two cigarette lighters, his first sighting of penguins was of two having it off complete with mating calls and flipper flapping.

The train line from Simons Town into the city was really useful and Glenn was there to help if I needed it. So, soon, I had the boat stored up and was ready to head out into the Atlantic.

The teeth I had capped in Mayotte were doing fine but I was still having major problems with the rest of them. I had found no cure in South Africa so now I planned to get them fixed in St. Helena. As I knew from my last visit to this little bit of Britain in the middle of the South Atlantic, there was a dentist there and the work would not cost me anything.

There were no dramas leaving; no fog or nasty wind. But there was definitely a nip in the air. Summer was over. As the boat scudded north it got warmer and soon I could prance around the deck again without warm clothes, or any for that matter. The fishing as usual was fantastic. I pulled in tuna and dolphin fish whenever I needed and twelve days after rounding the Cape of Good Hope, St. Helena popped up over the horizon.

The lady in Mozambique who had organized the rugby viewing, had asked me to say hello to her family if and when I was over in St. Helena. It turned that she was related to the customs officer who came on board to clear me in, so the story of my meeting in Pemba got around the village in no time. I said hello again to Ann in her restaurant and then went off to the dentist.

It turned out the dentist was really busy – or so he said. Maybe he was frightened by the sight of my rotten teeth. But anyway he refused to do the job. As an alternative, he said he could get in touch with his associate in Ascension Island. This dentist was 600 miles to the northwest but he was not so busy. So an appointment was made for me there.

I would like to have spent more time on St. Helena but I really did want my teeth fixed. I cleared out and went for a last beer in a bar overlooking the bay. Three guys invited me over to join them. They introduce themselves as the Baco Brothers, Johann, Arno and Peter. They had just sailed up from Cape Town on a catamaran they had built there. It had been their first attempt at sailing and they wanted to know what all the fuss was about. Members of the Royal Cape Yacht Club had warned them of giant waves, howling winds, and every chance of a shipwreck. They had in fact had a similar trip to mine, extremely uneventful. We drank more beer and then I left; but we would meet again.

Ascension was quite different to St Helena. It was more hilly than mountainous and the town more functional than the historic village. It was a major telecommunications site for Britain and I think America. It also had an airport.

I anchored close to the moorings and rowed the rubber ducky to the wharf. It had the same steps and platforms as St. Helena. The swell was small but I hauled the dinghy up onto the wharf and tied it off to the railing. It was early, so I had done the paperwork and was at the dentist by midmorning.

It was no good. The dentist himself inspired no confidence, the equipment looked second-hand or from a museum, and I was going to have to pay. I should have stayed in that bar in St. Helena and drunk more beer. With that thought in my head, I went back into town. The bar was busy, it was lunch time and they sold McEwan's Export, a prized Scottish beer that I had not tasted in years.

With a belly full of beer, I was feeling a little less grumpy but I had another surprise in store. When I arrived at the wharf the sea had changed dramatically. The rollers were coming in and the water rose almost to the top of the wall. Then it subsided maybe 15 feet or more down, before coming up again. A huge surf was breaking on the bank offshore and pounded on the steep beach to my left. I wondered how *Sea Loone* was faring

I pushed the dinghy into the water on the rise, holding a long painter. Then, when it came up a second time, I dived into it holding the oars. I landed in a heap but no problem. I sorted myself out and paddled out.

When I got to *Sea Loone*, she was going up and down dramatically and the swells broke into surf only meters behind. Fortunately, with no wind, there was little strain on the chain and anchor. I wasn't going to hang around though and half an hour later we had the anchor and sails up and we were heading west for Brazil. My stay in Ascension hadn't been much more than six hours.

I was now well north of Salvador on the Brazilian coast. So instead of heading south again, I turned west for Recife, once known as Pernambuco. I had been in touch again with Clark Stede in Chile and he was to fly over and meet me in Recife. Michelle was back in Australia

The rainy season was well under way as I approached the coast and the clear blue Ocean turned a muddy brown. Having cleared in, I anchored off a small restaurant inside the harbour facing the city. The water was filthy and the city was not much cleaner. But there was a market across the other side which had mountains of fresh fruit and vegetables.

I had acquired an email address in Richards Bay but was still pretty lost with the computer. But I found a local office to help contact Clark. It was all a bit difficult and up in the air.

Finally, one night, a huge storm passed over blowing a hooley and bucketing down with rain. A huge French trimaran which was anchored next to me, dragged its anchor and in the pitch dark was heading towards a low bridge on the city side. I chased it with the dinghy and woke up the crew, by which time they were getting very close to going under the bridge and leaving the mast behind. They managed to motor clear and I had to row like hell to get back to *Sea Loone*, soaked to the skin and freezing.

Next day the French guys arrived with a bottle of whisky as thanks and I decided it was time to get out. Islands of rubbish were floating past including branches of trees, a dead dog, and a pram, fortunately without the baby in it.

Clark never appeared and I didn't hear from him again for some time. I sailed north 100 miles or so and turned into Cabedelo at the mouth of the large river running up to Joao Pessoa. The approaches are shallow but there is a buoyed channel into the river mouth. I then tried to find my own way up the river to an anchorage and small jetty half way to Joao Pessoa. I dodged the sandbanks and arrived without going aground.

There were five boats already anchored there, more than I'd seen since Cape Town. Three were catamarans including the Baco Brothers I'd met in St. Helena. There was also the little Wharran catamaran I'd had tea with becalmed off Cape Agulhas. The other two were Taffy, a Welshman, his wife Shirley, and his "crew", a South African grey parrot called "Rubbish". There was also a Swedish single-hander, a young Olympic athlete with blonde hair, blue eyes and lots of muscles. The third catamaran was German. The wife, Bettina, ran a small bar at the foot of the jetty and the husband seemed to be doing a survey of the night life in the area. He was rarely seen.

With a train service down into Cabedelo or up into the city, it was a convenient place to anchor; although rowing ashore was hard work when the tide was ebbing strongly. Bettina's bar was popular most evenings and in another bar just down the river we could play a Brazilian form of pool. There were lots of pretty girls. They dressed provocatively and danced provocatively with smiles that would melt your heart. The youngest of the Baco Brothers got hooked and when Ron Llewellyn, a friend from Richards Bay, arrived he was caught in a matter of days.

A quiet few drinks in the bar could rapidly develop into fiesta, carnival or party. But this was Brazil. One evening a huge coach motored down the bumpy Lane. A dance group in native dress had arrived, complete with music. They danced and twirled around for an hour then jumped back in the bus and drove off.

Another evening a car arrived at Bettina's bar, backed up and opened the boot to reveal a massive sound system. They took over the place for the night. There were no complaints; it was fun.

The nasty weather I had caught coming to Simons Town had dismasted the little Wharren catamaran and he had drifted into Hout Bay. There he again had to bail out the two hulls and then find another mast. Undaunted, he found a crazy American as crew, and here they were in Brazil huddled under a canvas tent half the time in the pouring rain.

Bettina found me a dentist. She introduced me to him in the bar and we arranged to meet the following morning to have a look at my problems. He arrived at the wharf on a large motorbike. I jumped on the back and we shot off towards João Pessoa.

His clinic was new and looked unused compared to the place in Ascension. He certainly didn't seem to be very busy. But anyway, it was agreed that all the top teeth other than the two crowns, were to come out. The bottom set were all right. So then, back on the motorbike, we went into town. At the next stop we passed through a storeroom of equipment into another room with a dental chair. Here the technician made casts of my teeth. Days later, we made another visit on the motorbike to the technician's place and then a week later the teeth were ready.

By this time, everybody knew when the horror day was coming. All the teeth were to come out and the new ones jammed in immediately.

We took the motorbike to the dental clinic and the deed was done. Everything was pretty numb so no real pain. The new teeth were put in place and we were back on the motorbike back to the boat zooming down the highway. Although my mouth was filling with spit and blood, I dared not open it in case I spat out the new teeth.

When we stopped at the bar, I jumped off and dived into the bushes to clear my mouth. Back at the bar I had a reception committee that received my new white smile and I got a row of caparinias, rum and squashed limes that would take over from the dentists pain killers. An hour later I had no worries in the world.

The teeth had all come out cleanly and I had no problems after, which says a lot for the dentist. The total cost was one hundred and fifty dollars for everything, brilliant! The only problem, if it was a problem, was that my Brazilian girlfriend, who would stand on the end of the wharf and call out her love to me on the boat, was not happy with my new smile, and left me.

Bettina had worked for a radio station in Germany. Using quite a complicated tape recorder, she made weekly programs which she sent off for broadcasting back home. A while later she wrote a book about her life on the boat in Brazil.

We had more than one leaving party but finally, Bettina and I shared a market porter with his wheelbarrow, to store up fruit and vegetables and contraband cigarettes. I had heard from Nano and Mino, the couple that had lost their mast in Diego Suarez. They were in French Guyana, just around the corner. They had sent me a shopping list. So by the time Bettina and I had finished shopping, we had a massive load to pack into the taxi to take us home.

It would've been nice to have stayed on, seeing Brazil out of the rainy season when the beaches and bars really come alive. But arriving on a yacht, you were given only a six months' stay with absolutely no exceptions. So we all had to move on.

I thought of stopping in Fortaleza and again in some small islands just before the Amazon but I kept going. Having passed Natal and turned the corner, I had the wind and current behind me and it was easy sailing northwest towards the Caribbean.

One evening two hundred miles or more off the mouth of the Amazon, with strange up swellings in the water from the river, the sun had set and the full moon was just rising. Directly in front to me a strange shooting star came up over the horizon from the west. With strange effects on the water and the moon rising with little or no wind, it was totally unreal. Trailing a long fiery tail, the shooting star was aimed just slightly to the north of me. Now high in the sky and quite close, it suddenly broke up; one piece heading onwards and the other piece curving down trailing smoke and hitting the sea directly north of me.

By this time I was no longer worried. I had just witnessed the launching of one of the huge new Arian 5 rockets from the European space center in Kourou, which was where I was heading.

I arrived off Isles de Salut, Devil's Island, at dusk, having made huge allowances for the current. I recognized Nano & Mino's boat anchored there and turned the engine on to take me the last few hundred yards.

As I put the engine into gear, there were horrible noises. I opened up the engine box and saw that the gearbox was moving around independent of the engine. I stopped the engine and drifted on in the right direction. But now the depth sounder stopped working. By this time, Nano arrived in his dinghy but I had drifted close enough so threw in the anchor. What a palaver!

But it was good to have dinner with my friends, a few drinks, and then a good night's sleep. In the morning, I was able to sort myself out.

Next day I offloaded the vegetables, cheese, cigarettes, and booze and had another look at the engine. All the bolts had come loose and two had actually broken. I tightened up the loose bolts and hoped that would be enough to hold things together to get us up the river into Kourou.

It happened to be the weekend and Nano had a few days off from working in an engineering works. Mino had to be back the next day. She was one of the announcers on the local radio. So the next morning they shepherded me across the bar and into the river. Here I was able to anchor down from the town and close to a sailing school for kids sailing Optimist dinghies. Here the tidal stream wasn't quite as vicious as off the town, but still a worry if I was going to have to pull the engine.

In the end, the only real problem repairing the engine was finding the odd-sized bolts Volvo had used to bolt on the gearbox. The broken studs came out without a problem. Meanwhile, the Swedish Olympian had arrived and sorted out my other problem. He had a spare depth sounder of the same old-fashioned type as mine and, after a little negotiating, I managed to buy it off him.

The rocket range was now a huge going concern and very successful. The town was still really scruffy and like anywhere French, horribly expensive. There was a small marina where Nano kept their boat but the bars and restaurants was still prohibitively expensive. So the yachties still sat in the street or on a convenient park bench, to drink beer bought in the local Chinese store.

It was still a little early to arrive in the Caribbean, so I was happy to spend some time and practice my awful French. Nano and Mino had settled in and bought a Peugeot, a very small, typically French car. With the car we made two interesting trips inland. The first was to a village inland from Cayenne, the capital. Once you leave the coast road, which is sealed, conditions rapidly deteriorate. The village we were going to was popular with the people from Cayenne so the road was not too bad.

We passed through some dense forests and arrived in a huge valley which had been taken over by a population of Cambodians. The forest had been tamed and the land cultivated. The large village was native Cambodian with houses raised up high above the ground and a big market complete with stalls and eating places. It looked as if the whole valley had been lifted straight out of Cambodia and put down here.

We bought fresh vegetables and ate a meal of noodles with pork and vegetables. The people, small and smiling, were noisy and busy. I try to imagine what they would achieve in say twenty years, when they had already managed this in only a couple.

Our second trip out with the car was a little more adventurous. We took the coast road west to the Maroni River. There is a beach at the mouth of the river where the leather back turtles come ashore but unfortunately we were not there at the right time of year.

Turning inland, we came to Saint Laurent, the site of another old French penal colony. Across the wide muddy river was Surinam where petrol was a fraction of the price of French Guyana. Despite the large customs office built on the shoreline, there was a busy trade going on. Driving down the street, a guy would jump out from the alleyway, negotiate, and then be followed by young guys with jerry cans to quickly fill your tank and then dash off.

Loaded with petrol, we decided to drive up country to a waterfall reputed to be the largest and best in the country. We followed the map as the road got worse and worse and the sun got lower in the sky. At one point most of the road had slipped down the hillside. At another, a deep erosion channel looked as if it would swallow us up and the ruts were getting close to impossible for our small wheels.

We arrived at the end of the road at dusk. When we stopped the car, the mosquitoes descended in droves so we ate our bread and cheese with the windows wound up and then attempted to get some sleep. The heat of the day soon disappeared and it got really cold. It was one of my most uncomfortable nights ever.

We had avoided the mosquitoes but by early dawn, the ants had arrived, attracted by the remains of the food. Fortunately they did not bite. There were thousands of them. Gradually, the night's orchestra of tree frogs and whatever else joined in the cacophony had died down as the sun appeared over the forest trees.

It was agony climbing out of the car stretching our tortured limbs, but at least we had a spectacular waterfall to look forward only a short walk down the track. Not so, the waterfall was a huge disappointment. In fact it wasn't really waterfall at all just a series of rapids. Its only saving grace was providing us with a pool of water to slide into and wash away the grime of the trip.

The little car got back down to the coast road and on to Kourou without a hiccup, by which time we had more or less driven all the roads available in the country. There were a few small airfields inland servicing the old gold mines and rivers that were normally used for transport. But for the main part, the interior was left to the native people and nature.

October 2000 came around. There were no signs of any late hurricanes in the Caribbean so I set out for Grenada. I was keen to get some of the jewellery and carvings sold and get some money coming in. The piggy bank was almost empty.

The weather was good to me, no fishing boats appeared during the night, there were no squalls and I cruised quietly into Prickly Bay, Grenada. I dropped my anchor and complete my second circumnavigation of the world!

Book Four

Period: 2000-2013

1

THERE WAS NO time to rest and reflect. The following morning I set about sorting out my jewellery inventory on board.

I had a full selection of sand dollar earrings which had done so well during my last spell in the Caribbean. I had the bone carvings and pendants with the dolphins, whales, turtles etc. I had the native bone fish hooks, some with fancy lashings and some with inlaid pearls or the semi-precious stones bought in Cape Town. I had the Makonda carvings of families, skeletons, busts, letter-openers, walking sticks and so on. And finally I had lots of shells, tiger cowrie, tritons trumpets and helmet shells.

Before moving on I already knew that I would not want to stay in the Caribbean any longer than it would need to refill the piggy bank. I came up with a figure of $20,000. That would buy me at least four or five years sailing, by which time I would hope to find another money source.

The boat didn't need a lot of work. Although the engine wasn't really happy, it would at least get me through the Panama Canal and the canal itself was probably going to be expensive to transit. But $20,000 became the target to aim for.

Looking at the cargo I recorded that, at best, it would make only one third of the money I needed. So I knew had to either make a lot more jewellery or find a job and work for someone, not a pleasant thought.

Grenada was a good place to start my sales campaign. I had done business before with Jean who had a really interesting shop called Tikal near the Carenage in St. George's. I then found a small shop on Grande Anse where all the tourist hotels were. With Grenada covered, I sailed north to Cariacou, and then to Bequia and Mustique in the Grenadines all had shops I had done business with before. This made life easier. In St Lucia, I found some new customers in Rodney Bay and then called into Maogony Artisanat in the Saints north of Dominica.

When I arrived in English Harbour, I was surprised to find none of the big yachts at anchor. By November, they normally arrived to meet their agents at the beginning of the season. I cleared in and walked through to the yacht club in Falmouth Harbour where I saw that a giant new dock had been built. This was now where the armada of huge yachts and motor ships were tied up.

I went to see Scrim, the scrimshaw man, and did some business with an English couple with a gallery in Nelson's Dockyard. Then in the evening I wandered into the pub for a few beers at happy hour. I joined a large group loudly celebrating their arrival. When I went to leave at the end of happy hour, the girl at the head of the table persuaded me to stay promising to buy my beer.

I am easy persuaded. The girl was the chief stewardess on a motor yacht which looked more like the size of a cruise ship. They were all part of the fifty odd crew on board. I don't how long the ship was but I was impressed by the fact that, on one side, it had a fifty foot, fully-rigged yacht hanging on davits.

From English Harbour, I sailed over to St. Barts or St. Barthelemy to give the Island its full name. I anchored fore and aft behind Gordie's boat which was on a mooring in exactly the same spot I had seen it years before. Gordie had a new workshop in Gustavia and I walked in to find him working away on a huge canvas awning.

Work stopped and we had a cup of tea, the first of many. Miriam, Gordie's Peruvian wife, had become a serious alcoholic and had run away to St. Martin leaving Gordie with the two kids. The daughter had now flown the nest and was also in St. Martin, working. The lad had been to a number of different schools and was not doing well. Gordie was still living on the boat and now had a lovely petite French girlfriend, Noela.

So I settled into St Barts with Christmas on the horizon and the tourist season starting. I did a round of the shops successfully and then helped Gordie in his business. He was as usual snowed under with jobs at the beginning of the season, working a seven-day week and long hours. After a few cock-ups, I was able to take his finished jobs, awnings, sunshades, roller blinds etc. and fix them in place; usually in restaurants but also in villas. This freed him up to cut and sew the next job on the list. He paid me well, probably too well, but that was Gordie.

My sister and her husband Paul had organized a holiday for themselves in the British Virgin Islands. It was my suggestion, thinking I could take them sailing for a few days in the relatively calm water there. They were arriving in February.

In preparation for their trip, I left St Barts and sailed to St. Martin to do some business and then on to the Virgin Islands. I first stopped in St. John's in the US Virgin Islands, where a very fat, black, objectionable, immigration lady stamped "Cancelled" on my multiple indefinite visa and gave me forty eight hours to get out. Charming!

There was a cruise ship anchored off with a couple of thousand gay and lesbian tourists on board. They mobbed the shops with limp wrists and pouting lips, dressed to kill. It didn't help my sales campaign but at the end of a frustrating morning, I found a shop interested in all my remaining Makonda carvings. The really big pieces were already in a gallery in St. Barts. The following morning, I brought everything ashore and the deal was done.

I could now concentrate on the jewellery which was much easier to carry around and left a lot more space on the boat.

I beat back up to the BVI and anchored in Sopers Hole where my sister Di and husband Paul were due to arrive on the ferry, having flown from London into St. Thomas. Their holiday started badly. Di's back problems had returned the day before leaving. I met her hobbling off the ferry with two walking sticks. Fortunately the hotel room they were staying in had a jacuzzi which helped, but the only sailing we were able to do was a quick trip across to Jost Van Dyke and back. Paul refused to sail at all.

For me, the BVI had really gone downhill with hundreds of half built houses, rubbish everywhere, unfriendly locals and awash with cruise-ship tourists. The only highlight was me meeting Jamie and Marge on their yacht *Ave del Mar*.

We had both been in New Zealand both times we had been there. I asked them to invite Di and Paul on board. Their boat is, if anything, smaller and more cramped than mind. But I wanted to show the family that there were, in fact, others living a life much like mine.

As soon as their holiday was over and they had left, I beat back to St. Barts. Gordie was not quite so busy now and asked me to do some work on his boat. Helmut, his German friend had a source of teak from Trinidad so I rebuilt the cockpit and, having done that, rebuilt the main saloon.

May had arrived and with Easter over, the season had ended. Gordie still had plenty of work in the hurricane season and only moved the boat when there was a serious threat announced. He then took the boat into the lagoon in St. Martin. He and the boat had survived some serious hurricanes but on different occasions, the boat had been thrown up on the beach, the bow had been stove in and the rudder torn off.

Me, I was not going to stick around to take any risks. I sailed south to spend the next five months on the south coast of Grenada, hopefully watching all hurricanes passing north of me.

On the way south I visited all the shops. All of them reordered stuff and some invested a lot more. I would pass by again on the way back north. Usually the shops did not have a lot of money available for buying my stuff during this five month off-season.

When I arrived at Hog Island I found a number of old friends. Plastic from Zululand had brought over the huge Wharran catamaran in the hope of finding work for it. Mick and Allison arrived on *Lily Maid* which was now nearly 100 years old. The Aussies had arrived from St. Martin with Shane the Irishman who ran Atlas Deliveries. So the bar in the village would be busy.

Meanwhile, Wendy from Durban had sailed her aluminium yacht across and had opened a sewing shop in Woburn. It was a good crowd of people and Roger, who years ago had been persuaded to bring cold beers over to Hog Island on a Sunday, now had a small busy bar on the beach. There we could have a cold sundowner and the locals would sit in the corner and build huge joins to smoke us all out.

One day in September, Plastic arrived back from the village very excited. He'd just been in the village bar and on the television had seen the planes hit the Twin Towers in New York. It was September 11. We all took to our dinghy's and motored around to the marina at Mt. Hartman Bay where the Moorings Charter Co. were located.

There we found at least twenty Americans glued to the TV watching the Twin Towers get hit, burn and then collapse. We were all in shock that day!

The following day, back at our Hog island anchorage, the discussion started. I have to admit that there wasn't a lot of sympathy for the Americans but no one had any idea of how that single event would impinge on everyone's lives especially with respect to freedom of movement all over the world.

In October, I took stock of my first year. I shook the piggy bank and found I had managed to save $5,000. It was one quarter of what I needed before setting my sights on the Panama Canal once more. Unfortunately, that did not mean three more years, as my stock of jewellery was now seriously depleted and my Makonda carvings and shells had all gone. I had to do better.

I was back in St Barts by November, put the anchors down and was busy again with Gordie. As usual, he had an enormous amount of work to do with everyone preparing for the beginning of the season.

Eden Rock, a very exclusive small hotel, was one of Gordie's major customers. The main building was perched on a steep hillock in the centre of a long beautiful beach protected by a barrier reef. There were two restaurants and several cottages with rooms built into the steep cliff. There were awnings everywhere. Their clientelle included rock stars, film stars, billionaires of all sorts, all of whom could afford to pay thousands of dollars for just one night.

David, the owner, was a Yorkshireman who had made his first millions in Maggie Thatcher's privatization of Britain's public transport system. He ran the hotel partly, I think, as his private playground. His chief helper, another Englishman, was returning home and David mentioned to Gordie that he might be interested in employing me directly to organize improvements and sort out problems in the hotel.

When we met it was a bit of a"War of the Roses". I mentioned an hourly rate and David suggested half. I pointed out that I would initially be still helping out Gordie as I could not leave him in the lurch at the beginning of the season. David offered me a new scooter and a phone. I refused the phone but took the scooter and a half way reasonable hourly rate, no set hours and no overtime, but no limit to the hours I worked. I was to be paid in French francs monthly .

So it began. Long hours, seven days a week but some interesting and fun jobs with always lots of problems to solve. The roof leaked above the Garbo room,yes she'd stayed there. The drip landed next to the canopied four-poster bed. Nobody had yet been able to stop it. I looked under the eaves and found the drip. Where it landed on the ceiling I hung some guttering and tied it with string. The leak was now directed down the nearby wall well away from the bed, so problem solved.

Another problem one that took longer to fix was that the live lobsters were getting eaten by moray eels in the lobster pens under the dock. The eels could wriggle in anywhere and were highly motivated.

The hotel was paying a lot of money to store old or used equipment and furniture. Some stuff was in a room next to Gordie's workshop and some in two other stores across the island. David decided to get rid of the lot and I had to organize a sale. My incentive was that I was to receive a quarter of the proceeds.

The Dutch brothers whom I had first met in St. Helena and spent time with in Brazil, had just arrived in their catamaran. I asked them to be salesman for me on the day of the sale as I had other work to do. They had bought a lot of

Brazilian hammocks which they also brought along to the sale. Fortunately they had a friend with them who spoke French, though not very well.

I advertised in the local paper that the sale will take place at Gordie's workshop in Gustavia. On sale day, a large crowd appeared before we were ready to start. It was a riot. I had told the lads that everything had to go whatever the price. After all, if it didn't sell I didn't get my 25%. There were hammocks hung all the way down the street, a huge brass bed parked in the street outside, toilets on the pavement. By the evening, virtually everything had gone, a huge success and the Baco brothers hadn't had so much fun for ages!

After Easter when I told David I was preparing to go south, he wasn't happy. But there was no way I was risking the boat. Anyway, the hotel was more or less closed down for the hurricane season. The piggy bank was bulging and my mother surprisingly, had said she would pay for my airfare if I flew home. I had been away ten years since going home with Tracey.

I hopped down the island chain again and nudged the boat into the mangroves on Hog Island. With three anchors out on the bow and the stern tied into the mangroves I was happy to leave the boat. There were plenty of people to keep an eye on it and, as the saying goes. "June – Too Soon" for hurricanes, which, as I've said earlier, isn't always true.

I flew from the new airport on the south west tip of Grenada. It had been started by the Cubans but reluctantly finished by the Americans after they invaded. Mother greeted me with the question "why have you come home?". From this I deduced that I wasn't going to get my airfare refunded. An hour later, when making a few phone calls to friends down the road to say I was home, I was told off for making free use of her telephone.

I'm afraid I lost my temper with her and said a lot of things that had been stored up inside me over the years and which were better left unsaid. I then stormed out of the house. I wandered the streets in the dark and ended up at the door of my friend Kenny Hall. Kenny had helped me to build *Sea Loone*, years before. At least I had a bed for the night. After so many years away it was not a good homecoming.

I then went and to stay with my sister then with my cousin and saw a few friends. I had asked Sue, who had organized an amazing gathering of friends last time I was home, if she could have another go. Sue being a very organized and successful businesswoman surpassed herself.

I arrived from the Lake District to stay with Sue and Guy in Caldy on the Wirral just days before I was due to leave again. We drove out to the Wheatsheaf, an old thatched pub in the picturesque Raby Village, not far away. People started arriving from all over the country, many of whom I hadn't seen since first setting sail.

Maybe the most remarkable was an old girlfriend from when I first left home to go to University. Elaine had married an American airmen and I had not seen her since those days. She arrived in a taxi and I heard her laugh before I ever saw her. With that laugh, it couldn't have been anyone else even after nearly forty years.

After the pub, the party continued at Sue and Guys lovely home. It was the highlight of my trip!

I spent the last day at home with my mother, there was an unspoken truce but I was still pretty upset. When I left it was the last time I was to see her. Next day it was up-and-away back to Grenada and *Sea Loone*.

Back in the anchorage behind Hog Island on Grenada, all was well. I had a few jobs to do on the boat, made some jewellery and went diving for octopus, crayfish, and the occasional squat lobster which lived in the roof of caves in the reef.

There were occasional trips into the capital, St. George's and its market which involved the fifteen minute dinghy ride into Woburn village where, for EC$2.50, you could pick up the crowded minibus into town. Care had to be taken not to sit next to a large local mama because if the bus filled up you could get seriously squashed.

On the way back stopping for a cold beer at my local rum shop, Nimrods in the village, could easily develop into a day long piss up especially if Don Malmo or any of the other Australians arrived.

I set off early in October to get back to St. Barts and claim a good spot in the anchorage for the season. David in Eden Rock had not mentioned my working again in the hotel at the same time hadn't sacked me. He did however take the scooter back. Gordie was happy to lend me his car when he wasn't using it.

When I went back to the hotel, David was busy in Europe; but there were obviously lots of things that needed doing before the guests started arriving. I sat down and made a list, then went to see the manager, David's sister-in-law. She gave me the go-ahead to get started, so I began. I had Gordie make a number of new awnings and repaired others. The chef wanted some modifications in the main kitchen and by the time David arrived, I had a number of jobs going on all at the same time.

David reminded me of my mother's welcome when he returned and gruffly wanted to know what I was doing there. I showed him what had been done and what was being done; and by the time I finished talking he was pointing out other things that needed fixing.

However, while I was away, David had taken on a German guy to replace me. He was giving him a cottage, a car and paying him through the hotel. He seemed pretty busy doing other things so I just carried on often finding jobs that needed doing and things that needed fixing even before waiting to be asked.

By now the French franc had disappeared and it was Euro's. From the start, their value against the dollar was shooting up. I soon hit my target figure of $20,000.

As the season progressed my jobs petered out but not before I had a final fling. A millionaire property tycoon from California had booked the Eden Rock for a huge company party. The beach restaurant would be closed for a few days while a stage was built on the beach. The Beach Boys were coming in from California to perform.

We had to erect a huge marquee which would cover the beach and, because I was the only one around who knew how it was rigged, I got the job. I employed a dozen local guys and my friend Hans Klarr, who had just arrived on his crab-claw rigged Polynesian catamaran.

Two thirty foot poles had to be set up. While Hans wire-spliced, the others were pulling and heaving on the poles and then hauling up the enormous canvas. There were a few minor tears in the material so Gordie was hand stitching them, way up in the air. I shouted and cursed in French to get the lads heaving things tight. I then found myself praying that we wouldn't have any nasty squalls blowing through in the next twenty-four hours.

Everything was torn out of the restaurant, plants and flowers arrived, drapes were hung and finally everything was ready. The party people arrived, had dinner up on the Rock then went through some private bonding rituals on the stage before the band got started.

A huge crowd gathered from all over the island on the beach behind the stage and the Beach Boys played as much to them as to the Californians in front of them. But as it was Saturday night everything had to stop at midnight and a million dollars worth of partying suddenly came to an end.

By lunchtime the next day, I had the beach back to how it was and the restaurant back in business. I got my small share of the million and could call it quits. I was ready to sail away. David had just bought the hotel next door and had huge plans for the next year. It was quite satisfying for me to refuse the work after two years of our on-again, off-again relationship.

I sailed south back down the islands, on past Grenada to Trinidad. It was my first visit and the Anchorage was crowded with lots of tugboat and oil rigs being moved around. But I found a small marina, Humming Bird Marina, owned by Harold La Borde and named after all his boats. He remembered our night in Sydney with Mike Bailes years ago and I was able to bring him news of Mike, who was still in New Zealand. He found me a quiet little spot at the back of the Marina for the few days I was staying which was very kind of him.

Amazingly in the marina there was a huge catamaran called something like *Dee Cat* which had sailed out from Liverpool. I was told that, unfortunately, the owner had gone home to England with medical problems. Then I found out he was the policeman, Dave, who had turned up at my boat-building site in Meols in the police panda car so many years ago. It was the day when I took delivery of the steel rods for the boat, in the very early days in my boat-building project.

I bought a drum of anti-fouling paint in Trinidad and sailed up to Cariacou to haul her out and work on the bottom. The small yard lifted me out with a travel-lift and cleaned off the bottom with a water blaster. A friend, Mike, came to give me a hand and even with a break for lunch we had the boat ready to go back in the water by late afternoon. The yard owner thought I was joking when I told him that I was ready for him to put me back in already.

The rest of the summer was spent in Hog Island. It finished with a series of leaving parties. One day I actually had the anchor up to leave, only to be almost run down by another friend sailing in; so it was anchor back down and more beer!

But at last, after making my final visits to the shops, I left. In Bequia I watched the semi-final of the World Cup rugby. The reception was dreadful and not helped by the pouring rain. England seemed headed for the final so I sped north to be in St. Barts to watch it.

Sure enough, England won the semi-final game and I watched the final together with two other English guys, one a restauranteur I knew; the other my financial advisor, a banker who specializes in currency movements. We won! I was more surprised than elated and I was also told by the financier that my euros would continue to strengthen against the dollar. Maybe the piggy bank would burst? It was a good day!

A final party on the roof of Gordie's workshop overlooking Gustavia Harbour and I was ready to go. Previously my route to Panama had been from Grenada via Venezuela and the Dutch ABC islands, Aruba, Bonaire and Curacao. But there have been problems along the Venezuelan coast since a hurricane had caused huge damage and left a lot of people homeless and destitute.

A boat I knew from Port Elizabeth in South Africa had been boarded and robbed. They arrived in Panama City in serious straits.

Apart from that, the Dutch brothers had headed for Cuba when they left St. Barts. They were in a place called Luperon where they were having a fun time. The boys were serious party people and to spend more than one yeart in one place it was obviously worth checking out. It turned out that they had in fact never got as far as Cuba, Luperon was on the north coast of the Dominican Republic.

In a last discussion with Gordie we agreed that in seven years time when we were both seventy we would probably both be penniless wrecks but a small gun would sort the problem. In fact I now had 30,000 Euros to leave with which, carefully managed would get me close to three score and ten. It would also get me more than half way round the world. We would see.

Leaving St. Barts I called into St. Martin to buy new batteries for the boat. I also bought a Sony video camera with which I was going to make films that would make me rich and famous. I stopped for the night in the Virgin Islands and in Culebra. Then, with the wind behind me in perfect trade wind weather, I sailed west along the north coast of Puerto Rico. I passed the entrance to the San Juan harbour into which I had fled from a building hurricane in 1979. Then two more days across the Mona Passage to Hispaniola and then along the coast of the Dominican Republic, and I was off the entrance to Luperon.

Keeping the large hotel on the beach to the west, I followed the sketch I had been given and promptly went aground on a sandbank. I kedged myself off and cautiously moved deeper into the bay where I found the Dutch boys' catamaran. I anchored close by and within minutes a small work boat filled with officials arrived. There were six of them, all with forms to fill in and a fee to be paid. I paid with dollar bills and they all left happily. It hadn't been too expensive.

Johanne then arrived from the catamaran which I had first seen St. Helena in the mid-south Atlantic. We went ashore for cold beer and to catch up on each others news. The younger brother was in Holland looking after the business, and the other brother was down the coast indulging his latest passion, kite boarding.

To get ashore there was a long rough stone jetty coming-out of the mangroves with some floating pontoons where you could tie up the dinghy. The road ran inland from the jetty with the town strung along it. The rickety sheds with galvanized iron roofs became brick buildings as we moved inland and on to higher ground. Further on, there were shops and a bank which took over from the restaurants and bars.

In between chasing the girls and drinking vast amounts of beer and rum, Johanne and his brothers had rented part of a building and a yard. They were going into the business of making small fibreglass boats. They had a mold made to layup a dinghy about sixteen feet long and when I arrived, were preparing to make the first one. It was probably fortunate that I was there to explain some of the finer points. It was all completely new to them.

I quickly settled down into a fairly indolent life after St. Barts. In the daytime I helped dinghy production and in the evening share a "servicio" of rum with Johanne in the local bar. My Spanish wasn't so good but I soon realized that if you went into small scruffy bars at the bottom of the street, the owners and clientele were Haitians who spoke a sort of French. So conversation was much easier for me.

The other advantage was that the price and service were much better and the girls in the whorehouse nextdoor to our favourite bar, kept us entertained. Each evening a table was put out for us in the street, a large bowl of ice, a small bottle of rum and a bottle of lemonade. This was a "servicio". It cost less than one beer at St. Barts prices. The ice was continuously replenished. We were pampered.

Christmas came and went. It was now 2004. The boys were building a huge new thatch-roofed barn for their boat building. I was getting itchy feet so it was time to head for San Blas and the Canal before I got trapped by the rum and the girls.

Before I left, I anchored out in the clear water near the harbour entrance and scraped off the barnacles. Then I continued west to the Windward Passage between Haiti and Cuba. From there I turned south.

My first impression of the San Blas islands was that nothing had changed. I anchored behind one small island in crystal clear water and the following day went swimming around the reefs. I came back with a big slipper lobster and an even bigger spider crab which had been hiding under a dead platform coral, just as they used to.

There was not much water traffic. I saw a few Kuna Indians around in their canoes as well as a couple of sailing yachts quite far away. I decided to sail on to Nargana Village and find my Kuna friend, Jaime Filos. By now his baby who had been a ten-year-old boy last time, would be a twenty-year-old man.

When I arrived off the village, change was obvious. There were a number of yachts, some tied to docks others anchored off. There were restaurants and bars and even, in one, a pool table. Unfortunately Jaime and all the family were in Panama City. However his aunt was in the village and owned one of the restaurants. I showed her the photo of the family in nineteen eighty-three and then ten years later. More relatives arrived to see them.

In the restaurant they were using a cheese grater for grating coconut to squeeze for coconut milk. It was really inefficient so I brought my Polynesian rap ashore. They were amazed at how much easier it made the job and it did a round of the village before being returned to me. Within days one guy had fabricated a duplicate using a big old spoon. I took my new video camera up the Diablo River and filmed some woodpeckers and a large dragon-like lizard that could race across the surface of the river without sinking. Then I spent more time in the outer Islands diving and beach combing.

The population of San Blas had doubled between my first two visits. Now maybe the explosion was slowing down but not much. The coconuts and lobsters were no longer going to support the people. The visiting yachts now paid fees and the cruiseships, yes there was a cruise ship which visited, presumably also paid money, though I doubt it was very much.

Jamie and presumably a lot of other people had had to leave the islands for the big city to support their families. The closed guarded culture of the islands which existed when I first visited was falling apart, inevitable but sad.

I stopped for a couple of days in Porto Bello to film the ruins which had been tidied up for the coach tours from Panama City or Colon. Then I went on to the canal and anchored on the Flats to start the paperwork for yet another transit of the famous waterway.

2

THE FIRST TIME through the canal I paid fifty dollars for the boat to be measured for its "Panama Tonnage" and then paid for the transit. The Panama Canal Company had demanded a down payment of $100 but had sent more than twenty dollars back to England after I had arrived in the Pacific. The refund arrived at my mother's as a cheque from the Canal Company The second time, much the same happened but, without the measurement fee, I paid much less and got a lot more back.

This time, with the canal now entirely Panamanian, the story was going to be very different, as I soon found out. They first demanded an initial down payment of $2,000. I was promised that more than half of this amount would be returned to me as long as the transit went smoothly. However, if I caused any delays or any problems there would be no refund. I had to maintain a speed of five knots or more. This was going to be very difficult for *Sea Loone* but there was a lot of money at stake.

Panama ran on US dollars but the banks provided no exchange facilities. There were money changes in town but they were offering ridiculous rates of exchange. I finally had to use my brother-in-law, Paul, to arrange payment from the UK.

I found four line handlers to come with me through the canal. We were to leave in the late afternoon and lock-up into Gatton Lake where we would stop for the night before crossing the lake in the morning.

There were two other boats transiting with me, one a large American catamaran, the other a French ketch. They could both easily do six or seven knots so I was bound to be lagging behind. To make matters worse, our pilot arrived late so we were already miles behind the two other boats even on the way to the first lock.

It was dark as we tied up in the lock and pitch dark by the time we exited into the lake. The other two yachts were already in the lake and had found moorings to tie to. Meanwhile our pilot was busy on the radio and we were told that we would be carrying on to cross the lake in the dark. We would then anchor on the other side.

This had never been done before but really suited me fine. We set off down the buoyed channel, plying the pilot with beer and assuring him that *Sea Loone* was doing a good five knots. With food and lots of beer he was quite happy. We didn't actually arrive in the anchorage until one o'clock in the morning. The pilot got picked up by a launch and we settled down for a few hours sleep.

In the morning, our new pilot arrived and we motored the last few miles to the first down lock where we tied up to wait for the other two boats. We were miles ahead now so our problems were over.

In fact, when they arrived for the locking-down the catamaran was so large and powerful the French yacht tied to one side and we tied to the other side. So we didn't need to use our engine or our lines at all. We got towed from lock to lock and finally the American said he was happy to take us all the way to the yacht club. We remained attached all away. Perfect for me but my line handlers were a bit disappointed not having seen any of the lake, just flashing channel markers.

In the morning I telephoned the Canal Company and they assured me that all was well and I would be refunded the extra money. I still actually finished paying more than $900 for the transit.

In Colon there was a huge duty-free shopping centre. I had been in touch with my friends in the Marquesas and had a shopping list of things they would like. So I bought DVD players and such like. Now in Panama City I had a lot more to buy. I loaded up with tinned food and booze, and down at the market I ordered cigarettes. The cigarettes, I think, had been stolen.

I also found a shop with horse saddles close to the cigarette dealer so organized to pick up both cigarettes and saddles the next week. This I did, parking my taxi close and getting the vendors to bring everything to the taxi where I would make the payment. It was necessary to be very streetwise. I had the boat on a yacht club mooring. The yacht club itself had been burnt down probably by some dissatisfied yachty. But there was still a launch service going back and forwards. The launch operator got well tipped and he was goggle-eyed at the quantities of goodies going out to *Sea Loone*. He was especially surprised and puzzled by the three horse saddles.

As soon as I had everything aboard, which had taken a good ten days of running around, I sped down the channel into the Gulf of Panama. I had had no news of Whitey in Golfito, Costa Rica and for some reason thought he and Barbara had returned to the US. It seemed the officials there were as bad or worse than before, so instead of turning north, I headed south for Ecuador, somewhere new.

Pushing against the wind and current I expected a difficult trip but in fact had no problems. I tacked back and forwards a few times in light winds and arrived off Bahia de Caraquez early one morning having just across the equator a few miles back.

I had a crudely-drawn map of the entrance into the river which had numerous sandbars across it. There was also a name to call on the VHF for a local pilot. As it was, a yacht which was leaving came past and I gladly took on board the pilot he was using.

We made a convoluted route in, following waypoints on the pilot's GPS. Finally we anchored in a wide muddy river off a typically scruffy town. It was late June, 2004. I would be here sometime as I did not intend to set off for the Galapagos, and from there on to the Marquesas, until at least October

Part of the clearing in procedure required me to take a long bus ride to Manta, a large port further south. The immigration department there gave me a six months visa. I also I took advantage of being in Manta to visit a factory which made buttons and beads from the ivory nut, locally called tagua.

The factory had a shop and display counter where a number of people were buying things. I simply wanted to buy the raw nuts as material for my own jewelry. The manager was very abrupt and rude to me, but one of the customers took me aside and explained that the best place to buy the raw nuts was in the market in St. Vincent. St. Vincent was the small village directly across the river from where I was anchored; what luck!

The following day I took the ferry across the river and ambled up to the market. It took time but finally I was directed to a dilapidated shed across from the market where I found huge sacks of tagua. In Panama I had been offered nuts for a dollar each as a tourist item. Here, I could buy a hundred pound sacks for ten dollars.

I bought two; then hired a rickshaw driver to pedal me and the sacks back to the ferry. I had more help to load them on and off the ferry; then another rickshaw back to the dinghy dock. So at a total cost of less than thirty dollars, I had the whole deck inches deep in nuts which needed further drying and shelling.

My next trip inland was by the same bus was to a small village called Sosote where the ivory nuts were carved into tortoises, birds, seals, and so on. I wanted some sea turtles made. I made a drawing of what I wanted. Then I persuaded a local guy to make me one and send it to me by bus to see if I liked it. A few days later I picked up a parcel from the bus station.

The turtle still looked like a tortoise. So with my own nuts, I made my own example and put it on the bus to be delivered to my carver man. Two days later I got back what I wanted and ordered as many as he could make at the agreed price.

Within a few miles of the equator, you'd think it would be hot and sunny but the cold Humboldt Current which sweeps up the coast made for a cold damp start to most days, often with drizzling rain which I well remember from Liverpool. The damp air had got to the saddles. The leather had gone moldy and one even showed signs of termites in its wood frame. I brought spray and wax and employed a guy for the day to polish them up. I then took a bus to Chone, an inland town, to buy horse blankets and other bits, but the market was very disappointing.

Quite a lot of boats were anchored in the river, mainly Americans. There was even a yacht club with a swimming pool but it was normally deserted. There were lots of cheap restaurants and a few bars. None was very lively and on Sundays they were all closed.

There was however one lively American girl with a large ketch who organized some entertaining evenings. When she managed to charter her boat to three young English girls for a trip down the coast, I agreed to skipper the project. Linda was a great cook so we ate well and saw whales, frigate birds etc. There were also quite a few good anchorages.

In Florida, I had met the Chicago mafia; and once, in Golfito, I met a CIA man who was sure I was with MI6. In Ecuador, a friend of Linda's told me he was a hit man. He was quite open about it. I tried to imagine signing on the dole in Liverpool and filling in my occupation as "hitman". I never asked him what his rates were or which methods he preferred. In fact I thought of a barrage of questions to ask him but somehow it didn't seem like a good idea to risk upsetting him.

Come September and I had the usual itchy feet. It was easy to load up with fresh fruit and vegetables in the market. I had bottled pork and chicken in my monster pressure cooker. I had the last delivery of tagua turtles from Sosote. The rest of the cargo was fine . I had the horse saddles, DVD players, CD players, all my jewellery, a few carvings, lots of booze and fifty cartons of cigarettes, that is 10,000 cigarettes. My capital had shrunk from €30,000 to €24,000, plus $640 and the nest egg in UK of £9,600.

I cleared out for Galapagos and decided to give up smoking, a good test of my will power with thousands of ciggies on the boat. The wind blew me gently out into the Pacific and the current picked me up and pushed me along to Galapagos, the enchanted Isles.

I sailed into Wreck Bay in San Cristobel and anchored behind a fleet tourist boats. It was totally the wrong season for yachts and there were none at all in the bay. I launched the dinghy, attached the outboard engine, and motored over to the naval jetty. It was only a short walk to the Port Captain's office stepping around a few sea lions asleep at the top of the beach.

The Port Captain seemed in a good mood and friendly. After a short discussion, he agreed to my having a month in Wreck Bay and then another month in the Port of Vilamil on Isabela Island. This was going to cost me US$100 (Ecuador's economy now used US dollars). I pointed out to him that the Port Captain on Isabela was also going to ask for the port fees but he assured me that, no, there would be no further charges. Amazingly, this turned out to be true. I was not even charged a clearing out fee.

I was delighted. I had paid the same in 1983 for a miserable couple of days stay; so this time I had a real chance of having a good look around.

The next morning didn't start so well. I had left the dinghy tied alongside and during the night a sea lion climbed aboard, followed by all its friends. The final result was that the dinghy sank under their weight drowning the outboard engine. I hauled the dinghy up and then spent a few hours emptying out the engine fuel tank and the carburettor, and getting it going again.

The dinghy went back on deck and, in its place I blew up the Avon inflatable. From then on, I rowed ashore. At night I flipped the dinghy over so the sea lions couldn't do their enormous poos in it. A wildlife paradise has its drawbacks!

For the next few weeks, I walked for miles sometimes north along the lee shore with its rocks and cliffs and calm sea and sometimes south around to the windward shore where there was surf breaking on the long beach and a huge population of sea lions. Blue footed boobies and many other species of birds, allowed me to walk right up to them.

I dug out the video camera I had bought in St. Martin in the Caribbean and filmed everything from small crabs to sea anemones I found in the rock pools, and from birds to huge male sea lions. On two occasions a monster male sea lion lunged out at me from behind a bush, roaring and showing a vicious mouthful of teeth. I soon learned where they lurked and detoured around them.

Within a week of my arrival, another yacht arrived and anchored behind me. They were a French couple with a young daughter. I had met them in the canal on a much smaller yacht. Apparently, they been sailing for some time together with a large French catamaran sailed by a single man with a teenage daughter. In Costa Rica he had bought them the new much bigger boat and they had sold the old one.

The new boat had some rigging problems but was a vast improvement on their first boat. We were to meet them again in the Marquesas together with the catamaran.

Having seen all that was to see in Wreck Bay, I left for Isabela. The harbour there is very shallow. I made a long circle around the outside reef on which the sea was breaking dramatically. It was surprisingly calm once I worked the boat in as far as I could behind a row of rocky islets. A huge volcano reared up behind the town so we were often under the cloud which built up against it.

I rowed to the beach and walked into the town, more a village, to sign in with the Port Captain. The roads were all sandy and the few bars and hotel, very laid-back. The Port Captain welcomed me and told me I could stay as long as I liked!

The sea lions were still keen on using my dinghy and one morning I found one asleep on the aft hatch. How it managed to get up on deck between the lifelines without waking me, I have no idea.

On the rocks behind me I found my first penguins and there were iguanas everywhere. It was a magic spot! I shared it with a couple of fishing boats and a small coaster came in for a few days.

One morning a guy paddled out to see me in a kayak. He wanted me to take a tour of the volcanoes on horseback with him. If he could find a few more tourists in the village to make it worth his while, then he would paddle out and collect me early one morning. We had agreed on a modest price of $20 for the trip.

Some days later, he appeared at dawn and I followed him ashore with the rubber duck. He had found a Spanish couple and a mainland couple to make up the party. We all climbed into the back of a pickup truck and drove for almost an hour, way up almost to the rim of the first volcano. There we transferred to the horses.

They were more like ponies, not so far to fall, and mine had a pretty blond mane. Mine was also the slowest and had an addiction for a particular small roadside plant. Every time it veered off and lowered its head, it nearly catapulted me over its head; and every time I caught my privates on the knob of the western saddle.

The views were spectacular. Clouds cascaded over onto the caldera, hawks hovered over our heads and after a while, the whole of the west coast of Isabela came into view. We could also see the huge volcano on Isla Fernandino and Darwin's Volcano on the north end of Isabela. We parked the horses under a huge shade tree and walked down to some bubbling boiling fumerols. I had my video camera so continued making my epic film, including shots taken on the move on horseback.

After lunch we returned following the edge of the volcano. Then, leaving the horses, we plunged back through the clouds, down to the coast in the truck.

I had been told there was an English girl living in the village so I set out to find her. This was easy to do and I was invited to stay for a meal. It really was the most unlikely place to find a young English girl. But she had come on holiday, had fallen madly in love with a local fisherman and that was that. She had previously worked as a very well-paid secretary with the EEC in Brussels.

Here in Vilamil, money was very scarce, the only sources being a little tourism in the season and some fishing. Life was very simple. I agreed to pay for petrol for the trip to a rocky volcano sticking out of the ocean a few miles away, combined with some fishing for them to make a little money.

The fishing boat was a long Japanese pirogue with a massive outboard engine they had borrowed for the day. We shot out through a gap in the rocky islets and soon arrived at the volcano. The shore was lined with steep cliffs and there was a big swell running so we could not land. We saw fur seals as well as sea lions but we were catching no fish.

We set off again to a steep little pinnacle sticking out of the ocean to the east. Here we found a shoal of yellowfin tuna. On each circuit of the rock we snagged tuna on the two lines we were trailing but every time we tried to land them, the sea lions took them before we could haul them into the boat.

After an hour of hard work, they allowed us to keep two, nowhere near enough to make the trip worthwhile. While it was very frustrating for them, for me was an interesting day out. Had I not paid for the petrol, it would have been a disaster.

The last day of filming my nature epic, I visited the tortoises and flamingos; then walked for miles along the coast. Imagine my surprise when, having just filmed a very large marine iguana, I came round a clump of mangrove and there was a gorgeous girl posing in the middle of a rock pool in a very skimpy bikini. Another equally gorgeous bikini-clad girl was taking pictures of her friend.

Naturally I introduced myself. They were on holiday from Ecuador and staying in the village. When they showed an interest in my video camera, I gave them a demonstration and played it back to them. A little later they brought me to a very secluded small beach surrounded by mangroves and my nature epic began to show definite signs of becoming a "naturist" epic, or maybe worse. I was going to have to do some serious editing if the BBC were going to show it on British television.

On the way back to the village we were passed by a group of German hikers. They were elderly, overweight and had what looked like ski-poles to help them along. Unfortunately we caught up with them on the main beach where they had stopped to swim. They were all naked with flabby bits hanging everywhere so I saw the best and worst of the human form all in one day, ha! ha!

Having seen the west coast and the top of the volcano I was determined to sail around there before heading out. Maybe I could stop over for a night in Tagus Cove which I had heard about.

Once around the corner, the sea was wonderfully calm and I coasted along very close to the shore, using the slight land breeze. I saw more penguins but never saw the flightless cormorant, the last on my list of must-see things. I arrived off Tagus Cove late in the afternoon but there were two tourist boats anchored there and I had no permit.

So I turned the boat west and, once clear of land, set the self-steering gear and went to bed. I had a few thousand miles of open ocean in front of me. My next stop would be the Marquesas in French Polynesia.

My Galapagos film was rubbish; even the pretty girls didn't raise it above ordinary but my film of crossing in the Pacific, Galapagos to the Marquesas, wasn't so bad. There were no great storms and no disasters. The only excitement was a visit from a helicopter in the middle of nowhere, obviously off a tuna boat somewhere over the horizon.

For a yacht sailing around the world, the hop from Galapagos to the

Marquesas is the longest. There are no stops in between, just blue water. There's very little chance of storms or even gales and a tsunami would slip by unnoticed. No ships came into view to run over me and no whales tried to sink me. So there was plenty of time to relax.

It would be ten years since I had last been in Nuku Hiva and twenty years since I had arrived there for the first time. In those first ten years nothing much had changed. What, I wonder, had happened over this last ten.

I had news from Philippe who was still doctoring and through him, news of Justin Mahiatapu and his family. So I had lots of people to see again. I just hoped that whatever changes that happened weren't all for the worst.

Since leaving the Caribbean, my finances had declined rapidly with the transit of the canal, my holiday in the Dominican Republic, and then my stocking up with stores, saddles and electronic widgets in Panama but the boat was loaded and I had huge hopes for my jewellery business.

Thirty something days out of Galapagos, I rounded the East Sentinel and motored the last mile into the bay of Taeohae in Niku Hiva. The first thing I saw was a large cruise ship anchored which didn't go down too well. But I anchored anyway off the reef on the west side of the bay, close to two other yachts and some motorboats on moorings. There were half a dozen yachts anchored on the east side near the wharf. Ashore there were obviously a lot more houses, especially over on the other side of the bay. At least there were no high-rise buildings.

It was late afternoon by the time I had sorted the boat out and launched the dinghy. I had caught a big kingfish or wahoo, and threw it in the dinghy for Justin and then rowed ashore.

Justin's large house was hardly visible through the fruit trees which had grown enormously and then amongst them were little cottages. A sign told me this was "Chez Jullienne" so Justin's wife was now running a pension. Things have moved on and thankfully there were no more signs of the church.

I handed over the fish, and hugged and kissed the two of them. Justin was close to retiring from his job at the school. He was showing his age a bit but they were both well. I needed some sleep so we agreed to sort out any business the next day. Then I rowed back to *Sea Loone* and slept like a log.

In the morning I got a bit of a shock. Looking out, the cruise ship gone only to be replaced by a small grey warship with a large tricolor flying from its stern. On the bow, a large P was painted; but just in case it was a D for Duane, French customs, I locked up the boat and rowed ashore. I didn't want any visiters.

Not being much of a family person, I wasn't sure how many offspring Justin had. There were now two sons living on Justin's land up the hill behind the main house, another living over the other side of the island in Terra Desert, near the airport, and a daughter in Tahiti. They were all married and there were a number of grandchildren. Maybe there were more, I don't know.

Fara, one of the sons, was married to a French girl, Sophie, who had worked as a dental technician. They had a terror of a son called Kieni. That evening, Justin and Fara came out to the boat with a speedboat and tied alongside. I passed over the horse saddles, the electrical stuff, the booze and the huge box of cigarettes. Low in the water the speedboat headed for the shore and was back on its trailer and minutes later back in its garage. The grey ship had been Navy and had already up-anchored. I relaxed.

The next day I climbed the hill behind Justin's. There was a new road and at the top Philippe had built a house looking out over the bay. He was still working in the hospital. His wife was teaching and there were two boys. The children I had met in New Zealand were now full-grown and living in Tahiti. In fact I met them at Christmas and they had grown huge.

Philippe had sold his yacht and now owned a large speed boat on the moorings near me. He had a truck and a little car for commuting to the hospital. His youngest boy, now maybe ten, the same age as Kieni, was another little savage. Between the two, the roosters ran in fear of their lives. They were normally seen with a rooster on a string tucked under the arm. Philippe was well and happy. He also had only a few years to go before retirement and seemed to be taking life a bit more easy. The wife was still gorgeous and fit as a fiddle.

Out on the water, the catamaran on a mooring behind me was owned by Alain and Odile. Alain had sold the yacht he lived on here twenty years ago. He had then bought the catamaran in Australia and sailed it over here to do charter work. Odile was still working as a doctor in the hospital. They were living in an A-frame house on a precipice overlooking the main dock.

Stefan who had scuppered his yacht from twenty years ago, had now sold the big fishing boat that he had tried long-lining with ten years ago, and was occasionally working for the government. He and Flarise was still together in their house up the valley. At one time they had left and gone to live in southern Chile where Stefan had bought a small hotel. But it hadn't worked out and I'm sure Flarise was happy to be back on her island. Stefan was supervising small business enterprises that were receiving government grants, both here in Nuku Hiva and in the other islands.

The other person I knew from years ago was Rose who, with her husband, had run the hotel at the very western end of the Bay. Americans, they had arrived on a yacht and stayed. The husband had died a few years ago, the hotel had been taken over by some huge company, and Rose had been squeezed out. She was not happy and was intent on opening another hotel on lands she still owned.

In between time, she ran a small museum, boutique and a bar restaurant, rarely open but which she called the Yacht Club.

Tracey, who had left me, then left Philippe had also left her Marquesian husband. He had been the husband of Philippe's wife. Tracey had run off with a Frenchman first to the big islands and then to New Zealand. The Frenchman had found work in New Zealand, Tracy had married him, got pregnant by him and had the child , her second and a boy, in New Zealand.

Not that I wanted it, but no one had offered me citizenship anywhere in thirty years. Tracey had South African, British, French, and now New Zealand passports and was now living on the South Island , New Zealand with a half Marquesian daughter maybe ten years of age and a half French son some years younger. I was impressed.

The aerobics class she had started when she first arrived had developed into a dance group which had travelled as far as Tahiti specializing in the rather aggressive Marquesian dancing but also doing the lovely hip-swaying that had mesmerized me in Boa Bora years ago. There were now at least three popular local dance groups in town.

I imagined Tracey arriving back home on the Liverpool waterfront with her exotic dark-skinned beauties with their long black hair and huge smiles.

Having visited all my friends, I had all the news. The new hospital was completed. There were some new administrative buildings and the wharf had been tidied up. Pipapo still had a diving centre on the wharf, and next door was a yacht services company offering repairs, an internet service and a selection of jewellery and clothing.

The cruise ship I had seen was one of two which came up regularly from Tahiti during the cyclone season to avoid the rain squalls and high winds around the big islands. The larger ship was called the *Pacific Princess*, the smaller one the *Gaugin* after the famous artist who had lived here and was buried in Hiva Oa. The new sophisticated supply ship also carried passengers, had a restaurant and a small swimming pool. She was called *Aranui III*. She offered a tour around the island of the Marquesas loading and unloading cargo. It was a very popular trip and was fully booked from Tahiti.

So with the cruise ships plus visitors staying at the fancy new hotel and at "Chez Julienne" and a couple of other places, a small tourist business had developed. The wood and stone carvers were doing well and their work was brilliant. There were also a few bone carvers and lots of jewellery made from shell and seeds.

At weekends or whenever a ship arrived, the craft market would open in the village. It was a good opportunity to sell my stuff so when I met the French couple I had been with back in the Galapagos, they were keen to help me. Their large new boat had a few problems and they desperately needed to make a little money. So they took a selection of my jewellery, the bone carving, coral, ebony and so on, plus the remains of my sea urchin earrings. Altogether it made a nice display and it worked. I set my prices and they added half again.

My life settled down to a pleasant routine. I took the dinghy along the coast diving for whatever I could find. On the big tides I'd walk the reef early morning and hook out some octopus. The old ladies, from whom I had learnt the art of octopus hunting, were gone so I had the reef to myself. On his days off, I'd go with Philippe fishing with the speedboat, sometimes east and sometimes west.

We always took Philippe's friend, a local fisherman who knew the good spots for dropping a hook or trolling a line. We always came back with a huge ice chest full of fish including a couple of big wahoo or dorado caught on the move.

A couple of times we took the truck across the island, once over to the north coast and another time on the old road to the airport. That time, we had to leave the truck at the bottom of the zig-zag, the old road to the airport, then walk up onto the lip of the caldera, from there heading south with a 1000-foot cliff to our left. Eventually we arrived at a spot from where we were looking almost vertically down on Hakatea, Daniels Bay, almost 2000 feet below us. On the way back, we try to find the head of the famous waterfall but the impenetrable jungle made it impossible.

Meanwhile, I dug out my ivory nut, tagua, and after a few failures was soon making miniature tikis starting with the bench grinder and finishing off with a

Dremel tool. I was also making little manta rays as pendants from ebony wood. The ebony whales I had carved in Mtwara, Tanzania, had not been a success so I took them to Fara and Sophie's house up the track behind Justin's, and slice them up. Sophie was also dabbling with jewelry and had lots of tools from her dentistry days. It was great to be able to use their workbench for my basic cutting and grinding which was a bit messy to do on the boat.

I must admit I wasn't working too hard. The tagua turtles made in Ecuador got sold quickly and I could have made more but the tikis were fun and if I got bored I jumped in the dinghy and went exploring.

Canoe racing had become really popular, like the dancing, and just before Christmas, an inter-island competition was organized. The outrigger canoes were now fibreglass and quite sophisticated. The races were long distance from close to where I was anchored, going out of the bay and down to the south eastern part of the island past Taipi Vai and Hooumi.

As they reentered the bay, the drums started beating, echoing out across the water and a single woman's voice called out "Hane Mai" repetitively. On the beach three pretty girls stood in the surf with garlands of flowers for the winner. It was all very evocative.

The artisans, including my lot, cleared away the carvings and jewellery. Philippe's wife organized a huge feast, beer was cooled in large tubs of icy water and a dance band tuned up for the evening party.

At Christmas there was a dinner dance in town with Traecy's ex-group of dancers performing. Then on New Year, Alain and Odele invited me to a party at their house. A large catamaran had arrived in the bay. It belonged to the rich Frenchman and his daughter. It was he who had bought the yacht for the couple who were selling my jewellery. He had bought beer and wine for the party and catered food from the local restaurant.

It was developing into a really good party when I went out in the yard to take a pee. Unfortunately, I took a step too far and went head first over the edge of the cliff the house was built on. I came to a stop just before the vertical drop and clung on to a boulder I had butted it with my teeth. By the time I scrambled back onto the terrace, I was streaming blood from cuts and bruises and I realized I had knocked out my two front teeth.

I was a mess and so took early retirement. Later another party-goer fell off the dock wall looking for his dinghy and nearly drowned. So at least my drunken skydive wasn't the only story of the evening. The following day I made two new front teeth with a small piece of elephant tusk. They looked pretty good.

In the New Year, it was now 2005, I up-anchor and sailed overnight down to Tahuata. There are some good anchorage on the north shore and there were two people I wanted to meet. Teiki Barsenas lived in the main village, Vaitahu, and was probably one of the most famous of the Marquesian carvers. Using bone, whale's teeth, and shell, he made the most intricate pieces. He welcomed me into his workshop and showed me some of his work and photographs of pieces that were now distributed all over the world.

I was invited to lunch and left with some offcuts of miru, a type of rose wood which I could use. Incorporating the dark and light grains in the wood, I was able to make small shark hooks with ivory tips and fancy lashings which looked really good.

The second person I looked for was Cyril whose mother was chief in the village of Hapatoni. In the center of the village are the remains of a large ceremonial site built with huge squared off boulders. Stone platforms, pi pis, some of them huge, were all that remained of the old buildings and there were paved roadways, everything overgrown with huge fig trees. There was a new dock protected by a seawall in the corner of the bay. This allowed the cruise ships and the Aranus III to drop off visitors, not possible in the main village. So Cyril and others had a ready market for their carvings. Cyril was making some nice things but a lot of the smaller stuff, geared to the tourist trade, was not so good.

Before turning back to Nuku Hiva, I anchored in Hanamoenoe, well known for its beautiful white sand beach and the vicious sand flies, or "no-no's", which lived there. Last time I anchored here had been with Glenn, the South African, on *Blue Drifter*. Then, there had been a number of other boats but now I had the place to myself. It would be another two months before the season's yachties started arriving.

I remember collecting a bucket full of the beautiful Maritiana cowrie shells twenty years ago. They had disappeared but seem to be coming back. I also found a lot of orange lipped helmet shells. I spent hours scrambling along the cliff edge, away from the beach, peering into rock pools, finding octopus, lionfish, huge sea anemones and thick spinned sea urchins. In the water, I poked my nose into underwater caverns, turned over boulders and made a general nuisance of myself with the local marine inhabitants. One good-sized octopus finished off in the pressure cooker.

Back in Taeohae I had to get down to work making more tagua tikis and the new miru shark hooks which were selling like hotcakes. With the canopy strung up and a plank across the cockpit I had the two bench grinders set up with a small vice and the Dremel tool, like a dentist's drill, hung from the boom.

Waves broke on the reef nearby and there was the roar of surf from the centre of the bay when the swells pounded on the pebbly beach. The vertical sides of the inner caldera rose up immediately behind town. When it rained I counted seventeen waterfalls cascading down; one or two fell continuously. A few turtles popped their heads up now and again, manta rays and sharks passed by. It all made for a very picturesque backdrop to my workshop.

One morning early in March, I woke up feeling very, very, ill. I managed to get to the toilet and my guts emptied violently. Then I threw up. I also needed to pee and, when I did, it hurt like hell. I knew that my prostate, after ten years of quiet, had erupted again.

Fortunately, Odele was visiting their catamaran that morning and I managed to attract her attention. I was whisked off to hospital. That night I reckoned I had that near-death experience. My whole body shivered and shook. I felt so cold and yet somehow separate from my body. I must have eventually slept and by morning was nearer the land of the living again.

They pumped antibiotics into me and took samples to send to Tahiti. After three days I was well enough to wonder how much it was going to cost me in this fancy new hospital. A friendly lady came to visit and promised that she would see what she could do. Meanwhile, I got regular visits from Odile and Philippe.

Philippe had received a new machine, an ultrasound something or other, so we could look at the bits and pieces. We saw that the prostate had a lump which seemed benign and the bladder wasn't emptying properly. Obviously my body was wearing out. I would be sixty in November, what a horrible thought.

On the fourth day, they agreed I could go back to the boat, but only to sleep. Daytime I had to spend in the hospital garden with the drip reattached. At least I wasn't taking up the bed space.

The tests came back. They had isolated a possible bacteria but had knocked it off. The PSA was good, whatever that was, so I could pull out the needle from my arm and go home. I paid the bills for the laboratory work in Tahiti but never received a bill for the hospital bed, which was very kind.

In April, the cruise ship went back to sailing around Moorea and Bora Bora and my workers followed with their rich French friend with his catamaran. The wind turned south east so the anchorage became a bit rolly and the yachts started arriving from Panama. It was time for me to move on.

I had spent some time with Stefan at his house and on some of his trips around the island visiting small business enterprises. When we first arrived in Nuku Hiva, there was the third boat belonging to the Frenchman called Guy, with his Vietnamese girlfriend. He was the shell collector and treasure hunter on Cocos Island. He had spit up with his girlfriend and left Nuku Hiva for the Tuamotus, the huge area of ocean dotted with low lying atolls on the way to Tahiti. On British charts it is given the name the Dangerous Archipelago.

Stefan thought that, after all these years, he was still there on an atoll called Aratika. Justin confirmed this although he also had had no contact for years. So it was decided I would go to Aratika to see if I could find him.

Fara chopped down a huge regime of bananas from his jungle garden. I shook down all the limes from the lime trees around and I must have had twenty kilos before I finished. Then Justin provided a load of pamplemousse, Philippe's fisherman friend brought me a load more. The boat was loaded down. Whoever was living on Aratika, they were going to be very happy when I arrived.

It was probably going to be my last farewell. I doubted I'd be back so I was quite sad as I pulled up anchor raised the sails and glided out of the bay.

The bananas was still green but not going to stay that way long, so I didn't stop in Ua Pou or Tahuata. The weather was kind and I made good progress. Aratika wasn't visited by yachts but I had a couple of sketches of the two entrances into the lagoon. I decided to try the one on the lee side which had a shallow shelf of only nine feet to pass over, but shouldn't have a large swell coming in.

With the GPS system now working well, it was easy to weave through the atolls. No more hanging around trying to pinpoint my position with the sextant, like the first time. Still, trying to work out if the current was flowing or ebbing in the pass, was still not so easy. It depended not only on the moon and the tide, but also how big the swells were on the windward side of the atoll, pumping water over the reef.

When I arrived, I had to wait a couple of hours, hove-to. The pass was a swift flowing river, flowing out. The sketch I had was unnecessary as the French government had put markers on the side to the pass and there were lovely black and yellow striped pillars to line up with in order to stay in the middle of the channel. It was still very narrow when I eventually motored in and at one stage I was within feet of a steep coral wall and then skirting over coral heads which looked awfully close to the surface in the gin-clear water.

Once in, I had to motor-sail all the way across the lagoon some eight miles, avoiding the odd reefs which came almost vertically to the service from a depth of nearly one hundred feet. It was getting late in the day before I carefully edged up behind one of the windward motus, trying to find shallow enough water to anchor. As the visibility got rapidly worse with the setting sun, I found an open space among the coral heads and threw in the anchor. By the time I launched the dinghy, stowed the sails, and ate some food, it was dark. The boat was floating on a mill pond and I slept.

Early the next morning, with the two hp motor on the dinghy, I motored across to the motu further south where there was obviously a village. I passed across the windward pass into the lagoon. It was unmarked and it looked as if there were big breaking swells at the entrance. I had definitely chosen the best way in.

I motored up to a small house built on the edge of the lagoon. I could actually tie up to the veranda. Two young men sitting at table invited me in to have a cup of coffee. They had seen *Sea Loone* anchored not far away and wanted to know why I had come. I began to explain that an old friend, Guy Crombie, was maybe on the island and I was looking for him. The larger of the two lads interrupted me and told me I was talking about his father. Then looking behind me, he said that the lady coming towards us in a small launch, was his mother, Guys wife!

And so we all introduced ourselves, drank some coffee and then it was suggested that I go and collect *Sea Loone* and they would pilot me to the motu not far away, where the family lived. There I finally met Guy and the rest of the family. We had last seen each other in 1984. It was now 2005.

The island was a tiny paradise perched on the reef and the family were delightful. Guy had married the chief's daughter and as a wedding present had been given a large fish trap on the edge of the windward pass. The fish trap had supported them, the yachts had been sold and then Guy that got involved in pearl farming. He later specialized in growing the baby oysters through to the stage where he sold them on to the pearl farmers proper.

He was now semi-retired and building boats and a substantial new family home. The eldest boy I had already met. Then there was a younger boy with Down's syndrome then a small boy and little girl you would die for she was so pretty. The island was only about one hundred metres by three hundred metres covered on the lagoon side with coconut palms and, on the windward side, natural bush.

I was super popular when I brought the bananas, limes and pamplemousse ashore but they were not as isolated in as in the old days. A small freighter came every two weeks collecting fish and copra and delivering everything else. In fact, in the village there was a small shop with all the basics.

There was a larger village on the motu to the north but still only a total of one hundred people on the atoll. And yet the government had built an airfield which was now completed and they were expecting regular flights to start each week from Tahiti.

We ate dinner on the water's edge, swarms of fish came to take the scraps and clean the plates and even an octopus turned up one time. Guy didn't allow people to fish around the motu and also protected the coconut crabs, of which there were lots in the jungly part of the island.

I dug out my video camera and filmed the fish, the octopi, one actually climbed up my leg as I filmed him, the birds, fairy terns, noddies and boobies, and the corals and shells on the outer edge of the reef. I tried catching crayfish with my tangle net but only succeeded in catching a black-tipped shark which totally ruined the net. The kids caught coconut crabs for me to film. Time passed quickly.

Sylviana, Guy's wife, had quite a lot of black pearls and I still had quite a few cartons of cigarettes. So pearls, money and cigarettes changed hands. Luckily for me the shop had also run out of cigarettes and, with the supply boat not due for another week, the rest of the cigarettes left my boat. By now I had not smoked for many months.

I collected two sacks full of oyster shell and some really hard dark red wood called miki-miki from small stunted trees which grew almost in the surf on the windward coast. Both would be good for more jewellery making.

Eventually, I had to drag myself away and continue on to Tahiti. So one day, as the tide was running out, I got spat out of the lagoon through a maelstrom of breaking water into the deep blue ocean beyond. The tide was ebbing fast.

In Tahiti, I had to anchor down past the airport and then take a bus back into town. The traffic was horrendous and the crowded town centre daunting after the quiet easy life in the Tuamotus and the Marquesas.

The number one shop in Papeete for Poynesian artisanerie, "Ganesha", actually remembered me which was a good start. I also found a second outlet for my stuff, almost as good.

In Moorea, all the big hotels seemed to have closed down. The gallery which had saved my bacon last time I was there, was gone, Club Med was overgrown with weeds, but there was still some business to be done.

I moved on to Huahini and met my old hippy friends with a boutique. I also managed to contact Joan de Kat. His was the only yacht that had been in Aratika the previous year and Guy had said he was now based here. As usual, Johan arrived with some pretty young girl in tow. He still had the steel yacht from the flying saucer people. I was told Fafa was still on the motu in Bora Bora so I would go and see her.

I found a good gallery in Raiatea and then sailed across to Taha where I picked up a mooring for the night. That evening I had a beer at the hotel and sat with the manager. It turned out he was the son of the American guy I knew years ago who chartered his catamaran from the Hotel Bora Bora. Before I gave Plod the parrot to Joan and Fafa, he had wanted to have him. Apparently Plod had died But Lorita now lived with the father in his house on Bora Bora. It was strange drinking a beer with a guy who knew my parrot really well!

On Bora Bora I had to go and see Bi Bi with his shop near the wharf. He now had a second shop but nowhere looked very busy. I anchored off the Bora Bora Hotel and found the house of the American. Nobody was home but I found Lorita in a large aviary. She wasn't very friendly but then she never was but she was obviously happy. The aviary door was open if she wanted to leave.

I followed the new navigation markers past the airport and round to the windward side of the island inside the lagoon. It was a massive shock to find a huge hotel where I had once anchored as a lone boat in an empty lagoon.

Thatched cottages were strung out on stilts across the lagoon and the motu had been bulldozed to create canals, lakes and roads. They had even cut a channel through to the ocean. This seemed like a very dangerous thing to do. Another large project was dredging and bulldozing to the north and there were more hotels further on down the lagoon.

I had spent weeks and months anchored here where Joan and Fafa had their place on the motu. I knew the local family who made the pandanas thatch, had fished with them and even waded on the reef with them looking for crayfish. Now it was all gone, all but the double peak of the mountain towering over the lagoon.

Ashore on the motu I wondered where Fafa could be. The bulldozers had tamed and flattened the bush and so far only replanted it with stunted coconut palms. I followed the remaining narrow strip of bush over to the windward shore and found a battered old shed. It had been Fafa's workshop for making her pareos. It was now also her home.

Knowing that Fafa normally ran around naked I called out her name. She appeared, wrapping a pareo around herself. She had always been petite but with the salt air and the sun she seemed to have become almost mummified, all skin and bone. But she was well. She still smoked cigarettes which she rolled herself and her voice was as gravelly has ever.

The huge fare that Joan had built had finally collapsed and the land sold. Fafa still hung on to the little house simply because she had been there for so long. It was obvious she was never leaving, not still alive anyway.

Over the more than twenty years she had been on the motu, three cyclones had swept her house into the lagoon and three times she had reclaimed the bits and put it back together . We both speculated on what would happen with the next big cyclone. The hotel had removed the hardy bush which held the motus together so maybe the whole lot would be swept into the lagoon. We had high hopes!

Fafa was still making pareos but she didn't seem very busy. I suggested that with my sacks of tagua nut I could make a load of turtles with Stephen in Tonga, and send them to her. To avoid paying import duty I could send the turtles as parts which she could then glue together. She could then give them to the mamas on the wharf to sell, or sell the lot to the Japanese hotel with a turtle motif. Fafa could then send me half the money, easily making a thousand euros for herself.

I stayed a couple of days but the hotels depressed me so I promise to keep in touch with Fafa care of the post office and returned to Vaitape to clear out. By this time, a lot of yachts had arrived but I didn't have much contact with them. Each year's group seem to bond together and have a little interest in outsiders.

I sailed straight through to Tonga coming in the windward channel and anchoring off Panga Motu facing Nuku'alofa, the capital. The next day, I motored over to the fishing harbor early before the wind picked up, and with some help from other boats, managed to get anchored with stern lines out to the wall.

It took most of the day to clear-in with customs and agriculture & fisheries, and then walk into town to the Immigration Department. With the boat well tied down, the second anchor out and the awning rigged, I rowed across to the fish dock and went looking for the Blue Marlin, the latest popular bar.

It was just across the road, a huge place owned by a New Zealander married to a local girl. This was now the after work drinking place for the local businessmen and at five o'clock I recognized an English guy, Ralph, who had made leather pouches for me in his shoe factory. He was now a farmer and there were a lot of stories in between.

In the morning, having reconnected with the locals and drank too much beer I was a little hung over. I had a couple of months before heading down to New Zealand but things moved slowly in Tonga so if I was going to do any business, I knew I'd better get started.

When I left Bora Bora, I left my few remaining pieces of bone carving with Fafa. So I needed to find Steven and see what we could do. My stay in French Polynesia had been both enjoyable and profitable. I had made around €6,000 and $6,000. So now I had €31,000 and my £9,600 UK money, more than I had leaving St. Barts. Maybe I'd make seventy years of age before buying that little gun.

I had mentioned wanting to see Stephen when I was in the immigration office. He duly arrived at the boat soon after breakfast driving a quite respectable looking 4 x 4. In fact, by Tongan standards, it was immaculate. He looked well and was obviously prospering.

We drove into town to see his new shop, "Art of Tonga". It was in a new building on the main street and he had a fabulous collection of stuff from huge two and three metre carvings of fish and whales, to tiny pieces of jewelry all made in wood, whalebone and shell.

From the shop we drove out to his house, still the same one but bigger again and with another showroom attached. The workshop was now on some more reclaimed land and beyond that, he had created a Tongan village. It had traditional houses and a place to offer a traditional Tongan feast to the tourists and cruise ship passengers. Besides this, Stephen explained, he had another shop in Vava'u the popular northern islands in the Tongan chain, another in Hawaii and an outlet on the US mainland.

Fortunately for me, business was pretty slack. There was certainly nobody doing much in the workshop although there was plenty of bone and boxes of shells lying around. There were also some huge lumps of wood waiting to be turned into leaping marlin or whatever scattered around outside.

Stephen was happy to offer me the same price as ten years ago for the basic dolphins, whales, rays and so on. This surprised and pleased me. I knew I could turn a profit so we made a list of the basics just to get started. I would give him some starting capital the following day and then talk about all the other stuff.

A few days later I returned to the house. There was a local bus that would take me there. The workshop was now a hive of activity. The boys were cutting and grinding, sanding and polishing. The results were piling up and looking good.

One poor apprentice had the unenviable job of grinding off all the oyster shells from Aratika and polishing them. Steve and I had agreed that one sack paid for the other to be polished for me.

In another corner, the turtles were getting made from a sack of tagua nut. I had provided one sample and away they went. Each polished unit finished up as a group of parts in a little plastic bag, head, four flippers and a carapace. There were one hundred to be made.

A month later, most of the work had been done. There were dolphins, double dolphins, two types of whales, rays, turtles, octopus, and sharks. Then there were lots of different fishhooks in bone, wood-and-bone and whalebone. There were Marquesian design turtles cut from oyster shell and tiny sparkling turtles cut from trocha shell, the shell that pearl buttons were originally made from.

The Marquesian tikis made from bone didn't work out very well but I really liked the larger whales that Stephen had carved from whalebone. They varied from forty centimetres long down to fifteen. They were usually humpback whales with huge flippers, but there were also a couple of sperm whales. The whalebone found in the reefs in Ha'apai varied in texture and colour so each carving was quite different to the next. I bought all of them, plus a number of other pieces which took my fancy.

A few weeks later there was an exposition in town with all the local industries exhibiting their wares. Stephen was showing his carvings and jewellery including some dolls made from tapa cloth that his wife and daughter made. He also had an amazing chair carved from porous whalebone. The arms and back were humpback whales.

To complete the exhibit, he had to borrow back from me my carved whales and a whale tooth he had carved for me ten years before. He won first prize!

Most evenings I joined the palangi, white locals, to drink a few beers and tell tall stories. It'd been quite a while since I could drink cheap beer and natter away in English. Steve, an Australian, was a pilot for one of the airlines flying back and forth to Vava'u. If you heard his stories you would never fly with him. Ralph had done really well with a fish and chip shop until everybody copied him. He now had backpackers, some really pretty ones, working on his farm. Another guy was distilling rum from Fijian sugar but the locals had outsmarted him and made rum from industrial alcohol which killed the business, if not a few people.

Friday nights, the bar had live music and got so crowded that they usually ran out of glasses for the beer. Things often got a bit violent and the bouncers really had to earn their money. I usually went home early, , must be getting old.

By late October the harbour started filling up with the cruising fleet, all preparing to sail down to New Zealand. With a strong trade wind blowing, they often dragged anchor. At one time, I had three of them piled up against me. I was not impressed.

I said my goodbyes. I would be back in April and so set off south, 1000 miles to New Zealand. Stephen now had most of my US dollars and I had to make more than a thousand strings and toggles for the pendant; plus eyes to drill for the animals and fancy lashings for the fish hooks. It would keep me occupied on the way south, if the weather and the boat behaved.

3

AFTER A FAIRLY ordinary two weeks sailing, I turned into the Bay of Islands. It was already getting dark and I was not sure how easy it was to arrive at the new customs jetty in Opua in the dark. So I radioed the authorities to say I would anchor off Russell till the morning. No problem they said until they changed their minds and I had to go back out to sea until the morning.

I duly arrived, bleary-eyed, off the customs dock in the morning. With the tide running and no one to help it wasn't easy coming alongside. The dock was on the breakwater protecting a huge new marina full of fancy boats. There were new buildings for the marina and the old swamp was now a boat yard with more buildings.

Cut off from land on the customs dock, I could only wave to Ken and Jos and other friends who came to meet me. But the paperwork got done fairly quickly and I motored up the river to find somewhere to anchor.

There were mooring buoys everywhere but I eventually found a spot way up past Ashby's boatyard in really shallow water. I jumped in the dinghy and rowed ashore then walked along the railway line to the boat yard. I found the old path, Ken's "Ho Chi Min" trail up through the woods and into Ken and Jos's back garden. I was home, or as close as anything you could call home. Jos made a pot of tea and between the two of them I got all the news.

There were two things I needed to get organized as soon as possible. Firstly, I needed to buy a car and secondly, in not much more than a week it would be my sixtieth birthday. I wanted to have a party!

I had Andy Ball's telephone number in Whangarei and called him up using Ken's telephone. Andy had stayed in New Zealand when the owner of the boat yard and of a huge steel fabrication company, had asked him to work for them. Andy was a brilliant fitter, turner and engineer. He had spent time training apprentices so, with the backing of the company, he had been given residency in New Zealand at the age of sixty. He was now semiretired.

Balize his boat, built in Birkenhead docks where I launched *Sea Loone*, was on a mooring in the Whangareii River. He agreed to meet me off the bus and together we would go around the car auctions in Whangarei.

Ken and Jos were happy to help me with my birthday party and agreed to let me have it in their garden. With their legendary Christmas parties, they were well practised.

The day I met Andy in Whangarei wasn't a good day for looking for a car. There were no actual auctions happening and very few cars around the NZ$1,000, which was all I was prepared to pay. We eventually chose a very ordinary looking saloon car being sold at the right price. It was a Subaru which I'd never heard of, and under the bonnet was a complicated looking engine with a lot of bits which I didn't know the use of.

Initially I was nervous; but I finally came to love it. When I put my foot down, the car squatted down and took off. It was a racehorse dressed like a donkey!

Andy and his wife, Val, were living in a "retirement village" in the hills some way out of town. In fact it was a really nice practical little house they had built with minimal maintenance and even a gardener, so he didn't have to mow the lawn. But the "retirement village" bit didn't go down at all well with Andy.

While I was in Whangarei, I drove down to the Riverside Marina where I knew I'd find Alvah and Diana and their new boat. I had last seen Alvah in Lost Loone Bay in Panama when I was still with Tracey and they had come up from Cape Horn with the old wooden boat. A lot of water had passed under the bridge since then.

They had gone through the Panama Canal back into the Caribbean and spent a few years in Florida. They bought the new boat in Colombia, a French steel boat which they fitted out to follow what Clark Stede had done, sailing through the Northwest Passage, but without the aid of an icebreaker. Their new boat was called Roger Henry. The book Alvah wrote after this epic voyage is called "North to the Night".

I hadn't seen Alvah since Panama and the last time I had met Diana was in New Zealand on the Coromandel Peninsula where she was looking after her very sick father. At the time, Alvah was freezing cold, stuck in the ice on the North coast of Baffin Island with only the cat for company through the nine months totally dark winter. It's a good story.

We met in the marina. We had too much to talk about but we had lots of time and anyway, they would be in Opua for my party.

With the car I got around and quickly met my old acquaintances. Jos's friends Dorothy and George helped with the party and lots of people showed up including Ian Walkley from the fibre glass factory in Keri Keri, and Bernt &

Janet who had come to live in Opua from down south. They were the couple who had emptied out their huge hoard of tinned food into *Sea Loone* when we had left the British Virgin Islands for the Pacific the first time. They had stayed working for the Moorings Charter Company for another year before heading to New Zealand to settle.

The Liverpudlians, Charlie and Janet, arrived. Their boat, a Nicholson-32 *Quark*, was on a mooring below us. They had crossed the Atlantic with *Sea Loone* in 1978. Andy, the other scouser, arrived with Val. Their boat *Balize* was registered in Liverpool as is *Sea Loone*. Andy and Bernt had worked together for the Moorings Company in Tortola. Alvah and Diana arrived from Whangarei and Dick and Jane from Kati Kati. They were still kiwifruit farming in a leisure sort of way. Alvah, Diana, Dick and Jane and myself had all spent months in Richards Bay, South Africa together.

It was a small world and a grand party!

Ian in Keri Keri had split up with his wife. He had kept the house and the factory but sold the kiwifruit farm. He had moved across the road to live with Coleen who had a piece of property running down to the river. He still used the factory but had the house rented out. He was busy building a huge geodesic dome out of fibreglass and, together with Coleen, was installing a large waterwheel in the river. They lived in a pretty wooden cottage next to the river. The dome was to have a pond in the middle and living space above it. It was an amazing project. The water wheel also was out of the ordinary as I was to discover when I spent some time with them.

Down the road, Henry and Yanick Waklam had had a few problems. Yanick had been told she had cancer. She had got seriously into holistic medicine and yoga etc. and was now cured. The only problem was the green gunk she tried to force down my throat when I visited. Henry had been seriously injured when Yanick had crashed the car.

The first time I saw him he was dragging himself around on the lawn fixing a strange mechanism he had constructed which moved a large solar panel to track the sun across the sky. He was recovering. The macadamia nuts were history and now they were concentrating on olive trees. Henry's boat, *Operculum*, was in Noumea, New Caledonia, with the eldest son, Ivan. I would look him up.

Having caught up with all my friends, I then went on a sales campaign and over the next few weeks, managed to enlist a dozen or so boutiques and galleries to buy my stuff. I went as far north as 90-Mile Beach, to Monganui, Keri Keri, Pahia, Russel and Kawa Kawa and down to Whangarei.

I then planned a trip south to Kati Kati where I had been invited to stay with Dick & Jane. I took the Old Russel Road and found a fantastic art gallery perched up in the hills. They took a lot of my simple pendants and also some more complicated hooks and a couple of carved whales. From there I went down to Ocean Beach where Alvah and Diana had bought a house. They were busy working on their next sailing trip.

They planned to sail north to Japan and then on again to the Kamchatka Peninsula in Russia where they were hoping to see some rare wildcats and lynxes. From there they would head across to Alaska and then back to New Zealand.

In between time, Alvah was giving after dinner speeches to corporations which somehow increased their ability to make money. He had learned all the language required and Diana had showed me a photo of Alvah up on a stage in a shiny suit. I only got a glimpse before it was snatched away. I also got a glimpse of the video film some American company had organized with Alvah and Diana trekking up into the Kuna Yala, the Darian Gap in Panama. I was roaring laughing and Alvah got pissed off.

In that film Diana had shown the women weaving cloth and baskets and decorating them. That had all been "dust binned". What they really wanted was Diana in a cooking pot and Alvah, their hero, coming to the rescue.

The next day I spent in Whangarei and joined an artists' cooperative which had a gallery right on the waterfront. The ladies organizing it were very sympathetic and in the end, made a great display of all my stuff. As a result, it all sold like hotcakes before Christmas.

That night I stayed with Andy and Val in their village with a long unpronounceable name. I was shown the garage which turned out to be a sophisticated workshop with lathes, a milling machine, band saw and so on. Andy still repaired air tools for the old company and did odd jobs for people such as me. Val was still working in town in Arthur's Emporium, my favorite shop in all New Zealand. It was a place where you could find almost anything.

I had been in touch with Tracey in South Island and she was coming up to Auckland for a final examination to become a qualified masseur or masseuse. I spent the night in a backpackers hostel and then wandered around town waiting to meet her.

In the afternoon I drove up to the museum and strolled around the Polynesian exhibit which showed a lot of Mouri stuff and stuff from Papua New Guinea. There was little or nothing from Polynesia proper. At the entrance there was a café and a Museum shop. I went out to the car and collected my bags of stuff and a Marquesian stone tiki. I left with the promise of a nice fat cheque being sent to me at the end of the month and lighter by two heavy stone tikis and a bag of pendants.

At teatime I met Tracey, now a few years older and a mother of two. Last time we met was in Richards Bay, South Africa, when she was visiting her mother in Durban. . The baby must now be a little girl of say ten who had a brother a few years younger. We had a few drinks but she had people to see and I had a long drive to Kati Kati in the morning. Too much to say, too little time.

Dick and Jane were fine. They had built a new house away from the road looking down on their cow pasture and a little river. The kiwi fruit were behaving themselves, no plagues of insects. They had bought an old charter yacht and the elder son was living on it in Spain. The younger son was in Cambodia running his own night club and backpackers. Dick and Jane had a good life. I wondered if, in their shoes, I would still get itchy feet.

I met Elizabeth one evening in the Opua Cruisng Club. She was staying in a backpacker's motel near Pahia. She was much the same age as me and lived in Devon but liked to spend the English winter in New Zealand. To cut a long story short, she left the backpackers and moved on board *Sea Loone*. She also gave up her hire car and used mine; and put some of what she saved in the *Sea Loone* kitty.

It worked out well. Most mornings she was off playing golf and I had the boat to myself. In the evenings, NZ gets cold so it was good to have someone to to keep me warm. Spending so much time alone, I was losing whatever small social skills I had. Jos, my mother figure, wasn't so keen on the situation to begin with but Elizabeth won her over and then of course they conspired against me as women do.

Meanwhile, I had work to do on the boat and time was pressing. Christmas and New Year had come and gone and by April it would be time to head north. Elizabeth joined me on some of my trips around to restock the shops and to buy things for the boat.

I bought a computer and so got involved in all the stuff that goes with it. I wanted to edit the video films I have made but didn't make much progress. I was given computerized charts of the whole world but wasn't very impressed with them. I also got programs for weather, cruising notes and so on.

The one thing that really got me hooked was films. I could count on one hand how many films I had seen in the last thirty years. Now I could have DVD's of any film ever made and lie in bed watching them. I was given or loaned copies and suddenly realized that the modern sailor watched his boat navigate across the computer screen and in between watched movies. No wonder you rarely saw them.

Jos & Elizabeth bottled a dozen jars of peaches and another of pears to take with me and Elizabeth help me clean and paint *Sea Loone*'s bottom when I hauled up on Doug's railway. Elizabeth then had to fly back to Devon to get on with a massive renovation of cottage in Dittisham that she owned.

A few days before leaving, a young German girl, well actually more Bulgarian, decided she would like to join me on the trip to Tonga. When she first visited *Sea Loone* it was low tide and the keel sat on one of Andy's mooring blocks. The boat was heeled over dramatically. She was not impressed. A fancy American yacht had also offered her a birth so I was a bit surprised when she came back to me, cap in hand, and said she preferred a berth on *Sea Loone*.

No problem. A few days later after a lump of bad weather had passed by, we set off north. As we left the bay, we were met by some huge ocean swells, the sky was overcast and there was a definite winter chill in the air. I'm sure the poor girl must have been a little nervous. I certainly was. But in fact the next few days of steady south easterly wind pushed us rapidly north. Within a week we could have showers in the cockpit without getting hypothermia and then the blue skies and puffy tradewind clouds arrived and pushed us up to Tonga.

We arrived late in the day off the south coast of Tongatapa and I anchored behind Eua, the mountainous island to the southeast. Morning found us entering the Piha Passage and by lunchtime we were anchored off Panga Motu in fifteen feet of flat calm limpid water. Miglena, the crew, was delighted.

Anchoring stern-to in the fishing harbour with the crew was easy. There was even someone to take the stern line ashore for me. In the pub that night Miglena was promised a selection of tropical vegetables by Ralph's mate, Patrick. Patrick was Tongan but had spent a lot of his life in Australia. So Miglena got instructions as to what to do with the vegetables as well.

The next morning, Stephen Fehoko told me he was off to Hawaii in only a few days. He had been invited to demonstrate canoe building there. He would be away for a few weeks. In between time, the boys would get on with my order but I knew that without Stephen, things would not go very quickly.

I decided to make a trip up to Ha'apai and see if I could find any old whalebone. Stephen gave me the names of a few islands he thought might be worth visiting.

I spent the next weekend on Panga Motu with Miglena and her vegetables, playing darts with the locals in the bar on Sunday. I found a good berth for Miglena on the ferry going north up to Vara'u and then set off myself for the islands in Ha'apai.

Anchoring off some of the little islands was really difficult, the surrounding reef dropped into deep deep water. The first island where I found any bone was called Mango. I anchored precariously on live coral and rowed ashore where I was shown a huge whale skull and a number of vertebrae. I told the owner to get in touch with Steven who might be interested. But for me, the porous bone was of no use.

On another island, I dodged through the reefs and then dinghied ashore. A small boy took me up to the school where the teacher spoke English. I was taken into the teacher's house near where the children were all lining up in the schoolyard for the start of the day. I sat down in a scruffy lounge chair in a very dirty room.

The boy banged on the bedroom door and the teacher appeared. He looked vacantly around, leaned against the wall and slid to the floor. Obviously he had drank so much kava overnight he was away with the fairies. The kids were now singing the national anthem outside. Perhaps they taught each other.

I managed to explain to the boy what I was looking for and he and a few mates shot off to retrieve what they thought I wanted. They came back with two vertebrae which was rather disappointing. I wasn't having much success and time was passing.

Further north again I anchored off Ha'afeva, quite a large island with a road running north-south and another heading across the island to the west side. I had bought a bicycle in New Zealand from Arthur's Emporium and already it had been useful cycling down to Stephen's house and into town from the fish market.

I now took it ashore to see what I could find. Having peddled up and down I took the road to the west side to see what sort of anchorage there was there. So far nobody had been very helpful but at the end of the road I met an elderly man with a young boy with Down's Syndrome. Again were some problems with language but I knew the Tongan words for bone and whale.

The old man was sure he had what I wanted. I must follow him back across the island to his house. He had an even older looking bicycle than mine. With the boy perched on his handlebars, we set off. They flew along and I had difficulty keeping up through the sweet potato, manioc and taro plantations and into the coconut trees on the east side.

The house had a big yard, a few outhouses and an enclosure for chickens. The old man climbed up on the roof of a hen house and lifted down a long piece of bone. I was immediately excited. It was obviously heavy and therefore solid bone. It turned out to be one side of the lower jaw of a sperm whale. There was still sockets where the teeth had been but it was badly chewed up with wormholes in it and it was covered all over with grey and black crud.

Still it was massive and not easy to lift. Under all the growth, there must be a lot of usable dense bone. It was just what I wanted. After consulting with his wife, the price was set to be equivalent of twenty dollars. It was a good deal for me and a fortune for them .I tied the bone to the handlebars and then the saddle and pushed the bike back down the road to the dinghy.

I got back to Tongatapa only a few days before Steven. There was still work for the boys to do and I presented Steven with the whale bone and asked for as many whales as possible from the piece; and to bag the offcuts for me to make Marquesian tikis.

I had heard from Elizabeth back in Devon. She had decided to fly out and meet me in Fiji. It meant that I would have to get a move on but of course in Tonga things don't work like that. The result was that I was a little late leaving by the time I had waited until Stephen and the boys had finished the carvings. I could not complain. The whales were fantastic as were the pendants.

So I set off Fiji. The weather was perfect but the wind very light so we drifted west. By the time I anchored off the yacht club in Suva, Elizabeth had been there already for a week, had made friends with all the barflies and had the bloody Coast Guard looking out for me.

I must admit to not being very keen on Fiji. The kava drinking, ceremonial or otherwise, doesn't turn me on and the Indians, I reckon, get a very raw deal. But anyway Suva is lively and has a great market. I bought lots of DVDs for almost nothing, went to the dentist for a new set of teeth and Elizabeth bought some war clubs to beat up her neighbours when she got home.

I chose the wrong day to sail around to the west side of the island and we had a rough night beating into nasty waves. Poor old Elizabeth got seasick and I wasn't in the best of moods, but we sailed into Musket Cove and recovered a bit.

Fiji beer was good and the bar and the yacht club was always lively. Getting in conversation with a few people that I knew, and maybe drinking too much beer, ended up with my foolishly agreeing to sort out a large catamaran which had hit the reef. It had damaged one keel and lost the other.

I spent long, sweaty, hot days hauling out the fifty-odd foot boat on a trailer using a bulldozer, then jacking it up off the trailer and sitting it precariously on breeze blocks borrowed from a building site.

With epoxy resin and fiberglass cloth, two Fijian helpers and little else, I rebuilt the keels and set the boat back on the trailer to be returned to the water. In between times, Elizabeth had helped a Norwegian friend to sew up new covers for my settees with the material I had bought in Suva. She then spent a few days sailing in the islands with her and her husband. I had not been much of a companion.

When the catamaran job was finally finished, the Australian owners who chartered the boat complained loudly at how much I had charged them. I really shouldn't have bothered and Elizabeth would have been a lot happier.

From Musket Cove we sailed up to Lautoka where I had to clear in again. Elizabeth had gone ahead of me from the inlet where we anchored, a few miles south of the town. She got a lift on a train which had been doing track repairs. They were already harvesting sugarcane so the track was busy. I imagine it's quite rare for a train to stop and pick up hitchhikers.

Elizabeth's holiday did not improve. I got ill again with my waterworks and we tied up in the marina while I recovered, by which time it was time for her to fly home. She had thought about sailing to New Caledonia with me but returning to Fiji for the flight home wasn't really possible.

Looking back it was just as well. The trade winds were really having a go and now and again, seas came right over the boat. Life down below with hatches closed wasn't very pleasant and on deck, nasty cold salt water was flying everywhere.

The compensation was that 1,000 miles of ocean flew under the keel in no time. I surfed through the Havannah Pass as I had done once before and found a lovely little bay inside Prony Bay to anchor and recuperate.

As soon as the anchor was down and sails stowed, I slid over the side into the limpid, gin-clear water. The palm trees and white sand beach were backed by heavy bush. Then, above the red and yellow volcanic rocks were bare. The birds were singing and I was completely alone; perfect! A fresh water shower, tuna steaks for dinner and a motionless bunk for a long sleep.

Two days later I set off through Canal Woodin between Ile Quen and the mainland; then across the lagoon to Noumea, the big city. The big marina close to the city centre still provided a free birth for a day to clear in. So, in late afternoon, I tied up in a berth next to another elderly looking concrete yacht flying an Australian flag.

The immigration police arrived promptly and then the agriculture and fisheries officer which was a new thing. By five o'clock the customs hadn't yet arrived so I could now not bother with them. I wandered over to the pub for a couple of cold beers. With high-rise apartments all around hundreds of the yachts in the marina, this was the real world and a bit intimidating.

Early next morning, I took advantage of the fresh water tap and filled the tanks, put my washing to soak and washed the encrusted salt off the boat. My Australian neighbour appeared on deck lifting out a large backpack. He wasn't young, in fact approaching his eightieth birthday, he told me. He made regular trips from Sydney up to New Caledonia and Vanu'atu. He looked very fit and I began to think about my retirement plan which basically was "life ends at seventy".

When I asked him about the backpack he explained that he was off to catch the bus just around the corner there was a steep hill overhanging the bay. The backpack contained a paraglider. He was going to jump off the top into the prevailing wind and soar back and forth over the bay. Bloody hell, I could see my retirement plan might need some serious revision. The pension scheme might need boosting and spreading out to last a little longer.

I left at lunchtime and found a place to anchor among the moorings just outside. There I found I was among friends. I saw Henry Wakelam's old boat *Operculum* and met his son, Ivan, on his own boat nearby. Then on a small, beautiful, wooden sloop was a young German I hadn't seen since French Guyana the first time I was there, twenty years ago.

Farther out I saw an aluminium yacht which had to be Marie Christine who had been doctoring here for some years. She was just preparing to leave for the Philippines; so that night I was invited to a going away party in town. There I met a lot of old friends, and made some new ones.

One new friend was a girl living on *Fleur d'Ecosse* in the marina. This was the boat that had belonged to Ron Falconer when I met him and his wife and baby living on Suvarov Island in the Cook Islands in 1984. He had written a book about living on another small atoll, Caroline Atoll, which she lent me to read.

Marie Christine was intending to spend some time in south east Asia so maybe we would catch up with each other there.

I took my bicycle ashore. It hadn't enjoyed the trip on deck from Fiji and was getting very rusty but it made life very easy pedaling around town looking for suitable outlets for my stuff. I finished off with three really good places. One was a very posh gallery with very expensive jewellery and some Marquesian carvings. They had a smaller place downtown where they put a lot of my things on display in the window.

Another gallery near the museum filled a whole cabinet with all my carved whales which I left "en depôt" that is, on commission. Then a few days later, I found a place out of town in Baie de Citron that had an amazing collection of carvings from the Solomon Islands, Papua New Guinea, and a few things from Fiji. The owner, Raymonde, was a petite Vietnamese lady. She had it seemed a lot of different businesses and was always on the go; but we did some serious business.

I had found a pile of greenstone grit near the marina. It looked perfect for making tikis. So I dug out my old molds and made a dozen. The shop in town took one and Raymonde took the rest. I filled the bilge with bags of greenstone grit. The tikis really did look good.

On the Saturday morning I went to the flea market which they held each week next to the vegetable market, really close to the marina. There I met Sylvie and Max who lived on an aluminum yacht "Histoire d' Amour". They had been in the Marquesas and had also sold jewelry there next to my stuff. They made rings, bracelets and necklaces with beads and wire.

They did really well and Max was amazingly clever at twisting up wires into extraordinary shapes. Having been in New Caledonia for a year, they were thinking about heading down to New Zealand. I pointed out that they would have to sell everything for almost the half price here but seeing as the cost of living was half, it worked out and there were plenty of markets which they could try.

One day in the marina I was talking with some people and saying that I was planning to go back to New Zealand. They pointed out a Canadian yacht which had just come up from New Zealand and had left a car there which they had not yet managed to sell.

I wandered over to their boat and explain that I was returning to New Zealand and would need a car. I had sold the Subaru to Ken and Jos reluctantly, but they had loved it. I pointed out that I normally paid around $1,000 thousand dollars for a used car. They said they were really keen to sell me the car at that price. The wife didn't know what make the car was but said it was green and very nice. So, sight unseen, I bought a nice green car of unknown make or age. I paid for it in Central Pacific francs which they could use to help pay the marina bill.

Before setting off back to New Zealand, I sold a couple of whales, collected the rest, sold a few more pieces of jewelry, and promised to keep in touch with Raymonde if I was ever passing again. Then I was off. I had made a good wad of Central Pacific francs which I took to the bank and converted to euros at the set rate.

New Caledonia is a long way west of Tonga; so heading down to New Zealand, I was going to need to keep close to the wind. As it was I got pushed west and at one time I was close to hitting Norfolk Island. Fortunately, after that things got better and I eventually arrived off the north coast of New Zealand and loosed sheets to sail down to the Bay of Islands.

Having cleared in on the customs wharf, I motored up the river and found a spot beyond all the moored boats which looked deep enough to anchor in. At low tide, the keel sank into the soft mud but *Sea Loone* stayed upright. As the tide came back in, all the moored boats swung around in the current. I followed nearly an hour later.

Looking down towards Opua there was a boat yard, buildings, and hundreds of yachts tied in the marina or on moorings but for the rest of it, I had the wide shallow river winding into the hills, the bays full of mangroves and the hills covered with native bush, mainly tea tree, all to myself with no boats or houses to be seen.

I had dinner with Ken and Jos and caught up with all the news. The next morning they were happy to drive me down to Whangarei to find my new green car. We drove down in the Subaru I had sold them, which, thank God, was working well.

We found the farm where the car was stored and drove into the yard. There were a number of new looking cars parked so we went to inquire where mine was stored. It turned out to be one of the cars in the yard, bottle green, shiny, and very new looking. It was a Kia. I had never heard of one but it was made in Korea and had a key which you pointed at the car and it blinked, burped and opened the doors. Amazing! Apparently the Canadians had paid five thousand dollars for the car so I had a real bargain.

Ken and Jos left me and I drove into Whangarei to get a road worthiness certificate and then register the car at the post office. It was great although I must admit I missed the get-up-and-go of the Subaru.

It was still pretty cold in early December. I was used to the tropics, so even twenty three degrees felt cold; and at night it could go down to sixteen degrees. So I was happy when Elizabeth arrived to keep me warm. I had a load of jewellery put together and had made some more green stone tikis. We did a tour of the shops all of whom wanted to restock for the Christmas, summer season. Things had obviously sold well last year, so I again did well.

Lots of round-the-world yachts were arriving in Opua as usual. Unfortunately a memo from a meeting of local yachting businesses had leaked out in which it had been suggested that the bills for foreign visitors should be padded. This did not go down well and at the same time a dispute over the fuel dock left the visitors with no way to refill diesel tanks. As a result, many simply carried on down the coast.

Out in the main channel there was a really unusual looking vessel. It turned out it was owned by a friend of mine I had met years ago when he was living on a large concrete yacht. Eric was French, short and strong, with dreadlocks. Not so well-dressed, he wasn't going to be invited anywhere posh.

His new yacht was a hundred foot Dutch side trawler complete with funnel above the aft accommodation. He had bought her in Holland for very little money. The steel topsides were rusting away. The hull apparently was not so bad and the engine was a monster and almost new. He had then bought the complete rig for €10,000, off a huge luxury yacht which was being rerigged and set it up on the trawler. The main mast was enormous, as was all the rigging.

He had sailed across the Atlantic and now the Pacific. In Margarita Island in Venezuela he had loaded with super cheap fuel and persuaded the pretty young bar owner on the beach to come with him. She came with her dog, spoke no English and little French. The fuel had more or less run out and Eric was looking for somewhere to start fixing his rusty decks and bulkheads.

Sylvie and Max had arrived on *Histoire D'Amour* and had a table on the green in Pahia for the weekend market. Before Eric set off south to Tauronga to start work on his boat the six of us had some hilarious dinner parties on the trawler. I had bought a little LED Chinese garden lantern with a little solar panel. It shone from the rigging and helped me navigate home on a dark night. They were cheap at NZ$3.00 each so Eric bought two, one for the front and one for the back of *Pictoris*, the trawler.

Just before Christmas, Holger arrived on his new catamaran. This was now the third time we had met, the first in maybe 1989 when his catamaran became a parallelogram coming into Kuru in French Guyana, and had to be abandoned. The second time was in Tonga in 1994 with his Chinese wife and a trimaran, which again he had to leave to be sold because his business in Taiwan needed him.

Now he had an old ex-charter catamaran in which he had got as far as New Zealand with his wife and daughter. Things were going well but the boat needed some work and he was going on down to Whangarei to haul the boat out.

The daughter, maybe seven years of age, had me amazed. She could speak English to me ,turn to Holger and speaking German and then shout something in Mandarin to her mother in the galley; and there's me still stumbling along in my poubelle French after all these years.

With business organized, Elizabeth and I went off touring. We stopped in Auckland Museum which had completed its renovation. The shop was much larger but obviously not as discerning as before although they did buy a few bone hooks.

We stopped with Dick and Jane in Kati Kati for Liz to stock up on avocados and then drove onto Taupo to stay with Eddie, my ex-boss from Liverpool University. Eddie had taken early retirement and had become something of a real estate expert. He had a lovely new home in which he lived with his ex-secretary.

Ken and Jos in Opua had a nice little business collecting seeds from native trees; sorting and drying them and sending them off to seed merchants all over the world. Elizabeth and I had some idea of what they wanted so kept our eyes out for different trees. We came back with some good stuff but also a lot of common rubbish.

We motored around Taupo Lake, visited the trout farm, watched bubbling hot springs and mud pools, and gazed in awe at the scenery. I imagined if Ruapehu or the other big volcanoes really woke up, I'd want to be a long way away.

We went to stay with Alvah and Diana on the way home. Diana mentioned that a new gallery had opened not far away so we decided to all go for a lunchtime drink in the pub calling in the gallery on the way. The lady proprietors seemed interested in my goodies but as usual there was no room to lay anything out. So I tipped all the little bags of pendants on the floor adding a few tikis and some bone whales.

The lady join me on her hands and knees and I spread everything out and gave her a price list. Meanwhile, Alvah and Diana and Elizabeth were discreetly keeping in the background. Half an hour later, back in the car, we headed for the pub. Alvah was not happy about how I conducted my business. Why hadn't I got a nice display case. I explained that if the woman is prepared to get on her hands and knees, she's interested. If she started sorting through it all then she's going to buy. No problem.

Alvah was still not happy and seeing as I now had $500 in my pocket I had to buy the drinks.

Alvin and Diana was still working on the preparations for the trip back to the cold north. The cat was now old and fat with the tips of its ears still missing from frostbite north of Baffin Island. I was sure he was not the least bit keen on going back into the ice again. They would have to leave in the spring and I had to leave too

I had planned to go to Australia, stop again in Gove, and spend a little time on the north coast. However, every time I heard about Australia, it was about more petty bureaucracy making it more and more difficult to visit with a yacht. The cost of clearing in was now over$300. Gove was no longer an entry port, special permits were required for the north coast, and just now I heard that the captain of any vessel at any time, even at anchor, could be breathalysed and prosecuted for being drunk in charge of a boat. Ridiculous! Apparently yachts now put up two black balls in the rigging when at anchor to indicate that there was no one in command.

With all this in mind, I moved on to Plan B. This entailed leaving to head south into the Roaring Forties; then head back east all the way to Rapa, an island south of the Tuamotus. Rapa had the strangest volcanic plugs which looked like huge basalt penises rising thousands of feet into the sky.

From Rapa, I would reach north back to the Marquesas and spend a year there and in French Polynesia. Not only would it be really good to be back there, but I also could probably make it profitable. The down side was the sailing into the Roaring Forties.

Having decided on Plan B, I ordered a new mainsail from Hong Kong and some new standing rigging made up in Whangarei. The forward hatch was a bit suspect so I rebuilt that and made a new fuel tank. Ian and Colleen in Keri Keri were happy for me to use a corner of the fibreglass factory. Their water wheel project hadn't advanced but they were busy making the last few sections of the giant geodesic dome.

Down the road, Henry was on his feet again and Yanick was still trying to feed me green gunk. She had joined a cooperative where everyone exchanged goods and services without using money. Yanick's currency was olive oil.

I bought a load of small bits for the Dremel tool, a new bench grinder and a large band saw which could make life a lot easier. Then I contacted Steven in Tonga to see if he could get stuff made and sent down to me. He thought this was possible but also said that he may be coming himself in a month or so. I sent him a list of what I wanted and as usual, said I'd take anything else he thought I'd like. By this time, he had a good sense of how my mind worked.

In February, Elizabeth and I decided on another trip around and she wanted to take a tent and do some camping. I wasn't keen but we borrowed a tent anyway. The idea was to stay again with Dick and Jane in Kati Kati, and then travel up the Coromandel Peninsula, camping as we went.

Fortunately, we extended our stay with Dick and Jane where we had a very nice, large, double bed. Then I heard from Stephen to say he was at his cousins in Auckland and had my stuff. So our camping trip was not going to be too long.

In fact, we only camp one night in a lumpy, tussocky field with a primitive loo at the other end of the field. There were peacocks making child strangling noises and dogs trying to get into the tent. We couldn't light a fire so I had no coffee, no sleep then had to pay twenty dollars for the privilege. No more camping for us.

The following night I found a bird observatory where we could stay on the Thames Estuary. At high tide we followed the birdwatchers down to the water's edge and borrowed a pair of binoculars to watch a very strange New Zealand wader, small, grey brown, nondescript except that its bill was bent to the left, or was it the right? Anyway, I had heard about such a strange bird, and there it was.

There were bunk beds in small cabins, a fantastic library and a huge kitchen. There were only a few people staying, a Dutch family with two children, serious tick-hunters, who had just come down from South East Asia. They were out to see every bird in the world.

The other person of note was a South African who had just spent months in Antarctica on big trawlers, policing their catch. His main interest was the albatross and he showed us really good photographs of all the different species.

I'd like to have stayed at least another night but I needed to see Stephen before he left. Elizabeth was a bit out of her depth talking about our feathered friends. She had never met such fanatics but even she admitted it was better than that bloody farmer's field.

It took a bit of searching before we found where Stephen was staying. It was a nice bungalow with a large garage. The garage was a scene of great activity, not much different to Steven's workshop up north. His cousin was making pendants from pearl shell, probably from Aratika, and Stephen was finishing off some of the hooks I had ordered. Everything had been done and he had a load of really nice little whales which I also took. I paid out a large wad of NZ dollars and promised I'd see him in Nuku'alofa in a year and a half's time.

We motored out to Ocean Beach to see Alvah and Diana on the way home and find out how they were progressing with their plans. Alvah looked a bit uncomfortable. He said he had people coming to dinner and we couldn't stay. I was a bit suspicious and asked who was coming. He had the Pardy's coming for the evening.

For the past twenty years, Lynn and Larry Pardy had written the definitive how-to-sail and where-to-go books. They were not my favorite people, which Alvah well knew and he wanted me out of there as soon as possible .I didn't want to meet them either, so we left.

My nearest neighbour in the Kawa Kawa River was Lorraine who lived on an old wooden motorboat on a mooring. She spent most of the night on her computer and slept all morning, snarling if I ever came near. In the afternoons, she spent time growing a huge variety of vegetables on the foredeck. She earned money as a photographer.

Occasionally the local fishermen who put flounder nets out, caught a snapper and would give it to me in passing. I would share it with Lorraine and we'd have dinner together.

By this time Elizabeth had returned to her house building in Devon. Lorraine agreed to make me a catalogue of my jewellery, photographing each piece. She would print out a number of copies and also make me a CD. We agreed a price and did the work in a house she was looking after in Opua.

That morning it started raining. Half way through the process of photographing the pieces, we began to realize that the rain was serious. In fact, we got a phone call from the local plumber whose office and showroom were flooding just down the road. We drove down to see if we could help but the water was already over the sandbags and still rising. So we had to abandon the place and return up the hill to the house. Behind us the road collapsed and then further down towards Pahia, the road just slid away into the valley. Similarly, the road over the hill to Kawa Kawa washed away and Opua was cut off.

Lorraine finished the photography and I made it back to the boat, dodging trees and Islands of weeds swishing down the now red, brown river. A huge log had got stuck across the catamaran in front of me which I managed to clear but smaller stuff kept wrapping itself around my anchor chain. It was still pouring down and there was news of houses in Opua slipping down the hillsides.

In the evening it stopped raining and by morning the floodwaters were dropping but Opua was isolated. The local tourist boats set up a ferry service down the river to Pahia and this remained the only way out for a whole week.

Lorraine's catalogue looked great with a carved whales tooth on the cover. "Pelagic Art". There were over sixty items, some unique, one-off single pieces; others, as many as you want.

The new mainsail arrived from Hong Kong and fitted perfectly. But the new rigging, when it arrived from Whangarei, had to be sent back. I'd always used 7X7 galvanized wire. It looked like the riggers did not know much about galvanized wire and had used the wrong wire. They then discovered there was none of the right stuff in New Zealand and had to order it from Australia.

In fact, they found some 19X1 wire which was even better than the 7X7 wire; so finally I was happy. I hung the wire up in Ken and Jos's garden and doused it with boiled linseed oil before taking it to the boat.

4

By April 2007, I was ready. The boat was good. Even the engine seemed to be behaving itself. I set off down the river. I had not been farther south than thirty five degrees. Now I was heading into the Roaring Forties to find strong cold westerly winds in order to sail back to the east.

The first few days out I made some fair progress, edging towards 40° south. One day I managed to hook up the computer to my little Sony radio and got a weather-fax picture of the South Pacific, east as far as the Cook Islands. There was a tropical depression between Tonga and Fiji which would no doubt be heading my way. The following day, sure enough, the depression was heading south and would probably curve eastwards.

In addition, a large depression just below forty south was heading east from South Australia. It all looked a bit ominous. The next day I lost the radio signal and was left to tap the barometer but I knew what was going to happen. The two lows would join up and I was going to get a little more westerly wind than I really wanted.

It started twenty four hours later and for four days blew like hell. I dropped all the sails and tried to run with it under bare poles. I put out a long warp with a length of chain on the end to keep the stern to the wind and moderate my speed. In the Fasnet gale this had worked well. But not this time!

Whatever I did, *Sea Loone* remained pinned down sideways on, heeled over at 45°. The wind was slicing the tops off the waves and hurling spume across the surface. The thick cloud and pouring rain was made worse by the dark and gloomy conditions, even at midday. But for me, what was far worse was the freezing cold. We surfed sideways towards Rapa a few thousand miles ahead.

At one stage, the mainsail flogged its way free of the boom; so before the new sail destroyed itself, I went out to tie it down again. It's hard to describe how difficult such a simple job had become. I wrapped myself around the boom, horribly exposed, standing on the cabin top. I fought the sail into submission, lashing the jib sheet around and around the boom and the sail until I finally pinned down the last little flailing piece of sailcloth. Then, hand hold by handhold, I eased myself back onto the deck and along into the cockpit.

By the fourth day, life had become damp and salty but pinned over as we were, the movement wasn't too dramatic. Nothing had broken. The only problem was a persistent leak and I couldn't find where it was coming from. Every hour I had to pump out a gallon or more of water. It was very worrying.

When the weather eased enough to sail again the leak disappeared. For a few days we made progress in lumpy seas and then the wind started to rise again. The screaming wind in the rigging started all over and again, we were pinned down and pushed sideways. The leak started again. The low-pressure system was now in front of us and had developed into something huge and slow-moving. So the high pressure system coming up behind was squashing the isobars between and it howled! At least, now and again there was some blue sky so it wasn't so gloomy but it was still freezing cold.

Two days into the second beating, I found the leak. Pinned over at such an angle one side of the boat was permanently submerged so the bilge pump, which had an outlet just below the deck, was working backwards. There was no valve but on the up roll, lying on the deck, I jammed a cork into the outlet, problem solved.

I kept going after the weather eased. I had no really dry clothing. There was salt everywhere and I was bitterly cold. By now I was south of the Australs approaching the longitude of the Tuamotus. At this point, I was just too miserable to carry on so I angled north into warm water heading back to my little island paradise, Aratika.

A week later the weather improved. There was blue sky and it was much warmer. Another week and I passed a few of the western atolls of the Tuamotus and in the morning, I approached Aratika. This time the tide was flowing into the lagoon. I actually felt I was going downhill as we swept into the pass and were spat out into the lagoon. By late afternoon, I was anchored off Guy's motu, the horrible nightmare days in the Southern Ocean, just a memory.

Guy and the family were not home. The house and workshops were closed. In the morning a speedboat arrived. It was Guys father-in-law. The family were in Tahiti working, with the kids in school there. The father then handed me a cell phone and I talked to Guy in Tahiti. Amazing.

I was free to stay on the island as long as I wanted. There was water in the tanks and I could help myself to whatever food was in the deep freeze. I had brought Guy a number of beer making kits which were popular in New Zealand and Australia. He often ran out of beer when on the island and crates of Hinano, the local beer, from Tahiti were incredibly expensive.

I settled into a pleasant life working a few hours on the jewellery, walking the outside reef at low tide, snorkelling along the inside and collecting more miki miki wood, pearl shell, and trocha shell for carving. I also found some strange twisted roots which made new bases for the larger carved whales.

The first time I went to the village, only twenty minutes away with the dinghy and outboard engine I found the shop closed but I found the girl's husband in one of the sheds built on stilts over the water. He and a couple of other guys were busy opening oysters, removing the pearls and replacing them with new seeds.

He was happy to open the shop when they had finished the batch of shells. So I sat with him and watched. The secret of how this was done was known only to the Japanese the first time I was here in Takaroa, the Japanese had visited each year to seed the oysters they had prepared. Now the locals did it themselves and I was shown how.

It was a little complicated but basically the shell was eased open slightly, a pocket was cut in the body close to the muscle, and a piece of mantle placed in the pocket together with a small sphere of freshwater mussel shell. The oyster is then carefully placed in a net bag and lowered into the lagoon below the shed.

A week or so later if the seed hasn't been spat out, the oyster is taken out into the deep water of the lagoon and suspended there for over a year. There is now a tight control over the thickness of the mother of pearl that has to be deposited on the seed before it can be extracted and sold.

When the time is up, the pearl is removed and replaced by another seed. This can happen maybe three times before the oyster is finished. Each time a larger seed can be inserted and less time is needed to form the pearl.

I was watching the first pearls being removed and the second seed being put in. The first pearl prized out was small but perfect, with a green lustre. I was given it and told to pass it on to my girlfriend. The second pearl had a definite red tinge, quite different. This was also passed over. I had to strenuously refuse any more. I knew that in Tahiti these would sell for maybe €100 each.

With that batch of oysters seeded and lowered into the water we walked up to the shop where again I had difficulty getting them to accept money for what I needed in the shop. Later in my stay I visited again to buy some reject pearls. These were pearls that were pitted or were white or matt black because the wrong piece of mantle had been inserted. I particularly wanted whitish ones to make my jewelry and also wanted some "keshi" pearls.

Keshi pearls were pearls formed naturally from pieces of grit or whatever. They were usually very odd shapes but pure mother of pearl and, I thought, lovely. There were no keshi pearls but two large bags of rejects. We agreed a price per piece and I sat on their porch in the shade selecting what I wanted. I finished off with maybe half a kilo which I could use and counted them up.

Under the new rules of the cooperative in Tahiti, these pearls were not to be sold. In fact, much better looking ones were often rejected and crushed so the price was negligible. When I passed over the money, another large handful was added as a bonus.

Two weeks into my stay, the father-in-law visited again to say Sylvania was coming to stay for a week as she had community business in the village. I could order anything I wanted from Tahiti so I asked for a dozen eggs. On Thursday, I was picked up from the boat and we shot across the lagoon in the speedboat to meet Sylvania and the aeroplane which now regularly visited once a week.

There are one hundred people on Aratika and most of them were at the airport arriving in speedboats and tying up to the new dock. At least a third of the population was actually working. There was a ticket office with an arrivals and departures desk, baggage handlers, a coffee shop and so on. Just before the plane arrived, a fancy new red fire engine drew up. And then a van with flashing lights and a man with a large bat in each hand to direct the plane onto the parking stand.

With all the people running around, I never saw how many people disembarked from the plane, but it did include Sylvania with a number of boxes and bags, including my eggs.

Sylvania stayed with her father in the village and visited the island a few times. She dug out some frozen chicken for me. When I mentioned keshi pearls, she went over to the new house now almost completed. She came back quite upset. A bag of good pearls and one of keshi pearls had disappeared as had a few other things.

It turned out a nephew had stolen them and gone off to Tahiti. I was shocked, but it seemed that such occurrences were not uncommon. The idea of "ownership" was a lot looser here so stealing, borrowing, sharing and so on all had fuzzy edges. I was probably more annoyed than Sylvania at the loss of the keshi pearls because I wanted them.

Sylvania flew away the next Thursday and a few days later, the local schooner arrived with, among other things, a box of dry biscuits I was waiting for.

I had been on the island for a month and once had to move my anchorage when a small front passed through. I was now waiting for another front which would give me a push east towards the Marquesas. It arrived one morning, the wind swinging into the north and the barometer dropping just a little. I motored across the lagoon after untangling the chain from the coral heads and sped out of the lagoon.

For three days I managed to sail due east. When the wind finally clocked around from south towards the east, I could head for the Marquesas now well north of east with the sheets slightly slacked. What could have been a hard beat had become a pleasant sail.

As the sun began to paint the horizon with morning light, Ua Pou appeared on the horizon directly in front of me. I didn't get that huge satisfaction of a landfall as I did when I used to navigate with a sextant but still, a difficult trip had been completed. Nuka Hiva was just over the horizon to the north and I would be anchored in Taeohae by the evening. I was looking forward to spending a whole year in one of my favourite places.

It was now July 2007 and there were still quite a few yachts in the bay; but they would have to move on rapidly if they wanted to cruise all the other Pacific island groups before the end of the season.

I found Sophie and Fara in their new house up on the hillside behind Justin's place and got all the news. Justin was now retired but Julienne was still running the pension. Philippe had also retired from the hospital and the family had moved to Raeiatea, west of Tahiti in order to school the children.

Odile was still working at the hospital and in fact was now chief medical officer but Alain had had a major setback. On one of his charters with his catamaran, he had fallen asleep in the early morning approaching Ua Huka, the island to the east of Nuku Hiva, and sailed straight into a cliff face. One bow was completely destroyed and the other holed. The boat had filled with water but somehow or other he contacted Pipapo, the dive boat operator, and they had towed the catamaran, completely awash, back to Nuku Hiva. There they got it lifted out on the new dock wall and with a grant from the government, he was now undertaking a massive rebuild.

I left clearing-in until as late as possible as I was worried about the boat being allowed to stay more than one year in French Polynesia. I sent off my catalogues in the post to Tahiti, Moorea, Huahini, Raeatea and Bora Bora. I had also emailed the boutiques and galleries.

It was now impossible to pay with a cheque made out to cash and I could not open a bank account. But the post office had a wonderful system for sending money between the islands. It was like a postal order and was called a "mondat". So my customers could pay in at the post office and I would sign my mondat in the post office in Taiohae and be paid out there and then. It worked perfectly. I soon had orders from everybody and sent off parcels all over the islands. The postmistress got to know me well and waved and smiled if a mondat had arrived.

At the same time, the yacht services office on the wharf had changed hands and was now run by a local, Moitai, who was happy to sell some of my stuff. Pipapo's wife in her little boutique next door, also sold a lot.

On my side of the bay, Rose, the American lady, was still battling to build a new hotel and exhibited a lot of my things in her museum. So with that all organized I could settle in. I had the bandsaw and the bench grinders in the cockpit with the Dremel tool suspended from the coach roof, a small factory.

After a few hours' work, the batteries would go down and I would stop work for the day to let the solar panels recharge them. Occasionally, I'd have to stop because my hands were aching; but usually I wasn't working so hard.

A local friend, Damas, did some bone carving in his workshop near the beach. He agreed to carve some Marquesian designs into some of my larger bone hooks. I could do the lashings and we would split the rewards. It sort of worked, but in the end, he owed me a lump of money which dragged on a bit.

I got bored making little tikis and started playing with the pearl shell. I began making pretty pendants and inlaying pearls into the shell. I made a small copy of a hand adze with a Marquesian cross design carved into it and a fancy lashings above. They sold faster than I could make them so I was kept busy.

On the sail up from New Zealand, I'd had begun to notice a swelling on the side of my neck and began to have difficulty swallowing. Alone out on the ocean, things like this pray on your mind. So in Taiohae I went to consult with Odile at the hospital. It was a goitre, a swelling of the thyroid. But apart from swallowing, the thyroid was still doing its job properly. The problem was, if it kept on getting bigger, it might throttle me.

I wrote to my cousin, John, back in England. He was now a chief orthopedic surgeon in Newcastle. I was told that if I was going to have it out, I had to come home. It was a tricky operation so I tried to ignore the whole problem.

The months passed rapidly. I had revisited most of my favourite diving sites, seriously reduced the octopus population and found a few collectible shells.

In November, Odile contacted me to say that a thyroid expert would be arriving in Hiva Oa and staying a couple of days. I had to dive in and clear off some growth on the bottom of the boat and on the propeller. Then motoring out of the bay the engine overheated. A fish had blocked the inlet pipe for the cooling water. So I was late starting then had very little wind. The result was I arrived in Hiva Oa at the same time the doctor left.

I hadn't been in Hiva Oa, since1983. There was a new dock and they were busy dredging the inlet but it was still a long hike into town. At least I found another outlet for my goodies and then sailed over to Tahuata to see Teiki and Cyril.

In all the islands there was great activity for a big festival of art and dance to be held in December in Ua Pou. Visiting dance groups, sculptors and artists would be coming from all over Polynesia including Hawaii, Easter Island and the Cooks. I did some business with Teiki but Cyril was really involved making the complicated costumes for the hundred-strong island dance troupe. I had already seen the huge dance group in Nuku Hiva practicing for the event.

On the way home I stopped in Ua Pou and had dinner with the dentist whom I knew. Round the corner the French army were putting in a new dock for one of the festival sites.

A few weeks later together with four other yachts, I returned to Ua Pou and anchored off the new dock for the festival. A swell was running so, although you could land people at the dock, you couldn't tie up even a small dinghy. We all went ashore in a large inflatable; then the driver anchored off and swam in.

The festival site up the steep-sided valley was overhung by one of the huge volcanic plugs, a Havana cigar jammed into the ground and rising 1,000 feet into the air! The huge old ceremonial stone platforms have been cleared and thatched roofs built as they would have been in ancient times. Then a large area was cleared for dancing.

Another site had been prepared in the south of the island which I never saw and then there was a huge covered arena in the main town, Hakahau, and another covered area for the exhibits of craftsmanship.

The logistical problems were huge. Thousands of people had to be found a place to sleep and then provided with food. The schools, halls, and so on had all been commandeered and the main harbour was full of ships and boats. The

Army had come up with a transport ship and the governor's launch arrived. The cruiseship *Gaugin* arrived with some spectators. It was organized bedlam but fantastic!

The dancing groups and drums were amazing; from swinging hips to thumping haka and from the Marquesian "pig dance", with scowling muscle men to the "bird dance," with a delightful long-haired girl prancing delicately.

I filmed it all with my video camera but never caught the atmosphere. I watched the re-enactment of a battle between two valleys where one victim was finally carted off to be barbecued and I fell in love with a heart-stoppingly beautiful girl from the Australs. I could have been her grandfather, never mind.

On the last day we all piled on one boat and motored around to Hakahau for the final evening's dancing. We jammed the yacht in amongst the boats in the harbour and all trooped ashore. Most of the craft work had been and gone which was disappointing, but the dancing that evening was great.

We sailed back to our anchorage in the dark with children fast asleep in the bunks and the rest of us sprawled all over the deck. By the time we rounded up into the bay, anchored, and then got ferried to the different boats, we were all very very tired.

Christmas 2007 was the usual dinner dance in town and for New Year, the Mahiatapu family invited me to a huge kai kai feast with Justin and Julienne and the three brothers, a daughter and lots of sundry wives and husbands and kids. There was a pig, a goat, and octopus, prawns, shellfish, and mounds of taro, breadfruit, rice and so on. They had prepared enough to feed an army.

The only mistake I made was trying some specially prepared prawns and fish. I had always steered clear of eating poi, breadfruit which had been buried in the ground to ferment and fester. The dish was called fafaro I think. As soon as I took my first mouthful I realized my mistake. I made it to the nearest bushes before throwing up. It was absolutely disgusting. The family thought it was very funny as I washed my mouth out and settled my stomach with another bottle of beer. The recipe for the dish was simple, the prawns and fish were left in a bottle of sea water to rot for a few months.

So 2008 arrived. My life was pretty organized but then everything changed completely. There was a message for me to call my sister in England. I walked around the bay to the first telephone kiosk and using my plastic telephone card, managed to get through easily. I remember I was standing looking out over the bay where to the right *Sea Loone* and a few other boats were anchored and, to the left was the wharf with small boats. Looking south Ua Pou sat on the horizon with its distinctive outline.

My mother had, at last, died. It was not unexpected and, for my sister, must have been an enormous relief. My mother had tried and succeeded in making my sister's life as unpleasant as possible over the previous ten years getting worse as she got older. She died in a nursing home after an accident in the flat had put her in hospital. I can't say I grieved myself as we were never close.

What really affected me was that, over the later years, Paul, my brother-in-law, had assumed power of attorney over my mother's affairs and so she had been unable to spend all the money she had, not that she hadn't tried. And so out of the blue there was a flat to be sold and a large lump of money.

Whatever schemes mother had, if there was anything left my sister and I had long ago agreed to share half and half. And so suddenly there was I in a phone booth in the middle of nowhere being told that I had maybe £100,000 coming to me.

When you consider we left England in 1978 with £1,000 which lasted us a year and now I still budgeted around 3 or4,000 euros then this huge amount was difficult to imagine. My piggy bank was still full from the Caribbean. Now with this I was rich. .I could throw my crude retirement plan out of the window.

In March, I reanchored the boat a little further from the reef, tied everything down and flew home. I had a residence certificate from the town hall in Taeohae and with that, got my pensioner's card for Air Tahiti. This entitled me to half price fares to Tahiti but then I had to pay a huge amount of money for Air New Zealand to fly me to New Zealand, then Hong Kong, and on to London. I couldn't go the other way as America wouldn't accept my passport.

Once in England, cousin John had arranged for me to see a surgeon for my thyroid and a urologist to examine my prostate, Paul had promised to help me out with my finances, and Elizabeth would put me up in Dittisham in Devon before I went up north.

In Dittisham I realized that life in the village required at least fifty times the money I had. A small cottage cost millions. Still, working in an office in London and helicoptering into a pretty thatched cottage for the weekend didn't compare with Taeohae. I did have to admit that the beer was better and actually cheaper.

Elizabeth's cottage was still a long way from finished but when fully restored it was apparently going to sell for over one million pounds, ridiculous! I helped with the work for a week and then Elizabeth drove me up to the Lake District to Di and Paul's. Elizabeth could play golf with Di on their private golf course and Paul helped me open a UK bank account which was far from easy, and then deposit some money with the building society.

My mother's flat in Wallasey on the Wirral where I had built *Sea Loone* was up for sale but there was no great interest. It'wasnHt likely to generate more than £100,000. We were having to pay for its upkeep so in fact, at the time, it was costing me money.

In t'ree yearsH time I would reach the age of sixty-five and Paul had made inquiries on my behalf about how much old age pension I would get from the UK Government. I had actually contributed very little during my time working at the University and the jobs I had taken while building the boat. However, Paul was told I would receive approximately twenty pounds a week. I thought that was very generous. £1,000 a year went a long way in my lifestyle but the news was even better. The UK Government had a scheme through which I could increase my pension by buying stamps over the next few years, before I reach sixty-five.

The bank was offering a miserable five per cent interest so the pension scheme looked really good. Paul would pay in the maximum he was allowed every few months, a total of maybe £4,000 but my pension in 2010 would be at least £90 a week!'In one year, IHd get my money back and I could sit back and watch my bank balance grow week by week.

In Newcastle, John, my cousin introduced me to his friend, a surgeon, and he examined my thyroid. It wasn't seriously enlarged or debilitating, so we agreed to leave it for a year or two and see what happened. I was worried about taking pills every day if the thyroid was removed. Forgetting, running out, or losing them over the side could all be fatal.

The urologist was a waste of time as was the dental hospital .I would go back to Fiji to sort out my teeth problems.

March, April and England was cold. In fact I found it bitterly cold. It seemed to seep into my bones and I had neither the body fat nor the clothes to keep it out. But the locals seemed to be inured.

With cousin John, Heidi and the two boys we went hiking up a hillside in the Pennines to collect some frog spawn. There were still patches of snow here and there and we scooped the spawn out of a small pond half covered in ice. I tried to imagine frogs bonking in that freezing water; impossible. But only a few days later with a hellish cold wind blasting down the main street in Newcastle, I watched the local talent sashaying along in tiny miniskirts and bare midriffs. I was just a pair of eyes peering out from a mound of clothing.

The finale was just before I left. We planned a pleasant stroll along Hadrian's Wall. We found a picnic table high on the ridge looking north into Scotland and ate sandwiches in a sleeting rain. I couldn't get the mantra "what am I doing here...what am I doing here?" out of my head.

I was not looking forward to the flight home from Manchester via London, Hong Kong, New Zealand, Tahiti and finally Nuku Hiva. It started well when they changed my first flight directly to London Heathrow saving me a bus trip across London from Gatwick. But then the Air New Zealand manager refused to allow me to continue because I had no return ticket from French Polynesia. He lost a lot of face after a huge argument, and I was allowed to continue. They had to hold the Tahiti flight a few minutes in Auckland because we were late and I dashed across and was up in the air again in no time.

In Tahiti, my luggage arrived first and all alone. I don't think they had put it in the hold. So when I passed through customs with no-one behind me, they wondered where I had come from. We laughed and joked and the taxi driver whisked me into town for a few hours sleep before the last 1,000 miles to the Marquesas.

Fara's brother was waiting for me in Nuku Hiva with his Land Rover taxi to drive me over the mountain, across the caldera and down into Taeohae. The new road was spectacular. Then one of my fishermen friends gave me a lift out to the boat and then gave me a nice fish for my dinner.

Apart from the black sand in the middle of the bay seriously eroding the anchor chain, *Sea Loone* was fine. It felt so good to be back in my own little world, strip off all those clothes and look out over blue water at the spectacular scenery.

By this time it was April and the annual flotilla of round-the-world yachts was arriving. As the years went by, they got bigger and bigger and more and more sophisticated. This usually meant that after a long trip to arrive in Nuku Hiva, they had a few problems and had to hang around for weeks waiting for parts.

My jewellery business was still doing well and I sent more parcels off to the big islands. In the Marquesas, the cruise ship season was coming to an end but the tourist season in Moorea and Bora Bora was just beginning, with a huge influx in July for the "Quatorze" festival.

I spent time in Anaho Bay on the north coast of Nuku Hiva and then sailed down the coast of Terre Dessert on the west side. When I arrived back in Hakatea, there were a number of yachts, a few of whom I had met. This is the bay to anchor to walk up to the waterfall.

I was invited on board one of the yachts to socialize and, as we sat talking, we were hailed from the beach by a long-haired Marquesian with tattoos all over his face and body and a massive bone necklace. He looked the perfect cannibal and was calling my name. I rowed ashore. I knew it was Damas and sure enough he had more of the money he owed me on the carved hook transaction.

Back on the yacht with a large amount of money clutched in my hand, the visitors were a little awestruck, gobsmacked as we say in Liverpool.

My year was almost up and I had to visit all my outlets in Tahiti and the other big islands before I left. So after a lot of hugging and kissing, I tore myself away and sailed out of the bay.

By the time I arrived in Tahiti, the boat had been in French Polynesia for more than a year. This could have been a problem. Fortunately it was a busy day for customs and I think they assumed I had just arrived, having only looked at the month not the year, so nothing was said.

As promised, Ann in the shop "Ganesha" bought all my remaining whales carved from the huge jawbone I had found in Tonga. She also took all my little tikis, Damas's carved hooks, and other stuff. It was a very good start.

Moorea was disappointing. All the big hotels were closing down and the island seemed dead. Both the businesses I had done business with were gone but arriving in Huahini, everything was good. Again, in Raiatea, the gallery was pleased to see me. And finally there was Bora Bora. It had been raped and pillaged, the lagoon ruined by dredging and now surrounded with hotel shacks, the motus bulldozed and canalized. It was heading in the same downward direction as Moorea.

I sailed around the lagoon to the windward side passing a huge dredge starting another massive project, and anchored to one side of another hotel, more or less completed but with no obvious customers. I found Fafa's place perched above the steep shoreline. The jungle to the left was in stark contrast to the neat rows of coconut trees that were part of the hotel grounds, to the right.

I hadn't had much contact with Fafa since my last visit. Since then there had been the tagua nut turtle project. She had at last received the parcel of turtle parts from Tonga. I think the parcel went to Hawaii on route. But I had heard nothing since then.

Fafa came to the door thinner and more weather beaten than ever, but looking fit. She sat me down and prepared coffee. Before I could make any inquiries, she excused herself and I could hear her in the old workshop tossing stuff around. She came back with the cardboard box I had sent to her three years ago, the turtles.

So what happened? Within a year of my last seeing her, Fafa had been granted a pension from the government. They had augmented it because of the cost of living in Bora Bora so he she had found herself with lots of money. Therefore she had stopped work. No more jewellery, no more pareos and no turtle project. They were still in the box; one hundred bodies, one hundred heads and four hundred flippers!

Fortunately Fafa had not had to pay import duty as part-made craft work was exempt. But now they were in French Polynesia it would be silly to me to take them back to Tonga. So I spent the next week putting them all together and mounted them on pieces of coral gleaned off the beach. They looked good.

I phoned Rose in Nuku Hiva as she had bought some of the original turtles I brought from Ecuador. I offered her a discount and time to pay. No problem. A few days later a large box was winging its way from Bora Bora to Taeohae. If and when I got paid, I would get my original money back, plus a few times more.

I did some more business with Bebe in the village and got a part payment from Rose with a mondat. I then had to take my shoebox of lovely Polynesian francs and change them into Euros. I was off to Tonga and had already emailed Stephen to tell him I was arriving in a few weeks.

I angled south for a couple of hours to avoid the lumpy water behind Bora Bora and then turned west for Beverage Reef. With the boat squared away and the Aires wind vane happily steering, I dug into my piggy bank to see how my finances were. I found I had:

€ 22,535
US$ 2,376
$NZ 1,290
Fiji $ 50

I still had around €2,000 owed to me from the Marquesas. Under normal circumstances, I would be very happy with this situation, five years out from St. Barts. But in fact there was now also £60,000 in a building society in UK earning me 6.5% interest and another £10,000 in Barclays Bank. These sums made my efforts over the eight years of the new millennium look rather meager.

Since my last visit to Beverage Reef only a few years ago, a very severe cyclone had passed by and the effect was dramatic. At least the top two feet to the reef had been torn away. There was no sign of any part of the wrecked trawler and even the two metre cube concrete ballast blocks had disappeared. At low tide, little or nothing appeared above the surface. Thank God I had been a long, long, way away in New Zealand at the time. I stayed only a few days and carried on to Tonga.

With *Sea Loone* tied stern-to in the fishing harbour and the paperwork completed, I joined the five o'clock crowd in the Billfish and caught up with all the local news. The next day I met Steven and his boys set to work to replenish my stock. I gave Stephen himself the remaining pieces of ivory to see what he could make with them. We had worked together so often that little had to be said. There were a few new things worth trying and I had brought another sack of pearl shell and a kilo of substandard pearls.

By the end of October, the harbor was filling up with the cruising yachts set to go south to New Zealand, and when November came I set out myself. It was a reasonably quick and easy trip down but, damn, New Zealand hadn't yet warmed up and I was freezing!

The jewellery business wasn't going to take up much of my time and I had grand plans to spend some of my new found wealth. I contacted Andy, my Liverpool mate who was now semiretired on a New Zealand pension. He agreed to help me install a new engine in *Sea Loone*, and I was going to fit a roller furling gear for the headsail. The roller furling job was a bit complicated and I would have to make some serious modifications on the bow.

I organized to haul the boat out in Whangarei in January close to Andy's place by which time I planned to have bought the new engine, the reefing system and most of the other bits and pieces. The propeller, propeller shaft, exhaust system, and lots of other stuff had to be changed too. Mark, the welder in Opua, agreed to make the new bow fitting and I gave him the old engine.

On the day I hauled out, the crane arrived, removed the mast, pulled out the old engine and dumped it in Mark's lorry. It then picked up the new engine, just delivered, and drop it into the boat. The new engine probably weighed less than half the old Volvo and was half the size; so we could slide it into a corner of the main cabin while we prepared the new beds for it to sit on. The weather remained perfect and Andy and I worked like dogs. We had it all together inside a month and I painted the top sides after knocking away a load of loose concrete. The crane returned to reinstall the mast, a coat of anti-fouling was put on the bottom, and we relaunched.

The new engine was from Yanmar so their man came along on the trial to make sure we had it all right. We zoomed up and down the river at over six knots. Andy and I weren't over pleased that we should run the engine so hard without running it in but the Yanmar man was adamant it was okay. I still think he was wrong as subsequently we had a few problems. A year later we discovered that the new propeller was badly out of balance. With that fixed, the engine ran more smoothly.

The engine cost me over NZ$10,000 (€5,000) and, with the roller furling and all the extra parts, I spent twice as much. I paid Andy for his time but nowhere near enough. His expertise was worth more than money, a true engineer.

April, I planned to leave to sail to Tonga, New Caledonia and then Australia. Michelle who had sailed with Clark on *Asma* and had spent time with me and Jean on our desert island in Chagos, and who had sailed the North West Passage with Clark, was now living in Queensland. Clark and Michelle had gone their separate ways, and Michelle had married and had two young boys.

They were living in Mooloolaba and had a dock at the end of the garden that I could use. The husband Harold, another German, had a large yacht there but there would be room for me. So I planned to stay in Mooloolaba for the next cyclone season. I would then do another trip home to UK for a month and then sail on around Cape York into the Indian Ocean.

I would not be returning to New Zealand so made all my goodbyes reluctantly and off we went again. The jewellery business had been brisk and went a long way towards paying for the engine. My new source of income remained untouched.

Raymonde in Noumea was keen to do some more business with me and asked for some tapa cloth as well. So I kept busy in Tonga making up things. Steven and the boys worked as well. I had to stop in Fiji to get some new teeth which didn't take too long and then I continued through to Noumea.

It was in New Caledonia with time on my hands that I decided to write this book. Quite often, usually after a few beers I had told a few tales and then been asked if I had written a book and if not, why not. So many books have been written, many by close friends, that I had always been a little reluctant.

In the early days I was quite scathing of people like Hal Roth and the Pardys who seemed to sail around purely in order to write a book and persuaded hundreds of people to follow in their footsteps. Tragically, those idyllic faraway anchorages are no longer threatened just by fleets of yachts. They have been followed by cruise ships and resort developers!

The young people with refurbished old boats or maybe home build boats looking for adventure, looking to see the world, working from place to place etc. have been replaced by rich retirees with large complicated yachts and wives who would love to be back home. They now sailed from marina to marina and dined in restaurant after restaurant.

Now maybe, there would be some interest in how it was, a sort of history book describing the short era when, with a small boat, you could drop out of the system, off the map.

With my new found wealth and my impending pension I was being drawn back into the system. Already I'd had to open a bank account with a solid address in Britain, somewhere for the pension to be deposited. I also had a blue plastic visa card which I had not yet used. I was back in the fold, even the Australian government, unasked, had given me a four year multiple entry visa presumably because I was old and respectable.

I spent a month in Prony Bay, New Caledonia, scribbling away in a wonderful isolated anchorage and hiking up into the hills in the afternoons. But I soon got bored and sailed back to town to clear out for Australia.

I gave away the last of my ivory nuts, my toucan's beak, my raccoon's tail and other stuff which would excite the Australian officials when they came on board. Other stuff was put away discreetly .The turtle shell remained on the bulkhead where it had been for thirty years.

Unknown to me the weather was about to turn nasty. When I returned to the boat after clearing custom, I discovered that the boats around me had all moved out. A deep tropical depression was due to pass over us during the night, bringing serious wind and rain.

I found Stef and my other French friends anchored in the south west corner of the harbour close to the marina. So I chose a spot close by and did the same.

By midnight, the wind was howling. Stef's large, scruffy, steel yacht dragged past me heading for the main wharf, his diminutive Brazilian crew struggling with chain on the foredeck. A few others dragged. As I've said before, it's a French thing, a sport for them. They all disappeared into the murk.

Come morning things were settling down. Stef had managed to stop his drift before the wharf but one other yacht had ended up on the boulder break-water much the worse for wear.

I delayed for a day and then set off, but the wind was all over the place and it rained intermittently. Australia requires me to give them my date of arrival. By the time I arrived, they were getting worried. They weren't as worried as I was as I motored into the Bundaberg River. I had been told of sniffer dogs, underwater cameras, huge fines for barnacles on the bottom and so on.

Early the next morning, I steered the boat up to the quarantine dock which was surrounded by barbed wire. A pretty young girl in a brown uniform helped me tie the boat up. She was from the Ministry of Agriculture and Fisheries (MAF). She would charge me over Aus$400 for her inspection and could make my life hell.

As soon as she came down below on the boat she zeroed in on the turtle shell. I countered her shock horror with a copy of the Maryborough newspaper, a town just up the road. It had a picture of me, Jean and the turtle on the front page, admittedly a few years ago, but still. I then explained, I was a zoologist. She was interested and had started a course herself so I showed her the little photo album of my Australian biologists, Kathryn and Fiona, in Madagascar.

The first photo showed Kathryn holding the spear and Fiona holding up a huge mud crab, both up to their knees in muddy Malgash mangrove swamp. The MAF girl exclaimed and pointed to Fiona. She had worked for her on a project some years before.

Well, from then on, she wanted to know everything and when the customs officer arrived, another girl, she was also shown all the photographs. Neither girl showed any inclination to poke around further in the boat. I could have had an elephant in the for'd cabin. Wonderful, except of course for the money which I still had to pay!

An hour later, I was off down the river again and heading for the channels behind Fraser Island. These would take me south to exit the Wide Bay Bar and on to Mooloolaba. It's an interesting trip following the convoluted channels and catching the tide just so, to arrive at the other end of the island.

I spent a couple of days doing it and then motored out over the Wide Bay Bar. There was some big swells coming in and as I tipped over the top of them, the propeller shaft started knocking again I thought Andy and I had fixed it but apparently, not so.

I arrived late in Mooloolaba and found a slip in the marina for the night before contacting Michelle. She would have to come down and pilot me into the canals where her house was situated. The marina wasn't the least bit keen on having me as I had no insurance. I was finally allowed to stay for one night for fifty something dollars.

The next morning Michelle, still slim, dark-haired and gorgeous arrived with her youngest, a lad of seven or eight years and we extracted ourselves from the marina slip without bumping anyone. Then we set off down the canals into suburbia.

The houses were built quite close together each with its own dock with a sailing boat or sports fishing boat tied up. Some were obviously very expensive places, as reflected by the exotic boats on the dock.

We turn into a side canal and then again into another, a cul-de-sac, and there was Michelle's small house with Harold's fancy fifty-odd foot yacht tied alongside. We rafted up and then I met Harold himself and the elder son.

I already had some inkling that the marriage wasn't going well but soon realized that there was almost a war going on, with the boys in between. Fortunately, before I became piggy in the middle, I had organized an air flight home, paid for with my little blue plastic card. Oh so easy and also a bit scary. *Sea Loone* was left securely tied up on the neighbour's free dock. A communal taxi pick me up and drove me down to Brisbane not far down the coast.

For the first time in all the thirty years I had been away, I returned to England for a visit in midsummer. The weather was perfect, the countryside green, and flowers bloomed everywhere. I was enchanted. Why, I wondered, was I wandering around the world when here at home was England's "green and pleasant land".

With my sister and Paul, I took walks into the hills and around the lakes and did the same with John, my cousin and family, into the Pennines and along the Northumbrian coast. It was easy to forget the realities of dark nights in winter, with the pouring rain, sleet, snow.

My thyroid had not grown any larger according to the experts. My waterworks were stable and my Fiji dentist had botched up some repairs to my teeth. So all was well in that direction.

I had had more thoughts of writing the book. I had made a few false starts and made contact with Steve Williams an old school friend, who years ago in the Cayman Islands had tried to persuade me to put pen to paper. Steve was now living in the US but flitting all over the world with regular stops at his office in London. So out of the blue, returning from a lecture tour in Germany to London, he was jumping on a train to Newcastle and would stay one night to discuss the book.

We met on the railway platform in Newcastle after thirty years. Bald as a coot and a bit roly poly but still very recognizable, Steve was his usual effervescent self and over the next twenty-four hours filled me with enthusiasm to start writing. He was adamant that a story needed telling and was keen to take on the onerous task of editing and finding a publisher.

So the seed was set and I determined to start again as soon as I return to Mooloolaba and *Sea Loone*.

Clark Stede, hearing that I was now staying with Michelle, decided he would fly over from Chile to see us. He promised to help with the book project, having already written his book and many magazine articles. We had last been together in Dar es Salaam when Jean died, so meeting again would be interesting. Michelle was a little ambivalent about Clark's visit, still harbouring a few grudges about the value of an island in Chile she had been left with when they split up.

Clark had hired a car on arriving in Brisbane. From years of living in the mountains with his horses, he was darkly tanned and very much the South American gaucho.

Michelle had given me a small tape recorder used by typists and secretaries, the plan being for me to talk into it and she would type out the results. It wasn't going to work. I really wasn't comfortable with it so Clark offered to buy me an amazing computer program which allowed me to talk to my computer and it would type out whatever I said. I spent days with it. Maybe I talk too fast, or maybe there's still too much Liverpool scouse in me, or other bits and pieces I've picked up over the years but it typed back gibberish.

Meanwhile in the house, the war continued with Clark and I now both sandwiched between; so we took off into the hills to see some horsey friends of Clark's. They turned out to be "dinky di" true blue Australian's living in the Boulder Country way inland from Brisbane. Clark went off horse riding with the elder daughter and I went off trekking with the half-aboriginal mother. Father was an old drover from way back but shy and taciturn and the young daughters were just fun. With my video camera, Clark and I made a little film and it wasn't bad.

Back in Mooloolaba, with Clark set to return home, he decided to try his hand at marriage counseling. It was a disaster and after he left, I was in a difficult situation. I had found Harold to be a really nice guy and Michelle I loved; but the two together didn't work. For the two boys it must have been hard. For me; I just had to walk away.

The Queensland coast was a developers dream and was now an almost continuous strip of housing estates, condominiums and such like. It had huge highways, malls, advertising hoardings and all the razzamatazz of Miami Beach. It was not difficult to leave all that behind but sad to leave Michelle there so unhappy.

It was now December. The cyclone season would really be getting going soon. I could spend another season in the Mary River hoping not to get flooded out, or try to find somewhere safe to the north, not easy. The obvious answer was to beat back out into the Pacific and head south for New Zealand again.

I said a weepy goodbye to Michelle before sailing down to Brisbane to clear out. The weather was horrible and I got caught in the shallow banks with a lee shore, beating through the dark night with nasty steep waves.

Harold had found me a little GPS gadget which, plugged into the computer, put my boat on the electronic chart. I was skeptical but that night, as I tacked back and forth with the depth sounder sometimes registering only a couple of feet under the keel, it was a Godsend.

I was pretty haggard by the morning but was close to the marina where I could clear out with customs. The following day I set off for New Zealand threading back through the sand banks and finally into the deep blue ocean. The wind was north east so I pushed the boat off the coast expecting that, at any time, the wind would turn and push me back towards Australia.

I envisioned a hard bash to windward wet and cold, but in fact the wind stayed fair and ten days later I was due north off Cape Reinga, New Zealand. A front came through from the south and stopped me dead for two days but I was happy. The worst was over, I had my easting, the game was won. I sailed into the Bay of Islands on December 23 and, the next day, was propping up the bar in the Opua Cruising Club.

Ken and Jos were happy to see me and I anchored *Sea Loone* close to my old neighbour, Lorraine. She already had a flourishing vegetable garden covering the foredeck of her wooden launch. A friend had found me another nice little car to buy and so I settled into another summer season in New Zealand.

Learning from my previous times in Australia, I had put all my jewelry business away while I was there. If something cost more than a can of beer, then forget it they bought the beer.

So now, in New Zealand, I dug everything out of the bilges and started on my rounds. Andy, my Liverpool friend and engineer, puzzled over my engine problem. We finally took the propeller down to the expert in Whangarei and found it badly out of balance. At last we had found the answer to the nasty knocking noise.

In truth, I had little to do and sitting in my quiet anchorage up the Kawa Kawa River, I had every opportunity to get on with writing the book. Unfortunately, I found it difficult to pin myself down and turn my mind back all those years to the days when I had started out on the building of *Sea Loone*. I was easily distracted and always had someone to go and see or some small job I wanted done.

The New Year of 2010 rolled around. In November, I would begin to receive my pension from England which could seriously smooth out the ups and downs of my finances so it seemed to me a good time to finish the story of my wandering life. Before I left New Zealand again, I had bought two thick pads of writing paper and a bunch of biros. Steve, poor boy, was going to get my writings in long hand. I say poor boy as my writing is not very legible longhand and my spelling is atrocious.

Sailing into Ua Pou,
Marquesas

The drums Taeohae,
Nuku Hiva

My island paradise, Aratika

*Sailing slowly north off
New Britain*

*My rebuilt
Solomon Island dinghy*

Micronesia necklace

Body surfing with Stef & Chris, Western Palua

Fishing boats, Phillipines

Mangrove crabbing

John & I hunting the toko

Bat cave El Nido,
Western Palawan

*Sailing dhow,
Madagascar*

*Local crew,
Madagascar*

*Polly leaves
Richards Bay*

Polly in Capetown

*Alma in her garden,
Botswana*

5

I LEFT NEW Zealand again in April 2010 but not long before I left I had, for me, a really memorable weekend staying in a cottage just north of Auckland. My friends, Dick and Jane, were travelling up from Kati Kati and had rented a cottage perched on the end of a long peninsula pointing south east into the Hauraki Gulf. They were bringing their younger son, his girlfriend, and their new toy, a sportfishing boat on a trailer.

I hadn't seen the son, James, since Brazil years ago. He had obviously inherited some of his father's craziness. He now owned and ran a huge backpackers and nightclub somewhere in Cambodia. The girlfriend was Cambodian, a real live wire you could almost fit in a matchbox.

The high point and reason for mentioning the weekend was that one day, we took the boat to visit an offshore island which was a bird sanctuary. I had seen a number of the unusual New Zealand birds but that was one I never expected to see. Rediscovered up in the high mountains of South island and filmed by a BBC natural history team, the takahe had become quite famous. It looks like a giant moorhen, with blue plumage, a huge reddish beak and massive feet.

We were following a path across the island with bell birds calling, silver eyes and small parakeets and there it was, a takahe, walking down the path towards us! I had no idea they had a breeding programme on the island. I was flabbergasted. The bird was quite unconcerned. He walked up to us and was obviously interested to know if we had any sandwiches.

I said all my goodbyes again before leaving for Tonga, although there was one friend I couldn't say goodbye to, Hans Klar. He was still in jail in Auckland. I had expected to meet him when I arrived in New Zealand and when I cleared in in Opua I saw his new boat, a very strange looking, crab-claw rigged catamaran he had built in West Africa. Apparently, when he arrived in New Zealand, they discovered that South Africa had a prison sentence awaiting him.

Last time we had been together was when I employed him in St. Barts to set up the stage for the Beach Boys concert at Eden Rock. Hans refused to tell me why he had a prison sentence and, knowing his brother, I guessed there was a slight chance it may have something to do with drugs. With the world as it is, I dared not visit him in Auckland if that was the case.

In fact, later, I discovered it was something quite different. In April, there was still a great argument as to whether Hans should be extradited to South Africa, repatriated to Switzerland or remain rotting in New Zealand. The South African prison option would be very unpleasant and maybe life threatening. I wished Hans luck as I sailed north.

Stephen was waiting for me in Tongatapu. Besides jewellery I had an order for large carvings, tikis and masks which Stephen could provide. And in the market I found a lady to produce a load of tapa cloth pieces with different designs printed on them.

This was definitely my final time in Tonga before heading west so there was lots of stuff to be made. Steven's youngest daughter was soon to be married in America so Steven needed the work to finance his trip there. As it was, with all the work done, at the last moment Stephen was still short of some money to freight some of his work to America, so I bought up most of the carvings that remained in his workshop and gallery.

While all this was going on a strange story came to light which became international news. Some Tongans have been having gold teeth made at the dentist and, when questions were asked, more than a dozen gold ingots were confiscated. A week or two later, a girl was stopped boarding a plane for New Zealand with another lump of gold.

It piqued my interest so I asked a local friend to make inquiries. A few days later I had a meeting with some people on the other side of the island. A wreck had been found in only seventy feet of water. There was more treasure to be found and I was asked if I could either buy it or find a buyer for it in Australia. The talk was about few kilos of gold, worth a fortune.

It was an amazing story and gave me some sleepless nights. But in the end too many people talked too much, a rich American got involved as did the new King.

I drank a lot of beer on my last night in the Billfish. Steven had already flown off to Salt Lake City and I set off for New Caledonia.

I stopped briefly in Suva, Fiji, to have some new teeth made. In the end they were cheap but not very good. By the time I arrived in New Caledonia a specialized type of termite had started chewing on the tapa cloth. Fortunately only one piece was really badly damaged. A large Hawaiian tiki had also had a termite problem and had to be written off. But everything else was satisfactory and as I had arranged, I got paid close to a million Central Pacific Francs, almost €10,000. So my piggy bank was bulging again.

After that, my jewellery business was going into retirement. I sailed out of Noumea and anchored in an isolated little corner way in the back of Prony Bay intending to do some serious writing. It went well. Each morning I got a little more done in the in the afternoons, I went hiking in the hills. I saw no one.

A week or two later I pulled up the anchor to return to Noumea for stores and to contact Elizabeth in Devon. She was planning to come out and visit. There was little wind and I motored down the bay and turned into the Canal Woodin. I was using the electric autopilot I had just bought in New Zealand, a new experience for me. It turned out to be a horror story.

The Canal is not only deep but also steep sided, with a narrow shelf of reef along the cliff edges. I went below to make coffee and looking out of the window a minute later, realize that the boat had turned sharply to port. I shot into the cockpit and as I unleashed the tiller and pushed it hard over, *Sea Loone* climbed up on the reef, heeled over and turned sharply to starboard.

The tiller tore out of my hand and jammed against the side of the cockpit. The boat, slowing only a little, turned through 180 degrees and fell back into the deep water. Unfortunately the last part of the boat on the reef was the rudder. The lower half got bent almost at right angles.

I could only just steer a course so I headed for the nearest place to throwing in the anchor. I then plunged over the side to see what damage had been done. The bottom of the keel was untouched, the turn of the bilge, the belly of the boat where it had scraped along the coral, was only slightly scratched. The only damage was the rudder but that was serious!

Back in Noumea, the marina haul-out refused to lift me as I had no insurance. I couldn't just drop the rudder out while afloat as the skeg was also badly damaged at the bottom. And I certainly couldn't sail on to Australia or down to New Zealand.

There were some small boat yards on the other side of the commercial harbor. It was a more scruffy area frequented by the poorer sailors and the French sea gypsies.

The first yard I visited had a hydraulic crane, normally easily capable of lifting my boat. But it was in very poor condition and the owner wouldn't lift anything more than six tons. He directed me to another yard that he was in the process of buying.

The owner of that yard had been acting very strangely and no longer had any business, but he did have an old travel lift which would haul me out. With the prospective new owner's help and a lot of pleading from me the man agreed to lift me out. So the next day I motored over into his dock.

Lifting the stern high in the air and dropping the bow, once we were on dry land, enabled me to drop out the rudder and then *Sea Loone* was propped up and I was left to sort out my problems.

The yard was closed and empty but there was a fair amount of useful junk lying around including a large solid steel work table. With the rudder stripped of its fiberglass and plywood cheeks, the steel plate was easy to straighten. But the shaft which was inch and a half stainless steel, also had a small kinking in it and that was going to be very difficult.

With the rudder bolted to the table, some long levers and large G-clamps, I started trying to bend it. My first effort nearly killed me. A G-clamp flew off and shot over my shoulder nearly taking off my head. But the shaft had moved a little. I constructed a plywood screen and by the end of the day had everything perfectly straight.

I then had to knock away the broken concrete on the base of the skeg and sort out the inch-bolts which came down it and held the pintle. That all got glassed up with epoxy resin. The rudder cheeks got replaced with very expensive marine plywood and also glassed over with epoxy.

By the end of the week, I had the boat ready to re-launch with the bottom painted and the rudder ready to slip into place. I found a helper and when we lifted the boat, two of us lifted the rudder into place. The gudgeon fitted perfectly and I was back in the water.

I was €1,000 poorer but things could have been ever so much worse. I returned to the old harbour and cleaned up the boat. Elizabeth was due to arrive from England.

With my new found wealth I decided it was a good opportunity to sail up into Southeast Asia. This would allow me to avoid the bureaucracy in Australia and to visit Borneo and the jungle I had seen on BBC TV fifty years ago. I intended sailing up the coast of New Caledonia to the Solomon Islands. From there I would sail past New Britain, New Ireland and head for the equator and then Micronesia.

From Palau I would sail to the Philippines, down the coast of Palawan to Borneo then on to Singapore. From Singapore I would sail north up the coast of Malaysia and through the Malacca Straits to Thailand on the eastern edge of the Indian Ocean. From there my route would go south across the equator again to bring me back onto my old tracks and headed towards Madagascar.

When Elizabeth arrived, we returned to Prony Bay for a quiet week exploring the valleys and waterfalls and then stored up and set off north. Elizabeth had been nervous about continuing with me up to the Solomons and looking back, maybe it wasn't a good idea.

Within a day's sail of Guadalcanal, thunderstorms buildup and the wind gave up. And so it remained hot, humid and windless. The population had spilled out onto even the smallest of islands and the whole thing rather depressed me. On top of this my dinghy was stolen and as Christmas arrived in Gizo in the north of the Solomons, I came down with a really nasty dose of flu.

I was unlivable with, lay in bed and sulked. Elizabeth fled across to John's boat, *Fajola*. He was an English physicist with a New Zealand girlfriend, Chris. Christmas came and went, Elizabeth flew home and, only partly recovered, I cleared out heading for the equator. There was little or no wind and I drifted around for weeks. Any plans I had to stop anywhere were null and void.

After five weeks and just across the equator, I found a little wind and headed for Palau, a group of islands popular with divers. The whole time I was sailing, I had a tropical ulcer on my ankle which had worried me. I had cleaned it, kept it dry and poured antibiotic powder into it. Fortunately it had not got any bigger, but it also had not gone away. As soon as I arrived in Palau, I went to the doctors for a course a strong antibiotics.

I anchored off Sam's Diving Center in water nearly one hundred feet deep surrounded by raised coral cliffs. The water was crystal clear. Each day, hundreds of scuba divers went out to dive the different sites. I was not allowed to sail a yacht around without special, very expensive, permits.

With another stroke of bad luck, I came down with another dose of flu, this time a strain of Asian flu which was plaguing the island. I spent days at the doctors, my lungs on fire.

A month later fully recovered, I set off for the Philippines; now not so far away and a good wind was blowing.

It was harvesting time for the rice when I arrived at the first little island in the Philippines. The broken down dock where I tied my dinghy was covered in rice drying in the sun and the road to the main town where I could get some money was a single lane, the other lane covered for miles in rice.

Small children were leading huge buffaloes pulling primitive carts and sledges loaded with rice. Nobody was going to starve.

I left the Solomons with a wreck of a dinghy I had found being used as a painting platform. I had repaired a large hole in the bow but I really needed to build a new dinghy. In Noumea I had met Mick, a New Zealander I had known for some time. With his wife and young boy they were heading for Cebu in the Philippines. Mick had built a big, very racy catamaran in aluminium. The inside was still completely bare and he planned to finish the job in Cebu. It seemed a good place for me to head to build a new dinghy.

When I arrived there were four catamarans hauled up in the mangroves, all the same design and all being worked on by teams of young Filipinos. They were using sheets of fiberglass to form the interiors which was really convenient for me.

I took patterns off an aluminum dinghy on the beach, laid up a few thin sheets of fiberglass and cut them to shape. In no time, I had the basic dinghy tacked together under a tarpaulin sheet strung between the bushes. I laid up more fiberglass until I thought it was strong enough, fixed plastic pipe around the gunnel, glassed in two bulkheads in the middle and cut the boat in half in between. . So in less than two weeks I had a nice two-part dinghy, the front half nesting in the rear when I loaded it on deck.

I also refurbished my Solomon Islands dinghy, adding a centerboard and fitting the old rudder and sailing rig which I still had from the stolen dinghy. I now had two dinghies, one taking up the foredeck and the other nesting under the boom.

Mick and his boys were doing an amazing job on the catamaran and would soon have it finished. It was a lot of work but the end product was worth a lot of money.

John and *Fajola* arrived as I finished my project and we sailed down to the island of Bohol where Steph, my friend from Noumea, was staying with his new Filippino girlfriend. There was still very little wind but of course at any time of the year in the Philippines, a typhoon could arrive. So we were always on the lookout for places we could duck into if need be.

In Bohol, I particularly wanted to find a tarsier, a rare and very unusual monkey, quite distinct from all others. I found them caged and very badly treated then later found a so-called sanctuary which wasn't much better. I'm sure at least on the Bohol, in a few years they won't exist.

Weeks and months passed and I had drifted west to Negros where I discovered I had amoebic dysentery. Luckily it was cured by a load of pills. Then, I sailed on north around the tip of Palawan to meet Steph again. We met in a primitive little town where an odd Englishman was building a very odd looking the boat on the beach. We took our bicycles ashore and cycled for miles along dirt tracks and foot paths. There was lots of birdlife, wildflowers and fruit trees, small rice paddies in all the valleys and everywhere, lots and lots of people.

Steph was heading across to China and I was going to sail against whatever little wind there was, south west down the west coast of Palawan towards Borneo. There were some interesting places to visit including two which attracted some tourism.

The first was El Nido, a large bay filled with towering precipitous islands with vertical cliffs. In the cliffs were caverns in which the swifts that were the source of birds nest soup, nested. In the evenings huge numbers of bats also left these caves to form weird undulating clouds in the sky as they headed for the mainland to feed.

The second place was the Underground River. This you entered at the base of the sea cliff and you could travel by boat for miles. Hundreds of tourists packed into long canoes to do the trip which rather put me off the experience.

The rest of the west coast of Palawan was pretty untouched and without the huge numbers of people normally found in the Philippines. In one large bay I went hunting for a toko. It's a large gecko almost a foot long which shouts its name loudly, particularly at night. I had never seen one. With the help of a local Filippino lady and her gardener, we first found a stash of toko eggs attached to some bamboo. Later we cut down a hollow branch overhanging the water and I pounced on the toko which fell out.

The toko had some colorful patterning on his body and a striped tail. He opened his huge bright red mouth and fastened himself on my thumb. It took some time to persuade him to let go.

I kept him for a few days but he remained very aggressive. So I took him back to where I had found him and letting him go.

I kept the eggs in a box to see what would happen and two weeks later was rewarded with a hatchling. Only three inches long, the first thing the baby did was bite me. Tokos obviously don't make good pets.

I made slow progress down the long coast beating against what little wind there was and dodging the reefs. One morning, having tacked out to sea overnight, I was caught by a huge purple-black storm front. The wind picked up to over forty knots and the seas built up and I was surrounded by a lot of reefs. For once in its life the computer and the little attachment which showed my boat on the chart screen, came to life. However, the chart was horribly inaccurate and useless.

Luckily, Steph had put some tracks on the chart from a yacht that had passed this way before. One track was less than a quarter of a mile away and headed into a convoluted anchorage only a few miles away and across the wind. Even though the chart was inaccurate the track had to be correct.

By this time I had no sails up and was drifting sideways in big breaking seas. I started the engine and motored with the howling wind on the beam and waves breaking over the cabintop to arrive on the track and then followed it. According to the chart, we passed over a lot of reefs and one island. Certainly I passed really close to breaking reefs and an hour later I found myself in more sheltered water. Finally, I threw in the anchor in the middle of a huge sheltered bay in only eight feet of water.

During the day a number of large fishing vessels joined me in the bay and we sheltered there for two more days before the wind and sea calmed down. I was really grateful for Steph's little purple track on the computer.

Four more days sailing and I finally reached the southern tip of Palawan. From there I headed across the Balabac Strait to the small town of Kudat in Sabah, the most eastern state of Borneo and Malaysia.

I anchored in a small circular bay which was soon to become a marina. There were a few yachts and some local fishing boats, all tied stern-to to the seawall. Surrounding us was an expensive international golf course and to one side, a luxury hotel. A small group of Army commandos were camped in one corner and went out each day with high-speed launches. Not many years ago the area was controlled by pirates and avoided by yachts. Now they were only running contraband fuel to the Philippines.

Unlike the Philippines, Malaysia was rich and thriving. The main road from where we were anchored was a concrete dual-carriageway. I realize that the Borneo I dreamed of no longer existed. In fact the coastal forest had disappeared to be replaced by oil palm plantations which were spreading rapidly up into the mountains.

Near Sandakan, there was a major river which was navigable up to one hundred miles inland with the yacht. There were wild elephants fording the river, and orangutans in the trees on the riverbank, together with many other species monkey and exotic birds. It sounded fantastic until I found out more. .

The hundreds of square miles of riverine forest had been cut down and replaced with oil palm. But along the riverbank a fringe hundred yards wide had been left for the wildlife or what was left of it. No wonder the elephants were swimming around in the river. I gave it all a miss.

In Kudat there was a large boat yard which catered mainly for large fishing boats. They had a massive travel lift capable of lifting over a hundred tons. I decided to have *Sea Loone* hauled out and I would fly home again. The cost of being out of the water for two months was the same as one, so I went home for that time. It was too long away really and maybe I outstayed my welcome but it was summer in England which I loved and the beer was as good as ever.

The sound of karaoke music blasting out across the water with some dreadful singing that went with it, had been left behind in the Philippines. Here the sounds were different. The evenings were quiet but early morning prayers blasted out from the tops of the mosques didn't make a good start to the day.

Before I left Kudat heading for Singapore, the rest of the toko eggs started hatching. All the babies were as unfriendly as the first. They now live in a nice little golfer's shelter where they can call out "toko toko" without annoying anybody.

I made slow progress along the coast of Borneo and arrived a few days before Christmas in Victoria Harbour on the island of Labuan facing the kingdom of Bruneii. A huge new oilfield was being opened up so there were more than fifty, large, strange, oil-rig service ships in the anchorage. The harbour at the top end where I was anchored, was covered in a foot thick layer of mainly plastic rubbish.

I had a night out with a Welshman on a weed covered yacht next to me and a Danish guy involved with the supply ships. The next day I found some tinned duty-free New Zealand butter. I couldn't see me enjoying Christmas anchored in this dump, so when the wind picked up, I left.

Christmas Day found me out in the China Sea. It was blowing a gale. The shallow waters of the South China Sea made it very bumpy but at least we were moving forward. A few days later, the new little navigation machine I had acquired in New Zealand, the "AIS", whatever that stands for, showed a huge fleet of ships anchored in front of me. They were waiting to enter Singapore but anchored miles out to sea.

The closer I got, the busier the sea traffic. There were ships everywhere in two continuous lines, one going out and one coming in. I found a place to anchor for the night close to the shore behind two huge ships. In the morning, I carried on around Singapore Island and into the channel behind. I anchored again close to a high bridge linking Singapore to Malaysia, with a row of fish traps in front of me.

Continuing the next day, I arrived at the main causeway across to Singapore and tied up in a cheap dilapidated marina on the Malaysian side in Johor Bahru. It was New Year's Eve and there were quite a few boats in the marina, so I joined the party they had organized. Tomorrow would be 2012 and I needed a short break from the sailing before starting up the Malacca Straits to Thailand.

During the gale in the China Sea, the tiller had broken off leaving only a stub on the rudder shaft. It was an old propeller shaft, 1 inch in diameter, and had rotted through. With bits of aluminum angle and a length of two by four I had made a temporary replacement. But now found a machine shop to make a proper repair.

I also had to make a trip over to Singapore. My new engine had problems and I needed parts. The raw water pump needed new bearings and seals and I thought I had problems with the drive plate. The alternator was eating up the belts that drove it.

I found the Yanmar main office in Singapore but got no help at all from them. I was sent to a spare parts business up the street where I got the parts I needed but no help with the drive plate or the realignment of the alternator.

A few days rest, a rebuilt pump and with the new tiller installed, I set off up the Malacca Straits heading for Thailand. With little or no wind, I motored most of the way, dodging the fish traps, fishnets and the large islands of rubbish floating on the tide. Most nights I anchored on the muddy coastal shelf or found a small town and anchored among the local boats.

In Georgetown, Penang, I anchored off a Chinatown built on stilts and spent a couple of days there exploring the old town.

The last stop in Malaysia was Langkawi and I found a pleasant anchorage on the west coast off a large marina. As I motored into the marina with the dinghy, a girl called me from another dinghy. It was Wendy, an old friend from Hog Island, Grenada; and in fact even further back than that, in Durban,

South Africa. As in Hog, she was busy with a sewing business and had been in Langkawi some years. She was able to show me around and to lend me her scooter. I did a tour and, on several evenings, got invited out.

Langkawi is a duty-free island so, before leaving, I spent the remains of my Malaysian money on booze. A short breeze allowed me to sail to the first set of islands going north, but the next day I motored. The autopilot was working again after I had replace some parts from a pilot I found discarded in the marina.

The island I intended anchoring off that night was spectacular with its sheer-sided cliffs and tight little coves with small sandy beaches. Unfortunately, all the shallow areas were taken up by large tourist charter boats and the beaches all had large tourist speedboats drawn up on the sand. It was obviously a very popular spot but still, the water was really dirty with huge amounts of plastic rubbish floating about. I had to find an anchorage in another island close by where a dozen or more huge charter boats were moored for the night.

The next day I motored into Ao Chalong, Phuket, another large shallow bay with a long pier for the ferries and charter boats. There were also a couple of hundred other yachts either anchored or on moorings.

Going ashore at low tide was impossible unless you wanted to wade knee-deep in mud. Fortunately, my new dinghy was very light so I could drag it up among the tree roots above high tide. Another few steps and I arrived at the bar, restaurant, yacht club run by a large jolly Australian.

Another few hundred yards brought me to the main street of Ao Chalong which was solid with bars, restaurants and massage parlors. This was heaven for a large number of elderly, overweight, single-handed sailors with no need to go anywhere else and no wind to do it anyway.

In Langkawi one morning, I found I had started peeing blood. I think I had passed a bladder stone. It was very painful and was followed by a bladder infection. So in Phuket I visited the hospital. After an Xray and talking with a young doctor, I left with a fistful of pills. The hospital was a little run down and very busy.

The next week I found that my old friend Taffy had had some more problems with his heart and was back in hospital. When I visited, it was quite a different hospital, more like a luxury hotel. Taffy seemed in good spirits and was soon to be released with a large bill I think. Later I was on board his boat and met his wife Shirley and the parrot "Rubbish". I'd met them last in Brazil, years ago.

I ate ashore, enjoying the Thai food and traveled around a bit on a hired scooter, a very dangerous occupation competing with hundreds of other mopeds zooming around everywhere.

There were several huge food warehouses and supermarkets in town so, as my next destination was Madagascar, I stored up a massive amount of food. I dug out the pressure cooker and bottled pork and chicken for the long passage across the Indian Ocean. I also swapped a load of paperback novels in the yacht club.

With all that food on board I thought it a good idea to get some new teeth. My Fiji set was hopeless. I found a pretty young dentist with an equally pretty assistant, and they did a much better job. The pills I had got from the hospital didn't effect any miracle cure but I was getting better. So on the Saturday, I went to the fruit and vegetable market and loaded up.

With that done, I had to leave. So I cleared out and then motor sailed around the island to an outside bay where the water was clear, to scrape off any barnacles that had taken up residence. The next morning I was set to pull up the anchor went another yacht sailed in from the north. I immediately recognize the boat. It was Marie Christine, my doctor friend from Noumea who's leaving party I had attended when I was last there.

She had just sailed down from the Andaman Islands. We went ashore for lunch and caught up on stories from years ago and of course, discussed my medical situation. She really thought I ought to have some more tests done and wait around a bit. But I was set to go so she gave me some more antibiotics. The next day, March 12, 2012, I set off for the northern tip of Sumatra and the 3000 miles or so to Ile Ste. Marie on the west coast of Madagascar.

As I slowly drifted towards Sumatra, I met up with shipping coming and going down the Malacca Straits. Often as many as eight ships showed up on my AIS machine. Nearly all were heading for the Persian Gulf, or the Red Sea and Suez. Once across the ship lanes I saw far fewer but there was no abatement of the plastic rubbish. It followed me almost to the equator, hundreds of miles south.

With no wind I drifted on. Only the occasional thunderstorm provided a few minutes of squally wind. I filmed sail fish as they circled the boat, their huge fins out of the water; and one day, a little turtle, only six inches long, came and chewed on the grass growing along my waterline.

I expected more wind as we crossed the equator but in fact the trade winds didn't show up till past eight degrees south. I was forty four days out and had only done 1200 miles, an average of thirty miles a day, very, very slow. I was still less than half way to Madagascar.

I passed to the east of Chagos where I normally stopped. The British government had made it very difficult and expensive to stop there, with huge restrictions on where you could go and for how long you could stay. Egmont was not on the list and I had no insurance policies for either me or the boat.

In a way I could understand the new restrictions. Salomon Atoll had become something of a holiday resort for yachts and, as a result, the fish and lobster population had been seriously depleted.

Once the trade winds started to blow, my speed picked up and I could catch fish whenever I wanted. April had now been and gone and I decided to head directly for the north coast of Madagascar rather than farther down the east coast. As usual the wind and seas picked up dramatically as I approached Cap d'Ambre, Madagascar's northern tip.

I passed close by the Cape early in the morning and then, in the lee of the land, sailed rapidly along the coast to the second of three deep, convoluted, bays each with a very narrow entrance. I carefully navigated the way in, in not very clear water and at nine in the morning, dropped anchor, seventy-two days out from Phuket.

I had seen some cattle in the scrubby vegetation and, in the distance, a few people. But here in the anchorage I was alone. I jumped over the side and swam around the boat before making a big meal with Thailand pork. Then, having tidied up a bit, I slept for twelve hours, the boat hardly moving. When I awoke the next morning, the birds were singing.

A few days later I left to continue around to the west coast. There was a very low tide with the full moon and lots of people on the reef as I sailed past. There were more people than I expected, the population over the last twelve years having obviously increased dramatically.

Turning inside the barrier reef I now headed south. I anchored off Nosy Hara, the spectacular volcanic plug I had stopped at the last time. Little seemed to have changed until a small launch arrived, dropped off some French tourists on the beach, and then came to ask for my permit. Things obviously had changed.

The fish eagles were still nesting on the cliff. The youngster could already fly and I watched him soar back and forth crying to his parents. The turtles were coming ashore and laying eggs. They were leaving their tracks up the beach and the locals seemed to be digging them up as soon as they laid them, despite a large sign on the beach saying "National Reserve".

I sailed slowly on towards Nosy Bé spending a few days here and there. I found the octopi were still thriving in Nosy Mitsio. With coconut milk from Thailand, they were delicious.

In Nosy Komba I had dinner with Stephano. His village now had two schools and many more houses. He had recently installed a hydroelectric system on the river so there was hydro power and electric light. He had a few young student teachers helping him and with them, I went to visit the lemurs, the giant tortoise, a couple of large friendly boa constrictors and the amazing chameleons.

Finally, I arrived in Nosy Bé. I cleared in and anchored in the same dirty little harbor, tying up the dinghy among a load of pirogues, dhows and rusty work boats. My visa was for only three months and the time passed quickly.

In Crater Bay, just past Hellsville, there were lots of charter yachts, mainly catamarans; but there was little or no work for them. Not only had here been some political unrest but there was now a general fear of Somali pirates. The stories would have put off any holidaymakers. The cruising yachts it seemed had also been put off visiting and, in the time I was in Madagascar, I saw only half a dozen.

As a result, I had the whole cruising ground more or less to myself. This suited me. I spent days and weeks in deserted anchorages. The only boats I would see were sailing dhows or sailing pirogues. Some of the latter were quite large. With their long outriggers and lateen rig, they sailed extremely fast. Nearly all the cargo-carrying up and down the coast and between the islands, was done by sail and there seemed a lot more boats than twelve years previously.

I wasn't completely isolated. I met a Swedish couple and took them on a long walk to a village I knew. I climbed Nosy Ankarea with a French guy, you needed to know to know the way up the thousand-foot cliff and I wanted to film the paradise flycatchers which lived in the forest on the top. In Russian Bay, I met a German guy who was married to a local girl and had built a house there. He had some interesting stories to tell.

Just as my three months was up, I decided to treat myself to a weekend of debauchery in Ambotoloaka. I spent the evening drinking and dancing and then chose the most voluptuous young lady to invite back to the boat. She was wearing a long slinky dress and high heeled shoes which she had to remove when we arrived at the steep streambed which was part of the route home to Crater Bay. The last quarter of a mile she did bare foot and the rest of the night bare as well.

On the Monday I cleared out for South Africa and very, very, slowly headed down the coast. I again spent some time in Russian Bay. While filming a fish eagle stealing a fish out of a fisherman's net, I managed to drop the video camera. I was standing in two feet of water so it was the end of the camera and the end of my filming.

Further down the coast I found bays and river mouths to anchor in. I swapped two pieces of gill net for three litres of wild honey. I had a kilo of vanilla from Nosy Komba but had already eaten all the dried bananas.

My last stop was in the Barren Islands about half way down the west coast. From there I headed out into the Mozambique Channel passing between Ile Europa and Bassas da India. The current was all over the place, sometimes pushing me north, sometimes south west.

I picked up the Agulhas current south of Maputo and headed down the African coast. Off Cape St. Lucie, a small front overnight gave me headwinds. I hove to close to the beach and with the current, was still heading down the coast at two knots at right angles to the ship's heading. By morning I was a skip and a jump away from Richards Bay. By lunchtime I was tied up in the Small Boat Harbour. It was October 20, 2012.

Tied up opposite me was *Ouais Ouais* last seen here in Richards Bay in maybe 1987. I was back in South Africa.

Having cleared in, I had a few beers with Frank and Elise on *Ouais Ouais*. Then Plastic turned up. Plastic had been in Hog Island, Grenada with me in 2000 but he had also been in the Zululand Yacht Club back in 1987.

Elise was now a well-known scrimshaw artist and had exhibited her work all over. They were heading next for New Zealand having to avoid Australia because of the bureaucracy. In fact, they left at the end of the month and then took four months to get to the South Island NZ and I'd thought I was slow!

Simon Gossip was still in the harbour. His old steel work boat had rusted out from under him and he now had an old wooden launch. He's a big man and could still consume large quantities of beer while watching the rugby matches in the pub. He was a great help as I sorted myself out and was able to come up with a large drum of anti-fouling paint for *Sea Loone*. On the first big tide, I put the boat on the slipway and, over two days, cleaned the bottom and applied the new paint.

On the way across the Indian Ocean, the new genoa I had had delivered to Borneo had rotted out. There was obviously something seriously wrong with the material. Here in Madagascar, Lee Sails had agreed to replace the sail and have it delivered to me, free of charge. So I asked them to deliver it to Richards Bay. They also very kindly made some small alterations to the shape of the sail for me.

The sail arrived first in Johannesburg and customs there demanded import duty. For goods delivered to a ship in transit, this is normally not payable. For two weeks, S. African customs was rude and unhelpful, threatening to destroy the new sail if payment was not made. I paid but, from that day on, refused to buy any more substantial things for the boat in South Africa. I really did need a new toilet and stove and would also have bought some more solar panels.

I was keen to get south and meet Glenn in Cape Town and I wasn't looking forward to the trip down the coast. Just to make things more interesting, a few days before I left, I bought a baby African Grey parrot. I had seen the advertisements in a supermarket and couldn't resist the temptation. Only hatched a few weeks earlier, the baby was an ugly lump of gray skin, a large beak and massive feet. Its patches of gray down were streaked with spilled food and excreta.

I wedged a cardboard box into a corner on the floor of the cabin and put rags around the bird to stop him from rolling around too much. Every six hours, I had to shovel a type of porridge down his throat, large quantities in and large quantities out!

I left early the next morning with a cold drizzle falling and a south west wind still blowing. Nobody was awake as I untied from the dock except me and Polly.

The wind was due to switch around so I beat out into a big sea, the waves breaking over the bow and flooding along the deck. Polly didn't seem overly concerned. It certainly didn't affect his appetite.

As I arrived at the fifty fathom line where the south-going current was judged to be at its strongest, the wind turned. I tacked about and headed southwest at nearly 7 knots. It even stopped raining and by lunchtime, the sun was shining as we bowled along nicely.

I called Simon on my telephone to say goodbye and then phoned Lindsay, the Australian, who had been moored in front of me. He came up with the latest weather report. It sounded good for a few days.

I passed Durban and, off the Wild Coast, really picked up the Agulhas current. I was doing eleven knots at one time. I passed East London and approaching Port Elizabeth, called Lindsay again and also Glenn in Cape Town. They both assured me that nothing nasty was heading my way, so I kept going. Cell phones certainly have their uses I was discovering.

Polly was getting through huge amounts of porridge and feathers were beginning to appear. His attempts to walk around were unsuccessful. The roll of the boat was not helping him.

Off Mossel Bay the wind dropped and then turned against me. But only for a few hours, and then we were off again. Ten days after leaving Richards Bay I turned into False Bay heading for Simons Town. But then, because Simons Town had no place for me due to a big ocean race about to leave from there, I had to turn to the right side of False Bay and head for Gordon's Bay.

Glenn had arranged a place for me and I could call the yacht club on the telephone. So when I came into the little marina between the two large protective breakwaters, there was a guy waiting there to take my lines. It was all too easy.

Simon's Town is very English. In Gordon's Bay it seemed the first language is Afrikaans, the people were extremely helpful. My waterworks was still playing up so the club secretary took me in her car to her doctor. I got some more pills and then got taken to the nearest supermarket to get some fresh vegetables and meat.

The next day Glenn arrived. It's a long drive from Noordhoek where he still lived and he had had to go out of his way to find some more of Polly's special porridge. Polly had got through a kilo already but he was growing. He had doubled in size and feathers were sprouting everywhere. There were even some stubs of bright red above his bum where his tail feathers were sprouting.

Glenn, of course, I had not seen since I was last in Cape Town twelve years ago. He had two daughters already well grown and I was looking forward to meeting them and, of course, Collette, his lovely wife.

With all the racing boats taking off for St. Helena I could cross the bay and take a berth in Simons Town. Again, the telephone came in handy and Dave Gomersall, who I always knew as Neutron Dave from when he played music in

New Zealand, was in the marina to direct me to my place and catch my lines. Dave was also living in Noordhoek under Table Mountain and not so far from where I now was.

The Yacht Club and marina were now really expensive but I had no other choice in the matter; the main harbour in Cape Town was even more expensive.

At Christmas time, I was invited with Glenn and his family to a party up on the mountain in Constancia. There were a lot of interesting people, the rich and the famous and a lot a teenage girls all set to become high maintenance wives. After that, I had quite a few nights staying with Glenn in Noordhoek.

Polly now had lots of feathers and had moved into a proper cage. He had at last got the hang of using his big feet and was now concentrating on flapping his rapidly growing wings. He seemed to enjoy trips in the back of Glenn's car and wasn't the least put off by Glenn's two huge Greek shepherd dogs.

After Christmas, Peter arrived from Switzerland to stay in one of the two cottages in Glenn's garden. Pete and I had traveled across South Africa and Namibia twelve years before. He now kept a large four-wheel drive Landcruiser in Cape Town and each year, traveled around extensively. So Pete agreed that together we should drive up to Botswana and visit Alma, my old girlfriend from Richards Bay. Alma had stayed with me for a while in St. Barts. She was now living near Lobatsi on a farm with an English guy, Bill.

I left Polly with Dave and his family. His daughter was totally in love with Polly. Peter and I fueled up the car and set off north. The main road was in good condition but once we left it, they were either long delays due to extensive roadworks that went on for miles or massive potholes to weave around.

We met Alma and Bill at the Botswana border post. She was her dazzling laughing self, quite unchanged. Bill was a huge friendly Englishmen. We stayed with them for a week. The climate was quite mild and the land quite green in contrast to the stark desert and cacti I had expected. There were three different types of weaver birds in the garden. I also spotted the nest of my old friend, the paradise flycatcher. Walking in the bush a real pleasure.

We drove back south over some spectacular passes. You could see forever across the veldt and where there was more soil and water, they were miles of maize being grown turning the landscape bright green.

Closer to home, we passed through orchards of peaches, apricots and apples. Peter knew where there was a fruit-drying factory and I bought kilos of sun-dried apricots and currants to take with me on *Sea Loone*.

Once I had returned to Simon's Town it was time to move on. But I discovered a huge problem. With the panic over avian flu, the ostrich farms we had passed through in Oudtshoorn were no longer allowed to export to the New World. This meant that unfortunately Polly was also banned and had to find a new home.

Luckily much to the delight of his daughters, Dave's family agreed to take him and I had to sail on alone again.

Stored up, I sailed around to Cape Town Marina to clear out. Customs refused to refund me the duty on the sail and the marina charged me a fortune for the one-day visit. This left a nasty taste in my mouth after a really enjoyable month or two in False Bay.

I had a mainsail to deliver to a friend in Salvador, Brazil so that was where I was first aiming for. I decided not to stop in St. Helena which turned out to be a bad idea. I cut too far south, lost the wind and so finished up with another long slow transAtlantic passage.

It was already May by the time Salvador hove over the horizon. it had been windy with heavy rain squalls for the last three days and the channel into Bahia de Todos Santos was really rough. With the outgoing tide, there were big breaking waves one of which had the cheek to jump into the cockpit.

My friend Ron lived in the town of Itaparica on the island of the same name facing Salvador, on the opposite shore of the main channel. I wove between a dozen or more anchored ships and, once out of the main channel in the lee of the island, it was calm easy sailing. Just as well, because when I went to start up the engine and motor into the anchorage of the town, it refused to work.

So I had to beat up to windward and then, dodging a couple of sandbanks, sail into the anchorage. I dropped anchor with sails flapping, behind a large French catamaran and then, with the sails down, made myself a well deserved cup of coffee.

Ron's house was on the main street of the little old town and his back yard dropped down to the waterfront. *Sea Loone* was anchored just offshore. Since I had last seen Ron here in Brazil, he had sailed back to Australia via the Panama Canal and then returned via Cape Horn. Off the Cape he had upended the boat and lost the mast and nearly his life.

He eventually got to Brazil where he settled for a few years and where he found a beautiful young girlfriend whom he dragged off to the Caribbean and married. Now back in Itaparica, the boat sat dejected on a mooring while Ron, his wife and a little boy of perhaps two years of age, lived in a house.

I spent the best part of a month in Itaparica and over lots of beer, Ron filled me in on his adventures over the last twelve years. The new Brazilian currency, the Real, was pretty stable but the cost of living had rocketed. Still, people seem to be a lot better off, a fact that was brought home to me in a very unfortunate way.

The girls had always been pretty and loved to party. They now watch soap operas and novellas on the TV all day while drinking Coca-Cola etc. and eating fast food. They were now, to put it bluntly, fat. I realize this is a terrible generalization but still, not far from the truth.

When I left Itaparica heading north, I was looking forward to returning to Cabadelo just north of Recife where, the last time I was in Brazil with Ron and a number of other good people, we had had a really good time.

The trip north was good and the weather and wind were kind to me. But when I motored into the river entrance, the engine started blowing black smoke and quit. I had to turn and sail across the mouth and anchor. The tide was already turning, beginning to ebb. So I decided to remain anchored for the night and in the morning with the next flood tide and the engine only working at low revs, I crept up the river to anchor off the village of Jacare.

Things had changed in Jacare. The Englishman who had had a boat yard there for years was retired and two marinas had been built, one filled with French yachts. The few small restaurants were now five or more and huge with a tourist market behind. Every evening a mass of coaches and cars arrived to watch the sun set while some local guy in a small boat played Ravel's Bolero very badly. Fortunately, by late evening, they all went home. But after a few evenings like this, the whole circus became annoying, especially the Bolero.

The little houses in the village now all had TV, cars and so forth. They still fished the river with long gill nets, but the fish were getting smaller and the girls were getting bigger!

There were only a couple of boats on anchor in the river and the others in the marina were empty. Brazil now only allowed a three-month visa for most people, so they had gone home for a few months. It seemed a good time for me to clear in, I had not done so as yet.

I now had three months before it was time to head on to the Caribbean. I wanted to arrive in Grenada in October. Before that I planned to stop in

Fortaleza on the north coast and buy Brazilian bikinis. By chance, I had two girls I knew both from Fortaleza and both returning there in September. One was coming from Florida and one from France. The last time I bought bikinis, it had gone really well financially. This time I would do it for fun as much as for profit.

I pottered around on the boat and took the train down to either Cabadelo or up to Joao Pessoa, the big city. The book was moving along.

A few weeks before leaving I tried the engine and it again refused to start. This time I couldn't fix it. I decided the cylinder head was blocked with soot and I didn't want to start looking for parts and then trying to fix it on anchor in the river. There was nothing for it but to scrap my plans to stop in Fortaleza which was not a place to go in under sail. Instead I cleared out down the river heading for Tobago and from there to Trinidad where I could get the engine fixed.

There was a lot of wind when I left the river and one hour of really rough wet sailing over shallow water took me out to where the depth of water was at last over twenty feet. Here I could free off the wind and head north. We passed Natal doing more than six knots and then turned to head for the Caribbean with the wind almost directly behind, the sea quite calm and very comfortable sailing.

We gobbled up the miles. Although we slowed down a bit as we approached Tobago, altogether we made really good time. I tacked into the anchorage on the south west corner of Tobago and anchored among a dozen other boats. It was the weekend so I had to wait till Monday to contact the Dutch lads in Trinidad.

Johan was back in Holland but Arno and Peter had agreed to meet me at the Dragon's Mouth in Trinidad and tow me in if the tide and wind were not good. I even bought a new cell phone so I could talk to them as I arrived.

So the following day I left. Initially, I got swept westward by the current but with the boat hard on the wind, I managed to claw myself across to the north shore of Trinidad. Once there, I idled along overnight to be in the Dragon's Mouth, The Bocas, early the next morning.

Sure enough, there was no wind and the tide was ripping out, so the lads drag me along with the rubber ducky and their fifteen hp outboard. It took a while but we finally arrived and I anchored off the TTSA (Trinidad & Tobago Sailing Association).

First things first, I had to visit the hospital. After weeks of diarrhea in Brazil I was constipated for the whole trip to Trinidad. The hospital soon sorted that out with some soapy water!

Next I met an English guy having work done on his engine in the TTSA yard. His mechanic had agreed to look at my engine. It was a disaster. Messing with the valve clearances, one of the valve caps unseated and fell off into a cylinder. On the way in, it bent the valve and ruined the seating. Then it broke up and embedded itself in the piston. One piece jammed in the edge of the piston and scratched the cylinder wall. The engine was buggered. It was especially annoying to find out that the original problem had only been a blocked exhaust where the water injected.

I was quoted a minimum of 22,000 TT dollars to have it repaired. I could see the job taking forever and wondered in any event, how good was it going to be. The local agent agreed to sell me a complete new engine for 40,000 TT dollars, it seemed the better option so I bought it. The cost came to nearly €5,000. It made me sick for a few days just thinking about it. Still, in less than a week I had the old engine out and the new one installed.

The Baco brothers, as I called my Dutch friends, had left the Dominican Republic where I had last spent time with them, and had sailed to Trinidad. There they had sold their South African-built catamaran and had spent the last seven years building a huge exotic catamaran in a shed just down the road from where I was now.

The catamaran was already finished and in the water. In a few weeks they were sailing it up to St. Martin. I stored all the bits of my old engine in the bilge and left the head and the block in their shed. Arno and Peter had a car which was great for stocking-up in the supermarket or in the Sunday fruit and vegetable market in Port-of-Spain.

My plan to arrive in Grenada and meet Steve, my old school friend and now my editor, had been put on hold. He was not now going to have a break from his busy life before January. It was just as well for my book writing and ground to a halt with the engine problems. Now hopefully I could put everything back on track.

I cleared out for Grenada. The engine worked well as I motored out of the Dragon's Mouth. Then, with all sails set, we beat north in a stiff breeze. By morning I was off the Grenada coast and could free off to enter Secret Harbour and do the paperwork to clear in. By afternoon I had up anchored again and moved round to Hog Island, my old stomping ground.

And so I had completed my third circumnavigation and it had taken just as long as the previous times. Hog Island looked just the same apart from the new bridge which was already rusting away and unused.

I was anchored next to Mick and his family on *Lily Maid* and went for beers ashore on the island at Roger's Bar. I knew most of the people here so there were no nasty shocks. Next week I will have my sixty-eighth birthday coming up. Steve will be here in the New Year, 2014 and maybe this story will get published for you to read.

For me, the big question is... what now?

CHRONOLOGY

1970   *Sea Loone* planned and starts. 1970-77: Building at Meols, Wirral, Merseyside
1976   *Sea Loone* launched at Birkenhead

VOYAGES

1977   Shakedown to Anglesey. Then to Milford Haven (winter)
1978   Ireland, Bayona, Madeira, Antigua
1979   Jamaica, Dom. Republic, Rosy Roads Naval Base, Azores
1980   Spain, Madeira, Cayman
1981   BVI.
1982   Down Island, Venezuela
1983   Panama Canal, Costa Rica, Pacific
1984   Bora Bora, Tonga NZ (Christmas)
1985   Tasman Sea, Sydney Australia (Christmas)
1986   Solomon Islands, Cairns, Bundaberg Australia (Christmas)
1987   Darwin, Chagos
1988   S. Africa, Richards Bay, Durban (Christmas)
1989   St. Helena, Brazil
1990   BVI, Grenada (Hog Island), BVI (Christmas)
1991   BVI, Hog
1992   Venezuela, San Blas, Brazil
1993   Costa Rica, Marquesas (Christmas)
1994   Tahiti, NZ (Christmas)
1995   Tonga Fiji, New Caledonia
1996   Up the Aus. Coast, Darwin
1997   Chagos, Madagascar
1998   Richards Bay, Madagascar, St. Helena, Richards Bay (Christmas)
1999   Richards Bay, Cape Town, Richards Bay (Christmas)
2000   RB, Cape Town, St. Helena, Brazil (Christmas)
2001   Fr. Guyana, Caribbean, St. Bart's (Christmas)
2002   Eden Rock, St. Bart's (Christmas)
2003   Grenada, St. Bart's., Dom. Republic (Christmas)

2004   San Blas, Panama Canal, Ecuador
2005   Tahiti, Tonga, NZ (Christmas)
2006   Tonga, Fiji, New Caledonia, NZ (Christmas)
2007   Back to Marquesas via Tuamotus'
2008   Tahiti, Tonga, NZ (Christmas)
2009   Tonga, New Caledonia, Mooloollaba , Australia, NZ (Christmas)
2010   New Caledonia and north, Solomon Islands (Christmas)
2011   Philippines, Borneo, China Sea (Christmas)
2012   New Year Singapore, Madagascar, Richards Bay, Cape Town
(Christmas)
2013   Brazil, Trinidad, Hog Island Grenada (Christmas)

Acknowledgments

Were it not for Steve Williams's enthusiasm I would never have started writing. His continued encouragement kept me going and his hard work and expertise converted my awful scribbles into legible type. I apologise to him for frustrating his attempts to make my style more upbeat.

I thank Heidi Williams for proof reading and correcting some of my atrocious grammar and thanks also to Michelle Poncini and Clark Stede for pushing me forward in the very beginning.

BIBLIOGRAPHY

de Kat, Joan, *Adieu Misericorde*

Falconer, Ron, *Together Alone*

Haskamp, Bettina, *Azorenhoch*

Haytor, Rebecca, *Oceans Alone*

Jacobsen, Holger, *Destination Paradise; Guten Tag*

Llewellyn, Ron, *Sailor, Soldier, Lover*

Neale, Tom, *An Island to Myself*

Simon, Alvah, *North to the Night*

Stede, Clarke, *Northwest Passage*